BY ORDER OF
THE PRESIDENT

GREG ROBINSON

BY ORDER OF THE PRESIDENT:

FDR

AND THE

INTERNMENT

OF JAPANESE

AMERICANS

HARVARD UNIVERSITY PRESS

Cambridge, Massachusetts and London, England | 2001

Library of Congress Cataloguing in Publication Data

Robinson, Greg, 1966–
  By order of the president: FDR and the internment of Japanese Americans / Greg Robinson.
  p. cm.
  Includes bibligraphical references and index.
  ISBN 0–674–00639–9 (alk. paper)
    1. Japanese Americans—Evacuation and relocation, 1942–1945. 2. Roosevelt, Franklin D. (Franklin Delano), 1882–1945 I. Title

D769.8.A6 R63 2001
940.53'089956073—dc21

2001024609

For my parents, Ed and Toni Robinson,
and in loving memory of Joyce Fath (1916–1990)

CONTENTS

"He who gathers together not the rumors, the gossip, the legends that inevitably surround and becloud the real facts concerning a great man, but the actual things that that man wrote and said, connecting them briefly but clearly with an account of what he did so that they will be understandable, has performed a valuable service, not only for the historian of today but even more so for the historian of the future."

FRANKLIN DELANO ROOSEVELT, introduction to Harold Garnet Black, *The True Woodrow Wilson*, 1946

INTRODUCTION

ON THE AFTERNOON of November 21, 1944, nearly three years after the United States entered World War II and just two weeks after he was elected to a record fourth term, President Franklin Delano Roosevelt held a press conference. FDR looked forward to these biweekly rituals, which were a notable innovation of the Roosevelt White House. The atmosphere was informal and lively. FDR's assistant Stephen T. Early would bring the group of White House correspondents into the Oval Office, where they would crowd around the President's desk. Roosevelt, who fancied himself an old newspaperman from his college journalism days, was on a first-name basis with many reporters, and he would greet his favorites with a joke, genial teasing, or some social chatter. Unless the President had an opening announcement to make, the reporters would then proceed to ask whatever questions they wished: unlike some of his predecessors, FDR did not demand that questions be submitted in advance. Smilingly, confidently, Roosevelt would field the queries, answering

"JAPANESE PEOPLE

FROM JAPAN WHO

ARE CITIZENS"

directly if he chose, otherwise responding off the record, hinting vaguely at his thoughts, or adroitly sidestepping the question. These comments to the press, with their mix of gossip, candor, guile, and wit, were pure Roosevelt—FDR at his most stimulating, complex, and seductively charming.

The November 21, 1944, conference—number 982 of Roosevelt's presidency—opened with a plea by the President for industry to continue full production for the war effort and for employers to maintain wartime wage levels once peace was restored. Reporters proceeded to quiz FDR about the budget, the situation in Poland, scheduling of wartime conferences with Churchill and Stalin, the appointment of a new ambassador to China, the future of Lend-Lease aid, and other matters.

At one point early in the conference, Warren B. Francis, correspondent of the *Los Angeles Times,* took the opportunity to ask the President about the widespread rumors regarding the West Coast Japanese-American population: "Mr. President, there is a great deal of renewed controversy on the Pacific Coast about the matter of allowing the return of these Japanese who were evacuated in 1942. Do you think that the danger of espionage or sabotage has sufficiently diminished so that there can be a relaxation of the restrictions that have been in effect for the last two years?" Francis's question sparked this response from Roosevelt:

> In most of the cases . . . I am now talking about Japanese people from Japan who are citizens . . . Japanese Americans. I am not talking about the Japanese themselves. A good deal of progress has been made in scattering them throughout the country, and that is going on almost every day. I have forgotten what the figures are. There are about roughly a hundred—a hundred thousand Japanese-origin citizens in this country. And it is felt by a great many lawyers that under the Constitution they can't be kept locked up in concentration camps.

FDR added that approximately 20–25 percent of these citizens had already "re-placed themselves" around the nation, and he argued that the rest could easily be dispersed without "discombobolating" the population. He then commented that in any given county, such as one "in the Hudson River Valley or in western Joe-gia [Georgia] probably half a dozen or a dozen families could be scattered around on the farms and worked into the community.

After all, they are American citizens, and we all know that American citizens have certain privileges . . . 75 thousand families scattered all around the United States is not going to upset anybody."[1] Roosevelt concluded by stating that in permitting such releases from the camps, the government was also "actuated" by the achievements of the "Japanese" in the combat battalion in Italy, which was "one of the outstanding battalions we have."

Francis, explaining that the concern on the Pacific Coast did not relate to the relocation of the interned Japanese Americans elsewhere in the country so much as to their return to the western states, pressed the President for comment on whether the military orders excluding Japanese Americans from the West Coast would be lifted. Roosevelt asserted blandly that he knew nothing about it, and made no further comment.

The President's comments at the November 21, 1944, press conference mark one of his few public references to the most tragic act of his administration: the internment of Japanese Americans. In December 1941 the Japanese launched a surprise attack on Pearl Harbor, America's principal naval base in the Pacific, bringing the United States into World War II. Several weeks later, in January 1942, a group of U.S. Army officers, anxious over a possible Japanese invasion of the West Coast and encouraged by California politicians and nativist interest groups eager to drive out the "Japs" and seize their property, began to press for the removal from the coastal areas of all people of Japanese ancestry. Japanese Americans were singled out from other "enemy" groups such as Italian Americans and German Americans as innately untrustworthy on racial grounds. The complete absence of any documented case of espionage or sabotage by Japanese Americans only proved to the military and political leaders of the anti–Japanese-American movement that there must be a concerted plan for future subversion by Japanese Americans at an appointed time.

By the end of January 1942, the question of removal had evolved into a tug-of-war within the Roosevelt administration. The War Department, led by Secretary of War Henry L. Stimson, favored mass "evacuation" of West Coast Japanese Americans as an emergency military measure, while Attorney General Francis Biddle, seconded by FBI Director J. Edgar Hoover, contended that mass evacuation was unnecessary. On February 11, 1942, President Roosevelt ended the debate by orally granting Stimson his consent to take whatever "reasonable" action the secretary deemed necessary. Eight days later, FDR signed Executive Order 9066, which authorized the army to establish military areas from which any civilian could be excluded and to provide these "evacuees" with transportation and other assistance.

Although the text of Executive Order 9066 did not specifically mention Japanese Americans, it was intended to apply to them exclusively. Prior to the war, the Japanese-American or Nikkei community was made up of several distinct groups. First-generation immigrants from Japan, who were known as Issei, were resident aliens. Although the vast majority of Issei arrived before 1907, when immigration from Japan was restricted, and virtually all before 1924, when it was banned entirely, and were thus longtime U.S. residents by 1941, they were nevertheless forbidden by law from ever becoming naturalized citizens. The second generation—the Issei's American-born children, the Nisei—were, by birthright, American citizens. Among the Nisei was a third group, the Kibei, American-born U.S. citizens who were brought up and educated in Japan. All three groups were interned.[2]

Under the authority of Executive Order 9066, the army removed more than 100,000 Japanese Americans from the Pacific Coast states during spring 1942. After being rounded up by the army, Japanese Americans were first placed in temporary "assembly centers" under army custody. They were then sent under armed guard to confinement in the ten camps in the interior operated by a new civilian agency, the War Relocation Authority (WRA). The conditions in the camps were harsh. Most were set up on remote, arid lands where the climate was blisteringly hot in summer and frigid in winter and where dust storms were common. Schools and medical care were initially scarce, and food remained of poor quality. Comfort and privacy were all but impossible to secure in the uninsulated, barren, and hastily constructed barracks into which families were crowded. The camps were surrounded by barbed wire and armed guards, and in some cases guards shot "escaping" internees and beat "troublemakers." Perhaps even more damaging than these privations, especially to a proud population accustomed to hard farm labor, were the stigma and psychological impact of segregation and incarceration.

The internment of Japanese Americans in the camps continued throughout the war years. Although two thirds of the internees were American citizens, they were incarcerated without any charge, trial, or evidence against them. Since they were permitted to take to the camps only what they could carry, they were forced to abandon their homes, farms, furnishings, cars, and other belongings or to sell them off quickly at bargain prices. Thus, as a result of Roosevelt's executive order, the vast majority of the West Coast Japanese Americans lost all their property.

In the months that followed the initial confinement of Japanese Americans, government leaders determined, as a matter of policy, that the internees should be gradually released from the camps in small groups of families or individuals and relocated throughout the country east of the Rocky Mountains. They hoped thereby to lessen anti-Japanese-American prejudice and foster the postwar assimilation of the internees into American society. However, even after the WRA and army devised a system of bureaucratically slow and largely fictive investigations of internee "loyalty" by military boards to determine eligibility for release, only a small percentage of the internees were able to leave the camps. The West Coast remained off limits to all people of Japanese ancestry, and even outside the West Coast, the internees had difficulty obtaining the guarantees of employment and housing required for resettlement due to the prejudice and stigma of disloyalty that marked them.

In addition, Japanese Americans faced restrictions on entry into the armed forces. The U.S. Navy remained closed to them throughout the war, and the army fully opened its doors to Nisei only in 1944, although in 1943 a small fraction of young men from the camps, along with Nisei troops from Hawaii, were recruited for the army's segregated 442nd Combat Infantry Battalion (the outstanding "Japanese battalion in Italy" to which Roosevelt alluded in his November 1944 press conference).

After the army finally lifted its orders excluding Japanese Americans from the West Coast in January 1945, the pace of resettlement increased. Nevertheless, many of the internees remained in the camps. Those who had been found "disloyal" remained ineligible for release until the end of the war, while others feared violence against them if they left, or stayed because they had literally no place to go. The last camps did not close until 1946.

The internment was not simply an error of official overzealousness but a tragedy of democracy. Its human costs, in the blood and suffering of its victims, were insignificant compared with the military casualties of World War II or with the millions of civilians slaughtered in the Rape of Nanking and in the Nazi death camps. Even within the history of the United States, the treatment of the internees pales in comparison with the enslavement of African Americans or the destruction of Native American nations. The special stain of the internment is that an unpopular group of American *citizens* was singled out on a racial basis and summarily dispossessed and incarcerated without charge. By arbitrarily confining American citizens of Japanese ancestry, the government violated the essential principle of democracy: that all citizens are entitled to the same rights and legal protections.

A comparison of the treatment of Japanese Americans with that of other ethnic groups is telling. There was discussion within the administration regarding the mass removal of West Coast German and Italian aliens under the provisions of Executive Order 9066, and enemy aliens of various nationalities who were considered potentially dangerous were rounded up on an individual basis. However, unlike Japanese Americans, whether aliens or citizens, enemy aliens from other groups were granted speedy loyalty hearings at which the accused were allowed to present witnesses and evidence to demonstrate their loyalty.

It is difficult for many Americans at the turn of the twenty-first century to conceive how government officials who were fighting a war dedicated to the preservation of democracy could have become so caught up in the pressures of the wartime emergency that they implemented a profoundly undemocratic policy. It seems especially perplexing that such an action could have taken place during the administration of Franklin Roosevelt, a President justly celebrated for his attachment to human rights and his dedication to creating government programs to serve the needs of ordinary Americans. Yet, the President signed Executive Order 9066, which provided the legal basis for the internment, and his interventions into the ensuing policy were decisive in determining its character, duration, and consequences for the internees.

Perhaps because FDR's signing of Executive Order 9066 appears so uncharacteristic, his role in approving and carrying out the internment has been almost completely ignored. Instead, the policy has been seen primarily as a result of pressure from the military, combined with the anti-Japanese hysteria (manipulated by interest groups) that swept the West Coast in early 1942. In the words of a recent critic, the internment literature has focused on the actions of lesser officials, "almost to the point where history has absolved [Roosevelt] of any responsibility. In this way, time has been kind to FDR."[3]

If FDR's responsibility for the internment is to be fairly assessed, the extent of his knowledge of the policy and the nature of his active participation in formulating and executing it must be determined. Nevertheless, the principal goal of any examination of Roosevelt's actions must be an understanding of his motives. Why did the President sign Executive Order 9066, which violated all the democratic principles he so eloquently espoused, and what drove his conduct of the ensuing policy?

The full answer is necessarily complex, and many different elements, such as presidential leadership, administrative style, political calculation, national morale, and wartime propaganda must be explored. In addition, more personal and less immediate factors come into play. Here FDR's statements at his November 21, 1944, conference provide important testimony as to his sentiments. His words reflect the very principles that underlay the internment policy: the conviction that Japanese Americans, even native-born, were essentially Japanese; fear of their disloyalty; disregard of their citizenship rights; advocacy of their dispersion away from the West Coast; and a focus on public opinion in determining their status. Most of all, FDR's comments betray an astounding casualness about the policy and an indifference to its effect on its victims.

Official policy is, of course, the product of many people's contributions, and the influence of any one individual's ideas, even those of the leader who bears the ultimate responsibility, is not unlimited. Yet all leaders draw from their accumulated experience, emotions, and vision as well as from the conditions and forces at hand in making their decisions. In this case, Franklin Roosevelt's view of Japanese Americans as immutably foreign and dangerous was a crucial factor in his approval of the internment. To understand how Roosevelt evolved these beliefs, we must examine the nature of the American society in which Roosevelt spent his early life and investigate how his attitudes toward the presence of people of Japanese ancestry in the United States were shaped by dominant social and intellectual patterns of the period.

A RACIAL FEAR EMERGES

FRANKLIN ROOSEVELT grew to adulthood at the
end of the nineteenth century, a period marked by
the emergence of Japan as a serious power on the
international stage. In the decades that followed the
"opening" of Japan by a fleet of American gunboats
in 1853, the Japanese undertook a drastic program
of social and technological reform. Japanese leaders
sought at all costs to protect the nation's independence and avoid the colonization or quasi-colonization
to which most other Asian countries had been subjected. Within fifty years, Japan had developed a modern bureaucracy and navy, defeated China in two
short wars, begun to compete with European nations
for trade, and claimed special interests in China and
Korea. In 1904–05, Japan defeated Russia in the Russo-
Japanese War, becoming the premier military force in
East Asia.

 Japan's increasing economic and diplomatic self-
assertion led to tension with the established powers.
Although the European nations admired the Japanese
for their achievement in forging a new society, they

were reluctant to grant the upstart nation an equal place, especially as Japan's status as an Asian nation challenged their notions of white racial superiority. Japanese sensitivity to discrimination compounded the problem. Having struggled valiantly to industrialize and "catch up" with the West, many Japanese considered racial prejudice and unequal treatment of Japanese nationals an unbearable affront to the honor of the nation.

Japan's success likewise gradually altered its relations with the United States. At first, most Americans sympathized with Japan. Not only had the United States "opened" Japan, but in their own drive for empire during the late 1890s, Americans had also been forced to struggle for acceptance by the Europeans. However, as Japan rose to power, U.S. leaders began to focus on Japanese expansionism as a potential threat to national security.

The hostility over security was exacerbated by the racial difference of the Japanese, which triggered a host of negative images and reactions in the American psyche. Generations of settlers from Europe had transplanted into the culture of their new country a traditional European "orientalist" view of Asia as an exotic, backward, and barbaric land. In addition, the migration of a sizable population of Chinese laborers to the western United States during the third quarter of the nineteenth century had stimulated a backlash of resentment by white laborers and nativists. In order to justify their calls for the exclusion of Chinese immigrants, these groups helped manufacture and disseminate a series of racist stereotypes of Asians as treacherous, servile, and uncivilized. In 1882, the year Franklin Roosevelt was born, Congress obliged nativists by passing the first of several Chinese Exclusion Acts. In addition, by the turn of the century "scientific racism" had become a dominant force in American thought. Adapting and distorting the work of Charles Darwin and his followers, some social scientists asserted that human life was governed by the evolutionary competition for resources between opposing "races" and that therefore the Japanese were innately hostile to people of European descent. Prominent Americans, drawing on elements from all these sources, warned that Japanese expansionism represented a "yellow peril," an Asian challenge to "Anglo-Saxon" and Christian civilization.[1]

Franklin Roosevelt, unlike many Americans, was attracted to Asia and Asian civilization from his earliest days. Roosevelt's fascination with Asia was nourished by numerous family connections. His maternal grandfather, Warren Delano, was involved in the China trade (in which he made, lost, and remade a fortune) and lived for ten years in Canton (now Guanzhou).

Roosevelt's mother, Sara Delano Roosevelt, often recounted to her son vivid stories of the girlhood trip she had made with her father to the Far East in the mid-1860s. The Roosevelt estate at Hyde Park, where FDR grew up, was full of vases and artifacts that his grandfather Delano had brought back from China, including a large temple bell which dominated the front room.[2] Because of his family background, Roosevelt in later years referred to himself as an "old China hand" (although he never visited China or studied Chinese culture in any formal way), and he spoke frequently, if sometimes paternalistically, of his attachment to China.

Roosevelt nourished a similar, though less intense, interest in Japan. Members of both sides of Roosevelt's family had traded with or visited Japan, and the Hyde Park estate contained Japanese porcelains and other cultural artifacts.[3] Warren Delano had been part-owner of the boat that brought over Manjiro Nakahama, the first reported Japanese to settle in the United States, in 1843. In 1934 Roosevelt proudly wrote Nakahama's son that he remembered his own grandfather's stories of the elder Nakahama as the Japanese boy who lived across the street from the Delano house in Fairhaven, Massachusetts, and often went to church with the Delano family.

The young Roosevelt also made friendships with numerous Japanese. In 1902, during his college years at Harvard University, Roosevelt met and grew close to Otohiko Matsukata, the son of a distinguished Japanese mercantile and political family, through Matsukata's friendship with Roosevelt's cousin Lyman Delano and his family and through Matsukata and Roosevelt's common membership in Harvard's Delphic Club (where they each gained a reputation for generously providing liquor). Roosevelt also became friendly with Ryozo Asano, a friend of Matsukata who was a Harvard classmate and friend of FDR's brother-in-law G. Hall Roosevelt. In 1911 Asano and Hall stayed with FDR and his family at their summer home at Campobello, New Brunswick.[4] In 1915, during his tenure as assistant secretary of the navy under President Woodrow Wilson, Roosevelt became friendly with Captain (later Admiral) Kichisaburo Nomura, the Japanese naval attaché in Washington. In addition to their professional relationship, he and Nomura met socially on several occasions over the following two years, and Nomura also became acquainted with Eleanor Roosevelt (possibly at a dinner which the Roosevelts attended at the Japanese Embassy in November 1915).

Roosevelt maintained these friendships into his later life. For example, in 1919 Matsukata wrote asking FDR to assist one of Matsukata's colleagues in lobbying the Wilson administration to approve the laying of a new trans-Pacific wireless cable. The following year, he sent a telegram congratulating FDR on his nomination for the vice presidency.[5] Matsukata and Asano again renewed their contacts with Roosevelt after he entered the White House in 1933, and he conferred privately with each of them in order to keep himself informed on the state of Japanese liberal opinion.[6] Meanwhile, Roosevelt and Nomura kept up their relationship through correspondence. In 1937 Roosevelt wrote Nomura, "As I have often told you, I hope the day will come when I can visit Japan. I have much interest in the great accomplishments of the Japanese people and I should much like to see many of my Japanese friends again."[7]

As FDR's affection for these various individuals demonstrates, he did not share popular racist views of Asians as innately menacing or uncivilized. Still, despite his friendships with Japanese and his genuine interest in Japanese culture, Roosevelt adopted an increasingly wary position toward Japanese power during the first decade of the twentieth century. This shift has often been interpreted as a by-product of FDR's Chinese chauvinism. He favored China over Japan whenever the two countries were compared—in a letter he wrote in 1898, he told his parents that a Groton lecturer on China "ran down the poor Chinaman a little too much and thought too much of the Japs."[8] In 1923 he admitted that the pro-Chinese attitude of many Americans, among whom he clearly included himself, made it difficult for them to see the Japanese point of view.[9]

However, it is easy to exaggerate the strength of Roosevelt's feeling for China in his foreign policy. A more important cause of Roosevelt's shift was his evolving perception of Japan as a potential military and economic rival of the United States, a view catalyzed by his reading of the works of Admiral Alfred Thayer Mahan. In his seminal books *The Influence of Sea Power on History* (1890) and *In the Interest of America in Sea Power, Past and Present* (1897), Mahan had promulgated the thesis that a nation's greatness was directly dependent on its control of the seas, and he strongly urged the United States to live up to its potential greatness by augmenting its naval strength and joining other nations to preserve a stable world order.[10] Mahan's books and articles were enormously influential. In the United States, they were largely responsible for reviving the navy, which had shrunk significantly in size and power after the Civil War. Under the leadership of Mahan's disciple President Theodore Roosevelt, the American navy attained an unprecedented level of technical and strategic capability. On the international level, Mahan inspired several other countries—notably Japan—to concentrate on naval strength as a source of national prestige and political power.

Franklin Roosevelt first discovered Mahan's *Influence of Sea Power on History* at the age of eleven, and he reread it repeatedly, to the point where, as Sara Delano Roosevelt later recalled, he had practically memorized it.[11] He received a copy of Mahan's *Interest of America in Sea Power* at Christmas 1897 and quickly absorbed it as well. The following spring, he cited Mahan in his first surviving public "speech," a Groton debate in which he was assigned to oppose the annexation of Hawaii.[12] Roosevelt continued to rely on *The Influence of Sea Power on History* in later years. In 1922–23, he several times spoke of his plans to draft and publish an updated edition of the work.[13]

Having thus learned from Mahan to pay particular attention to the role of naval power in international relations, FDR grew concerned that the Japanese naval buildup might presage expansionist ambitions in the Pacific. Many years later, in 1934, Roosevelt would recount a conversation he had had in 1902 with a Harvard classmate, a "Japanese boy of Samurai class" (obviously Otohiko Matsukata, who had an aristocratic background and was the only Japanese student then at Harvard). This "boy" told him of the existence of a secret Japanese fifty-year plan to establish complete dominance over East Asia and the Western Pacific through a naval buildup, war with an Asian and a European power, and then a takeover of Manchuria, China, and the Philippines.[14] Whatever was in fact said during the conversation, the young Roosevelt clearly took away from it the conviction that Japan's desire for naval power was not designed simply to protect against encroachment by the Western powers.

FDR's nascent concern over Japanese naval power increased exponentially after Japan's victory in the Russo-Japanese War of 1904–05. When Japan first became embroiled in a war with Russia, virtually no one believed that the small island nation could defeat a major European power with an imposing army and fleet. Many Americans felt great sympathy for the Japanese "underdogs" confronting the Russian empire; they included Eleanor Roosevelt, who wrote her fiancé Franklin: "Everyone is talking war madly at present, and the Japanese certainly seem to have made a good beginning. I do hope they will win for I suppose that their defeat might bring about an international war. Besides they are, from a distance at least, such a plucky and attractive little people, don't you think?"[15]

By March 1905, when Eleanor and Franklin Roosevelt married and took their honeymoon cruise to Europe, Japan was close to victory. FDR showed his budding political and strategic interests during the voyage by befriending a group of six Japanese naval officers en route to England, from whom he sought information on Japan's strengths and motives. He wrote to his mother from the ship, "I have had several interesting talks with [the Japanese] though their English is not voluble, and I find myself giving out more information than I receive." Eleanor added in her own letter to Sara that Franklin had spent a great deal of time *"trying* to talk to the Japs."[16]

Meanwhile, President Theodore Roosevelt, who had initially offered private support to the Japanese cause, grew concerned that the total defeat of Russia would destroy the balance of power in Asia. He thus offered to act as a mediator between Russia and Japan, and he succeeded in brokering the Treaty of Portsmouth, which ended the war without crippling Russia's strength in the Far East. "It's nice news, isn't it?" Eleanor and Franklin wrote to Sara from England when the news of the treaty reached them. "We had really begun to think it would not be and Uncle Ted must be gratified to have done so much toward it."[17]

While FDR took enormous pride in Theodore Roosevelt's accomplishment, Eleanor later recalled that he was more interested in the unexpected efficiency of the Japanese navy and in the implications of the Treaty of Portsmouth on the naval balance of power, particularly its provisions granting Japan de facto control of southern Manchuria and awarding the Japanese new naval bases in Asia.[18] Like Mahan, who had written a series of articles on the war for *Collier's Weekly* and the *National Review,* he now considered Japan to be America's chief rival in the Pacific.[19]

In the half-dozen years that followed 1905, FDR practiced law and served in the New York State Senate. Although no record remains of his views about Japan during this period, FDR evidently remained heavily influenced by the personality and ideas of his cousin and hero President Theodore Roosevelt. The young FDR admired TR so greatly that he cast his first vote for President for him in 1904, despite the Democratic voting tradition of the Hyde Park branch of the Roosevelt family, and he attended the inauguration in March 1905. The young Roosevelt also enthusiastically supported TR's imperialist foreign policy, including his subjection of the Philippine independence movement.[20] It is therefore important to examine the evolution of TR's own policy toward Japan.

Perhaps even more than his younger cousin, Theodore Roosevelt openly esteemed Japan. The Japanese "character," with its military spirit and emphasis on honor, epitomized his vision of national greatness. TR was so impressed by *Bushido: The Soul of a Nation,* Inazo Nitobe's 1905 book on Japan's warrior code, that he ordered sixty copies for friends, and he tried to persuade Americans to take up judo as a popular sport. He sympathized with Japanese resentment over unfair treatment by Europeans.[21] However, despite his affection for the Japanese, TR considered Japan a potential rival for world power. In 1905 he told a friend, "What a wonderful people the Japanese are! They are quite as remarkable industrially as in warfare. In a dozen years the English, Americans and Germans, who now dread one another as rivals in the trade of the Pacific, will have each to dread the Japanese more than they do any other nation."[22]

In order to defend the United States and its Pacific island territories against the Japanese threat, TR sought to build up a strong naval fleet in the years after 1905. In 1907, in a gesture meant to demonstrate America's strength in the Pacific, the President sent the navy's "Great White Fleet" on an around-the-world cruise, including a stop in Japan.[23] In the meantime, TR sought to placate Japan and avoid war in order to give the navy a chance to complete its building program. He negotiated the Taft-Katsura Agreement of 1905 and the Root-Takeshira Convention of 1908, in which both countries pledged to maintain the status quo in Asia and the Pacific. TR likewise encouraged the Japanese to establish a protectorate over Korea and to increase their trade with China. He believed that these actions not only would distract Japan from challenging American interests in the Pacific but also would exert a civilizing influence on the backward Koreans and Chinese, just as U.S. occupation acted as a "civilizing" force in the Philippines.[24]

Theodore Roosevelt's conciliatory foreign policy toward Japan was soon undermined by domestic events, in the form of controversy over Japanese immigrants in the United States. As Japan industrialized during the last third of the nineteenth century, many impoverished farmers and factory workers sought to improve their prospects by emigrating to Hawaii and the United States, as well as to Canada, Brazil, Peru, and other nations. By the early 1900s, some 150,000 people of Japanese ancestry lived in Hawaii, more than any other ethnic group, and Japanese workers dominated the islands' plantation labor force. Meanwhile, another 150,000 Japanese had settled on the U.S. mainland, mainly on the West Coast. The immigrants were initially welcomed for their willingness to work long hours for little money. However, as the number of immigrants increased and as the Japanese farm workers began to use the savings they had accumulated to buy land of their own, self-interest, greed, and bigotry fanned the flames of anti-Japanese sentiment among white commercial, labor union, and nativist groups. Mobilizing the same hostile stereotypes that they had employed a generation before against the Chinese (whose exclusion had created the very demand for agricultural workers that the Japanese had originally filled), anti-immigrant agitators conjured up racist images of the Japanese as menacing and immoral. Nativist forces also drew on the "yellow peril" anxieties aroused by Japan's new power in the Western Pacific by claiming that the immigrants had been sent to the West Coast to prepare the way for a future Japanese military conquest. Ignoring the fact that Japanese farmers owned barely 10,000 of California's 500,000,000 acres of farmland, white agitators charged that the Japanese were seizing control of the state's food supply.

In 1905, shortly after the end of the Russo-Japanese War, the California legislature passed an official resolution calling for the legal exclusion of Japanese immigrants. A year later, in October 1906, San Francisco's school board (encouraged by the labor-friendly *San Francisco Chronicle* as well as by Mayor Eugene Schmitz and local political leaders) issued an order providing that children of the Japanese "race" would henceforth be required to attend the separate Asian schools to which children of Chinese ancestry had already been relegated. The board's avowed purpose for this action was to reduce Japanese immigration.

The board's action, though blatantly racist, was scarcely noticed by most Americans. However, it aroused immediate and impassioned protest from the Japanese government, which followed the treatment of its overseas nationals with intense interest. In the eyes of many Japanese, discrimination against Japanese people anywhere was not only an insult to their human dignity but an intolerable reminder of the days of unequal treaties and Western domination. Such an assault on the nation's honor could be avenged only by war against the perpetrator.

President Theodore Roosevelt was ambivalent about the segregation policy. Despite his concerns over war, the President was sympathetic to the idea of restricting Japanese immigration. Like most educated Americans of the period, TR's views on society were heavily marked by the work of Herbert Spencer, William Graham Sumner, and other Social Darwinists, who had adapted Charles Darwin's biological theories of evolution and natural selection to the study of human society. According to these so-called Social Darwinists, humanity was divided into different races, which were made up of groups of people living in separate environments. Over multiple generations, these races evolved specific biological characteristics which promoted survival in that environment. Each member of such a race inherited these physical and character traits from birth and passed them on to their children. Unlike the majority of Social Darwinists, who used the Darwinian principle of "survival of the fittest" to justify notions of white supremacy, TR considered the Japanese substantially equal to whites in their level of civilization, and he in fact believed that Japan had much to teach the West. Nevertheless, he shared the Darwinists' view that the Japanese were fundamentally different according to what he termed "the great fact of race." That is, over the generations that the Japanese "race" had remained isolated from the West, the Japanese people had developed personality traits that were distinct from those of whites.

TR wrote a friend that the disparity between the races was not serious when it was a matter of interaction between small numbers of educated people, but that large-scale immigration of Japanese was not possible because the two populations could not be merged. Ordinary Americans naturally felt hostility and resentment when forced into contact with large numbers of people whose essential nature diverged so strongly from their own, and the Japanese could not undo in a few generations the biological conditioning they had acquired over countless centuries. TR likewise opposed immigration because it would likely lead to intermarriage, which he wished to avert at all costs. According to Social Darwinist theory, social cohesion within a "race" grew out of its members' shared biological characteristics. Intermarriage between different races led to the birth of "hybrids"—children who possessed no clear and unified set of racial characteristics and who thus remained without any social identity. TR warned that "it is not only undesirable but impossible that there should be racial intermingling and the result is sure to bring disaster."[25]

TR's feelings about inherent racial differences were overshadowed, however, by his distress over the San Francisco school board's segregation policy. TR was offended by the naked racial bigotry of Californians, and he privately fumed that the board had enacted a provocative policy without considering the injury it would inflict on the national pride of the Japanese. If the policy was not halted, the President warned his advisors, it might well draw Japan into declaring war on the United States, which was unprepared for such a conflict. The President's fears were shared by his longtime friend Admiral Mahan. Mahan wrote TR that he took the possibility of war seriously, although he believed that war was ultimately worth risking to restrict Japanese immigration.[26] Mahan warned the President that the Japanese had caught the Russian fleet while it was divided and had crushed each part in turn. The U.S. Navy should remain massed in case of attack by Japan, so that the same thing would not happen to them.[27]

In his annual message to Congress on December 3, 1906, TR sought to defuse the crisis by publicly appealing to the California school board to abandon its decision, which he termed "a wicked absurdity." To further mollify Japan's concerns over racial equality, he made the formal gesture of requesting Congress to permit Japanese aliens to be granted citizenship, although he knew Congress was unlikely to comply. (Japanese, like other Asians, were barred from naturalization by the federal Alien Act of 1798, which restricted naturalization to white immigrants.) When the school board persisted in its decision and its members complained of federal interference in local affairs, TR invited Mayor Schmitz and a delegation from San Francisco to the White House in early 1907. He succeeded in getting the board to rescind its decision in the national interest. In return, Roosevelt pledged to limit Japanese immigration, a pledge he kept by signing an executive order barring the migration of Japanese laborers from Hawaii to the U.S. mainland. Later that year, the President negotiated the first of two so-called Gentlemen's Agreements with Japan. By this agreement, the Japanese government "voluntarily" agreed not to provide exit visas to the United States for laborers, and Roosevelt promised not to legally restrict Japanese immigration. The agreement thus provided a face-saving device for both governments.[28]

Despite Theodore Roosevelt's attempts to calm Japanese-American tensions, they rose once more in January 1909. Although Japanese Americans owned a minuscule fraction of California farmland, their success at turning dry and infertile land into profitable farms aroused envy and resentment among whites, and consequently an act to bar Japanese aliens from further land ownership was introduced in the California legislature. As in the case of immigration restriction, the President privately favored the legislation in principle. He wrote shortly afterward, "The Japanese certainly object to Americans acquiring land in Japan at least as much as the Americans of the far Western states object to the Japanese acquiring land on our soil . . . Wherever there is settlement in mass—that is, wherever there is a large immigration of urban or agricultural laborers, or of people engaged in small local business of any kind—there is sure to be friction."[29] Mahan privately wrote that if the Japanese were not controlled, their immigrants would soon fill up the entire western portion of the country and cause "interminable trouble."[30]

Despite his private support, TR knew that the Japanese government felt strongly about the discriminatory aspects of an alien land act, and he was not yet prepared to risk war with Japan over this matter. Thus, he prevailed on Hiram Johnson, California's popular Republican governor, to have the bill killed in order to avoid antagonizing Japan. In 1911, after Theodore Roosevelt left the White House, another alien land bill was introduced in California, and TR's handpicked successor, William Howard Taft, pursued a similar course. He persuaded Johnson once more to prevent the bill's passage on national security grounds.

Theodore Roosevelt (like Taft after him) used the influence of the White House to prevent open anti-Japanese discrimination, which he believed carried a real risk of war with Japan. However, he was well aware that the presence of people of Japanese ancestry on the West Coast was a chronic source of conflict between the two nations, and he privately believed that racial differences made the presence of Japanese immigrants in American society a source of agitation and menace. The fact that even Teddy Roosevelt, who admired Japan and hoped to avoid unnecessary conflict between the two nations, sought to restrict Japanese entry and settlement in the United States no doubt sent a powerful message to his younger cousin that the Japanese presence in America was dangerous and undesirable.

After he left the White House in 1909, Theodore Roosevelt confined his opinions on Japanese immigration to private letters and conversations. Yet various others in positions of influence commented publicly on the subject in the years after TR's presidency. Perhaps the most widely read analysts of Japanese-American relations during this period were Homer Lea and Admiral Mahan, each of whom would contribute in important ways to FDR's views on national security and "the Japanese peril."

Homer Lea, an American a few years older than FDR, had become interested in China while at Stanford University and had traveled to Peking at the time of the Boxer Rebellion in 1898 to join the Republican Army. Despite constraints imposed by his small, hunchbacked body and his foreign race and nationality, Lea became a close advisor to Republican leader Sun Yat-Sen and ultimately rose to the level of Commanding General of the Republican forces.[31]

In 1909, after an absence of more than a decade, Lea returned to the United States, which he found to be a very different place from the one he had left. First, the U.S. economy had recovered from the serious economic depression of the 1890s, and the country was experiencing a wave of prosperity. The strong economy had lured a major influx of immigrants, mainly from eastern and southern Europe. Lea grew concerned that the country had become dangerously complacent and heterogeneous, and he aired his fears in a popular book, The Valor of Ignorance. In it, he argued that prosperity had dampened the vital military character of the nation, and "mass" democratic government and the influx of immigrants of foreign "races" had diluted its patriotic spirit. "If there is any such thing as patriotism, then a naturalized citizen is an anomaly . . . He not only cannot share in national ideals, but he cannot comprehend them."[32] In order to survive, Lea claimed, America's "Anglo-Saxons" would have to renew their original God-given militant characteristics, take control of the army, and organize to defend their empire.

Lea argued that the main threat to the United States was from Japan. The Japanese, he wrote, naturally sought to expand their empire over the globe, just as the European "races" had. The Japanese would soon conquer the rest of East Asia, where their military was dominant, and would follow up with a swift movement into the Philippines, Hawaii, and Alaska, which were not defensible against a rapid strike. Once this was accomplished, the Japanese would strike at the West Coast of the United States. Lea believed that America would not be able to withstand such an attack. The Pacific Coast was extensive and sparsely populated, and it lay far closer to Japan's naval strength than to the center of U.S. naval power.[33]

Lea asserted that the climactic conflict between Japan and the United States would be set off by the presence of Japanese immigrants on the West Coast. He pointed out that the federal government denied naturalization and suffrage rights to Japanese aliens because of their racial difference, and the immigrants experienced social and legal exclusion in West Coast states. The imposition of what Lea called "caste in a republic" provoked great outrage and a desire for revenge among the Japanese and provided a pretext that the

Japanese government could exploit to gain international support for their war of conquest.

Although Lea identified Japanese immigrants as the trigger for danger, he did not propose any policy for solving the "problem" created by their presence.[34] Like TR, Lea asserted that Japanese were innately different from "Anglo-Saxons" and could not change their long-developed "racial character" to conform to occidental ways. Perhaps because of his long experience with the Chinese, Lea was careful to note that the racial difference of the Japanese did not in itself imply inferiority. (He may, however, have absorbed his fears of Japanese aggression from the Chinese.) Rather, he stated that the "non-assimilability" of the Japanese heightened the potential for friction and hindered the kind of commonality of view and interest between Japan and America that promoted peace between the Anglo-Saxon countries.[35]

The Valor of Ignorance caused a sensation not only in the United States but in all the nations engaged in the vast military buildup that would eventually explode into World War I. Lea's depiction of a "yellow peril" was not new, but his military experience and his knowledgeable discussion of the strategy, tactical dispositions, and potential landing areas involved in a Japanese invasion of the West Coast lent credence to his argument. Within a short time Lea's name was known to military and political leaders throughout the world. He was invited by Kaiser Wilhelm to view German military maneuvers, while his work was considered required reading for English military strategists by Field Marshal Lord Roberts (the dedicatee of Lea's second book) and was even praised by Lenin. In Japan, the book sold 40,000 copies and went through 24 editions in a single year, despite being briefly banned by the government.[36]

In spring 1913, as the flames of anti-Japanese sentiment continued to blaze on the West Coast, the California legislature again considered restrictions on Japanese land ownership. The treatment of the Japanese attracted significant attention, both at home and abroad. In mid-May, Sir Valentine Chirol, a well-known British journalist, wrote an article in the London *Times* deploring discrimination against the Japanese. Admiral Alfred Thayer Mahan replied to Chirol with a letter that the *Times* printed in June. Because of both men's prestige as political commentators and because Mahan's letter represented, in the *Times's* phrase, "the clearest analysis that has yet been written of the American attitude toward Japanese immigration," the exchange received significant media coverage.[37] In response to public interest, both Mahan's letter and his subsequent correspondence with Chirol were immediately excerpted at length in *The New York Times,* and Mahan subsequently published his text as an independent article.[38]

Mahan's letter began by disclaiming any prejudice against Japan, which he recognized as a "great power." He stated, however, that the question of whether America was prepared to grant a country's nationals right of entry was not connected to that country's status. American public opinion was strongly against the granting of immigration rights to the Japanese. "Be the causes what they may—economic, industrial, social, racial or all four, and if there be any other motives—the will of the people is the law of the government."[39]

For Mahan, the primary fact was that the Japanese were, as he put it, "unassimilable" with Europeans (that is, Americans). "The question is fundamentally that of assimilation, though it is idle to ignore the fact that the clear superficial evidences of difference which inevitably 'sautent aux yeux' and are due to marked racial types, do exacerbate the difficulty." Because of their divergent culture and history, the Japanese people were unable to adapt to the spirit of American institutions, despite their absorption of Western "methods."[40]

Mahan took particular exception to Chirol's suggestion that discrimination against the Japanese represented a "color bar" of the kind that America had fought a civil war to overcome. He pointed to the Austrian empire and to the British troubles with the French in Canada and the Boers in South Africa as evidence that "racial" conflicts were not necessarily based on a "color question." Even more, he vehemently denied that the Civil War had been fought for the abolition of slavery, let alone for the granting of equal citizenship rights to African Americans (which he belittled as a postwar "party political measure," however mingled with humanitarian sentiment). Instead, Mahan presented America's history of trouble with its "inferior" black population as a demonstration of the limited potential for assimilation of other races. He turned the very absence of such inferiority among the Japanese into the ground for excluding them:

> While recognizing what I clearly see to be the great superiority of the Japanese as of the white over the negro, it appears to me as reasonable that a great number of my fellow-citizens, knowing

the problem we have in the colored race among us, should dread the introduction of what they believe will constitute another race problem, and one much more difficult because the virile qualities of the Japanese will still more successfully withstand assimilation, constituting a homogenous foreign mass, naturally acting together, irrespective of national welfare, and so will be the perennial cause of a friction with Japan even more dangerous than at present.[41]

Like Lea, Mahan feared the Japanese for their strength, not their weakness, and he connected the presence of Japanese Americans with the threat of war with Japan. Also like Lea, Mahan stressed that the Japanese were not assimilable. However, Mahan proposed that it was precisely their lack of inferiority to whites—a trait that would logically have made them attractive as immigrants—which made them resist assimilation. Unlike Lea, Mahan placed the onus for any trouble between Japan and the United States entirely on the presence of Japanese Americans themselves and on what he deemed to be their hostile and disloyal behavior.

In March 1913 Woodrow Wilson was inaugurated as President, following a victory over both Theodore Roosevelt and William Howard Taft in the 1912 presidential election. Wilson's new secretary of the navy, Josephus Daniels, a longtime North Carolina newspaperman, appointed young Franklin Roosevelt to TR's old position of assistant secretary, a post that FDR, with his love of ships and the navy, coveted more than any other.[42] Daniels had little experience in foreign policy, and Roosevelt, although just 31, swiftly took de facto control of much of the Navy Department's business.

Within weeks of taking office, FDR was confronted with an international crisis over Japanese Americans which mirrored those faced by Theodore Roosevelt a few years before. That spring, the California legislature passed a new Alien Land Act, which barred the Japanese and all other "immigrants ineligible for citizenship" from owning real property. The act's progress through the legislature sparked mass protests and calls for retaliation in Japan, and in mid-April when an extreme Japanese nationalist in the Japanese Diet called for a retaliatory blockade of the West Coast of the United States, both countries recognized the extent to which bellicose passions had been aroused. However, unlike TR and Taft, Wilson (who had earlier sent the legislators a private message encouraging them to pass such legislation as long as it did not clearly single out Japanese immigrants) maintained that the federal government was powerless to intervene. He made only belated and half-hearted efforts to oppose the act.[43] With the outspoken approval of California's popular governor, Hiram Johnson, and no effective opposition from Washington, the legislature passed the act and Governor Johnson signed it into law on May 19, 1913. As a result, Issei (immigrant alien) landowners in California were henceforth forced to lease their farms, to rely on white friends or agents to hold their property for them as the "legal" owners, or to register property in the names of their American-born Nisei children, who were citizens.[44]

The navy began preparing for the possibility of war with Japan over the Alien Land Act in early spring 1913. On March 13 the Joint Army and Navy Board put together a naval war plan recommending that a fleet of ships be assembled at Manila in readiness for war in the Pacific and urging that further ships be sent to reinforce Pearl Harbor and the Panama Canal. Admiral Bradley Fiske, the navy's "official strategist," gave Navy Secretary Daniels a confidential memorandum warning that it was "probable" that Japan would use the upcoming Alien Land Act as a pretext to declare war and to seize the Philippines and Hawaii. Japan would then fight a defensive war and hold on to those territories through the ensuing military stalemate until the United States gave in and surrendered control over its Pacific colonies.

Thus, almost immediately upon taking office, FDR became active in making plans for a possible war with Japan. According to later testimony by Daniels and Rear Admiral Fullham, Roosevelt expressed his agreement with the Joint Board's recommendations as soon as he received them, and he passed them on to the secretary as his own. Through his assistant Louis Howe, he leaked the Joint Board's plans to the sympathetic *New York Herald* in order to put public pressure on Washington.[45] FDR also expressed his agreement with Fiske's memorandum. In mid-April, he asked the navy's operations division to keep him apprised of the pace and progress of Japanese ship construction.[46]

FDR's efforts to prepare for war went into high gear after he received a confidential letter from Theodore Roosevelt in early May. The ex-President apologized for presuming to give advice, but he repeated Mahan's warnings of 1907 about keeping the fleet undivided in case of a Japanese attack: "I do not anticipate trouble with Japan, but it may come, and if it does it will come suddenly. In that case we shall be in an unpardonable situation if we permit

ourselves to be caught with our fleet separate. There ought not to be a bat-
tleship or any Formidable Fighting ship in the Pacific unless our entire fleet is
in the Pacific."[47]

On May 18, the day after California Governor Johnson signed the Alien
Land Act, the assistant secretary wrote TR that he had actually opposed the
Joint Board's plan to send a squadron to the Pacific, in order not to divide the
fleet: "I have 'butted in' and made them devote all their energies to two main
objects: 1. Preparing the fleet as a whole in the Atlantic and getting it in
shape. 2. Planning to make our little squadron in the Philippines and the
armored cruisers on the Pacific Coast do all the damage and cause all the
delay possible." He was clearly thinking in terms of a Japanese invasion not
only of the Pacific islands but of the West Coast, since such "damage" and
"delay" clearly referred to measures to be taken against an invasion force.

To Roosevelt's chagrin, Secretary Daniels and President Wilson vetoed all
plans for war mobilization. Daniels admitted that the navy was not prepared
and that Japan could seize Hawaii, Alaska, and the Philippines if war broke
out. The President agreed that any war plans were thus not only premature
but needlessly provocative.[48] FDR complained to his cousin that the administration was reacting timorously to the threat from Japan, and he argued vainly
that American ships based in Shanghai should be moved before war broke
out, to avoid capture or internment. "The Cabinet has taken the position that
we can't move a ship anywhere for fear of arousing the Jap Jingoes . . . nor can
we concentrate any of the other ships in the Pacific."[49]

In the face of administration opposition, the assistant secretary turned to
other methods for encouraging preparedness. He commissioned a group of
like-minded officers to assemble a secret contingency plan "in anticipation of
war with Japan," which incorporated many of the Joint Board's rejected proposals, including transfer of battleships from safe waters, increases in naval
enlistment, and organization of two squadrons of light ships to patrol the
Pacific while the main fleet remained in the Atlantic.[50] In his remarks to the
press, however, he followed the administration line and continued to make
what the San Francisco Examiner termed the "customary official denial" that
there was any danger of war with Japan or that the navy was mobilizing for
war. On May 20 he denied that the navy was preparing for war, and on May
26 he denounced the whole idea of war as "preposterous!" On May 29 he
added that "there is no Japanese scare. Japan doesn't want war and neither
does the country. The trouble is not a national one. It is a California question

purely."[51] Though made in furtherance of the party line, this was a somewhat disingenuous statement considering the continuous maneuvering, both open and secret, that had taken place between Washington and California. However, FDR seized on the "yellow peril" as a lever to call for increased naval preparedness. He commented pointedly that the "jingoes" who made "bellicose statements" about Japan were performing a service in educating the population to the state of naval armament, notably the fact that Japan had 159 heavy ships (though less total tonnage than the American fleet), while the United States had only 146.[52] He cited this disparity to further his case for an American naval buildup.

By midsummer 1913 the war scare with Japan had cooled as a result of cautious diplomacy on both sides, although the Japanese government continued to denounce the Alien Land Act and to make formal protests. However, Franklin Roosevelt, who had been sufficiently concerned about the threat of Japanese attack to engage in secret defense planning and contacts with opposition leaders after his superiors overruled his recommendations on war mobilization, continued over the succeeding years to consider war with Japan an imminent threat. He remained in contact (using his assistant Louis Howe as go-between) with Admiral Fiske and other figures who had been responsible for planning the defense of the Pacific Coast in case of war with Japan.

In April 1914, while on the West Coast, Roosevelt received a copy of Homer Lea's second book, *The Day of the Saxon*. Although that work was primarily devoted to an analysis of Europe, Roosevelt was "stirred," in his own later description, by the passages dealing with the Pacific Coast problem and the threat of invasion by Japan.[53] The section restated the general ideas Lea had presented in *The Valor of Ignorance*: "For Japan not to possess the control of the Pacific is to lose her sovereignty in Asia. Because of this Japan draws near to her next war—a war with America—by which she expects to lay the true foundation of her greatness. The Republic's indifference to the development and potentiality of Japan, its submersion in the ebb and flux of party politics, its heterogeneous racial elements, the supremacy of the individual over the welfare of the nation, and, finally, the nation's vain and tragic scorn of the soldier, predetermines the consummation of this fatal combat."[54]

What stirred FDR? No doubt Lea's dramatization of the vulnerability of the West Coast to attack was impressive. However, Roosevelt had already been anticipating war with Japan for a year by this time, and it was his business to be aware of the disposition of forces in the Pacific. In January 1914, three months before he was "stirred" by Lea, he had told *The New York Times* that the Pacific Coast was so poorly defended along its 1,800-mile border that "if I couldn't secretly land on this unprotected coast and I was Japanese I would commit Hari-Kari."[55]

Instead, Lea's work was perhaps more important in feeding Roosevelt's perception that Japanese immigrants were the source of U.S. conflict with Japan. Roosevelt had not previously commented on the reasons why he continued to believe a Japanese invasion was likely, but the question of the immigrants would undoubtedly have been on his mind while he was on the West Coast. Although the specific case of Japanese immigrants does not figure directly in the brief precis of the "Japanese question" in *The Day of the Saxon*, the concatenation of immigration and racial conflict lies at the core of Lea's thesis in that book as well as in its predecessor. In Carey McWilliams's words, Lea's most original contribution was the way in which he "correlated the domestic 'peril' and the overseas 'peril': he made them one."[56]

In addition, Roosevelt's association of Japanese Americans and conflict with Japan might well have been inspired by his contact with Admiral Mahan. In May 1914, only one month after he was introduced to Homer Lea's work, FDR contacted Mahan directly for the first time. The navy, he explained, was likely to revive plans to divide the fleet following the imminent opening of the Panama Canal, since the time required to reunite the fleet in case of war would thereafter be considerably reduced. Roosevelt asked the admiral, as "a public service," to write a series of popular historical articles on the perils of dividing naval forces. FDR suggested that, if possible, such work could be published "in some paper like *Collier's Weekly* or *The Saturday Evening Post*, where it would reach a very great number of people."[57]

Mahan wrote the assistant secretary that he would be happy to help by contributing such an article.[58] He also took the opportunity to warn Roosevelt that West Coast defenses should be reinforced, given that the threat in the Pacific so much exceeded that in the Atlantic. Mahan emphasized that danger of war with Europe was remote, since the Europeans were busy with their own affairs and were not disposed to interfere in those of America. With the Japanese, however, there was imminent danger, because nationalist sentiment was involved in the Japanese-American rivalry. In an obvious reference to discrimination against Japanese on the West Coast, Mahan stated that Japan regarded as "an insult what we regard as essential to national security in forestalling and avoiding a race problem."[59] Roosevelt did not challenge Mahan's conflation of "national security" with "avoiding a race problem." Instead, he expressed vigorous agreement, telling the admiral, "I wish it were possible to speak quite frankly, and in public, about the excess of our danger in the Pacific over that in the Atlantic."[60]

The month after Roosevelt wrote Mahan, World War I broke out in Europe. Roosevelt threw himself into a "preparedness" campaign during which he called for the construction of a powerful navy, in part to meet the threat of naval attack by Japan. In a Navy Day speech in January 1915, he asserted that if the navy were not strengthened, the United States was in danger of losing not only its Caribbean possessions but "the Hawaiian Islands, Guam, Samoa, and the Philippines."[61]

However, as the United States became drawn into involvement in the First World War, Roosevelt increasingly turned his attention from the potential Japanese threat to the more immediate danger represented by German U-Boats in the Atlantic. He gradually relaxed his previous hawkishness toward the United States' de facto wartime ally, although once the war ended he began commissioning intelligence reports on Japanese espionage in the United States.[62]

By the end of World War I, Roosevelt's attitude toward international affairs had changed drastically. The carnage of the war dampened his interest in warfare and made him abandon much of his previous support for imperialistic ventures. He became an outspoken advocate of America's entry into the League of Nations in order to preserve world peace; and in 1920, running on a pro-League platform, he received the Democratic nomination for vice president.

Roosevelt's support for the League of Nations did not immediately diminish his suspicions toward Japan. In a newspaper interview published shortly after his nomination, Roosevelt argued that if the United States did not join the League and participate in international disarmament efforts, it would have to spend a billion dollars a year to build an enormous army and navy to resist potential threats from "great nations" such as England, France, or Japan.[63] The antimilitarism that had led FDR to support American entry into the League of Nations continued to grow even after the Republican landslide in the 1920 election convinced him that the cause was lost. Though he retreated from outright support for the League, in spring 1921 Roosevelt stated that he was "wholly out of sympathy with this talk about our having the greatest Navy in the world," and he called for international negotiations to foster naval disarmament.[64] "I take it that the easiest way to get Japan, Great Britain and the United States to cease naval competition is for them to get together and agree to stop."[65]

Despite Roosevelt's expression of confidence, Japan and Great Britain immediately launched aggressive naval construction plans. Fearing a naval arms race, in November 1921 President Warren G. Harding and Secretary of State Charles Evans Hughes convened the Washington Naval Conference, which brought together delegates from the United States, Great Britain, and Japan (later joined by France). In return for scrapping existing American ships and abandoning further naval building, Secretary of State Hughes succeeded in persuading England and Japan to dissolve their alliance and to scrap significant portions of their capital fleets. The Washington Naval Treaty, negotiated at the conference, fixed the proportion of capital ships in the American, British, and Japanese navies at a 5:5:3 ratio. In addition, Japan agreed to abandon completely its occupation of China's Shantung Peninsula and joined a nine-power agreement guaranteeing an open-door policy for international trade in China. In exchange, the United States agreed not to further fortify its possessions in Guam and the Philippines.[66]

Shortly after the treaty was signed, the young scholar Raymond Leslie Buell published what remains the most influential study of the conference. Buell described the Far Eastern aspects of the conference as a victory for Japan, asserting that "as a result of the Washington Conference, the intervention of foreign powers in the progress of Japanese imperialism on the continent of Asia is more impossible than ever."[67] Buell warned that peace could be maintained only if Japan embraced liberal internationalism over militarism, and he suggested that the United States support Japanese liberals by ending undemocratic practices against Japanese Americans in order to demonstrate to Japan that its own liberalism was authentic. Buell stated that America, like Australia and Canada, had the right to exclude Japanese immigrant labor "as an economic and racial necessity." He thus suggested formalizing Japanese exclusion in order to close loopholes in the Gentlemen's Agreement. However, to underline that such a measure did not constitute racial discrimination, he proposed that exclusion be accomplished by means of a bilateral treaty between Japan and the United States barring immigration from either country to the other, on the ground that Japan could not object to America being closed to Japanese immigrants if Japan were closed to Americans.

More importantly, Buell advocated granting naturalization privileges to those Japanese immigrants already in the United States and guaranteeing Japanese aliens full civil rights by formal treaty in order to end the insult of legal discrimination in the West Coast states.[68] Buell's intention was to promote liberalism and curb aggressive nationalism in Japan by proving to the Japanese that the Western democracies were prepared to cooperate internationally with them on an equal basis.

Buell's recommendations were not followed. Although many Americans cheered the diplomatic triumph of the conference and welcomed the slowing of the international arms race, anti-Japanese sentiment in the United States continued unabated.[69] A series of works—notably Hector C. Bywater's Sea Power in the Pacific and Walter Pitkin's Must We Fight Japan?—warned that Japan intended to annex America's Pacific islands and that war was inevitable. These weighed heavily against conciliation among the American public.

As before World War I, hostility to Japan was tied closely to the objections of nativist groups to Japanese Americans. Indeed, the issue of Japanese immigration played a significant role in the Senate's rejection of the Treaty of Versailles and membership in the League of Nations in 1919. Although President Wilson vetoed Japan's proposal to enshrine the principle of racial equality in the League's covenant, Henry Cabot Lodge and other Republican leaders in the Senate who opposed the League asserted that U.S. admission to such an international organization would mean the annulling of restrictions on immigration from Japan.[70]

However, unlike the situation before 1914, popular sentiment against Japanese Americans now focused mainly on their racial difference. The Hearst and McClatchey newspaper chains, along with politicians such as Senator James B. Phelan, attacked Japanese Americans through undisguised appeals to white supremacy.[71] Pressure groups such as the Japanese Exclusion League (later the California Joint Immigration Committee) and the California Anti-Oriental League, along with social scientists such as Jess Steiner and Eliot Mears, called for further restrictions on Japanese Americans, including a ban on the immigration of Japanese "picture brides" and the elimination of Japanese-language schools. Some even went so far as to suggest that since the young Nisei were (technically) dual citizens with Japan, they should also be excluded from land ownership. The Japanese immigrant community tried various ways to blunt the force of nativism. In December 1919 Issei leaders successfully lobbied the Japanese government to refuse visas to "picture brides" in order to remove a source of complaints from nativists. Meanwhile, Japanese-American organizations passed resolutions in favor of assimilation, petitioned the federal government for citizenship rights, and brought test cases challenging the alien land acts in the courts.

The task of Japanese Americans was made especially difficult by the establishment during the early postwar years of a powerful nationwide nativist movement, whose leaders advocated substantial or total restriction of immigration and forcible "Americanization" of newcomers.[72] A series of popular anti-immigrant works, beginning with Madison Grant's *The Passing of the Great Race*, published in 1916, encouraged and exemplified popular sentiment. Grant, a zoologist and anthropologist associated with New York's prestigious American Museum of Natural History (the laudatory introduction to his book was written by Museum Director Henry Fairfield Osborn), asserted that the percentage of Nordic blood in a nation's population determined its "strength in war and standing in civilization."[73] Building on the arguments of Homer Lea (whom Grant admired) about the decline of Anglo-Saxon influence, Grant stated that America's previously pure Nordic racial stock had been depleted due to declining birth rates and immigration of inferior races, who had debased the physical and moral qualities of the nation. "Our jails, insane asylums, and almshouses are filled with this human flotsam and the whole tone of American life, social, moral, and political, has been lowered and vulgarized by them."[74] If the Nordics did not begin to reproduce faster, the women of "the Great Race" would soon be forced to intermarry with members of the other races. However, such unions would lead to "race suicide," since the genes of darker groups always predominated over lighter ones.[75]

Although Grant was not concerned with Japanese Americans as such, his thesis served to inspire Lothrop Stoddard's *The Rising Tide of Color against White World-Supremacy* four years later. Stoddard's bestselling book (for which Grant wrote an introduction) stated that the Asian races, weary of white domination, would soon rise up, with Japan at their head, and challenge the Anglo-Saxon race for world domination. The white race, weakened by internecine war and declining birth rates, would be unable to stop the coming onslaught from the Orient unless proper steps were taken. In order to preserve the "race-values" and "race-culture" of the Anglo-Saxons, the nation must apply "rigid exclusion of Orientals" and other darker races whose immigration and reproduction threatened the biological strength of the population.

Stoddard and Grant agreed with Lea that Japanese Americans would become a hostile factor in the coming race war. Yet there was a new element in their contentions. Lea and his followers were primarily concerned about an actual military invasion from Japan.[76] In contrast, Stoddard identified the racial difference of Japanese Americans as an innate source of danger. He stated that "colored triumphs of arms are less to be dreaded than more enduring conquests like migrations which would swamp whole populations and turn countries now white into colored man's lands irretrievably lost to the white world."[77]

In 1921 two bestselling anti–Japanese-American novels, Wallace Irwin's Seeds of the Sun and Peter B. Kyne's The Pride of Palomar, were published. After the Kyne work was serialized in William Randolph Hearst's Cosmopolitan magazine, Hearst commissioned the young journalist Cornelius Vanderbilt, Jr., to compile a survey of public opinion across the country on "the Japanese problem." Vanderbilt solicited responses by sending letters to influential figures asking whether they agreed with the opinions stated in Kyne's novel. Vanderbilt's letter, like Stoddard's book, described the presence of Japanese Americans as a threat to the nation's institutions even in the absence of military danger from Japan: "Personal investigation over three years has shown me that we are drawing near unto the crossroads of America's future Oriental destiny. Japan's future penetration can mean nothing save a direct insult to us. Absolute exclusion of all Orientals will be the only solution of the problem."[78]

Approximately 300 prominent figures from around the United States, including some 35 congressmen, 10 state governors, and dozens of college presidents, newspaper editors, and authors, responded to Vanderbilt's letter.[79] The letters were assembled by region in the book. Perhaps not surprisingly, in view of the tendentious language of Vanderbilt's inquiry, at least 80 percent of the responses in every area of the country favored the complete elimination of Japanese immigration. In FDR's home state of New York, only Lyman Abbott, editor of the progressive journal The Outlook, explicitly opposed anti-Japanese legislation. More typical was City College President

Sidney Mezes, who stated that Asian immigration disrupted democratic society because "Orientals are fundamentally different in their economic, social and political outlook" and could not be assimilated. Edna Ferber (who went on to write a series of novels, such as *Show Boat*, which attacked racial bigotry) added, "No one could be blind to the plans of the Japanese in America, or to the methods by which they go about making those plans secure."[80]

Only a handful of Vanderbilt's correspondents mentioned the concerns that had fueled prewar nativism: the threat of war with Japan. Even more surprisingly, the majority of the writers ignored economic considerations. Instead, most of the authors based their opposition to immigration on the alleged racial difference and non-assimilability of the Japanese and on the need to preserve the United States as a "white" country against the threat of racial dilution.[81] In support of race-based exclusion, several correspondents pointed out (as Stoddard had previously done) that the Japanese limited immigration to their own shores and barred Americans from land ownership there.

Lobbying by nativist groups provoked an unprecedented wave of restrictive government action in the early postwar years. Despite the legal handicaps imposed by the 1913 Alien Land Act, Japanese farmers had tripled their land ownership and lease holdings, and the agricultural production from Japanese-held farmland in California was valued at $67 million, or one-tenth of the total value of the state's produce.[82] In 1920, following a voter initiative sponsored by nativist groups, California enacted a new and more stringent alien land law, which barred Japanese and other Asian immigrants from obtaining long-term leases on land. It also forbade them from serving as "guardians" of land owned by underage citizens, a provision later found unconstitutional by the courts. Henceforth the aliens could no longer protect their property by registering it in the names of their Nisei children.

In 1921 Congress passed the restrictive Johnson Immigration Act. Following the racial theories of Grant and Stoddard, it imposed a series of national quotas amounting to three percent of a given nation's representation in the population in 1910; these were designed to limit the representation of the "new" (non-Nordic) immigrants. Japanese immigration was unaffected, as it was still limited by the 1907–1908 Gentlemen's Agreements under which Japan had forbidden laborers to emigrate to the United States (such emigration became almost nonexistent after 1919, following the cutoff of "picture brides").

The following year, the U.S. Supreme Court (which had delayed hearing the case until after the signing of the Washington Naval Treaty for fear of alienating Japan by an unfavorable ruling) held in *Ozawa v. United States* that Japanese immigrants were ineligible for citizenship. Based on *Ozawa*, the Supreme Court upheld the constitutionality of California's Alien Land Law the following year. Between 1921 and 1925 fourteen states passed similar alien land laws.[83] The restrictionist campaign climaxed in the passage by Congress of the Immigration Act of 1924. This law limited immigration from each European country to two percent of that country's representation in the United States in 1890, thus excluding practically all immigrants from Eastern and Southern European nations, since the majority of immigrants from those nations had come to the United States after that date. In response to nativist pressure, Congress also enacted an absolute ban on Japanese immigration (transparently disguised as a ban on immigrants ineligible for citizenship). Since Japan's quota under the act would have been minimal, the ban was a gratuitous slap in the face which outraged the Japanese and embittered Japanese-American relations. (Indeed, Secretary of State Hughes had testified against the provision, which he claimed would undo the work of the Washington Naval Conference.) By discrediting the Japanese liberals and giving force to the claims of the extreme nationalists in Japan, the 1924 Immigration Act made an important contribution to the shift in Japan's domestic politics during the late 1920s away from liberalism and thus removed a barrier to the domination of the military during the 1930s.[84]

Franklin Roosevelt was not active in official circles while these acts were passed. He returned to private life in November 1920 following his defeat as the Democratic candidate for vice president. Then, in August 1921, he suffered a crippling attack of polio. He spent much of the following seven years trying to regain the use of his paralyzed legs, during which time he was largely absent from public life. However, in order to remain engaged in issues and to keep his name before the public in anticipation of an eventual return to politics, Roosevelt undertook numerous writing projects, kept up what he could of his law practice and business affairs, established regular correspondence with political leaders across the country, and became a prominent political supporter and ally of New York governor and presidential hopeful Al Smith.

Franklin Roosevelt's reaction to the postwar wave of nativism was ambivalent. He deplored open prejudice. He also was a politician from a heavily ethnic state, in which he had to work with ethnic-based political machines and voting blocs to attract majority electoral support. During the 1920s

Roosevelt expended a great deal of time defending Al Smith from nativist and anti-Catholic attacks. As Roosevelt's son Elliott later suggested, FDR's attitudes were shaped in part by his political interests. "Father's pragmatism saved him from bigotry."[85] Moreover, Franklin Roosevelt's vision of America during these years had broadened. While the youthful Roosevelt had described America as an "aryan" nation,[86] in early 1922 he responded to a suggestion by an expatriate American that the Boy Scouts of America (whose New York chapter FDR chaired) be restricted to "Nordic" youth by retorting that there were thousands of Jewish Boy Scouts and pointedly suggesting that the writer return to America in order to better "understand" the country.[87]

At the same time, FDR could not completely escape the influence of nativist ideas, which remained widespread in the nation and among his family and old friends. FDR owned a copy of Madison Grant's *The Passing of the Great Race*, although he made no recorded comment on it. He was also a life member of the Museum of Natural History, where Grant worked and where Henry Fairfield Osborn, an old family friend, was director. In addition, Roosevelt was aware of the political appeal of the anti-immigrant movement. As a result, he tried throughout the 1920s to find a safe intermediate position on immigration, as he did on the question of Prohibition (which sprang in part from similar fears of uncontrollable and immoral foreigners). He approved (or acquiesced in) restrictions and advocated efforts to "Americanize" immigrants, but he also denounced attempts to stigmatize foreigners. For example, in a 1920 interview, Roosevelt, then the Democratic vice-presidential candidate, expressed support for the restriction of unhealthy or feeble-minded aliens but opposed the literacy test (which had been enacted over President Woodrow Wilson's veto three years earlier). He guardedly praised the principle of immigration: "We have had the theory from the start of this government that we have room here for peoples from all countries who are anxious to come here and become Americans . . . We, all of us—some time or another—came from a foreign land to America, and all of us have a love for our native land. But first of all, of course, we should have a love for America and a loyalty for it."[88]

Roosevelt called for mass civic education in order to "Americanize" the immigrants and allow them to assimilate as quickly as possible. He proposed a policy of deliberate government dispersion of immigrants to rural areas on the model of the Canadian system, which he much admired. In a comment that would have great future significance for Japanese Americans, he observed that such dispersion would eliminate racial prejudice by eradicating the immigrants' cultural difference and enabling them to adopt American manners and customs:

> Our main trouble in the past has been that we have permitted the foreign elements to segregate in colonies. They have crowded into one district and they have brought congestion and racial prejudices to our large cities. The result is that they do not easily conform to the manners and the customs and the requirements of their new home. Now, the remedy for this should be the distribution of aliens in various parts of the country. If we had the greater part of the foreign population of the City of New York distributed to different localities upstate we should have a far better condition. Of course, this could not be done by legislative enactment. It could only be done by inducement—if better financial conditions and better living conditions could be offered to the alien dwellers in the cities.[89]

FDR later repeated these sentiments in a short-lived newspaper column, "Roosevelt Says," which he wrote in the *Macon* (Georgia) *Daily Telegraph* during spring 1925. As before, Roosevelt took an equivocal (and inconsistent) position. He denounced anti-immigrant nativism, reminding Americans that they were themselves the children of immigrants, and he hailed the addition of new European "blood of the right sort." Despite such racialist language, Roosevelt evidently did not mean simply "Nordics," since he explicitly praised the Bavarian and northern Italian immigrants in rural New York state. However, while claiming that he did not wish to discuss specific immigration quotas, Roosevelt declared that he agreed with the nativists that immigration should continue to be restricted for "a good many years to come" in order to allow the nation to "digest" (that is, assimilate and Americanize) the people it had already taken in. He added that such immigrants as were thereafter admitted should be the most readily assimilable so that quick "digestion" could proceed. He repeated his conviction that the way to absorb European immigrants was to disperse them throughout the country, as Canada had done. "If, twenty-five years ago, the United States had adopted a policy of this kind we would not have the huge foreign sections which exist in so many of our cities."[90]

Neither FDR's cautious support for immigrants nor his proposals for dispersing the newcomers into rural areas were intended to apply to Japanese Americans (who were targets of prejudice despite living largely in rural areas). Roosevelt preferred to avoid the entire touchy subject of Asian immigration.[91] Significantly, when Cornelius Vanderbilt, his Hyde Park neighbor, wrote in March 1921 to solicit his opinion on the Japanese-American question, FDR was evasive: "I am, of course, interested in the very important subject which you speak of, and should be glad to have a talk with you about it one day."[92]

On September 3, 1922, George Marvin, a journalist and editor whom Roosevelt had known since his Groton days, wrote his old friend to invite him to contribute an article on international affairs for the journal *World's Work*.[93] Roosevelt was intrigued by the idea, since naval and foreign affairs were the areas where he had the greatest knowledge and interest. He was also looking for ways to fight the boredom and depression he experienced after months of inactivity forced on him by polio.[94]

Roosevelt at first declined Marvin's invitation, not only because he was a habitual procrastinator but also because, as he claimed, "I am carefully trying to stay out of print on controversial subjects, and by all that is holy if I got started on any kind of article on international affairs my remarks would most assuredly be controversial." Nevertheless, he suggested that Marvin speak to him again on the subject the following month, remarking, "I may get so mad in the meantime over something that is or is not being done in Washington that the grenade inside me may burst."[95]

In early October 1922 FDR read an editorial in the Boston *Transcript* (based on William Howard Gardiner's article "Atlantic and Pacific Power" in that month's issue of *Current History*) contending that the agreement of the United States under the disarmament provisions of the Washington Naval Treaty of 1922 not to fortify the Philippines and Guam had assured Japanese naval supremacy in the Pacific. The *Transcript* editorial infuriated Roosevelt, who had been one of the few leading Democrats to back the conference. He considered the Washington Naval Treaty a major step toward peace, not only for the actual disarmament it accomplished but also for its psychological effect. FDR feared that a resurgence of militarism would lead to a costly and futile war. He thus decided that the editorial, which he referred to as an example of "thinking in terms of war rather than in terms of trying to remove the causes of war," required a vigorous response, and he abandoned his resistance to writing an article.[96] Marvin agreed to provide research assistance, and he quickly obtained up-to-date figures on armaments from the Navy Department. By March 1923 Roosevelt had produced a draft, which he entitled "The Japs—A Habit of Mind."[97] After minor stylistic editing and the insertion of additional factual material, the piece appeared as "Shall We Trust Japan?" in the July 1923 issue of *Asia*.

"Shall We Trust Japan?" was designed as a "plea for a pacific attitude" in the Pacific and for an end to the instinctive hostility most Americans felt for Japan. FDR's principal point was that, even though it had been "natural" in the past for Japan and the United States to consider each other as "the most probable enemy" and to plan for war with each other, the grounds for such rivalry, particularly in the wake of the Washington Naval Conference, no longer existed.[98] By freezing the size of the American and Japanese navies, the Washington Naval Treaty had reinforced and formalized an existing de facto naval "deadlock" in the Pacific. As naval leaders had long conceded, the Philippines were too large and too distant for the United States to mount an effective defense of them in time of war.[99] Conversely, under the treaty limitations, Japan could not possibly build and supply the overwhelmingly superior armada it would need to cross the ocean and invade and hold the West Coast of the United States. Thus, if war did break out, it would soon degenerate into a costly and futile stalemate.[100]

While many Americans still assumed that conflict with Japan was inevitable, Roosevelt considered such views not only outdated but dangerous, since they might spark an unnecessary war. As Raymond Buell had done the previous year, he took the position that the nation's Pacific colonies were militarily indefensible, and their only security lay in friendly relations between the United States and Japan. FDR expressed confidence that, once Americans abandoned their phobias over the "yellow peril," the underlying causes of U.S.–Japanese friction, such as commercial rivalry and Japanese ambitions in China, could be more easily managed. "If, instead of looking for causes of offense, we in all good faith confidently expect from Japan cooperation in world upbuilding, we shall go far toward insuring peace."[101]

Roosevelt addressed the all-important immigration question somewhat reluctantly—as he stated, it was impossible to discuss without arousing "unreasoning passions on one side or on both."[102] While he conceded that the Japanese, as well as such other Asians as the Chinese, Filipinos, and Indians, were a "race . . . of acknowledged dignity and integrity," he stated flatly that they should be excluded, on racial grounds, from equal citizenship and property rights with whites:

> So far as Americans are concerned, it must be admitted that, as a whole, they honestly believe—and in this belief they are at one with the people of Australasia and Canada—that the mingling of white with oriental blood on an extensive scale is harmful to our future citizenship . . . As a corollary of this conviction, Americans object to the holding of large amounts of real property, of land, by aliens or those descended from mixed marriages. Frankly, they do not want non-assimilable immigrants as citizens, nor do they desire any extensive proprietorship of land without citizenship.[103]

Roosevelt insisted that immigration should be restricted, either by legislation or gentlemen's agreements. Like Raymond Buell, he believed that such restriction was morally justified as long as it was reciprocal: "The reverse of the position thus taken holds equally true. In other words, I do not believe that the American people now or in the future will insist upon the right or privilege of entry into an oriental country to such an extent as to threaten racial purity or to jeopardize the land-owning prerogatives of citizenship. I think I may sincerely claim for American public opinion an adherence to the Golden Rule."[104]

In sum, Roosevelt's position was that the Washington Naval Conference had succeeded in eliminating (or at least indefinitely postponing) war at the cost of ending any possibility of American naval intervention in the Pacific. His goal was to avert useless conflict between the United States and Japan by identifying areas of agreement and potential cooperation between the two countries. He thus focused on easing tensions over the treatment of Japanese Americans, which he considered the chief obstacle to better relations. Although FDR recognized and sympathized with Americans' desire for racial purity and their belief that the Japanese immigrants could not be assimilated, he pointed out that there was no practical difference between America's exclusion of Japanese immigrants and Japan's own restrictions on immigration.

"Shall We Trust Japan?" received a significant amount of positive attention from the Japanese, who either overlooked or were indifferent to Roosevelt's position on Japanese Americans. Japanese newspapers reprinted sections of the articles and praised Roosevelt's statesmanship. Akira Fukami, a business acquaintance of Roosevelt's Oyster Bay cousins Archie and Kermit Roosevelt, met with FDR in November 1924 to invite him to join the Japan Society, though there is no evidence that he did so.[105]

The article received a more mixed reaction in America. In a comment that would later prove revealing, FDR complained to one correspondent about the attitude of "the jingo press" and of the difficulty of persuading public opinion of the facts of U.S.–Japanese relations when "the chain newspapers, such as those conducted by Hearst, cannot see their way clear to making sensational the fact that Japan and the United States have no reason for going to war with each other."[106] Frederick Adams, editor of The Baltimore Sun, invited Hector C. Bywater to reply to Roosevelt's article. Focusing on the threat of a Japanese invasion of the Philippines, Bywater charged that Roosevelt's pacifist policy meant conceding America's Pacific possessions to Japan, which would snap them up to provide needed outlets for her surplus population; and he noted that the naval construction program undertaken by Japan and other powers made lasting peace a dubious proposition.[107] Roosevelt (who had read Bywater's Sea Power in the Pacific during his initial illness) responded that Bywater's attitude was a reflection of the same old instinctive hostility toward Japan he had sought to combat; the greatest threat to peace was the breakdown of mutual trust. In any case, Roosevelt insisted, the Japanese would not want to take over the Philippines as an outlet for their surplus population because "the Japanese are not a tropical race."[108]

Despite the critical attention it received, "Shall We Trust Japan?" had little influence on either policy or popular attitudes toward Japan. The year after it appeared, Congress passed the Immigration Act of 1924, which deeply embittered U.S.–Japanese relations. Roosevelt nevertheless reiterated soon afterward both his friendly policy toward Japan and his racial justification of exclusion. FDR's Macon Telegraph "Roosevelt Says" column of April 30, 1925 (which came one week after his equivocal defense of European immigrants), was written during a diplomatic crisis with Japan prompted by the commencement of naval maneuvers in Hawaii. Roosevelt pointed out that the government had a perfect right to plan maneuvers to defend its coasts, to which defense the Hawaiian bases were central, but the official announcement that the maneuvers were designed to practice defending the islands in the event of a Japanese attack he considered unduly provocative.[109]

FDR added that the announcement paralleled the late campaigns by "troublemakers" on both sides of the Pacific. "Japanese jingoes" complained of the insult of exclusion laws and American attempts to control the China trade. Conversely, "dangerous agitators" in America, who wished to cut off competition from Japanese traders and exclude cheap immigrant labor, brought up the immigration "bogey" and warned of the need to check Japan's commercial and military might. By stirring up anti-Japanese feeling, such agitators had pushed through the Japanese exclusion provisions of the Immigration Act of 1924, but their irresponsible actions had aroused Japanese hostility and poisoned America's diplomatic relations with Japan.

Expanding the logic he had used in his *Asia* article, Roosevelt contended that instead of using economic arguments, America should instead have justified its exclusion law solely on a racial basis: "It is undoubtedly true that in the past many thousands of Japanese have legally or otherwise got into the United States, settled here and raised children who become American citizens. Californians have properly objected on the sound basic ground that Japanese immigrants are not capable of assimilation into the American population. If this had throughout the discussion been made the sole ground for the American attitude all would have been well, and the people of Japan would today understand and accept our decision."[110] FDR argued that if America now explained that its Japanese exclusion policy was based entirely on racial grounds, the tension it had caused between the two countries could still be defused. After all, the Japanese themselves were known to have strong taboos against intermarriage and did not wish their distinct culture to be polluted by racial mixing:

> Anyone who has traveled in the Far East knows that the mingling of Asiatic blood with European or American blood produces, in nine cases out of ten, the most unfortunate results . . . The argument works both ways. I know a great many cultivated, highly educated, and delightful Japanese. They have all told me that they would feel the same repugnance and objection to have thousands of Americans settle in Japan and intermarry with the Japanese as I would feel in having large numbers of Japanese come over here and intermarry with the American population. In this question

then of Japanese exclusion from the United States, it is necessary only to advance the true reason—the undesirability of mixing the blood of the two peoples.[111]

In sum, FDR's position in his two articles during the mid-1920s was that peace depended on "trusting" Japan to keep its commitments to respect the territorial integrity of its neighbors. FDR recognized that this meant adopting a friendly foreign policy that would support Japanese liberals against right-wing nationalist pressures. Like Raymond Buell, Roosevelt approved restriction of Japanese labor, on the model of Australia and Canada. However, he failed to propose that resident Japanese aliens be naturalized or that their civil rights be guaranteed, as both Buell and Theodore Roosevelt had done, and he justified legal discrimination and the denial of equal property rights against the Issei.

To some extent, FDR's position can be explained as a pragmatic response to the necessity of placating nativist public opinion in order to get Americans to accept peace with Japan. (Roosevelt's later comment, in another context, that Buell was an academic theorist who had never shouldered public responsibilities may be revealing in this connection.)[112] Roosevelt clearly considered the exclusion question to be a "bogey" which agitators on both sides used to stir up public opinion. Unlike in the case of European immigrants, there was no real middle ground to take on the Japanese-American issue: domestic political pressure was one-sided against the Issei, and there was little counterpressure for citizenship rights from liberals or ethnic voters. Despite Roosevelt's denunciation of the nativists as "troublemakers," he no doubt realized that an exclusionist position was the only politically realistic one, especially since formal exclusion made little practical difference, given that Japanese immigration was already so severely restricted by the Gentlemen's Agreements.

However, FDR did not simply express his opposition to Japanese Americans on pragmatic grounds, namely, that the Japanese presence in America was a source of unnecessary tension between the two nations or that Japanese laborers provided unfair competition. Rather, echoing TR's private thoughts and Mahan's letter of 1913, as well as the respondents in Cornelius Vanderbilt's book, he justified discrimination on the grounds that the Japanese were people of "oriental blood" and ipso facto "unassimilable." That is, Japanese people remained innately Japanese no matter where they lived, and were not capable of adapting to the very different conditions of life and culture in the United States. They thus provoked resentment among Americans, who saw them as alien and hostile.

This was not a particularly original or controversial position. Commentators from Admiral Mahan and Homer Lea on had spoken of the Japanese immigrants as incapable of Americanization. (Indeed, Roosevelt may have had Mahan's letter, with its repeated use of the term "unassimilable," in mind when he used the same word in his articles.) Meanwhile, Lothrop Stoddard and other writers had identified intermarriage as a form of conquest by the darker races. Roosevelt's articles represented a variation on both these positions. Those who had previously described Japanese Americans as nonassimilable had nevertheless objected to their presence in the United States primarily because it led to friction with Japan or hindered coastal defense in the event of a future Japanese invasion. In contrast, FDR had a genuine interest in wooing Japanese liberals by adopting a conciliatory foreign policy toward Japan. He did not anticipate trouble from Japan over Japanese Americans, although he was aware that the United States' treatment of immigrants was a sore point with the Japanese. At the same time, while FDR agreed with Madison Grant and Lothrop Stoddard that Japanese immigration and civil rights for Japanese Americans were a prelude to inevitable intermarriage, he did not consider people of Japanese ancestry innately hostile or menacing in genetic terms. He did not contend that if Japanese intermarried with whites, their children would inherit the characteristics of the "darker race."

Instead, on the model of Theodore Roosevelt, FDR's underlying assumption was that intermarriage was dangerous because it would break down the unified racial character on which the social cohesion and culture of a nation depended. The "half-breed" offspring of a marriage between Japanese and Americans would inherit two separate and contradictory sets of traits. They would have neither a Japanese nor an Anglo-Saxon racial identity, but would be biological and social misfits.

By the standards of the age, Roosevelt's position was commonplace, and in certain respects enlightened. He praised the Japanese as allies and even as friends, and he denounced demagogues who spread anti-Japanese sentiment to limit economic competition. He also was alert to Japanese sensitivities and expressed indifference as to whether restriction of Japanese immigration should be accomplished by law or by informal gentlemen's agreements. Still, the fact that Roosevelt's comments reflect the conventional wisdom of the period does not make them any less negative. FDR's thesis was that people of Japanese ancestry remained innately Japanese no matter where they lived— even if they were born and raised entirely in the United States, spoke only English, and absorbed American customs—and this made them undeserving of equal citizenship rights. Roosevelt's argument that bans on Issei naturalization and land purchases were necessary to safeguard against widespread "mingling" of the "blood" resembled the attempts of white southerners of the era to justify Jim Crow laws against African Americans on the grounds that they prevented miscegenation.[113] While Roosevelt's Japanese friends, who were all from elite backgrounds distinct from that of most immigrants, may indeed have felt their own racial pride and shared his aversion to intermarriage, they surely did not agree that discrimination against all people of Japanese ancestry was necessary in order to deter it. In any case, white–Asian marriage was statistically insignificant and had been illegal in West Coast states long before the conflict over immigration began. As FDR tacitly acknowledged in his "Roosevelt Says" column, the anti-immigrant laws were passed to reduce economic competition from Japanese-American farmers and landlords by stigmatizing the Issei as undesirables.[114]

Roosevelt's assertion that exclusion of Japanese immigrants was justifiable because Americans did not demand the rights of mass settlement and land ownership in Japan was simply an exercise in bad faith. Quite apart from the fact that white Americans had never, in fact, obeyed the Golden Rule—the United States held Asian colonies, and U.S. citizens enjoyed extensive property holdings and special legal privileges such as extraterritoriality in China and other parts of Asia—Japan was not a nation of immigrants and there was no large group of Americans wishing to emigrate to Japan. Thus, his contention that race-based exclusion was reciprocal was as dishonest as the legal doctrine that "separate but equal" Jim Crow facilities did not constitute discrimination against African Americans.

Most importantly, FDR's focus on preserving "racial purity," coupled with his insistence that Americans (whom he assumed were white) properly objected to the presence of Japanese Americans, reveals that he shared the eugenicist ideas and gentlemanly racism widespread among white Americans of his background and period. This genuine race-based antipathy was reserved for the Issei and their progeny, and by extension other Asian Americans; he never expressed such sentiments toward any other minority group (at least publicly). Both before and during his presidency, he openly praised

Jews and other white ethnics as good citizens. Even though his private views of African Americans were complex and ambiguous, he never advocated discrimination or justified Jim Crow. Roosevelt carried his view of Japanese Americans as irremediably foreign and potentially dangerous into later life, and it helped shape his policy toward them during the 1930s, as the United States and Japan moved toward confrontation.

WAR ABROAD,
SUSPICION AT HOME

WITH THE PASSAGE of the Immigra-
tion Act of 1924, fears of Japanese immigrants and agitation over the "Japanese problem" in the United
States largely disappeared. Although on the West
Coast, where 90 percent of mainland Japanese Americans lived, legal discrimination continued and nativist
groups commenced lobbying for further restrictions
on Japanese residents, nationwide hysteria about the
Japanese menace swiftly subsided. Franklin Roosevelt
could have been forgiven for thinking that the end
of Japanese immigration, although enacted for the
wrong reasons, had made possible a new era of peace-
ful cooperation between the two nations. In 1928, on
the eve of his return to public life as candidate for
governor of New York, Roosevelt was selected by
the Democratic National Committee to present the
Democratic position on international relations for
the influential journal *Foreign Affairs.* In the article,
"Our Foreign Policy: A Democratic View," he reiterated his confidence in Japan and his hopes for international conciliation and disarmament. Only a handful

of irreconcilables still believed that Japan posed a military threat to American security. Taking a slap at his onetime Navy Department allies in the "preparedness" struggle, FDR wrote that war with Japan had now become inconceivable except to "the most excited of the Admirals."[1]

However, Japan and America had begun to move apart. The 1924 Immigration Act outraged Japanese public opinion. Militant Japanese nationalists, already unhappy with the Washington Naval Treaty's "unequal" restrictions on the Japanese Navy, pointed to such "humiliations" as proof that concessions to international opinion were senseless since the Western nations were fundamentally opposed to Japan. They urged an ambitious program to restore national honor. By 1930 Japan's weak liberal regime was faltering under pressure from ultranationalists and the military. In April of that year, at the London Naval Conference, Prime Minister Hamaguchi, a leading internationalist, agreed to extend the Washington Naval Treaty's limitations on Japanese capital ship construction and obtained the emperor's approval for the treaty over the objections of the navy. Soon after, he was assassinated by a military fanatic, an act which crippled the liberal faction.

In 1931 the Japanese military attacked the city of Mukden in the Chinese province of Manchuria, a longtime Japanese sphere of investment and influence. By early 1932 Japan occupied the entire province, and the military-dominated government established the puppet state of Manchukuo. U.S. Secretary of State Henry L. Stimson opposed the Japanese occupation as a violation of treaties and advocated economic sanctions to force Japan to withdraw. President Herbert Hoover, a Quaker pacifist and isolationist, refused to approve unilateral measures against Japan that might lead to war. Great Britain and the other powers in the League of Nations were reluctant to get involved and refused to institute sanctions before having a commission study the situation. Hoover and Stimson ultimately settled on a policy of "non-recognition" of Japan's conquest and of Manchukuo. This so-called Stimson doctrine was controversial. Critics argued that it was too inflexible and that it alienated the Japanese without leading to any effective international action against them.

Franklin Roosevelt was silent on all aspects of the Japanese question during this period. In 1928 he was elected governor of New York. During the next four years, as he concentrated first on New York politics and then on organizing a run for the presidency, FDR remained deliberately aloof from all matters touching on immigration or foreign policy. He likewise carefully stayed away from such issues during his presidential campaign in 1932, with one important exception: in order to gain the indispensable support of influential isolationists such as the newspaper publisher William Randolph Hearst, who controlled the California delegation, Roosevelt formally disavowed interest in American membership in the League of Nations at the time of the Democratic National Convention. Although he did not share the isolationists' belief that America should remain aloof from international organizations, domestic politics—particularly when crucial for achieving office—took precedence over foreign policy principles.

The Japanese attack on Manchuria seems to have been decisive in turning Roosevelt away from conciliation with Japan. Ironically, his election to the White House in November 1932 was initially welcomed by the Japanese as an opportunity for reexamination of the non-recognition policy. In the weeks after election, the government-controlled Japanese press pointedly reprinted the pro-Japanese sections of "Shall We Trust Japan?" including FDR's suggestion that Japan be granted special rights in China. Numerous foreign observers and American commentators agreed that Roosevelt would likely distance himself from the unpopular Stimson doctrine, as he had from Hoover's policies on international debt repayment and currency issues.[2]

However, on January 9, 1933, Secretary of State Stimson visited the President-elect at Hyde Park to discuss foreign affairs. Roosevelt agreed with Stimson during their talk that Japan had temporarily reverted "to the old position of a feudal, military aristocracy" which had now overextended itself in Manchuria. The Japanese occupation would soon collapse, the military would be discredited, and liberal forces would re-emerge.[3] Roosevelt assured the outgoing secretary of state that he would not change U.S. policy in the Far East. A week later, he publicly stated that "American foreign policies must uphold the sanctity of international treaties," a statement universally seen as an endorsement of the non-recognition policy.[4] The new President explained to the British ambassador, Ronald Lindsay, that "there is nothing to be done at present and the question can only be solved by the ultimate inability of Japan to stand the strain any longer."[5] Challenged by Rexford Tugwell and Raymond Moley, his chief "Brains Trust" advisors, as to his reasons for committing himself to the Republicans' non-recognition policy even before he entered office, and before the League of Nations decided on whether to impose sanctions, Roosevelt explained that he trusted Stimson. When the two advisors protested that he was risking war, he replied that if his position meant war with Japan, it might as well come sooner rather than later. In any case, the President asserted, he could not abandon China, a nation with which he had longstanding family ties and the deepest sympathy.[6]

Roosevelt's embrace of the non-recognition policy signaled a decisive shift in attitude toward Japan. He never again manifested the trust he had shown during the 1920s. Instead, his wariness increased in the following years, as Japan solidified its hold on Manchuria and menaced the rest of East China. During the balance of his first term, in the early 1930s, FDR's policy toward Japan consisted of a series of actions designed to dissuade the Japanese from further militarization without provoking armed conflict. Roosevelt's strategy applied psychological and economic pressure—an intermittent and cautious forerunner of the "containment" policy later envisioned by George Kennan.

As part of this strategy, Roosevelt deliberately avoided warlike conduct toward Japan, including making any direct threats or renouncing trade agreements and imposing economic sanctions. He made various conciliatory gestures, hoping to spark a revival among Japanese liberals, who would restrain the military from further imperialistic ventures. He retained the popular ambassador in Tokyo, Joseph Grew, and he met for confidential talks in Washington with Japanese representatives, including future foreign minister Yatsue Matsuoka and Viscount Ishii. In May 1933 FDR made a bold proposal to associate the United States with world disarmament efforts by stating that America would abide by any multilateral pact, thus signaling to Japan his desire to avoid war. In December 1933 Roosevelt assured the Japanese that he had no intention of isolating them diplomatically, and he withdrew most of the American fleet from the Pacific to the Atlantic, as the Japanese had repeatedly requested.[7]

Even as FDR made conciliatory gestures toward Japan, he also prepared for conflict.[8] During 1933 Roosevelt rejected Japanese proposals for a bilateral non-aggression pact, and he began a program of naval rearmament within the limits permitted by treaty. He commented in a letter to a friend that, while he would prefer to come to an agreement with Japan, he was forced to undertake the buildup to enable the United States to equal Japan's naval strength. "The whole scheme of things in Tokyo does not make for an assurance of non-aggression in the future," he noted.[9] In December 1933 Roosevelt officially recognized the Soviet Union, Japan's Far East rival, in a move designed partly to counter Japanese influence, and he privately promised diplomatic support in any future war the Soviets might wage with Japan. Nevertheless, FDR declined Russia's simultaneous offer to discuss a bilateral non-aggression pact and expressed his support for a regional treaty that would include China and Japan, provided Japan would first abandon Manchuria.

Meanwhile, Roosevelt voiced increasing suspicion of the Japanese. According to his cousin Margaret Suckley, FDR commented in January 1934 that there was trouble brewing with Japan and referred to his 1902 Harvard conversation with Otohiko Matsukata regarding Japan's purported plan for gradual expansion through Manchuria and China and ultimate conquest of Asia. Roosevelt told his cousin, "It is a plan looking a century ahead, a thing we Anglo-Saxons can't do, and in considering what *has* happened so far, since 1900, [the Japanese] seem to be carrying out this plan."[10] When, in April 1934, Japan announced the Amau doctrine, which claimed East Asia as Japan's special sphere of influence, and warned the other powers not to interfere in China, Roosevelt's fears of Japanese imperialism were reinforced. He made no immediate response to the Amau doctrine beyond a diplomatic note asserting U.S. interest in China, but he scheduled a tour of Hawaii during summer 1934 which included inspection of military bases, a trip widely interpreted as a warning to Tokyo. By 1935 Roosevelt had evidently abandoned hope of moderating Japanese policy in East Asia. When a peace delegation led by the Reverend Harry Emerson Fosdick visited the White House to protest "provocative" American naval maneuvers in the Western Pacific, Roosevelt repeated his story of his Harvard conversation and stated bluntly that aggression "was in the blood" of the Japanese leaders.[11]

However, while Roosevelt may have been ready to "do something" about "bandit nations" such as Japan, his attention remained fixed on the economic crisis in the United States, and he did not wish to endanger the nation's recovery by disrupting unnecessarily America's profitable trade with Japan.[12] Japan was an important market for oil, steel, and raw materials, and a number of Japanese firms had American subsidiaries. In addition, the President's power to intervene in Asian affairs was circumscribed by strong isolationist sentiment in the country.

In December 1934, Japan announced its determination not to renew the 5:5:3 ratio of capital ships prescribed by the Washington Naval Treaty and demanded naval parity with the United States and Great Britain.[13] A second naval conference was quickly convened in London in January 1935, but it rapidly adjourned when the parties failed to reach agreement. Fearing a new naval arms race, Roosevelt requested a large defense appropriation in his 1935 budget. The new isolationist-dominated Congress sharply cut the defense request instead and in mid-1935 passed a Neutrality Act cutting off trade with all nations engaged in war, both aggressors and victims. Roosevelt, hoping to retain control over enforcement, reluctantly signed the measure into law. Realizing that his only hope for maintaining U.S. naval supremacy in an increasingly dangerous international environment was either to negotiate further limitations on naval strength among the Great Powers or to win public support for rearmament by placing the burden of blame on Japan for rejecting such limitations, the President sent a group of American representatives to a reconvened London Naval Conference in late 1935. There they proposed an innocuous agreement extending the treaty limitations on the naval strength of the Great Powers through qualitative curbs on various kinds of armaments. Japan responded by rejecting even a pro forma limitation on naval armaments on the grounds that it constituted discrimination against her, and the Japanese walked out of the conference. The United States and Great Britain, left to their own devices, signed a bilateral extension of the treaty which allowed them to mutually increase naval strength against non-signatories.

After the failure of the second London Naval Conference, Roosevelt moved decisively into the anti-Japanese camp. On January 3, 1936, shortly before the Japanese delegation walked out of the conference, Roosevelt made his annual address to Congress. He denounced the threat to the peace-loving nations, who comprised the vast majority of the world, by a few "European and Asian nations" who held "the fantastic conception that they alone are chosen to fulfill a mission and that all others must and shall learn from them and be subject to them." His reference to "Asian nations" was obviously directed at Japan. The President warned that the developing situation "has in it many of the same elements that lead to the tragedy of general war."[14] As if to confirm his fears, on February 26 the Japanese army attempted a coup against the government in Tokyo. While the military officers failed to overturn the government, several leading moderates were killed or wounded, and the episode sounded a warning to those that remained. They would subsequently become even more cautious in opposing the military's aims and designs.

In spring 1936 Roosevelt again asked Congress to grant funds for a massive program of naval rearmament. Administration lobbyists, bolstered by Japan's refusal to sign a naval limitation treaty, persuaded Congress that further ships and arms were needed to defend the Western Hemisphere. Roosevelt reassured pacifist leaders that Japan would soon be forced to cease her aggressive actions due to lack of raw materials and money. The Japanese, FDR said, could not "hold out much longer."[15] Unlike in 1935, the appropriation was quickly approved. In the following months, as FDR campaigned successfully for reelection, relations with Japan and other foreign policy matters were subordinated to pressing domestic concerns. However, Roosevelt had already begun to plan for the eventuality of war in the Pacific.

As FDR began planning for conflict with Japan, he turned his attention to Japanese activities in the New World. These had previously been of peripheral interest, as when, in 1933, he had commissioned a study of Japanese immigration and "infiltration" of Latin America. He had simultaneously communicated about Japanese activities in Mexico with Ambassador Josephus Daniels, his old Navy Department boss. In 1934 Roosevelt had asked the State Department to prepare a report on possible Japanese espionage on the West Coast of the United States.[16] In spring 1936, according to one witness, the President revealed his anxiety over Japanese penetration of the Americas: "His primary concern about Japan was in relation to South America. Should she, for example, try to lease for 99 years, say, some area of land in Ecuador— then the U.S. would have to act."[17] However, the State Department considered the Japanese danger in Latin America small.[18]

Meanwhile, the President focused his attention, for the first time, on the Japanese-American community. During FDR's early years in office, when his primary goal had been attacking the Great Depression through the reform program of the New Deal, the Japanese-American community had remained largely outside the administration's notice. There was little demand for relief or government assistance by the Nikkei community as a whole, which traditionally supported its own members. Furthermore, Japanese Americans on the West Coast were largely excluded from New Deal public works jobs during the 1930s as a result of discrimination by local authorities, although a few individual Nisei (notably artists such as Isamu Noguchi and Miné Okubo) did obtain federal government employment through the Works Progress Administration. The Japanese-American community itself was too small to form a useful electoral bloc in the New Deal coalition. The Issei, as aliens, did not have the right to vote, while most Nisei were too young to exercise the franchise. There were no Japanese-American or other Asian-American staffers in the White House, or even any advisors with links to such communities, to keep Roosevelt informed about their concerns. In his many speeches cele-brating America's ethnic diversity, the President never cited Japanese or other Asians as a constituent American group. On the contrary, in a rare communi-cation to the Japanese-American community, he explicitly linked the Nisei with Japan by praising their efforts to strengthen friendly ties between Japan and the United States.[19]

Meanwhile, Japanese immigrants remained excluded under the 1924 Immi-gration Act. Although Japan did not officially attempt to persuade Roosevelt to repeal the ban, the administration was well aware that the issue loomed over diplomatic relations between the two countries. However, FDR knew that the question of Japanese immigration was still explosive on the home front, and he was not prepared to work for repeal of restrictions which he had previously endorsed. The administration thus acted defensively to dispel any hint of change in policy. In January 1934 Roosevelt received a joint letter from twenty members of the California and Oregon congressional delega-tions, warning of the unfortunate consequences of any attempt to alter the Japanese exclusion policy and institute a Japanese immigration quota. The Japanese and other Asians, the letter alleged, would never be satisfied with "equality," and they would derail the entire quota system. Although Roose-velt privately expressed disdain for the attitude of the writers (he told his advisors to bring in "the most responsible of California Congressmen" to dis-cuss the matter), he pledged not to bring up the immigration question with the Japanese.[20]

In April 1934 Secretary of State Cordell Hull and his assistant William Phillips, upon learning that Japan was about to launch a diplomatic offensive, assumed incorrectly that any such demarche would include proposals for immigration reform. They strongly urged FDR to inform the Japanese gov-ernment, should it raise the question, that not only was there no foreseeable hope that Congress would repeal the exclusion law but that even to promise to consider the issue officially would "create a new increment of criticism of the administration and . . . inject new and inflammatory irritants into the sit-uation as between the United States and Japan."[21]

The supremacy of West Coast nativist interests over administration policy on Asian immigration was tellingly demonstrated by Roosevelt's actions in regard to the Philippines. In 1933, just before FDR took office, Congress passed the Hare-Hawes-Cutting Bill, which would grant independence to the commonwealth after ten years, conditioned on the maintenance of existing American military bases. In response to pressure from West Coast commercial and nativist groups, the bill also contained provisions ending free trade between America and the Philippines and limiting Philippine immigration to the United States, which had hitherto been unrestricted, to fifty people per year until independence, after which time further immigration would be barred. In October 1933 the Philippine legislature rejected these terms. The legislature passed a resolution stating that the bill's military and economic provisions were unacceptable and the ban on immigration was "objectionable and offensive to the Filipino people."

The Filipinos then commissioned Manuel Quezon to visit Washington and press Roosevelt, whom they perceived as sympathetic, for a better deal. FDR met with Quezon in early 1934. Although he was willing to make concessions on the military base and economic issues, he flatly refused to support any alteration in the immigration provisions of the bill and suggested instead that the Filipinos erase the insult by enacting reciprocal restrictions. With the President's vague promise to correct afterward any "imperfections or inequalities," the FDR-endorsed Tydings-Macduffie Bill quickly passed through Congress and was reluctantly approved by the Filipinos.[22]

On the domestic front, the immigration issue remained largely dormant. The Japanese-American community did not lobby strongly for repeal of the 1924 Immigration Act. Instead, through organizations such as the Japanese American Citizen's League (JACL), founded in 1930, the young Nisei leadership took advantage of the end of immigration to challenge the dominance of the older generation Issei within Japanese-American communities. The JACL's chief concern was Americanization of the Japanese, including naturalization of the Issei immigrants, who remained "ineligible to citizenship" under the 1790 Naturalization Act. The JACL lobbied for naturalization rights for Japanese aliens through newspaper articles, speeches, and educational activities.

Roosevelt's attitude toward naturalization of Japanese immigrants is unclear. In 1935, following a long personal campaign by Tokie Slocum, a Japanese-American veteran of World War I, Congress approved by an overwhelming margin the Lea-Nye Bill, which granted citizenship to some 500 U.S. Army veterans from "oriental" countries. The bill's chief sponsors were pro-New Deal California Congressman Clarence Lea (who would, ironically, later become one of the chief instigators of the internment of Japanese

Americans) and Senator Gerald Nye, a leading isolationist. Roosevelt signed the measure into law on June 25, 1935.[23]

Despite his willingness to act on popular measures, Roosevelt had no interest in upsetting politically powerful nativist and anti-Asian forces by granting citizenship to more than a handful of Issei. During the same period, he refused, evidently on racial grounds, to grant citizenship rights to other Asian peoples. In 1933, after indigenous leaders in Guam heard reports that Roosevelt had expressed support during a private conversation for extending American citizenship to the colony's mixed-race Chamorro population, they organized a petition for citizenship which received almost 2,000 signatures. However, the secretary of the navy secured the President's agreement to oppose any citizenship bill based on the petition on the ground that the Chamorros "are Orientals."[24]

Although he had little contact with Japanese Americans, Roosevelt grew concerned about the Japanese-American community as relations worsened between the United States and Japan. In the event of war between the two countries, he believed, the community was a potential source of pro-Japanese fifth columnists. Thus, beginning in spring 1936, he made significant efforts to investigate and neutralize any possibility of disloyal activity. His efforts focused on the Japanese-American residents of the then-territory of Hawaii, known in Hawaiian usage as the "local Japanese." They accounted for one third of the islands' population and represented the most important segment of the plantation labor force on which the territorial economy depended.

The government's concern about the Japanese Hawaiians was not new. The army's War Plans Division had long feared that the local Japanese in Hawaii would support Japan in case of a Japanese invasion of the islands. In the early 1920s, the division, led by its assistant chief of staff, Colonel John DeWitt (the future chief instigator of the internment), produced a "Project for the Defense of Oahu." The project, which formed part of a "Joint Defense Plan" (so called because it involved both army and navy forces) to be used in case of conflict with Japan, included contingency plans for imposing martial law in Hawaii, suspending the writ of habeas corpus, instituting registration of Japanese "enemy aliens," and selectively interning those believed to be dangerous. This plan, with minor modifications, remained in effect into the 1930s.

In 1933 the Hawaiian branch of G-2 (Army Intelligence) compiled a new 15-volume report, entitled *Estimate of the Situation—Japanese Population in*

Hawaii. The report presented an apocalyptic picture of Japanese-American disloyalty and danger. Both first- and second-generation Japanese in Hawaii, it stated, displayed Japanese "racial traits" such as "moral inferiority" to whites, fanaticism, duplicity, and arrogance. Under the influence of these traits, the report asserted, the local Japanese population resisted Americanization, while Japanese schools and churches inculcated their loyalty to the militarists in Japan. As Hawaii's Japanese population increased, the territory would lose all its American character and become Japanese in fact if not in name. The white population of Hawaii, the report concluded, was convinced that in any war with Japan the majority of the Japanese population would prove disloyal and that there was a large segment of it prepared to commit sabotage and "seriously interfere" with the defense of the key island of Oahu. A series of reports on Japanese organizations in Hawaii by the FBI and G-2 during the following two years further confirmed the subversive and pro-Japanese nature of the local Japanese population.[25]

The army's Hawaiian Department sent the completed reports to Secretary of War George H. Dern. Though Dern may have shown them to Roosevelt, there is no evidence that the President was so informed. What is known is that Dern turned the reports over to the War Plans Division. Based on the army's "findings" that the Japanese population would be actively disloyal in event of war, the War Plans Division feared that the army would not be able to defend the entire territory and recommended the drafting of a more stringent Joint Defense Plan. After an unexplained delay of almost three years, an Army-Navy Joint Planning Committee began to revise the contingency plans for Hawaii. In May 1936 (less than one month after the London Naval Conference broke up), entering Secretary of War Harry Woodring approved a revision of the former Joint Defense Plan to include active intelligence efforts, among them surveillance of the local Japanese in order to prevent an armed uprising by local Japanese or a sneak attack by Japanese invaders and local Japanese partisans.

On May 25, 1936, the Joint Planning Committee submitted a report to the chief of naval operations, who passed it on to the President. The report described some of the problems of defense of the islands in the case of a massive Japanese invasion. It questioned, for example, whether the main island of Hawaii, with its thinly populated west coast, should be reinforced to guard against attack. The report centered on the difficulties of meeting the threat to security posed by contact between Japanese commercial vessels and

Japanese Americans in the Hawaiian Islands. Japanese tankers routinely stopped in Oahu, where "many of the visiting Japanese naval personnel have close relatives among the local Japanese residents." Ship's officers delivered mail from Japan to the locals and visited "hotels, tea-houses, shrines, temples, and schools" to spread subversion:

> Aside from the espionage activities of the visiting Japanese vessels, they serve as a direct medium of contact between the Japanese residents of Hawaii and their homeland, and the personnel of these vessels are naturally looked to for interpretation of conditions and events in Japan. The visiting Japanese naval personnel make most of the opportunity. Through lectures, moving pictures, exhibitions, etc. is born home to the local Japanese the 'greatness' of Japan, her virility, and her absolute superiority over all other countries. In fact, every effort of Japanese naval personnel ashore here appears to be deliberately calculated to advance Japanese nationalism and to cement bonds of loyalty.

FDR reviewed the report and replied that in order to deal with the local Japanese "threat," the Joint Planning Committee should make contingency plans to cover "the Japanese population" of all the islands, not just Oahu. Referring to the possibility of invasion, he asked the committee for suggestions as to whether the government should reinforce the island of Hawaii, which he knew had no ports and thus little military value, or fall back on Oahu in such an event. Impressed by the description of subversive activity between Japanese sailors and the local population, the President commented, "One obvious thought occurs to me—that every Japanese citizen or non-citizen on the Island of Oahu who meets these Japanese ships or has any connection with their officers or men should be secretly but definitely identified and his or her name placed on a special list of those who would be the first to be placed in a concentration camp in the event of trouble."[26]

This memo has often been seen as a precursor of the government's later establishment of the internment camps, and even as proof that the internment was actually the realization of a longtime design in Roosevelt's mind to put Japanese Americans in concentration camps.[27] Although there are clear commonalities between the action suggested in the memo and the later events—most importantly Roosevelt's reference to "concentration camps" and his failure to make any distinction between enemy aliens and American citizens of Japanese ancestry—there are also significant differences. Roosevelt's 1936 memo was limited to Hawaii, a territory belonging to the U.S., not a sovereign state thereof. Furthermore, the memo proposed action to be taken only in the event that the territory came under direct attack, and following the imposition of martial law. While the memo approved the summary internment of suspicious Japanese Americans regardless of citizenship, it did not contemplate mass imprisonment or mass evacuation of the entire local Japanese population. Indeed, there never was a mass removal of Japanese Hawaiians during World War II.

Yet, even without overstating its connection to future events, the memo is significant. It is the first sign of the President's personal interest and involvement in the question of "control" of Japanese Americans by the military, and of his growing acceptance of the idea, disseminated by the military, that the Japanese-American community in Hawaii constituted an inherent and undifferentiated threat to national security. It demonstrates the President's willingness to tolerate arbitrary action against Japanese Americans in the name of preserving security and his indifference to the constitutional rights of those citizens and aliens involved.

This trait appears even more clearly in the exchange of memos that followed. After reviewing Roosevelt's suggestion for concentration camps, the secretaries of war and the navy sent a letter informing the President that military intelligence units had long retained a general list of Japanese-American "suspects" to be interned in times of danger.[28] Roosevelt evidently decided that these lists would suffice, for he quickly dropped his proposal for a special list. Ironically, in view of the critical attention that Roosevelt's concentration camp proposal has received, the army's plan was far more restrictive and arbitrary. The President's plan called for the confinement only of those against whom there was at least some prima facie evidence of subversion—namely, contact with Japanese ships. In contrast, the army's lists, as Roosevelt must have realized, were made up of local Japanese teachers and merchants who were selected for internment simply because of their prominence in the Japanese community.[29] They were, in essence, hostages who would be held to assure community good behavior.

In that same letter, the secretaries of war and navy informed the President that they were instituting a program of employment discrimination on a racial basis whereby they would assure that future civil service vacancies in defense installations in Hawaii would be filled by "selected citizens of unquestionable loyalty rather than by citizens generally of alien extraction whose loyalty may be questionable." Despite the arbitrary and clearly invidious nature of such a measure, FDR did not raise any objection.[30]

The President's Hawaii memo served as the catalyst for more intensive government surveillance of any contact by Japanese Americans with Japanese. In May 1937 Roosevelt appointed the secretary of war to chair an interagency committee to find a "practical means" of curbing Japanese espionage, and he subsequently approved the committee's report, which called for, among other things, legislation to control ownership of fishing boats by aliens and for surveillance by the customs service of all individuals entering or leaving Japanese "public vessels" in Honolulu, in order to avert any secret entry of Japanese.[31] He asked Admiral William Leahy to investigate Japanese crab fishermen to assure that they were not engaging in subversion.[32] In May 1937, following reports of activities by Japanese spies meeting Japanese-American contacts on the West Coast, the War Department compiled a report on Japanese activities in "lower California" and Mexico. (Although "lower California" generally refers to the Mexican state of Baja California, the fact that lower California is identified separately from Mexico indicates that the report may have referred to the "southern California" portion of the United States.) Upon receiving it, Roosevelt complained that the report was based on second-hand and patently inaccurate information. "The citation of naval visits to the coast line of lower California as evidenced is wholly absurd—the officers and men see nothing of what goes on one hundred feet back from the beach. I should think G-2 could arrange for some individual or individuals to cover the whole of lower California and prepare a careful check. It should not cost much or take any great amount of time."[33] Within a few months, the War Department compiled a revised report, which minimized the numbers and activities of Japanese residents in Mexico.[34]

Roosevelt's efforts during 1936–37 to investigate and restrict Japanese Americans in Hawaii and the Pacific Coast were a direct outgrowth of his fears of Japanese invasion. Except for his acceptance of employment discrimination in the territorial civil service, all of the President's actions appear to have been reasonable precautions to guard against espionage or to prepare for the eventuality of direct Japanese attack. Roosevelt's orders came in response to military reports, which represented the most reliable information available to him—there was no FBI office then operating in Hawaii. As his response to the War Department's report on Mexico indicates, FDR did not accept military fears of a Japanese threat entirely at face value. Nevertheless, his actions demonstrate his readiness to assume that Japanese Americans, whether alien or U.S.-born, were potentially disloyal and to take preventive measures. He did not make any similar effort to keep tabs on Americans of German or Italian ancestry during this period, despite the presence of Nazi agents in the United States and the propaganda activities of pro-Axis groups such as the German Bund.

In July 1937 Japan crossed the Marco Polo Bridge and launched a full-scale invasion of northern China. Japanese planes bombed civilians in Shanghai, Canton, and other cities, and the Japanese Army brutally repressed all opposition, engaging in torture and mass execution of Chinese resisters. In December 1937, after a protracted bombing campaign, the Japanese Army conquered Nanking, the seat of the Chinese Nationalist government. Over the following six weeks, Japanese soldiers engaged in wholesale looting, rape, and murder of the city's population, killing at least 100,000 people and possibly many more.

Roosevelt was outraged by the Japanese atrocities, which he considered a violation of all civilized behavior. He was particularly stricken by the despoiling of China, a nation to which he felt a personal attachment. However, the isolationist mood in the country limited his ability to respond. In May 1937 Congress passed a new and strengthened Neutrality Act, banning trade with belligerent nations or travel in war zones. Roosevelt tried to work out a settlement in China by convening a Nine-Power conference in Brussels under the auspices of the Washington Naval Treaty, but Japan refused to attend. The President then tried to prepare public opinion for strong collective action against aggressor nations, and in a speech in Chicago on October 5, 1937, he proposed international agreements to "quarantine" them. However, the speech did not arouse what FDR considered a sufficiently strong public response to support taking such action, and the following day he disavowed the idea of economic sanctions. In December 1937 Japanese planes deliberately bombed and sank the U.S.S. *Panay* while it lay at anchor in the Yangtze River. The American public reacted with outrage, and Roosevelt denounced the attack. However, when Japan apologized for its action and offered compensation, American public opinion forced FDR to accept the Japanese apology and abandon any thought of retaliatory action.

During the two years that followed, Roosevelt avoided invoking the Neutrality Act to cover China, and he provided moral and financial support to the

Chinese government in its struggle against Japan. FDR considered imposing sanctions against Japan and toyed with various schemes for economic retaliation.[35] However, he did not take any definite action. Roosevelt was primarily concerned with the threat of Germany and Italy, especially after Hitler swallowed up Czechoslovakia in 1938, and he was reluctant to commence action against Japan in the face of opposition from Great Britain, whose leaders remained focused on Nazi aggression in Europe and feared war in the Far East.[36] Also, despite the strength of anti-Japanese sentiment in the United States, public opinion remained strongly opposed to foreign entanglements. FDR was thus forced to rely on moral suasion and rearmament to pressure Japan to withdraw from China.

By mid-1940, however, Roosevelt had adopted a get-tough policy with Japan. Hitler's invasion of Poland in September 1939, and especially the fall of France in June of the following year, increased Roosevelt's anxiety about fascist aggression and pushed him to take stronger defensive measures. In August 1940 he traded fifty overage destroyers to Great Britain in exchange for leases on British naval bases in the Western Hemisphere. In September Roosevelt signed the Selective Service Act, which authorized the first peacetime military draft in the history of the United States. Sixteen million young men, including thousands of Nisei, registered for the draft. After Japan signed the Tripartite Pact with Germany and Italy in September 1940, Roosevelt could more easily connect Japan with the warlike behavior of Hitler and Mussolini. Cabinet changes also contributed to the shift in policy. In mid-1940, Roosevelt appointed Henry Stimson and Frank Knox, two interventionist Republicans, as, respectively, secretary of war and secretary of the navy. The new Cabinet members, especially Stimson, the architect of the nonrecognition policy, were outspoken champions of standing up to Japan.

In late 1939 the lapse of the 1911 Japanese-American Commercial Treaty gave Roosevelt more leeway in instituting economic pressure against Japan. Early the next year the State Department succeeded in persuading American companies not to sell airplanes or parts to Japan by calling for an unofficial "moral embargo" on nations that bombed civilians. In July Congress passed a law granting the President authority to regulate exports of goods deemed essential to the American war effort. In late July, with the support of Stimson and Secretary of the Treasury Henry Morgenthau, Roosevelt used his power under that law to immediately halt sales of high-quality iron and steel to Japan, and he soon used his "licensing" power to eliminate sales of all strategic materials except petroleum. However, Roosevelt did not cut off sales of scrap metal to Japan despite criticism from pro-Chinese forces, who complained that the Japanese were turning the metal into planes and munitions. Pressed by his son Elliott as to why these sales were continuing, Roosevelt explained that scrap iron could not be considered an essential military item, and Japan would be justified in cutting off diplomatic relations or even declaring war if America committed such an unfriendly act. "We're appeasing Japan in order to gain the time we have to have to build a first-rate navy, a first-rate army."[37]

Roosevelt's get-tough policy translated into a crackdown on Japanese Americans as well. To some degree, this reflected a generalized fear, within the government, of "foreigners." In mid-1940 FDR transferred the Immigration and Naturalization Service from the Labor to the Justice Department, and he signed a law requiring all aliens to register with the government. Nevertheless, FDR and the military seem to have perceived Japanese Americans not only as aliens but as appendages of Japan. In October 1940 Navy Secretary Knox sent FDR a memo proposing fifteen steps to be taken "to impress the Japanese with the seriousness of our preparations" for war. These included the establishment of defensive areas by presidential proclamation, the transfer of the coast guard to the navy, and seizure of Japanese and German ships in or near American ports. Significant among the recommendations for action was Number 12, which read: "Prepare plans for concentration camps (Army-Justice)."[38] The terse (and cryptic) nature of this proposal suggests that the topic of concentration camps, at least of some kind, was familiar to Roosevelt, and the circumstances of the proposal suggest that Japanese Americans were the intended targets. It is not clear from the allusion to the Justice Department whether these camps were designed to control suspect individuals, like those contemplated in 1936, or whether Justice (which had jurisdiction over "alien enemies") had been selected to operate mass internment camps. In any case, Knox's suggestion that the internment of Japanese Americans would intimidate Tokyo indicates that he considered them essentially as adjuncts of Japan. At the same time, FDR stepped up security efforts. In June 1939 he ordered the army's G-2 and the Office of Naval Intelligence (ONI) to coordinate anti-espionage and anti-sabotage activities with the FBI. In June 1940 the FBI was granted control over cases against individual subversives. The ONI was assigned to watch over Japanese Americans.[39]

In November 1940 the FBI (which had just reopened its Honolulu office after a six-year hiatus) produced a long report on Hawaii that rebutted most of the military charges of Japanese-American disloyalty. The FBI reported that within the local Japanese community a "large esoteric inner circle" of some 1,000 "consular agents," Japanese school teachers, and Buddhist and Shinto priests was at high risk for espionage. Still, the FBI reported that this inner circle was a small group, most of whose members had resided in Hawaii for only a short time. Conversely, there was typically much less sympathy for Japan among either "the local born Japanese [whom the FBI reported made up nearly 80 percent of the Japanese population] or the alien Japanese who have been residing in the Hawaiian Islands for the greater part of their life-time." Indeed, the long-time resident aliens were even more "American in ideals and principles" than the American-born Japanese language teachers.[40] Since the Nisei, who were "presently believed by some to be loyal to the United States," risked having their loyalties turned by Japanese propaganda, the memo proposed that the government organize Nisei into pro-American and anti-Japanese associations.

In sum, the FBI report contended that the vast majority of local Japanese (except for a small, easily identifiable group which had not had time to assimilate) were American in their values and loyal to the United States. Although the FBI report did not refer directly to the Joint Planning Committee's description of Japanese Americans as massively disloyal, it offered a devastating critique of the committee's findings.[41]

The events of 1941—the fruitless peace negotiations and the tightening of the knot of war between Japan and the United States—are long and complicated. The story of the lead-up to Pearl Harbor is overshadowed by the dark controversy over Roosevelt's possible foreknowledge of the Japanese attack. It is enough to say that the positions of the two countries remained largely irreconcilable, although Japan made several very conditional gestures toward peace. The Japanese, burdened with the occupation of China, wanted solid security and economic guarantees. Roosevelt and Secretary of State Hull, though anxious for peace, absolutely refused to accept Japanese dominion in China.

In February 1941, after a moderate Cabinet led by Prince Konoye took power, the Japanese government sent Roosevelt's onetime friend Admiral Nomura, who was regarded as pro-American, as ambassador to Washington.[42] FDR was not receptive. He believed that a firm stand by the United

States could force Japan to leave China, and he was extremely skeptical about the chances for a negotiated resolution of the conflict. The President's skepticism that spring was undoubtedly heightened by his reading of the secret instructions Japan's government was sending its representatives via the MAGIC code, which the United States had broken.[43] Referring to a cable from Foreign Minister Matsuoka to Nomura defending the Japanese position, FDR called it the work of a man who was "insane." On the other hand, Roosevelt was willing to commence talks. He was absorbed during 1941 in preparing the country for eventual entry into the war in Europe on the side of Great Britain. He did not wish to be distracted by hostilities in the Pacific, which would require him to divert attention and precious resources from the European situation. As FDR wrote privately, "I simply have not got enough Navy to go around—and every little episode in the Pacific means fewer ships in the Atlantic."[44] Isolationist sentiment in Congress and among the public remained strong. Although the Lend-Lease Bill, which provided $7 billion of military aid to the allied nations, easily passed Congress in March 1941, in August the House of Representatives approved the extension of Selective Service by only a single vote. Roosevelt considered negotiations with Japan useful. Even though they were unlikely to lead to an agreement, they would in any case delay the outbreak of war in the Pacific and would persuade public opinion that the administration was doing all it could to secure peace. Thus, after a brief meeting with Nomura, Roosevelt invited him to confer with Hull, who was equally skeptical about peace with Japan.[45]

Over the next nine months, Nomura (later joined by Special Envoy Saburo Kurusu) met for numerous sessions with Hull in an attempt to negotiate a settlement. The two sides remained far apart, and Roosevelt refused to make any important concessions for peace. In July he commented that the Japanese were evidently undecided about whether to attack Russia, to attack the South Seas, or to pursue a friendly policy.[46]

Meanwhile, Roosevelt further tightened the economic noose on Japan. In July, following the Japanese takeover of military and naval bases in Indochina, the President froze all Japanese assets in the United States and restricted sales of gasoline to Japan (an order which led, by the beginning of August, to a full de facto embargo on petroleum products). At the Atlantic Charter Conference in August, Roosevelt told British Prime Minister Winston Churchill that he was primarily concerned with the war in Europe and still hoped to preserve peace in the Pacific. FDR refused to issue an ultimatum to Japan to curb its aggression, but he agreed to warn the Japanese ambassador that further Japanese expansion might lead to U.S. retaliation.

In August Nomura met with Roosevelt to propose a summit meeting between Roosevelt and Prince Konoye, the Japanese prime minister, to discuss peace. Roosevelt was at first inclined to accept the idea and even discussed whether Alaska or Hawaii would be a more favorable location for the talks.[47] However, in a demonstration of some inner suspicions toward Japan, he asked Nomura sardonically whether Japan planned to invade Thailand during the conference, "just as an invasion of French Indochina occurred during Secretary Hull's conversations with your Excellency?" He eventually allowed Hull to dissuade him from the meeting on the grounds that the Japanese were insincere and such a meeting would constitute appeasement. By autumn 1941 Roosevelt seems to have regarded a Far East settlement as impossible, although Hull persisted in talks with Nomura and Kurusu.

As Japan and the United States inched toward confrontation, the administration continued its efforts to monitor Japanese Americans in anticipation of a sudden attack by Japan. Roosevelt's concern about Japanese-American fifth columnists was not assuaged by the Honolulu FBI report describing the American values and loyalty of the local Japanese population. In February the army's list of "suspects" to be arrested in time of war was united with lists compiled by the Office of Naval Intelligence (ONI) and the FBI to form a master list of some 2,000 Japanese from Hawaii and the mainland. This list was further expanded in March after ONI staff officer Lieutenant Commander Kenneth Ringle led a midnight raid on the Japanese consulate in Los Angeles and uncovered additional information about Japanese espionage and names of Japanese sympathizers. The final master list, informally known as the "ABC list," was maintained by the Justice Department's Special Defense Unit, which had responsibility for control of enemy aliens in time of war. Like the earlier Hawaiian list, the ABC list was divided into different classes of suspects—but with the important difference that the list was restricted to Issei (and German and Italian) aliens, since American citizens could not be summarily detained. (The army maintained a separate list comprised of both Issei and Nisei to be arrested and held following a declaration of martial law in Hawaii.)[48] The "A" portion, like the earlier Hawaiian list, consisted of those considered "immediately dangerous," such as consular officials, Shinto priests, Japanese business and community leaders, and fishermen. The "B" portion contained "potentially dangerous" people whose loyalty had not been assessed by the FBI, while the "C" portion list contained those suspected of pro-Japan views.[49] The list was secret, but the existence of the controls was not. In response to inquiries about the status of Japanese Americans in case of conflict, Attorney General Francis Biddle promised "fair treatment" of Japanese "enemy aliens" but stated that in the event of war the administration had plans ranging from "paroling of those persons not suspected of subversive activity to those whose detainment would be necessary."[50]

In addition to reports from the FBI and military intelligence, the President had his own confidential agents reporting on Japanese Americans. In February 1941, with the aid of secret State Department funds (which were later supplemented by presidential emergency funds), Roosevelt hired John Franklin Carter to build up a network of secret intelligence agents.[51] Carter, an author and newspaper columnist who wrote under the pseudonym Jay Franklin, was a committed New Dealer and internationalist who had been a speechwriter and advisor during Roosevelt's 1940 reelection campaign. During the following months, Carter's staff issued confidential reports on such topics as Nazi influence in South Africa, political conditions in Martinique, and sources of support in Chicago for the isolationist group America First.[52]

In fall 1941 Roosevelt commissioned Carter to prepare a secret study of the "Japanese situation" on the West Coast and Hawaii. Roosevelt's concern was to detect both whether espionage or subversion was being conducted by Japanese agents and whether the resident Japanese communities would aid or support Japan in the eventuality of war with the United States. Roosevelt may have been influenced by a letter he received from New Deal Congressman John D. Dingell of Michigan, who wrote the President privately in August that the United States should prepare to place 10,000 alien Japanese in Hawaii in forcible detention in concentration camps and to hold the remaining 150,000 alien Japanese as a "reprisal reserve."[53] Carter selected Curtis B. Munson, a midwestern Republican businessman, as his chief informant, and assigned other agents to report back on related topics such as Japanese espionage efforts in Mexico. Around the beginning of October 1941, Munson reached the West Coast. While in Los Angeles and San Francisco, Munson met with Japanese Americans, with local FBI leaders, and with ONI's Lieutenant Commander Ringle, who had led the raid on the Japanese Consulate in Los Angeles the previous spring. Munson was heavily influenced by Ringle, a professional intelligence officer fluent in Japanese and familiar with the Japanese-American community.

In mid-October, Munson sent Carter a hastily written preliminary report on the "Japanese situation." After a brief disquisition on the complex psychology of "the oriental" and the general inability of whites to understand or predict anything concerning "the Jap," Munson stated firmly that, as hard as it was to believe, the "Japanese question on the Coast" was very simple: "We do not want to throw a lot of American citizens into a concentration camp of course, and especially as the almost unanimous verdict is that in case of war they will be quiet, very quiet. There will probably be some sabotage by paid Japanese agents and the odd fanatical Jap, but the bulk of these people will be quiet because in addition to being quite contented with the American Way of life, they know they are 'in a spot.'"[54]

Munson underlined that his greatest concern in case of war was not Japanese-American loyalty but outbreaks of violence against the Japanese population. He hoped that such violence would be confined to the odd beating by "irresponsible toughs," which could be dealt with by police action. Californians, he recorded optimistically, "like and trust the Jap out here far better than the east thinks they do." Munson concluded that, while someone should go on to Honolulu to complete the planned survey, there was really no need, since the navy had any potential threats well in hand. "Honoluluians from there say the Jap is probably 98% loyal to the U.S. and those who are not, the Navy and the F.B.I. has ticketed."[55]

Three days after Munson sent his letter, Carter passed it on to the President, adding tersely, "The essence of what [Munson] has to report is that, to date, he has found no evidence which would indicate that there is danger of widespread anti-American activities among this population group. He feels that the Japanese are more in danger from the whites than the other way around."[56] The following week Carter sent another memo, reporting that Munson's subsequent dispatches "confirm the general picture of non-alarmism already reported to you."[57]

While Munson prepared his final report and scheduled a trip to Hawaii, diplomatic relations between the United States and Japan grew steadily worse. On October 16 Prince Konoye resigned as prime minister, and a war cabinet led by General Tojo took office. Amid reports of Japanese plans to launch an attack, Stimson wrote in his diary that the administration wanted to force Japan to make "the first bad move—overt move." On November 5, FDR learned from the MAGIC intercepts that Japan was preparing one more effort before going to war. He feared that the Japanese, starved for petroleum, would push into the oil-rich Netherlands East Indies. Two days later he polled his Cabinet on whether to actively oppose such an invasion. A Cabinet member reported that "the President's question was whether the country was prepared for us to move into the Pacific and attack the Japanese convoy across the Pacific beyond a given line. Could this be done immediately or should we have to wait for an 'incident.'" The Cabinet agreed that action could be taken provided the American response did not require a full expeditionary force.[58] On November 10 the Japanese envoys presented what they told the President was Japan's final proposal for peace, which involved limitations on Japanese expansion and deployment of troops in China in exchange for American concessions on trade. Roosevelt informed the Japanese ambassador that their proposals were unacceptable.

On November 7, 1941, the same day that Roosevelt discussed with his Cabinet sending a naval task force against Japan, John Franklin Carter submitted Curtis Munson's 18-page final report on the West Coast to the President. In it, Munson forthrightly restated and expanded his previous conclusions regarding the loyalty of the West Coast Japanese-American community: "The Issei or first generation is considerably weakened in their loyalty to Japan by the fact that they have chosen to make this their home and have brought up their children here . . . They are quite fearful of being put in a concentration camp. Many would take out American citizenship if allowed to do so. The weakest from a Japanese standpoint are the Nisei. They are universally estimated from 90 to 98% loyal to the United States if the Japanese educated element of the Kibei is excluded. They are pathetically eager to show this loyalty."[59]

Carter stated in his covering memo that Munson's report was worth reading in its entirety. However, he prepared a summary which cited the five passages from Munson's text that he considered the most salient:

1) There are still Japanese in the United States who will tie dynamite around their waist and make a human bomb out of themselves . . . but today they are few.

2) There is no Japanese "problem on the coast." There will be no armed uprising of Japanese. There will undoubtedly be some sabotage financed by Japan and executed largely by imported agents. There will be the odd case of fanatical sabotage by some Japanese "crackpot."

3) The dangerous part of their espionage is that they would be very effective as far as movement of supplies, movement of troops and movement of ships . . . is concerned.

4) For the most part the local Japanese are loyal to the United States or, at worst, hope that by remaining quiet they can avoid concentration camps or irresponsible mobs.

5) Your reporter . . . is horrified to note that dams, bridges, harbors, power stations, etc. are wholly unguarded everywhere. The harbor at San Pedro could be razed by fire completely by four men with grenades and a little study in one night. Dams could be blown and half of lower California might actually die of thirst. One railway bridge at the exit from the mountains in some cases could tie up three or four main railroads.[60]

The President read Carter's covering summary (and possibly Munson's underlying report) immediately, which suggests its importance to him. Roosevelt's anxiety over Japanese-American threats to security, which had led him to commission the reports originally, was heightened rather than reduced by them. Munson's warnings about possible sabotage drove FDR into a flurry of anxiety. He sent the full report on to Stimson the next day, commenting, "Please read this and let me have it back. There is nothing much new in the first four paragraphs on page #1 [that is, Carter's cover memo] but paragraph five relating to the guarding of key points should be examined into."[61]

To some degree, Carter may have been to blame for Roosevelt's anxiety. He presumably wished to respond to the President's inquiries about security and to call attention to immediate dangers without repeating information he had already passed along. Thus, his cover note summary of "salient points" presented Munson's few comments on espionage and sabotage, including his brief and largely offhand reference to the fanatical Japanese with dynamite, as the essence of the report. In his urge to encapsulate Munson's comments on the danger of sabotage—the only portion of the report to which Roosevelt made reference—Carter excised Munson's crucial qualifying preface, "Your reporter is very satisfied he has told you what to expect from the local Japanese," which clearly indicated that the sabotage to which he then referred would be carried out primarily by paid Japanese agents, not by Japanese

Americans. In contrast, Carter minimized and distorted Munson's endorsements of community loyalty. His summary cited only the report's depiction of Japanese Americans as mostly loyal or "at worst" wishing to avoid concentration camps. This characterization, however, referred only to the Issei, not to the far more numerous Nisei, whom Munson had described as 98 percent loyal and "pathetically eager" to prove their attachment to America.

Whatever the reasons for Roosevelt's reaction to Munson's reports, it appears that he turned his attention during the following days to leading a concentrated effort to identify suspects and guard against sabotage in case of war. He apparently first asked for more information, because on November 10 Carter sent a supplementary memo. Carter's memo evidently related to forming a task force to protect installations from sabotage, for FDR responded on November 11, "This is a thing which you should take up directly with [William] Donovan [coordinator of intelligence and future director of the Office of Strategic Services] and, in conjunction with Donovan, also take up with [FBI Director J.] Edgar Hoover, in view of the fact that immediate arrests may be advisable. In regard to the protection of Pacific bridges, I suppose you should take it up with the army."[62]

In the days that followed, while Roosevelt and his advisors awaited further word from Tokyo on its "final" proposals, FDR asked the War Department for a confidential report on the West Coast Japanese Americans.[63] At the same time, the FBI sent the White House a response to a previous presidential inquiry on the situation. Much of the FBI report dealt with the espionage activities of secret agents from Japan, disguised as "language officers" or Japanese Navy personnel. The memo reported that the FBI had submitted 342 dossiers on suspect "Japanese" (actually the same Japanese consular agents in Hawaii whom army officials were monitoring) to the Justice Department. FBI agents were coordinating further efforts in Hawaii and the West Coast with ONI and Military Intelligence.[64] The report hinted at opportunity for widespread subversion by stating that the "majority of the Japanese on the West Coast and in the Territory of Hawaii belong to numerous Japanese societies." However, it did not describe Japanese Americans as a security threat—on the contrary, it reported the Japanese consulate's mistrust of Japanese Americans and insistence on being informed of Nisei who booked passage to Japan in case they were *American* agents.[65] The report found the Nisei loyal by omission.

Meanwhile, Carter expanded his anti-sabotage efforts. On November 14, 1941, he asked the Census Bureau for figures on the geographical and generational breakdown of the Japanese population in the United States. The anthropologist Henry Field, Carter's assistant, later claimed that on or about November 20 Roosevelt's secretary, Grace Tully, directed him on the President's behalf to have the Census Bureau compile a complete list of addresses by district of all Japanese Americans, but this story seems at least exaggerated.[66] On November 18 Carter sent Roosevelt a memo on the problem of defending against sabotage in which he described the meetings he had held, at the President's request, with Hoover, Donovan, and the War Department. Carter reported that the FBI and the military intelligence agencies were ready to arrest suspects on the West Coast whenever notified to do so, and that staffers from those agencies, along with Donovan, would be meeting with him to outline a program to control sabotage. Carter suggested that a coordinator of West Coast defense areas be appointed to lead the task. On November 27, 1941, the President signed an executive order establishing the Los Angeles–Long Beach Harbor Naval Defensive Sea Area.[67] This order permitted the army to tighten surveillance and impose restrictions on entry and exit from the area.

Meanwhile, as a result of Munson's warnings about the danger of anti-Japanese violence, Carter became engaged in planning efforts to protect loyal Japanese Americans. He commissioned reports from his agents on the state of opinion among white Californians. In the days that followed transmittal of the Munson report, Carter sent Roosevelt a report by Warren Irwin (who was also the agent responsible for monitoring Japanese activities in Mexico) on the "Possibility of Anti-Japanese Riots in Los Angeles" and Munson's report on the Japanese in California's Imperial Valley and in Utah (neither report is still extant). It is unclear how much Roosevelt was concerned with defending loyal Japanese Americans, but he was certainly interested as a practical matter in avoiding violence which could disrupt the war effort. Thus, he suggested that Carter take up both reports with Donovan and the one on riots with Secretary of War Stimson as well.[68] On November 18 Carter included in his memo to Roosevelt the comment that "Bill Donovan has undertaken to coordinate a publicity program designed to reassure loyal Japanese Americans and to allay white suspicion of their Japanese-American fellow-citizens. This has already started." Meanwhile, in response to concerns raised by Japanese-American leaders, in early November First Lady Eleanor Roosevelt officially asked the Justice Department about the treatment of Japanese-American aliens in case of war. On December 4, 1941, she publicly announced that no law-abiding aliens of any nationality would be discriminated against by the government. The President evidently approved, though there is no record of any further intervention on his part on the matter.[69]

Munson spent nine days in Hawaii in November 1941 and found the local Japanese community to be overwhelmingly loyal. Carter later stated that he met with Roosevelt on December 2, five days before the Japanese attack on Pearl Harbor, and "reported to him the findings of my intelligence assignment showing that the overwhelming majority of Japanese-American residents on the West Coast and in the Hawaiian Islands would be loyal to the United States in event of war."[70] This suggests that Munson contacted Carter from Hawaii to relay his findings.

On November 20 Japan presented a revised plan for a temporary modus vivendi, by which Japan would agree not to expand further in exchange for a resumption of American trade. The United States quickly responded with a proposal for a three-month truce based on Japan's withdrawal of troops from Indochina and her agreement not to invoke the Tripartite Pact with Germany and Italy if the United States became engaged in the European war. FDR hoped to avoid war if at all possible. He was nevertheless aware that war was likely—on November 25 he conferred with his military advisors about how to maneuver Japan into firing the first shot without causing too much damage to American forces. During their December 2 meeting, Carter asked Roosevelt when war was expected. FDR responded, "In a week, or ten days at the most."[71] On December 6, Roosevelt made a last push for peace. He wrote a letter to the Japanese emperor, stating that the only hope for peace was for Japan to withdraw its forces from Southeast Asia. However, the Japanese fleet had already begun sailing toward Pearl Harbor.

During the prewar years the President consistently regarded Japanese Americans as adjuncts of Japan and therefore as potential enemies, despite their American birth or decades-long residence in the United States. Although he was rightfully concerned for American security in the face of an aggressive and expansionist Japanese empire and took legitimate steps to counter subversion by agents of Japan, he did not confine his efforts to the network of "consular officials" sent over by Tokyo or to the spies they hired, virtually all of whom were Caucasians. Instead, Roosevelt automatically extended that hostility and suspicion to the entire Japanese-American community.

It is true that many Japanese Americans in Hawaii and on the mainland felt an attachment to their ancestral homeland as well as to the United States during the years before Pearl Harbor. Some Issei, and even a few Nisei, hosted Japanese sailors, wrote pro-Japanese articles (especially in the Japanese-language press), or raised money for the Japanese war effort in China.[72] However, most Issei and Nisei had little or no real connection to Japan, while thousands of Japanese Americans showed their patriotism by enlisting in the U.S. Army or volunteering for other forms of national service during 1940–41. Indeed, the Nisei were so overwhelmingly pro-American that, as the FBI noted, the Japanese suspected them as potential American agents. Yet, the President did not relax his scrutiny of the Japanese-American community, even after both the FBI and his own investigators, led by Curtis B. Munson, reported that there was no "Japanese problem." Indeed, his chief reaction to Munson's final report was to call for further repressive action and to personally supervise a secret campaign to guard against sabotage and prepare for the summary arrest of "suspects." While John Franklin Carter may have missed an opportunity to acquaint Roosevelt fully with Munson's description of the real situation, FDR seems not to have been listening to information that was, as he admitted, "nothing much new." He was in crisis mode, attentive only to immediate dangers. Roosevelt's actions show how overprepared he was to believe the worst about the entire Japanese-American community, notwithstanding the lack of any firm evidence of disloyalty and in the face of tangible evidence of community loyalty. He did not react in this way toward any other aliens, not even Germans or Italians, and certainly not toward any other group of American citizens. These actions suggest that Roosevelt's concern for security was undergirded by an implacable belief that Japanese Americans—Issei and Nisei alike—were dangerous and foreign.

FDR'S DECISION TO INTERN

ON DECEMBER 7, 1941, Japanese naval and air forces launched a surprise bombing raid on Pearl Harbor, the chief base of the U.S. Navy's Pacific Fleet. Roosevelt and his handpicked commander, Admiral Husband Kimmel, had clearly not forgotten the warnings of Theodore Roosevelt and Admiral Mahan against dividing the fleet in time of war, and the Pacific Fleet had massed together at Pearl Harbor in preparation for a possible naval engagement with Japan. In this case, however, the massing of the fleet left it vulnerable to attack by air, and Japanese bombers inflicted crushing damage on the American ships.[1]

American losses were compounded by other failures to properly prepare for an enemy attack. In the months before December 7, the War Department and the army chief of staff had repeatedly discounted the possibility of external attack on Pearl Harbor. They assumed that Japan's naval strength was insufficient to launch a full-scale assault on a heavily defended naval base thousands of miles from Japan. Rather, they

3

anticipated that the Japanese would strike at a closer and less defensible target such as Indonesia or the Philippines. As a result, they had warned that the primary threat to American military bases in Hawaii lay in potential sabotage by the local Japanese-American population—Roosevelt had not been the only high government official to suspect the "local Japanese" as potential fifth columnists. General Walter Short, the local army commander, had ordered the airplanes at Pearl Harbor grouped closely together for protection from local sabotage, which never occurred. Instead, the Japanese task force found the American planes clustered together on the ground and put them out of action with a single thrust.[2]

Radio bulletins and special newspaper editions swiftly spread word of the bombing of Pearl Harbor. The "sneak attack" shocked and outraged the country. Overnight, the rancorous divisions between interventionists and isolationists were forgotten, and the entire citizenry looked to the White House for leadership. Individuals and groups nationwide wired or telephoned the White House demanding revenge against Japan and pledging their aid in the war effort. On December 8 President Roosevelt addressed a joint session of Congress. Referring to the attack on Pearl Harbor as "a date which will live in infamy," he asked Congress for a declaration of war against Japan. The resolution passed both houses with only a single dissenting vote.

In the days that followed, waves of anti-Japanese sentiment swept the nation. In government halls, newspapers, and on the street, Americans expressed their hatred and mistrust of the "treacherous Japs." Rumors of Japanese invasion spread along the West Coast, and local authorities received reports from jittery citizens of sightings of strange aircraft, although these reports soon proved groundless.

The morning bombing of Pearl Harbor had barely ended when the government began putting into effect the plans that FDR had approved long before. On the afternoon of December 7, General Short met with territorial governor John Poindexter and told him of a massive campaign of sabotage by Japanese Hawaiians. Poindexter then agreed to sign a proclamation declaring unlimited martial law in the territory.[3] Martial law remained in effect in Hawaii throughout most of the war. Under its provisions, the entire population, including the local Japanese Americans, lived under direct military rule. As soon as martial law went into effect, the military instituted an immediate curfew and began rounding up "suspicious" Japanese.

Meanwhile, on December 7 and 8, the President signed proclamations authorizing the FBI to summarily arrest any aliens in the continental United States whom it deemed "dangerous to public peace or safety." In the next four days, FBI agents on the West Coast arrested as potential subversives some 2,000 Issei whose names appeared on the Justice Department's ABC list. At the same time, the navy ordered all fishing boats owned by Japanese nationals beached in order to prevent them from aiding Japanese ships. The Treasury Department froze all assets of Japanese nationals as "enemy aliens" and suspended their licenses to sell produce in order to protect the food supply from poisoning. Some Treasury officials even spoke hypothetically about taking over all Japanese-American businesses and setting up concentration camps. However, Secretary of the Treasury Henry Morgenthau ordered them not to panic, and he stated that he was not prepared to go the President and propose "suddenly mopping up 150,000 Japanese and putting them behind barbed wire."[4] As a result of the intervention of First Lady Eleanor Roosevelt, whose humanitarian sympathies remained intact, the Treasury Department restrictions were relaxed shortly afterward to permit each family to withdraw $100 per month for living expenses. After Germany and Italy declared war on the United States, these restrictions were extended to "enemy aliens" from those nations as well.

By the end of December, at the request of the War Department, the Justice Department prepared detailed lists of "contraband" items for enemy aliens. In accordance with these lists, FBI agents conducted warrantless searches and confiscated guns, cameras, radios, dynamite, and other possessions from West Coast Issei households. Justice Department analysts later determined that these searches did not uncover any proof of disloyal activity or any information that the department could not have gained from other sources. However, the searches created havoc in the households subjected to them. Issei, anxious to allay suspicion, destroyed their Japanese clothes, books, swords, and crafts.

In the weeks that followed the outbreak of war, there was no public outcry for government action to control Japanese Americans. During this time, Roosevelt immersed himself in shoring up the nation's defenses, shifting into a war economy, and establishing a war bureaucracy. He devoted little attention to Japanese Americans on the West Coast. On December 8, 1941, the same day that the United States declared war, John Franklin Carter sent

Roosevelt a copy of Curtis Munson's 20-page report on "the Japanese Situation" in Hawaii, which had been completed shortly before Pearl Harbor, as well as a companion report by Warren Irwin on Japanese activities in Mexico. It is not certain whether Roosevelt knew of Munson's conclusions about Japanese Americans in Hawaii before Pearl Harbor, but Munson had reported to Carter and Roosevelt by mid-October that he was almost certain that the loyalty of Japanese Americans in the islands would be equivalent to those on the West Coast, and he may have further briefed Carter and Roosevelt following his arrival in Hawaii. Carter did not summarize Munson's conclusions in his own December 8 transmittal memo, as he had done with Munson's previous reports, so he may have already given Roosevelt either an oral briefing or some preliminary version of Munson's report on Hawaii.

In the report, Munson made clear his belief that, as on the West Coast, there was no "local Japanese" problem in Hawaii, although he reported that there might be significant opportunity for military espionage by agents of Japan on Oahu. The Issei were predominantly loyal and could be expected to be quiet in the event of a war. Honolulu FBI agents estimated the Nisei to be 98 percent loyal. Munson was aware that this meant that "perhaps 1500" aliens and a larger number of citizens might still be disloyal, but he affirmed that only a fraction of those could be considered dangerous. Further, army intelligence had the names and addresses of these people ready, so that they could be immediately arrested at any sign of trouble.

Munson concluded by expressing a certain uneasiness: "We cannot say how loyal the Japanese in the Hawaiian group would be if there were an American Naval disaster and the Japanese fleet appeared off the Hawaiian Islands. Doubtless great numbers of them would then forget their American loyalties and shout 'Banzai' from the shore. Under those circumstances if this reporter were there he is not sure that he might not do it also to save his skin, if not his face."[5] Even under such extraordinary circumstances, however, Munson did not believe the United States had much to fear, since there were more than sufficient American soldiers in the islands to control any conceivable activity by the local Japanese. Munson concluded, "In fairness to them it is only right to say that we believe the big majority anyhow would be neutral or even actively loyal."[6]

On the next day Roosevelt casually passed the report to one Captain Beardall (his naval aide) "to review and return," without making any further comment. It is not certain whether FDR actually ever read any part of the report (any more than he may have read the text of Munson's previous reports). However, since the President was clearly familiar with the conclusions in the report, and may possibly have known of them even before the Japanese attack, the fact that Roosevelt did not question Munson's findings, reject them, cancel his assignment, or request further investigation in light of the attack on Pearl Harbor suggests that he accepted, at least provisionally, Munson's assessment that Japanese Americans were loyal.[7]

Directly after the Pearl Harbor attack, Roosevelt granted Navy Secretary Frank Knox's request that he be allowed to personally inspect Hawaii. Knox spent only 36 hours in Hawaii meeting with naval officials before returning to Washington. On December 15, after reporting his findings to the President, Knox told reporters, "I think the most effective Fifth Column work of the entire war was done in Hawaii with the possible exception of Norway." Four days later, Knox repeated his conclusions at a Cabinet meeting, stating that local Japanese fishing boats had furnished information on the location of warships and the Japanese consulate had engaged in espionage.[8] Knox claimed "there was a great deal of very active fifth column work going on both from the shores and from the sampans." Citing the danger of further espionage, Knox then "recommended to the President that the Secretary of War take all the aliens out of Hawaii and send them off to another island."[9]

Roosevelt diplomatically praised Knox's handling of the Pearl Harbor situation, but he did not approve any such removal. He may have realized that Knox, anxious to take heat off the navy for the disaster at Pearl Harbor, might have accepted rumors of Japanese-American treachery at face value. The secretary certainly had a preexisting bias. As early as 1933 Knox had warned of the danger of war with Japan and had publicly advocated the internment of every Japanese resident of the islands "before the beginning of hostilities threatens."[10] Roosevelt also had contrary information furnished by his investigators and by FBI director J. Edgar Hoover, who discounted Knox's assertions.[11] Since Roosevelt had great faith in Hoover's opinion regarding security matters, the FBI director's disagreement with Knox's assessment was undoubtedly a factor in staying the President from immediately approving dramatic action against the Japanese in Hawaii.[12]

Nevertheless, Knox's comments may have contributed to Roosevelt's doubts over disloyal conduct by Japanese Americans. Certainly, both Knox's willingness to believe that the local Japanese had engaged in fifth column activity and his refusal to distinguish between spies from Japan who were working for the consulate and the longtime resident or citizen Japanese population would be echoed in the military plans Roosevelt later approved. Even as Knox was making his investigation, Roosevelt's secret intelligence unit, led by Carter and Munson, was racing to reaffirm their conclusions that the Japanese-American community, both in Hawaii and the West Coast, was overwhelmingly loyal. On December 16 Carter sent Roosevelt a memo emphasizing that there was still "no substantial danger of Fifth Column activities by Japanese." He emphasized that Knox's December 15 statement charging that Japanese Americans had engaged in fifth column activity was erroneous. The only possible activity Knox could be referring to was "close physical espionage at Honolulu directed by the Japanese Consulate General." No doubt feeling it was old news, Carter did not mention that Munson had indicated that this espionage had been carried out entirely by Caucasians and by paid infiltrators brought from Japan. Carter warned of the continuing potential for sabotage at unguarded strategic points and strongly recommended the arrest of Hawaiian Nisei "suspects" (that is, from the military's lists) in addition to the "alien suspects" who had been arrested in previous raids. However, he also stressed the necessity for an immediate presidential statement "to reassure loyal Japanese and Japanese Americans" in the wake of Knox's false accusation.[13] Three days later, Carter again begged the President to make a statement, reporting that five Japanese Americans in California had already committed suicide in response to the dishonor of being suspected of disloyalty.

On December 22 Roosevelt received a further report from Munson claiming that the Japanese attack was the "proof in the pudding" of the previous reports. He was sure that the sources for his reports, notably Kenneth Ringle in Los Angeles and Mr. Shivers of the Honolulu FBI, had not changed their minds. They still envisioned no danger from the Japanese-American community on the West Coast and in Hawaii. Since the "measured judgment of 98% of the intelligence services or the knowing citizenry" was that the Japanese community was loyal, Munson was sure that his conclusions were "still good *after the attack*."[14] He added that Knox's accusations, which had already caused "some reaction of an undesirable nature . . . on the West Coast," were influenced by ignorant and racist naval sources who were "inclined to consider everybody with slant eyes, bad."[15]

Carter not only prevailed upon Roosevelt to verbally support Japanese Americans, but he and his staff devised an immediate plan of action in order to short-circuit the anti-Japanese violence that Munson had previously predicted and that Carter feared Knox's statement might help foment. On December 19 (the same day as the Cabinet meeting at which Knox made his statement recommending relocation of Japanese Americans in Hawaii), Carter sent the President a memo containing the highlights of a new "Program for Loyal West Coast Japanese" which Munson, who had remained on the West Coast, was then busy completing. Carter described the program (based largely on plans previously drafted by Lieutenant Commander Kenneth Ringle) as designed to preserve Japanese-American loyalty and assure "wholesome race relations." Its basis was the promotion of the Nisei, whom Munson and Ringle had both found to be overwhelmingly pro-American, to control of Japanese property and organizations. Carter was careful in his memo to Roosevelt to distinguish between the Nisei, whom he referred to first as "American-Born Japanese" and then as "U.S. Citizens of Japanese blood," and the Issei, whom he described as "Japanese-born residents ineligible for citizenship."[16]

Sensitive to the anxiety and terror sweeping Japanese-American communities, the authors of the Munson-Ringle plan called for the Nisei to be encouraged by "a statement from *high* authority" and accepted as volunteers for patriotic service in the Red Cross and civilian defense. With the assistance of an alien property custodian appointed for the purpose, the native-born Nisei groups would then take over control of Issei properties, such as produce stands and fishing boats, which the government had shut down. Eventually, "*INVESTIGATED* Nisei" would be permitted to take jobs in defense plants. By working through Nisei groups such as the JACL, which would be responsible for the conduct of the Issei, the government would be able to control Japanese communities indirectly. Carter pointed out that this system would have the dual advantage of enhancing the power of the loyal group while allowing the authorities "*to utilize Japanese filial piety as hostage for good behavior*" (that is, the young Nisei would be sure to take good care of their elders' property and refrain from disloyal actions in order to preserve it).[17]

Roosevelt read Carter's memo on December 20 and was clearly intrigued by the Munson-Ringle plan. His secretary noted for the file that she had "telephoned John Franklin Carter at the President's request, and suggested that he take the matter up at once with J. Edgar Hoover and the Attorney General."[18] Roosevelt's approval may have been influenced by William Donovan, who had continued his own focus on defending loyal Japanese Americans and who briefed FDR regarding a proposal he had received from the novelist John Steinbeck for cooperating with Nisei organizations to obtain better information and permit the Nisei to show their loyalty.[19]

Munson's complete plan arrived on December 22, and Carter immediately passed it on to Roosevelt with a recommendation that he read it.[20] The plan Munson described was much as Carter had summarized it. The persons and property of the Issei would be controlled by "unquestionably loyal Nisei," such as those in the JACL, who would in turn be "rigidly approved by and under the thumb of [government bodies], PREFERABLY OF A MILITARY OR NAVAL INTELLIGENCE TEXTURE." Munson pointed up the urgency of immediate action by including an extended description of the hardship faced by the West Coast community as a result of the suspension of produce sales and fishing licenses. Issei farmers and fishermen were cut off without any savings or source of income and were forced to depend on community handouts.

On December 23 Carter reported that he had met with Biddle and Hoover, as Roosevelt had requested, to share and discuss Munson's plan. He added that "both were enthusiastic and offered full cooperation" and that all had agreed Munson should return to Washington to direct a coordinated interdepartmental effort based on the plan's recommendations. The President was presumably satisfied, for he made no comment. However, he made no effort to discuss the plan's provisions with Carter. More importantly, despite Carter's pleas, Roosevelt failed in the days that followed to make any public statement in support of loyal Japanese Americans, thus leaving them alone to face the wave of hostility building up against them.

FDR did not keep himself informed about Carter's activities in the weeks that followed. The President was distracted by the Christmas holiday, which he insisted on celebrating in normal fashion in order to reassure the nation, and by strategic conferences occasioned by the three-week visit of British Prime Minister Winston Churchill to the White House. By mid-January 1942, when Roosevelt was able to turn his attention to the plan once more, the situation on the West Coast had changed for the worse. The military had begun to press for more coercive treatment of Japanese Americans, and popular pressure had grown for their removal from the coast. On January 13, 1942, Churchill's last day in Washington, Carter sent Roosevelt a memo complaining of the lack of progress on the West Coast Japanese program. The army, he explained, had sent on Munson's reports to General John DeWitt, the West Coast defense commander, but DeWitt had not made any response or implemented any part of the plan. The FBI and the Department of Justice, though sympathetic, had not accomplished anything much either, except for having federal attorneys make soothing statements and start up good-citizenship training classes for Nisei. Meanwhile, the other departments that were supposed to help coordinate plans for the West Coast had relegated their efforts to "executive committees" which were without any authority, with the result that dealing with them was excessively slow. Worst of all, no alien property custodian had been appointed, and until one was in place, no transfer of Issei property to Nisei supervision could take place.

The memo to Roosevelt also included what Carter termed a "despondent" report from Munson at the slowness of progress on the West Coast. Munson asserted forthrightly that Roosevelt had granted the plan his support. "We understood that this plan was approved and we were instructed to see that it was put in the right hands to be made effective." He affirmed that General DeWitt, to whom the army had forwarded his reports, had not taken any action. In a mixture of confidence and exasperation, Munson stated, "Your observer feels that DeWitt is the man to examine this program and either pass on it, alter it, or turn it down as he is the man on the ground and in a position to be thoroughly conversant with all the facts mentioned in this report."

By this time, Roosevelt had clearly lost interest in the Munson-Ringle plan. He made no reply to this memo and did not contact either the War Department or the Justice Department to expedite action. Two weeks later, Carter reported that there still had been no action taken on Munson's recommendations, which "were last sighted in the War Department." Carter enclosed a letter from British Intelligence, whose agents in southern California reported growing anti-Japanese sentiment and likely violence against Japanese-American citizens. He pleaded with Roosevelt to have "this job . . . done in time to prevent possible violence with dangerous repercussions in Hawaii" (presumably anti-white retaliatory rioting). Carter proposed that the President give someone immediate authority to attend to the "thankless but important duty" of controlling Japanese Americans. Since Munson (who had clearly soured on DeWitt) believed that Ringle would be best qualified to handle the task, Carter urged that Ringle be given the necessary authority.[21] Roosevelt's only response to Carter's plea was to send the memo for review to the secretary of state, which suggests that his primary interest in the memo was concern over infiltration by British Intelligence.

Why did the Munson-Ringle plan fizzle out? It was vulnerable from the beginning, since it was developed outside the bureaucracy and was thus dependent on Roosevelt's active support in the face of administration inertia. Carter had to ask Roosevelt for permission to reveal his authority to executive department staffers whenever he needed to get anything done. For a short time before Christmas 1941, the proposal enjoyed tacit support. Carter and Munson believed that Roosevelt had approved the plan, and FDR had encouraged Carter to coordinate government efforts in accordance with its provisions. However, during the busy first weeks of the war, many strategic and diplomatic matters required the President's close personal attention. He could not spare the time and energy required to push the Munson-Ringle plan, especially once Churchill arrived. Without the President's active participation, Carter made no headway.

In any case, Roosevelt's support of creative thinking about ways to assure the loyalty of the Japanese community was halfhearted. FDR's interest was less in promoting Japanese-American loyalty than in averting racial violence or food shortages that would hinder the war effort. Carter and Munson clearly understood this and based their recommendations on such practical considerations rather than moral or constitutional arguments. Yet they still failed to capture the President's interest and energy. FDR never committed himself or his prestige to the plan by making any public statement to reassure Nisei of his support and protection, as Carter and Munson recommended. Significantly, Roosevelt originally had Carter and Munson coordinate plans with the Justice Department and the FBI, not with the army, which indicates that he did not consider the problem at the time to be a military one. So long as there was no critical urgency in terms of the war effort, all other problems could be left to those who volunteered to take them on. Once the military began pressing for action against Japanese Americans, the President retreated from active support and let the plan die on its own.

Paradoxically, the Munson-Ringle plan, while well-meant and undoubtedly constitutional, would have represented an enormous restriction on the Issei, whose property and businesses would have been effectively confiscated and placed in the hands of Nisei receivers (who were themselves to be carefully monitored for loyalty). Munson stated bluntly that the aim of his report was "that all Japanese nationals in the continental United States and property owned and operated by them within this country be immediately placed under absolute Federal control." Even if Munson and Carter believed that such a restrictive program was the only way to assure a relaxation of the government's suspension of all alien activities, they did not explain why the same Issei community they had presented as predominantly loyal and whose innocence vis-à-vis Pearl Harbor they had just defended should be subjected to curbs solely on the basis of their ancestry. Instead, Munson and Carter advocated in practice the same harsh treatment of the Issei that they later denounced when applied against the Nisei.

Munson was no civil libertarian. Before Pearl Harbor, he had called for the immediate imposition of martial law in Hawaii to prevent enemy activities, and he was outspoken in favor of concerted action to curb the danger of sabotage. After Pearl Harbor, he proposed putting all individual citizens against whom there was evidence of disloyalty in protective custody.[22] In late December, at the same time that he proposed the plan for "controlling" Japanese Americans, he recommended that the Los Angeles–Long Beach Harbor Naval Defensive Sea Area, which his warnings about sabotage had helped create, be further expanded and fortified, and he stated explicitly that "operating officers should be allowed to remove all aliens from the zone." What would happen to these removed people, he did not say. Furthermore, in early January, Carter sent the President a two-page memo from Munson urging him to join with Congress in suspending the writ of habeas corpus in order to deal with subversion by a substantial group of Nazi agents who had become naturalized American citizens to escape surveillance.[23]

The Munson-Ringle plan may well have undercut its stated objective of protecting Japanese Americans. Even though designed to reassure the President that there was no Japanese fifth column and to appeal to his pragmatic temperament, the plan sent the clear message that both Issei and Nisei, irrespective of their loyalty, required government control. Although Munson recommended suspension of the writ of habeas corpus in order to restrict naturalized citizens from Nazi Germany, no mass control program was contemplated for any "enemy alien" groups except the Japanese—even groups like the Germans that were not composed of longtime residents like the Issei. The Munson-Ringle plan, though far milder than the wholesale relocation that was to follow, made the same race-based presumption of collective disloyalty, at least as to the Issei. Roosevelt's passive acceptance of that plan, however ephemeral, represents the first sign of his willingness to place restrictions on the Japanese Americans in the absence of any proof of subversive activity or intent. His failure to detect or challenge the presence of such ideas even at this early stage demonstrates that there was more to his acceptance of mass evacuation than immediate pressure from the military.

Ironically, the same week that Roosevelt received the Munson-Ringle plan, he remarked to his Cabinet that he wished to make a statement in support of the rights of aliens and naturalized citizens, in response to reports of such persons being fired from their jobs. On January 2, 1942, the President released a statement, drafted by Biddle, which warned employers to "adopt a sane policy" and avoid discharging loyal employees simply because they were aliens or foreign-born citizens, since such a policy was wasteful and unjust and played into the hands of the enemies of democracy. "Remember the Nazi technique: 'Pit race against race, religion against religion, prejudice against prejudice. Divide and conquer!'"[24] Though the statement did not specifically mention the Japanese "enemy aliens" or those of any other nationality, it equally did not exclude them, but instead referred to all "loyal aliens." The Japanese-American press interpreted the statement as a strong endorsement, and highlighted FDR's denunciation of racial bigotry. It was a hopeful sign within a climate of growing hostility on the West Coast.

During the first month after Pearl Harbor, as the President remained absorbed with wartime strategy, a coalition of concerned groups began to press for "control" of the Japanese Americans on the West Coast in the name of national defense. The first call for emergency powers came from the West Coast Defense Command, headed by General John DeWitt, a career officer with an undistinguished record of service in the United States, Hawaii, and the Philippines. DeWitt expected a possible Japanese invasion of the West Coast, and he repeatedly insisted to the War Department that West Coast Japanese Americans were communicating with the enemy and plotting sabotage.[25] During the week that followed the bombing of Pearl Harbor, DeWitt reported as truth rumors that a squadron of airplanes had passed over California. Naval investigators soon established that the rumors were unfounded. DeWitt also received a report (which turned out to be the invention of a disgruntled FBI agent) of an imminent uprising by 20,000 Japanese Americans in San Francisco, and he passed it on to the War Department. DeWitt's intelligence staff alleged that signals were being sent offshore from Japanese houses throughout

December and January. The FBI immediately discounted these reports and the Federal Communications Commission (FCC) soon discredited them.[26]

In spite of their lack of credibility, all these stories fueled DeWitt's anxiety. The general was determined not to take any chances in matters of security—especially after the military commanders who had been caught unprepared at Pearl Harbor were disgraced. Thus, he was predisposed to recommend action against the Japanese Americans. He had previously organized plans for incarcerating suspicious Japanese aliens in Hawaii, and he evinced a streak of racial animosity toward Japanese Americans as tensions rose. In his February 14, 1942, "Final Recommendation" in support of his request for relocation of Japanese Americans, he asserted that they were members of an "enemy race," regardless of their citizenship, and that their "undiluted racial strains" made them innately Japanese and a risk to national security. DeWitt refused to believe reports of loyalty in the Japanese-American community. He ignored Munson's recommendations, and he twice refused to see Ringle. Even the total absence of documented reports of sabotage by any Japanese Americans failed to make DeWitt reconsider his premise—on the contrary, he remarked in late January that this absence was proof that Japanese "control is being exercised" and that sabotage would begin on a mass basis once the signal was given.[27]

DeWitt discussed various relocation plans with his War Department superiors. On December 16 he suggested that a 100-mile-wide coastal strip be designated a military area and that any persons deemed undesirable by the military be removed, even though the FBI authorities who were responsible for control of "alien enemies" informed him that no American citizen could be summarily arrested or seized. On December 19 DeWitt recommended to the War Department that all enemy aliens (German, Italian, and Japanese) over the age of fourteen be moved inland. When Justice Department attorney James Rowe met with DeWitt in early January to coordinate efforts, the general told Rowe that he had no confidence in the loyalty of either the Issei or the Nisei.[28]

Nevertheless, DeWitt opposed wholesale evacuation for well over a month after Pearl Harbor. On December 26, 1941, in response to requests to remove both Japanese-American citizens and aliens from Los Angeles, DeWitt told Army Provost Marshal General Allen W. Gullion that it would be too great a job to move 93,000 people from the city and would alienate many loyal Japanese. In any case, DeWitt pointed out, "An American citizen is, after all, an American citizen." Though Gullion agreed, he feared that the army would not be able to defend the coast without a declaration of martial law or at least authority to detain civilians. Gullion had his aide, Captain Karl Bendetsen (a Stanford University Law School graduate who was promoted to colonel within three months as a result of his championship of mass removal), draft a memo to Roosevelt proposing that the War Department take over the control of "alien enemies" from the Justice Department, and he soon began to press DeWitt to recommend the evacuation of all Americans of Japanese ancestry.[29]

Neither DeWitt nor Gullion brought up the question of mass evacuation during their meetings with the Justice Department in early January. In fact, DeWitt referred to the whole idea of evacuation as "damned nonsense." Instead, DeWitt pressed for dramatic steps against enemy aliens, including army registration of aliens and creation of military zones from which aliens would be excluded on a "pass-permit" system. At the instigation of Gullion and Bendetsen, DeWitt also called for mass raids on Issei homes in order to determine whether inhabitants were aiding the enemy.

DeWitt's requests brought him into conflict with Attorney General Francis Biddle and his subordinates James Rowe and Edward Ennis—a conflict that shaped the eventual debate over evacuation. Biddle agreed to institute registration of aliens by the Justice Department (which Roosevelt subsequently ordered on January 14), and the Justice Department promised to approve creation of restricted military zones on an "as-demanded" basis. These military zones were composed of areas in and around barracks, ports, and other strategic facilities. Despite his protestations of emergency, DeWitt did not actually provide a list of restricted areas until January 21.

However, Biddle opposed taking further action. He did not believe that the Justice Department could approve arbitrary action even in wartime, especially against American citizens. He thought that the army might take such action under a military emergency, but from the Carter and Munson reports and his continuing contacts with FBI Director J. Edgar Hoover, Biddle downplayed the need for any mass control of "enemies." Therefore, while he agreed to "spot" raids, he refused to allow indiscriminate warrantless raids on Issei houses. He stated that if the army appealed to Roosevelt to overrule him, he would have the army take over the Alien Enemy Program, which he was well aware they had neither the interest nor the facilities to manage.

Though DeWitt did not raise the subject of evacuating either Issei or Nisei during his various conferences with Justice Department officials, and he continued to state that the Justice Department should handle control of enemy aliens, by the latter part of January his anger over Biddle's apparent recalcitrance nevertheless pushed him toward recommending a military solution to the West Coast alien problem. DeWitt was encouraged to challenge Justice Department control by Assistant Attorney General Tom Clark, whom Biddle sent out in mid-January to coordinate strategies with DeWitt and to monitor the California situation in the hopes that he would bring about a more reasonable attitude on the part of the army. Instead, Clark allied himself with Bendetsen in pressing DeWitt to request the broadest possible authority and in demanding that Biddle give the army whatever it wanted.

With the support of Clark and Bendetsen, DeWitt lobbied the War Department through Assistant Secretary of War John McCloy to reduce the Justice Department's resistance to dramatic action to root out possible subversives. On January 24 (the same day DeWitt stated that the absence of any sabotage by Japanese Americans "proved" that a sabotage campaign was being planned), Secretary of War Henry L. Stimson wrote Biddle that DeWitt had reported persistent ship-to-shore radio communication by the Japanese and that DeWitt's "apprehensions" had been "confirmed by recent military observers on the Pacific Coast" (presumably Bendetsen, who may have drafted the Stimson letter). The same observers related that, in the previous days, "not a ship had sailed from our Pacific ports without being attacked." Stimson insisted that "immediate and stringent" action, of an unspecified nature, was needed to deal with such dangers.

Even as the army and the Justice Department wrangled over the handling of Japanese enemy aliens, various interest groups, predominantly in southern California, organized a campaign to force all Japanese Americans away from the Pacific Coast. This movement, through inspired by Pearl Harbor, did not begin in earnest until several weeks afterward. Indeed, the Japanese attack on Hawaii served in many cases to inflame (or rationalize) preexisting suspicions and hatred of the Japanese Americans. In 1940 *Life* magazine had reported anti-Japanese sentiment and warned of the danger of subversive activity by Japanese Americans.[30] Even more neutral sources had expressed suspicion; in the same year, *Newsweek* reported tightening vigilance by West Coast federal authorities over Japanese-American potential spies and saboteurs and reported seizure by the FBI of a short-wave radio set belonging to a Japanese-American family in the vicinity of Washington's Bremerton Navy Yard.[31]

Stories likewise spread through West Coast areas in the months before Pearl Harbor that the Japanese-American population would be exposed to violence or forced into concentration camps in the event of war with Japan. It is not clear precisely how or when this idea originated, but by early August 1941 Japanese-American community representatives had begun asking Justice Department officials whether the Issei would be deported or sent to concentration camps in case of war.[32] Samuel King, Hawaii's congressional delegate, wrote Attorney General Biddle to receive his assurance that the widespread rumors of concentration camps for Japanese aliens in case of war were unfounded.[33] However, such rumors were still widespread in the Japanese community when Curtis Munson visited the West Coast at the beginning of October. Nor was Munson the only investigator to report these stories. In the October 11, 1941, issue of *Collier's,* Jim Marshall remarked that there would be a demand for concentration camps in California for those of Japanese ancestry in case of war, although the FBI and army and navy intelligence agents who had been continuously engaged in intensive surveillance doubted there would be any trouble.[34]

Similarly, in mid-November, the author and journalist Ernest O. Hauser reported after a visit to California that the Japanese Americans were "on the spot." Hauser claimed that those whose business it was "to keep an eye on our Japanese compatriots" estimated the Nisei at 50 percent actively loyal, 25 percent passively loyal, and 25 percent doubtful, with a negligible number actively disloyal. He added that even many Kibei, Nisei indoctrinated with Japanese values through their education in Japan, were patriotic Americans. He added that it would be unfair to treat Japanese Americans as a dangerous group in the event of war. Rather, the "actively disloyal elements" were Japanese sent across the Pacific Ocean and "planted" in the Japanese-American population for the express purpose of spying. Hauser stated that "alarmist patriots" were nevertheless spreading stories of Japanese-American plans for sabotage when war broke out—stories whose details precisely anticipated the rumors of planned sabotage that spread along the West Coast in early 1942 and formed the basis of the movement for evacuation: "When the Pacific zero hour strikes, Japanese Americans will get busy at once. Their fishing boats will sow mines across the entrances of our ports. Mysterious blasts will destroy navy shipyards and flying fields and part of our fleet . . . To add the final demonical touch, Japanese farmers, having a virtual monopoly of vegetable production in California, will send their peas and potatoes and squash full of arsenic to the markets, throwing the population into panic."[35] Hauser reported that many Nisei, though loyal, faced discrimination and had told him "with forced flippancy" that they were dieting in preparation for being sent to concentration camps once war broke out.[36]

The free-floating anxieties that led to these rumor campaigns exploded into mass hysteria following the attack on Pearl Harbor, which appeared to confirm them. Ironically, the West Coast was largely calm in the immediate aftermath of the attack on Pearl Harbor. On December 10, 1941, the *Los Angeles Times* published an editorial warning against vigilante activities by white "patriots."[37] But in the weeks that followed, a popular movement for removal of Issei and Nisei to concentration camps emerged on the West Coast. The motivation of the organizations and individuals involved was complex. To some degree, they shared the military's anxiety over a possible Japanese invasion and the possibility of "a second Pearl Harbor" on the mainland. General DeWitt and the army did nothing to allay these fears, if they did not encourage them. Conspiracy theories mushroomed. For instance, throughout January 1942, the broadcaster John B. Hughes gave a series of radio talks accusing Japanese Americans of subversive activity and hinting that Japanese-American control of agricultural production was part of a Japanese master plan. He intimated that the fact that Japanese Americans, many of whom were fishermen and farmers, had tended to settle in areas which lay near coast facilities or defense installations further "proved" their disloyal intent.[38]

Another element in the hysteria was America's outrage over Pearl Harbor and its desire for revenge against the "treacherous" attack. This translated easily to attacks against Japanese Americans who were identified with the enemy. The anger of West Coast whites was compounded by Japan's early military victories in the Pacific during January 1942, as the Japanese captured Manila and threatened Singapore. Issei and Nisei were insulted and spat on in the streets, and shots were fired into Japanese-American homes in southern California.[39] Newspapers and magazines ran wild stories about spy rings, alleging falsely that FBI agents had confiscated navy signal flags, illegal radios, and ammunition from Japanese-American homes. Nor were such stories confined to West Coast media. The nationally syndicated columnist Damon Runyon alleged that Japanese aliens in Los Angeles were enemy agents with transmitters, and a piece in the January 1942 issue of *Reader's Digest* "exposed" the plans of the treacherous California Japanese saboteurs.[40]

Greed and economic rivalry played a significant part in the anti-Japanese movement. To white farmers in California, organized into groups such as the Western Growers Protective Association, the Grower-Shipper Vegetable Association, and the White American Nurserymen of Los Angeles, the war emergency offered an opportunity to "kick the Japs out," rid the area of their hardworking competitors, and take over the fertile Japanese-operated lands.[41] As the Grower-Shipper's manager told *The Saturday Evening Post* shortly afterward, "We're charged with wanting to get rid of the Japs for self-ish reasons. We might as well be honest. We do. It's a question of whether the white man lives on the Pacific Coast or the brown man."[42] Racism and greed merged into each other. Merchants and businessmen who had an interest in removing competition from Japanese-American shopkeepers were heavily represented in local commercial groups that led the call for evacuation. As early as December 22, 1941, the Los Angeles Chamber of Commerce stepped into the fray and made the first call for the removal of Japanese-American citizens and aliens from the city.

The binding factor among these disparate social, economic, and military forces was racial animosity toward Japanese Americans. White Americans could not accept either the Issei or the Nisei as Americans and projected onto them all the popular negative stereotypes that had evolved about the Japanese since the beginning of the century. Japanese Americans were especially vulnerable to a hate campaign. Their community was small but racially distinct and easily noticeable, economically powerful, politically powerless, and concentrated into "Japantowns" (in part the result of several decades of residential segregation in the Pacific Coast states) which had their own foreign-language newspapers, schools, and institutions. Their segregation increased their visibility and vulnerability.

The evacuation movement, though catalyzed by the emergency, represented the culmination of a historic pattern of prejudice and legal discrimination against the "Japs" on the West Coast. Its ideology and rhetoric derived from those of the longstanding West Coast nativist groups that had lobbied for decades in favor of restrictions on Japanese residents. The war brought these groups increased visibility and influence and fostered the establishment of new local groups with similar goals. Groups such as the California Joint

Immigration Committee (the descendant of the Japanese Exclusion League), the American Legion, and the Native Sons and Daughters of the Golden West referred to the Pearl Harbor attack as confirmation of the danger posed by the presence of the "treacherous Japs," and they saw the events as an opportunity to overturn the existing constitutional bars to expulsion of Japanese-American citizens. They made public statements, organized letter-writing campaigns, and lobbied government officials for harsh measures against both Issei aliens and Nisei citizens.[43]

As the anti-Japanese movement grew and took political shape within California and the West Coast states, those involved sought to exert influence on the national government. During January 1942 groups and private citizens sent dozens of individual letters urging evacuation of the West Coast Japanese Americans irrespective of citizenship. Many of them were addressed directly to the President. The letters brought to the surface the powerful emotions aroused by the anti-Japanese hysteria—racial hatred, greed, mistrust, revenge, and fear of further "treachery." The first such request came on December 30, when a local chapter of the Military Order of the Purple Heart petitioned the President to move all Japanese away from coastal counties.[44] On January 2 a couple in San Fernando asked the President to "remove" the Japanese gardeners on the coast, since such *nasty dirty sneekie people* could not be trusted. Two days later, a man in Los Angeles wrote FDR not to "take chances" with citizens who could not be trusted but to move them to the interior. On January 5 a Long Beach man objected to Japanese being left "at large" when the Japanese Army in the Philippines was treating Americans harshly. The government, he insisted, must protect Americans against the "Jap menace" of sabotage, whatever the cost to individuals. On January 14 a Chicago woman wrote that she would feel better if the Japanese Americans were moved inland after the "costly lesson in Japanese treachery" at Pearl Harbor. On January 24 a Seattle woman wrote, "Kindly give some thought to ridding our beloved Country of these Japs who hold no love or loyalty to our God, our ideals or our traditions, or our Government—They should *never* have been allowed here." On January 29 a man from Orestat, California, urged the President to get rid of the "Japs" and send them "back" because they could not be trusted, and also because they "occupy all the best farm ground in California." He complained that Japanese-American farmers worked too hard and were willing to pay outrageous rents for the land they leased. "An American does not stand a chance against them."[45] The war had liberated the racism seething just beneath the surface of white Californians' envy of Japanese Americans.

It did not take long for California political officials to jump on the anti-Japanese bandwagon. Leland Ford, a conservative Los Angeles Republican facing a difficult reelection campaign, was the first congressman to do so. On January 4, 1942, he sent Secretary of State Cordell Hull a telegram calling for rigorous checks on the Japanese community, stating, "I do not believe we could be any too strict in our consideration of the Japanese in the face of the treacherous way in which they do things." On January 16 (a week after the California legislature considered and tabled a resolution calling for mass evacuation), Ford wrote Stimson, Knox, and Biddle calling for the evacuation and internment of Japanese Americans from the West Coast, a step which, he asserted, his constituents strongly favored, based on the mail he was receiving. Four days later, Ford repeated his proposal before Congress. In his speech, he set up a classic "Catch-22" situation for Japanese Americans by presenting internment as their patriotic duty—if any were loyal, they would prove it by volunteering to be locked up, while their unwillingness to be imprisoned was proof of their disloyalty.

Ford's letter shifted the terms of the debate from action against aliens to removal of aliens and citizens.[46] Attorney General Biddle replied that the Justice Department Enemy Alien Program's officials had matters well in hand and he saw no legal way to move citizens short of suspending habeas corpus.[47] However, the War Department was more welcoming. On January 24, Secretary of War Stimson wrote Ford a letter (drafted by Bendetsen) which stated that the task of relocation of the Japanese population would be enormous and complex, but the army was prepared to take on the task and had the facilities available if needed. The obvious implication was that Ford should lobby the Justice Department to transfer authority over the Enemy Alien Program to the army. Ford was soon joined by other Pacific Coast congressmen in an ad hoc committee chaired by Clarence Lea, dean of the California delegation, which held a series of meetings during the last part of January to determine how to pressure the Justice Department into agreeing to the internment of citizens.

During this entire period, Franklin Roosevelt was insulated from direct exposure to military and political pressure on the "Japanese problem" as he focused on planning wartime strategy with Churchill. However, by mid-January 1942 he had apparently turned his attention to the Japanese-American question. One factor may have been the dozens of letters he was receiving from the West Coast calling for action. While the President sent these letters to the Justice Department for acknowledgment, he normally paid close attention to his correspondence as a way of tracking public opinion. In addition, anti-Japanese-American sentiment was making its way into newspaper and radio accounts, a source of information which Roosevelt, an active reader of the press, could not fail to notice.

The President's interest may have been inspired by international developments as well. On January 14, 1942, the government of Canada issued an order removing all male Japanese nationals aged 18 through 45 from Canada's Pacific Coast province of British Columbia. The Canadian action received virtually no media attention in the United States, and it seems to have played no direct part in the administration's deliberations over evacuation. However, West Coast naval authorities expressed appreciation for the action and tacit approval of similar action in the United States.[48] While there is no evidence that Roosevelt was influenced by the Canadian government's actions, it is quite likely that he knew of them, especially as he was in daily contact with British Prime Minister Winston Churchill and in frequent communication with Canadian Premier Mackenzie King during the period. At the very least, the Canadians would logically have raised the question of coordinating their actions with the United States.[49]

On January 13, the same day Roosevelt received John Franklin Carter's "despondent" report about the lack of progress on the Munson-Ringle plan, writer Louis Adamic dined with the President at the White House. Adamic reported that Eleanor Roosevelt surprised the President by urging him to "do something" about aiding the one million enemy aliens, some Japanese but mostly German and Italian, who, she argued, were the targets of harassment and discrimination. Winston Churchill, who was also present at the table, commented that Americans might follow the British example of dealing with enemy aliens by means of examinations by loyalty tribunals: "We separated the goats from the sheep, interned the goats and used the sheep."[50] As "Roosevelt listened intently," Eleanor Roosevelt countered that the main problem was unjust suspicion and scapegoating of aliens.

Roosevelt then asked Adamic, a well-known champion of ethnic minorities, for his thoughts on the alien situation. Adamic asked, in a general way, for a campaign of government propaganda to counter anti-alien hysteria.[51] Roosevelt agreed, noting his statement urging employers against firing aliens or those with alien names. Encouraged to continue, Adamic then brought up the hysteria against the Japanese Americans on the West Coast. There was no reason, he asserted, to treat the Nisei population, the vast majority of whom were loyal, any differently from the second-generation populations of German Americans or Italian Americans in the East. Any disloyal individuals could be handled by the FBI and military intelligence. Adamic added that he "had reason to believe" that the hysteria for internment of "all people with Japanese faces" was stimulated by a combination of "chauvinistic groups and newspapers" and by "special agricultural interests" who wished to eliminate competition by Japanese farmers and should thus be resisted.

Adamic was taken aback by the harsh and peremptory reaction his comments received from Eleanor Roosevelt:

> "But some of the Japanese on the Coast *have* been caught as spies
> of the Japanese government," said Mrs. Roosevelt sharply.
>   The tone and finality of her words surprised me. The President
> looked thoughtful but said nothing.[52]

Eleanor Roosevelt had spoken publicly in support of both Issei and Nisei loyalty only two days before, and she ultimately opposed mass evacuation. The incident thus demonstrates not only the strain of the wartime situation but the misinformation to which the President was exposed. Eleanor Roosevelt frequently acted as a sounding board for her husband, and her information on intelligence matters undoubtedly came from him.

Another case of misinformation occurred on January 16. Attorney General Biddle recorded that at a Cabinet meeting, "Claude Wickard [the Secretary of Agriculture] raised the difficulties on the West Coast with the Japanese gardeners, people would not use vegetables produced by them and in one actual case a Japanese gardener confessed to putting very much too much arsenic in spraying vegetables. A conference has been suggested to work something out." While Roosevelt did not comment on this unlikely tale, such "evidence" (which was persuasive enough to push Wickard into later support for relocation) would not only have given him a false picture of Nikkei loyalty but (like the letters he was receiving) would have shaped his picture of community attitudes—a major political consideration in policy formation, especially in wartime.

Paradoxically, Supreme Court Justice Owen Roberts, who later dissented on the constitutionality of Executive Order 9066, may have contributed the most crucial piece of misinformation to Roosevelt. On December 18, 1941, the President appointed Roberts to lead a commission of inquiry into the disaster at Pearl Harbor. On January 18 and 24, just before the Roberts Commission report was released, Roosevelt met with Roberts for extended conversations.[53] While there is no record of these conversations, it is evident that Roberts was very much absorbed with the problem of Japanese Americans. According to Stimson's diary, Roberts met with the secretary of war on January 20 and told him that Japanese Americans in Hawaii were not trustworthy. "The tremendous Japanese population in the Islands he regarded as a great menace particularly as a large portion of them are now armed under the draft. He did not think that the FBI had succeeded in getting under the crust of their secret thoughts at all and he believed that this great mass of Japanese, both aliens and Americanized, existed as a great potential danger in the Islands in case a pinch came in our fortunes."[54] Whether Roberts expressed such sentiments directly to the President or through Stimson, FDR would naturally have been impressed by the testimony of such an "objective" observer and would surely have been tempted to draw the analogy between conditions in Hawaii and on the West Coast.

The Roberts Commission's final report on Pearl Harbor, dated January 23, 1942, was made public the following day. Ironically, in comparison with Roberts's inflammatory private comments regarding Japanese Americans, the report was exceedingly vague and innocuous. Not only did it not describe the Japanese Americans in Hawaii as a current danger or come to any conclusions about subversion or espionage, it did not mention the community at all. On the contrary, the report's only discussion of subversive activities was a brief comment in the text that espionage had been conducted by Japanese spies in Hawaii in the period before Pearl Harbor. "Some were Japanese consular agents and others were persons having no open relations with the Japanese foreign service."[55]

Nevertheless, the report's release attracted national attention and transformed public opinion on Japanese Americans. Newspapers throughout the country publicized the report in bold headlines, and their articles centered on the subversive activities of Japanese in Hawaii in preparing the way for the sneak attack. Neither the report nor the newspapers who publicized it distinguished between espionage by planted agents brought from Japan and hired Caucasian spies, on the one hand, and the longtime-resident Issei and Nisei populations, on the other. Rather, journalists and radio trumpeted the findings as proof of subversive activity by Japanese Americans. The *Philadelphia Inquirer's* headlines connected "enemy aliens" with "enemy spies," and the newspaper editorialized against the "infestation" of "enemy aliens and others who seek to weaken America's war program."[56] Three days after the report was released, the *Inquirer* ran a suspiciously timed, unsubstantiated, and later discredited report from the Navy Office of Public Relations that "Japanese Fifth Columnists" who had lived for many years around Pearl Harbor had deliberately driven their cars and jammed the roads on December 7 to hinder military traffic.[57]

The reaction among newspapers and politicians on the West Coast was even more extreme. Despite the Roberts Report's innocuous or ambiguous language, in the feverish anti-Japanese atmosphere of California it was taken as positive proof of Japanese-American disloyalty that legitimated all the previous rumors. *The Los Angeles Times,* which as recently as January 23 had defended the Nikkei as good Americans who "deserve sympathy rather than suspicion," called, on January 28, for immediate relocation of both aliens and American citizens. On February 2 *Times* columnist W. H. Anderson referred to the Japanese Americans as "vipers" loyal to Japan, who posed a "potential and menacing" danger to the country. Meanwhile, the popular newspaper columnist Harry McLemore stated bluntly, "I am for immediate removal of every Japanese on the West Coast to a point deep in the interior. I don't mean a nice part of the interior either. Herd 'em up, pack 'em off and give 'em the inside room in the badlands. Let 'em be pinched, hurt, hungry and dead up against it . . . Personally, I hate the Japanese, and that goes for all of them."

The release of the Roberts Report led army officials and California political leaders to unite in support of evacuation of both Issei and Nisei. On January 27 DeWitt met with California Governor Culbert Olson, a liberal Democrat. Although Olson had vacillated over steps to control enemy aliens, he now told DeWitt that the people of the state wanted "the Japanese" moved out. "Since the publication of the Roberts Report," Olson claimed, "they feel that they are living in the midst of enemies. They don't trust the Japanese, none of them." Two days later, California Attorney General Earl Warren (who would defeat Olson in the gubernatorial race in California that November) announced his support for evacuation.

Olson's and Warren's comments, in addition to the Roberts Report (perhaps as much for the blame it placed on the Pearl Harbor commanders for negligence as for its discussion of Japanese-American espionage activity), ended Dewitt's hesitation, and he informed the War Department on January 29 that he favored evacuation of all Japanese Americans, whether aliens or citizens, from the Pacific Coast. Although Secretary of War Stimson was still uncertain about evacuation, his chief deputy, Assistant Secretary of War John McCloy, agreed with DeWitt and Bendetsen that some action was necessary.

Meanwhile, in Washington, the Roberts Report led to strong pressure for evacuation by the Leland Ford–Clarence Lea committee, which claimed to represent the entire West Coast congressional delegation. On January 30, the day after DeWitt asked the War Department to evacuate aliens and citizens, the committee met with Karl Bendetsen, representing the War Department, and James Rowe and Edward Ennis of the Justice Department. Bendetsen informed the congressmen that DeWitt concurred in the need for evacuation, and while he could not speak for the secretary of war, who had the final authority, he believed strongly that the army was prepared to take over the Alien Enemy Program if the War Department were given authority. Afterward, the committee sent the President a detailed set of policy recommendations (drafted with the aid of the Washington lobbyist of the Los Angeles Chamber of Commerce, who sat in on the committee's meetings) for army control and evacuation of Issei aliens and Nisei "dual citizens." (The notion of "dual citizenship" was a longtime canard of the nativists, since the United States did not recognize dual citizenship and the provisions of Japanese law granting Nisei automatic citizenship had been abolished in 1925.)[58]

The Justice Department raced to counter Bendetsen's pressure. On January 29, the day DeWitt informed the War Department that he favored evacuation, Biddle issued a proclamation creating the 88 "vital defense areas" the general had requested, most of which were near shipyards and factories in the vicinity of San Francisco and Los Angeles. He ordered that enemy aliens leave these military zones by February 24. He further announced that the Justice Department was keeping tabs on all potential enemies of the United States and closely studying the situation before deciding on further action. He continued, however, to oppose mass evacuation of American citizens as unnecessary, and he publicly warned that persecution of Japanese Americans could easily drive loyal Americans into fifth column activities. Biddle's policy made him an unpopular figure on the West Coast. For instance, *The Los*

Angeles Times attacked him in an editorial on February 7, charging that Biddle's concern for individual rights, though laudable in peacetime, could not be permitted to interfere with national security in wartime.[59]

Biddle hoped to persuade Roosevelt to back him up. The President, however, was already beginning to talk about the Japanese Americans as a security problem. Interior Secretary Harold Ickes recorded that at the Cabinet meeting on January 30 (the first one after release of the Roberts Report), the conversation turned to the West Coast:

> The Hearst newspapers are putting on a typical Hearst campaign for the removal and sequestration of all the Japanese along the Pacific Coast. This would be a cruel and unnecessary step . . . In some places in California, people are refusing to buy Japanese truck farm products. The President told about a movie actress who said to him that she was afraid that the Japanese would poison their vegetables. This, of course, is purely hysteria . . . The President asked whether the Department of Justice was tapping wires and Francis [Biddle] answered that they were being tapped wherever it was considered necessary . . . There seems to be quite a disposition in Congress now to pass a bill permitting wire tapping, but since Pearl Harbor the administration has gone ahead regardless and undoubtedly will continue to do so.[60]

This diary extract shows in miniature the forces working on the President. Roosevelt was continuing to receive wild anti-Japanese reports from the West Coast and was aware of sensational newspaper accounts. It is not clear whether Roosevelt agreed with Ickes that the reports were hysterical, but he certainly was aware of Hearst's longstanding manipulation of anti-Japanese sentiment. Indeed, the young Roosevelt had deliberately stirred up the anti-Japanese press during the Alien Land Act crisis of 1913 in order to further military preparedness, and he had complained bitterly about the Hearst press's refusal to print the truth about Japanese-American relations during the 1920s.

The Cabinet, presumably at FDR's request, went on to discuss briefly the evacuation of Japanese Americans as a real possibility. The debate focused not on the wisdom of removal but on the manner in which it could be accomplished, and whether Nisei were to be included: "It would also be quite a task to move all of the Japanese out. Francis Biddle deprecated the lengths to which the Hearst papers and others have been going but he did indicate that the time might come that there would be certain areas where the President might suspend the writ of Habeas Corpus."

Roosevelt must have expressed interest in the situation and in Biddle's suggestions for suspending the writ of habeas corpus, because the attorney general sent the President a memo the same day describing the steps which the Department of Justice had already taken regarding arrests, registration of aliens, seizure of contraband, and creation of "prohibited areas." Biddle then explained the debate over evacuation:

> 5. The army is recommending "restricted areas," contemplating a strip of land along the West Coast reaching at times a width of thirty or forty miles. This will involve mass evacuation of 50,000 or 100,000 aliens. Alien enemies may be permitted in the restricted areas under special licensing. The problem of resettlement, reemployment, etc., is, of course, very great. We are cooperating with Social Security, the Labor Department, and other agencies of the Government in this program.
>
> 6. American born Japanese, being citizens, cannot be apprehended or treated like alien enemies; probably an arrangement can be made, where necessary, to evacuate them from military zones. Study is being made as to whether, with respect to them, the writ of habeas corpus could be suspended in case of an emergency.[61]

Given his previously expressed opinion that relocation was both unnecessary and harmful, Biddle's comments at the Cabinet meeting and in the memo are puzzling. In particular, he expressed a readiness to support and cooperate in the mass military evacuation of aliens and to use (or at least consider) the suspension of the writ of habeas corpus as a mechanism for moving out the Nisei if it became necessary. At first glance, the memo appears to represent a capitulation, with the attorney general agreeing to the army's demands for evacuation of all West Coast Japanese Americans and discussing ways in which the constitutional difficulties could be worked out. Such an interpretation would suggest that Biddle actually approved of mass evacuation so long as the matter was taken out of his hands and the Justice Department did not have to engage in any illegal acts.[62]

A kinder view is that removal of the Issei was a fait accompli by the end of January, as Ickes's Cabinet record suggests, and that the attorney general preferred to demonstrate his willingness to cooperate in the relocation of aliens in order to better persuade the President not to evacuate citizens as well. Biddle's inflation of the Issei population, which totaled less than 40,000, to "50,000 to 100,000" might thus be explained as the result of strategy rather than ignorance. In that case, however, Biddle erred in raising the question of suspending the writ of habeas corpus, even if he meant it as reassurance that the administration could still take such action if it ever became necessary. Presumably the attorney general wished to find a compromise policy that would simultaneously avert wholesale evacuation of citizens, satisfy the President's security concerns, and leave the Justice Department free to deal with dangerous individuals. If so, he succeeded, at least temporarily, for Roosevelt sent Clarence Lea's letter with the congressional committee's proposals to Biddle for preparation of a reply—thus demonstrating that he continued to consider the attorney general responsible for the Alien Enemy Program. Still, Biddle's reassurance that the legal obstacles to removing citizens from restricted areas could be evaded in an emergency was an invitation to the President to ignore constitutional issues entirely.

After sending his memo to Roosevelt, Biddle moved onto the offensive. Egged on by Rowe and Ennis (who were outraged by Bendetsen's statements to the congressional committee in support of evacuation), the attorney general contacted Stimson in an attempt to ward off further army interference with control of American citizens. On Sunday, February 4, 1942, Biddle, Rowe, Ennis, and Hoover met with Gullion, Bendetsen, and McCloy to approve a common statement and reduce West Coast hysteria. Biddle was fortified by a fresh report from Hoover, who had received Ringle's January 26, 1942, special report to the chief of naval operations, in which Ringle insisted that there was no serious "Japanese problem" and argued that security concerns were best handled on an individual basis. Hoover's report stated that there was no evidence of disloyal activity justifying the relocation of Japanese Americans. Biddle made clear that Justice would not handle the removal of U.S. citizens in any case. When Gullion asked angrily if Biddle would refuse to cooperate even if the army men "on the ground" determined that evacuation of citizens was necessary, Biddle responded that the Justice Department would be "through" if it interfered with the rights of citizens. Biddle then presented a joint press release for the War Department to approve, stating that the FBI had found "no substantial evidence of planned sabotage by any alien" and concluding that the Justice Department and the

War Department agreed that the military situation did not require removal of American citizens of Japanese ancestry. McCloy, however, did not want to foreclose all possibility of evacuating citizens, and he refused to approve the press release. The meeting broke up amid the disagreement.[63]

Biddle's offensive fostered an internal debate within the War Department over the question of the Nisei. Bendetsen and Gullion wanted all Japanese Americans removed. DeWitt was willing, if necessary, to accept a voluntary evacuation plan for the Nisei, although he was scornful over drawing a distinction between the threat posed by aliens and citizens, especially in view of the unanimous pressure in California for evacuation of all Nikkei: "A Jap is a Jap to these people now," he told McCloy. McCloy was willing to accept a plan for mass exclusion of Issei and limited, voluntary migration of the Nisei (a compromise suggested by Tom Clark, the only Justice Department figure to approve relocation, and by Governor Olson). Secretary of War Stimson favored relocation of the Issei from selected areas but was not interested in mass evacuation and doubted whether the Nisei could be included. On February 3 Stimson wrote in his diary that the Nisei were "more dangerous" as saboteurs than the Issei, but that any military evacuation could only be justified in order to protect specific facilities; a racially discriminatory policy was not acceptable.

Seeking to clarify the issue and resolve his own uncertainties, Stimson asked DeWitt to give a specific military rationale for the mass evacuation of citizens. Over the following days, as DeWitt (assisted by Clark) labored on a rationale to justify emergency military action against the Nisei, McCloy conferred unsuccessfully with Rowe and Gullion regarding various schemes for accomplishing the removal of the Nisei constitutionally, such as by removing all civilians from a zone and permitting all citizens except Japanese Americans to return.

After the beginning of February, West Coast public and political pressure for government action skyrocketed. On February 4, 1942, the Office of Facts and Figures (a government information service that was later absorbed into the Office of War Information) released a survey of public opinion on the West Coast during the previous week. The OFF survey revealed that the majority trusted existing government controls on the Japanese Americans but found that a significant minority, between 23 and 43 percent, believed further action was necessary.[64] On February 2, a meeting of 150 California sheriffs and law enforcement officers, led by state Attorney General Earl Warren, demanded that Japanese Americans be removed from California and warned of large-scale violence against the Nikkei if they remained. The following day, the West Coast House and Senate delegations, led by Hiram Johnson (the onetime California governor who had signed the 1913 Alien Land Act), publicly called for internment of both the Issei and Nisei, and Senator Mon Wallgren of Washington asked for the immediate "eviction" of all West Coast Japanese Americans. On February 4 California Governor Culbert Olson made a public speech charging that Japanese Americans had communicated with Japanese ships. On February 5 Los Angeles Mayor Fletcher Bowron made a radio address in favor of evacuation, in which he accused Japanese Americans of plotting sabotage and preparing a second Pearl Harbor. Bowron's address attracted widespread attention and was inserted in the *Congressional Record* four days later. On February 7 Representative Martin Dies of Texas, chair of the Communist- (and headline-) hunting House Committee on Un-American Activities, claimed that he had evidence that the Axis powers planned an imminent joint invasion of the United States, and proposed that all Japanese Americans be moved at least 500 miles from the Pacific Coast. On February 12 the distinguished national columnist Walter Lippmann, relying on false reports from Earl Warren and other sources on the West Coast, wrote the first of two columns stating that Japanese Americans were planning acts of sabotage. Lippmann was widely read and quoted in Washington, and his column lent authoritative support to the movement for evacuation. During this period, letters to Roosevelt and other government officials urging evacuation grew approximately fivefold in volume over the January total, reaching at least 200 per week. Many were inspired by, and cited, the anti-Japanese-American newspaper reports and speeches by public officials.

The rising hysteria stunned defenders of civil rights both inside and outside government circles, and they scrambled belatedly to organize pressure against evacuation. Fair Play committees and religious organizations released statements calling for tolerance, and the liberal journal *The Nation* published a pair of articles decrying West Coast pressure for removal.[65] However, public pressure against evacuation remained sporadic and ineffective. Within the White House, Archibald MacLeish and Eleanor Roosevelt joined Biddle in organizing opposition to mass evacuation. MacLeish, a Roosevelt friend and speechwriter who was director of the Office of Facts and Figures, had been monitoring the situation on the West Coast since shortly after Pearl

Harbor, and in mid-January he sent his assistants Ulric Bell and Alan Cranston to Los Angeles to persuade newspaper editors to moderate their coverage of Japanese Americans.[66] On February 3 he forwarded to McCloy the OFF study on West Coast public opinion with a cover note warning him not to make decisions on the basis of representations by local officials and pressure groups, and emphasizing that the majority of Californians favored existing methods of control. The same day, MacLeish sent Roosevelt's secretary, Grace Tully, material for a proposed presidential speech denouncing war hysteria and mentioned that his office was "trying to keep down the pressure on the West Coast."[67] On February 11 MacLeish sent Eleanor Roosevelt, who had already made a radio address in early January on behalf of the loyal Nisei and Issei, material for further statements. Shortly thereafter, the First Lady met with MacLeish and his assistants for a briefing on the Japanese-American situation designed to give her arguments to take back to the President, in order to dissuade him from taking extreme measures. However, much of Mrs. Roosevelt's time during February 1942 was spent responding to conservative criticism of her actions as director of the Office of Civil Defense, and it is not precisely clear when she raised the subject of Japanese Americans with the President. When she did, he told her coldly that he did not wish to discuss the matter with her.[68]

Under pressure from congressional and army sources, Biddle retreated further from his opposition to mass removal. Evacuation of citizens, he told a Senate committee on February 5, could be constitutionally carried out by the army in case of military necessity. Rowe and Ennis disagreed with this position. Rowe, a former White House staffer, wrote a back-channel memo to Grace Tully pleading with her to "please tell the President to keep his eye on the Japanese situation in California," which was becoming explosive, and added that if he suspended the writ of habeas corpus he would have a nasty fight with the Supreme Court.[69]

In response to his underlings' pressure, Biddle took the unusual step of soliciting an outside opinion from a trio of government lawyers and New Deal stalwarts, Benjamin Cohen, Oscar Cox, and Joseph Rauh, on the constitutionality of evacuating citizens. The Cohen-Cox-Rauh team replied with a hasty memo that affirmed the constitutionality of removing citizens on a racial basis if necessary for national safety. The memo asserted, "It is a fact and not a legal theory that Japanese who are American citizens cannot readily be identified and distinguished from Japanese who owe no loyalty to the

United States." Since Japanese Americans were not readily distinguishable to the "occidental eye," it was impossible to effectively monitor them for disloyal activity. Though the authors stopped short of recommending evacuation of citizens (which they later claimed to oppose), they agreed that it was up to the military to decide what restrictions were necessary, including the establishment of special defense zones from which people of Japanese extraction could be forbidden.[70]

Biddle still believed that no necessity existed for evacuation, and he clearly thought the President needed further lobbying on this point. He asked FDR for a meeting regarding the Japanese situation on the West Coast, which he referred to as "very disturbing and important."[71] The attorney general met with Roosevelt for lunch on Saturday, February 7:

> I discussed at length with [FDR] the Japanese situation stating exactly what we had done, that we believed mass evacuation at this time inadvisable, that the F.B.I. was not staffed to perform it; that this was an army job not, in our opinion, advisable; that there were no reasons for mass evacuation and I thought the army should be directed to prepare a detailed plan of evacuation in case of an emergency caused by an air raid or attempted landing on the West Coast. I emphasized the danger of the hysteria, which we were beginning to control, moving east and affecting the Italian and German population in Boston and New York. Generally he approved, being fully aware of the dreadful risk of Fifth Column retaliation in case of a raid.[72]

Roosevelt's reaction to Biddle's presentation, which was plainly not new to him, is not entirely clear. His comment about fifth columnists suggests that he was less concerned about whether West Coast evacuation was or was not necessary than with the situation on the East Coast. Roosevelt hoped to avoid a repeat of the scapegoating and hostility directed at German Americans during World War I, but he also wished to avoid driving innocent people into the arms of the enemy. Certainly, the attorney general did not go away satisfied of the President's strong backing. He thus turned to Stimson.

On February 9 Biddle sent the secretary of war a letter reaffirming his position that evacuation of the Nisei was unnecessary, but he did not demand a meeting. Stimson's prestige was such that Biddle was unwilling to challenge him directly to either provide specific evidence of such necessity or abandon the idea of evacuation. By February 9, however, Stimson had evidently made up his mind to approve evacuation of American citizens, despite Biddle's opposition and DeWitt's failure to provide a clear case for military necessity. Stimson was wary of the constitutional implications of the policy—more so than Biddle—and he felt doubts as to whether national security justified such an extreme step.

However, Stimson believed that a Japanese invasion of the West Coast was a real possibility. The war in the Pacific was going badly for the Allies. Japanese military forces were marching largely unopposed through Malaysia and racing toward Singapore. At the same time, Japanese invaders were steadily pushing back Filipino and American defenders in the Philippines. Under prodding from McCloy and the army, Stimson decided that national security required that all Japanese Americans be removed from the coast because their racial tie to Japan made them liable to commit disloyal acts, and white Americans could not easily separate the loyal from the disloyal. He wrote in his diary, "The second generation Japanese can only be evacuated either as part of a total evacuation, giving access to the areas only by permits, or by frankly trying to put them out on the ground that their racial characteristics are such that we cannot understand or trust even the citizen Japanese. The latter is the fact but I am afraid it will make a tremendous hole in our constitutional system to apply it."

On February 11, 1942, Stimson met with McCloy and Deputy Army Chief of Staff General Mark Clark (who opposed evacuation as costly and unnecessary). The secretary of war then determined that he ought not to decide the matter of evacuation on his own. He sent the President a memo, asking the question, "Is the President willing to authorize us to move Japanese citizens as well as aliens from restricted areas?" Stimson then asked whether the army should "withdraw" Japanese Americans from "the entire strip DeWitt originally recommended," which would include over 100,000 aliens and citizens, or take an intermediate position by evacuating the large cities such as Los Angeles and Seattle, or simply establish restricted areas around airplane plants and such facilities. (He made clear his opposition to the last proposal as "wasteful, involv[ing] difficult administrative problems, and more trouble than 100 percent withdrawal from the area.")

Stimson asked the President for a meeting to discuss the memo, but Roosevelt responded that he was too busy. It was indeed a troublesome time for FDR. On that day, the Japanese invaded Singapore, which was to fall on

February 15. The Japanese were also poised to take over the Philippines, and on February 11 the President and Stimson were forced to dissuade Philippine leader Manuel Quezon from declaring the islands neutral as a last-ditch move to avoid a Japanese conquest. Roosevelt's frustration and anger at the Japanese over these events undoubtedly made him less concerned about the rights of Japanese Americans.[73] In any case, Stimson managed to reach the President by telephone that afternoon. Stimson noted in his diary that the President was "very vigorous" and told him to do whatever he thought best. McCloy reported that Roosevelt had stated that if the army's proposal involved citizens, "we will take care of them too." According to McCloy, FDR said that "there will probably be some repercussions but it has got to be dictated by military necessity," and added: "Be as reasonable as you can." McCloy interpreted this to mean he had carte blanche to proceed with evacuation of all Japanese Americans.

Though Executive Order 9066 would not be signed for another eight days, Roosevelt's telephone conversation with Stimson marked his decision. DeWitt's final recommendation for evacuation of the "enemy race," which was sent to the President on February 14, simply confirmed this decision, as did the intensifying pressure from the barrage of letters, newspaper columns, and congressional lobbying that poured in during the week that followed the appearance of Walter Lippmann's column. A few days after his telephone call with Stimson, the President received a memo from the ad hoc congressional committee, entitled "Recommendations of the Pacific Coast Delegation Regarding Alien Enemies and Sabotage." The President sent the material to the secretary of war and asked him to send a reply to committee chair Clarence Lea, thus signaling clearly that the matter was now a military problem, no longer in Attorney General Biddle's hands.[74]

On February 17 Senator Thomas Stewart of Tennessee increased the pressure to evacuate by introducing a bill in Congress to imprison all Japanese Americans for the duration of the war. The same day that Stewart introduced his bill, the President issued his first executive order against the Nisei, which transferred jurisdiction to the navy of Terminal Island in Los Angeles harbor, which the War Department had already cleared of its large Issei fisherman and shopkeeper population. An executive order has the force of law, although it carries no provision for arrest or imprisonment of violators without congressional action. Navy Secretary Knox and Rear Admiral R. S. Holmes thereupon ordered all Japanese Americans to move off the island within thirty days and condemned all houses belonging to Japanese Americans. Within a few days, the deadline was reduced to a mere 48 hours, and the Terminal Island Japanese Americans were pushed off their property with nothing but the things they could carry in their hands or wear on their backs.[75] Later that day, Roosevelt granted Stimson and McCloy final approval of their mass evacuation plan and asked them to have an executive order worked up for him to sign.[76] Stimson and McCloy had been careful not to inform Biddle, whom they considered an obstructionist, of the President's shift. Stimson wrote in his diary that the Department of Justice had been unhelpful on the evacuation question but that "the President has been all right."[77]

In fact, Biddle, still unaware of Roosevelt's approval of evacuation, sent the President a memo on February 17, ostensibly to provide information if he was asked at his press conference about the subject of evacuating Japanese Americans. Biddle explained that the demands for evacuation of Japanese Americans (including those from special interests who "would welcome their removal from good farm land and the elimination of their competition") were based on the grounds that attack on the West Coast and sabotage were imminent; but he maintained that, on the basis of his most recent information from the War Department and FBI, neither proposition was true. Biddle took Lippmann and other columnists to task for whipping up public anxiety through unsupported charges, an act he compared to crying "Fire!" in a crowded theater. Not only was evacuation unnecessary, but it would materially disrupt agricultural production.[78]

Presumably in response to the memo, Roosevelt informed Biddle that he had approved mass evacuation of Japanese-American aliens and citizens. Biddle's resistance then quickly ceased. On the evening of February 17, he held a joint War Department–Justice Department meeting at his house. Rowe and Ennis, who had no idea that any steps were contemplated against the Nisei, were shocked and outraged when Provost Marshal Gullion took out the draft of an executive order authorizing evacuation, but Biddle did not protest. Rowe helped clean up the language of the order and reluctantly submitted it to the Bureau of the Budget for Roosevelt to sign. Once presented with the executive order prepared by the War and Justice Departments, Roosevelt signed the order without further discussion or inquiry into the basis of the policy.[79]

On February 19, 1942, the President issued Executive Order 9066. It stated that to grant "every possible protection against espionage and against sabotage to national-defense material, national-defense premises and national-defense utilities," the President authorized the secretary of war and the military commanders he designated to prescribe military areas "from which any or all persons may be excluded, and with respect to which, the right of any person to enter, remain in, or leave shall be subject to whatever restriction" they cared to impose. It further authorized the military to provide transportation and accommodations for any excluded people and to accept assistance from state and local authorities. The order's text did not specifically mention Japanese Americans, the West Coast, evacuation, or internment. Nevertheless, nobody inside or outside the government had any doubt that the purpose of the order was to give the army the power to remove the Japanese Americans from the Pacific Coast.

What the order meant, in substance, was that the President and his military advisors determined that the Japanese ancestry of 112,000 Americans made them so likely to engage in subversive activities in the event of a Japanese invasion of the West Coast that they were to be collectively deported from the excluded area (which ultimately included the entire Pacific Coast of the United States). The army was empowered to take these people and move them away from their homes and businesses to unspecified areas inland. The determination of their disloyalty resulted not from any judicial finding or any reliable evidence of their individual or collective involvement in espionage or sabotage. In fact, not a single documented case of any such activity had come to light.

Seventy percent of these "disloyal" people were American-born U.S. citizens; their average age was 18 years old. The remaining 30 percent were virtually all permanent residents whose average age was over 50 and who had immigrated to America decades earlier. Yet this community of native-born Americans and longtime residents was assumed, because of the racial identity of its members, to be indistinguishable from the Japanese enemy. In contrast, no other alien population was confined as a group solely because of the ancestry and appearance of its members (although individual German and Italian "enemy aliens" deemed dangerous were detained), and no other American citizens, regardless of ethnic background, were subjected to such treatment.

The order's bland language concealed an unprecedented assertion of executive power. Under its provisions, the President imposed military rule on civilians without a declaration of martial law, and he sentenced a segment of the population to internal exile (and ultimately forced incarceration) under armed guard, notwithstanding that the writ of habeas corpus had not been suspended by Congress (to whom such power was reserved by the Constitution).[80] More importantly, Executive Order 9066 was unprecedented in the extent of its racially defined infringement of the basic rights of American citizens. The evacuation was not limited to the approximately 30 percent of the Japanese-American population that consisted of immigrant "enemy aliens." If it had been, it would still have been arbitrary, but it would clearly have fallen outside the guarantees of due process and equal protection of the laws granted to American citizens by the Constitution. The federal government had violated the fundamental liberties of non-citizen populations on racial grounds before—such as in the Fugitive Slave Acts and the expulsion of the Five Civilized Tribes from the southeastern United States. The novelty and danger of Roosevelt's order lay in its infringement of the constitutional protections inherent in American citizenship.

What led Roosevelt to approve the relocation of Japanese Americans? His ostensible motive was military necessity, or at least satisfying the expressed (or perceived) needs of the military. Certainly, the President defended his decision exclusively in terms of military factors. When Biddle objected that the evacuation was unnecessary, the President remarked that it must be a military decision, and he repeated that view in Cabinet meetings.[81] The army might be wrong, but Roosevelt considered it best equipped to decide what was needed to win the war.

Further confirmation of this conclusion comes from John Franklin Carter's pseudonymous novel, *The Catoctin Conversation,* in which the character "Roosevelt" explains that the internment was entirely "a matter of martial law": "The army asked for special status on the Pacific Coast. After Pearl Harbor, they were entitled to get what they said they needed. Once they had this status, they decided that the Japanese Americans must move east of the Rockies. I had no choice but to back them or discredit them." Carter's fictional alter ego then presses "Roosevelt" to admit his responsibility as commander-in-chief for allowing the army to commit a wholesale violation of the rights of citizens of Japanese origin, even though he knew from Carter's survey that the Japanese Americans were loyal. "Roosevelt" agrees that the action was wrong but maintains that "the army said it was necessary" and that he "accepted the army's judgment."[82] Given Carter's intimate association with FDR during the time when decisions about Japanese Americans were being made, this exchange, though fictionalized, probably represents an informed description of Roosevelt's actual views on the subject.

Nevertheless, the question of "military judgment" is by no means so simple. Even if Roosevelt merely accepted that army claims of necessity were accurate, it would not settle the question of his *motivation* for accepting them. It is true that the President generally deferred to the military on defense issues and saw his own task as giving the military whatever it said was necessary to defend the country. However, like the army planners in Hawaii who were so bent on protecting airplanes from nonexistent saboteurs that they left the planes open to a Japanese attack, Roosevelt's preoccupation before Pearl Harbor with discovering subversive activities by Japanese Americans shows how prepared—even overprepared—he was to believe military claims of fifth column activity after Pearl Harbor, even in the face of strong evidence to the contrary.

In any case, the evidence indicates that his decision to approve the evacuation was not in fact based on strictly military considerations. Roosevelt was not faced with a clear-cut military recommendation. There was dissension within the military itself over how best to deal with Japanese Americans. The President also failed to consult General George C. Marshall and the Joint Chiefs of Staff, his principal military advisors, before signing Executive Order 9066. The chiefs were conducting their own investigation of the West Coast situation during February. On February 4, one week before Roosevelt authorized evacuation, Marshall's deputy General Mark Clark and Admiral Harold Stark testified before the Lea-Ford committee that the danger of invasion was effectively nil and that coastal defenses were perfectly adequate. A week later Clark wrote the secretary of war that he believed mass evacuation was undesirable and unnecessary.[83]

Roosevelt was no doubt also aware that the navy brass (following the report of Lieutenant Commander Kenneth Ringle) opposed evacuation or took no position.[84] Roosevelt considered himself an old navy man—his allegiance was so marked that his chief of staff, General Marshall, once complained, "At least, Mr. President, stop speaking of the army as 'they' and the navy as 'us!'"[85] Because of his knowledge of naval matters, he often interfered in naval policy. In contrast, he felt less familiar with army policy and tended to leave the army alone. Unlike Stimson, the President did not demand the specific basis for the claims of military necessity. FDR did not even wait for DeWitt's final recommendations, which provided the (spurious) justification of military necessity that undergirded the army's case for evacuation, before granting Stimson his blanket approval to proceed.

Moreover, FDR did not approve all measures requested by the armed forces in connection with Japanese Americans, even when military necessity was presented to him as a justification. He did not, for example, support Navy Secretary Knox's December 1941 recommendation for immediate removal of Japanese aliens in Hawaii, even though the islands, unlike the West Coast, had actually been attacked and were under martial law. Although Roosevelt later gave his support to a plan for the incarceration of 100,000 Japanese Hawaiians, he refused to suspend the writ of habeas corpus in order to do so, and in the end there was neither a mass evacuation nor internment of Japanese Hawaiians.

Moreover, if military necessity had been the sole criterion for action, the President would have approved military proposals for similar control of other enemy aliens who posed a potential threat to security. Roosevelt was certainly aware of the problem of espionage and disloyal activities by Italian and German "enemy aliens." A few days after Pearl Harbor he told Biddle, "I don't care about the Italians. They are a lot of opera singers. But the Germans are different. They may be dangerous."[86] During his February 7 meeting with Biddle, the President expressed concern over subversive activities by Italians and Germans on the East Coast. Three days later, following the sinking of the cruise liner *Normandie* in New York harbor while it was being refitted for military use, Roosevelt ordered an investigation as to whether enemy aliens had been employed on the project and could have committed sabotage.[87]

However, the President did not approve General DeWitt's request to remove West Coast Italian and German aliens en masse, and he specifically refused to permit any evacuation in accordance with Executive Order 9066 on the East Coast. In April 1942, Eighth Army General Hugh A. Drum, the East Coast defense commander (DeWitt's Atlantic counterpart), proposed evacuating dangerous German and Italian aliens. Biddle took Drum's request as a sign of his intent to order mass evacuation, and he protested that such a move would lower morale and damage the region's economic and political structure. With Stimson's agreement, Roosevelt ordered Drum not to evacuate any person without prior approval.[88]

In the manuscript draft of his memoirs, Biddle contrasted the East Coast situation to the evacuation on the West Coast. He noted that, in military terms, the East Coast would have been the logical place for an evacuation of aliens. "There was more reason than in the West to conclude that shore-to-ship signals were accounting for the very serious submarine sinkings all along the East Coast, which were sporadic only on the West Coast." There would also have been greater reason to suspect disloyal activity from the numerous German and Italian aliens than from the much smaller Japanese population on the West Coast (indeed, even in California, Italian aliens outnumbered Issei). There were, in fact, established pro-Nazi and pro-fascist patriotic societies such as the German Bund on the East Coast, though Biddle did not mention them. "But the decisions were not made on the logic of events or on the weight of evidence, but on the racial prejudice that seemed to be influencing everyone."[89] Biddle's indictment of Roosevelt's motives is manifest, despite his tactful use of the passive voice regarding the decision to evacuate and his generalized attribution of racial prejudice.

If military necessity is an insufficient explanation for Roosevelt's approval of evacuation, what does explain it? As Milton Eisenhower, who as first director of the War Relocation Authority supervised the internment, perceptively stated, "The President's final decision was influenced by a variety of factors—by events over which he had little control, by inaccurate or incomplete information, by bad ⌐ ᴐunsel, by strong political pressures, and by his own training, background, and personality."[90]

The press of events and the lack of reliable information have historically been used to justify Roosevelt's decision to sign Executive Order 9066. According to this theory, the attack on Pearl Harbor led to widespread fears over a possible Japanese invasion of the West Coast. In the emergency atmosphere, army officers did not have sufficient information to make an informed decision about whether Japanese Americans represented a security threat, and they acted hastily to protect the country. It was precisely on this basis that the wartime Supreme Court, in *Hirabayashi v. United States* (1943) and *Korematsu v. United States* (1944), upheld the constitutionality of the military's actions. Champions of the internment such as Walter Lippmann, John McCloy, and Fletcher Bowron each relied on this narrative construction of events in their later apologias for their actions. Stating that they were correct to favor evacuation in the wake of Pearl Harbor and the Roberts Report, they claimed they honestly believed that Japanese Americans posed a security threat or that they accepted the conviction of the military that the threat was real. Other latter-day figures such as the historian Page Smith and the internment denier Lillian Baker have also based their interpretation of events on this narrative.

The narrative has, however, been largely discredited, both by reputable historians and by the report of the U.S. Commission on Wartime Relocation and Internment of Civilians. The narrative denies the obvious importance of such factors as historical anti-Japanese prejudice and economic resentment in prompting calls for evacuation. Instead, it assumes that the army's expressed justification for the evacuation represented a complete and accurate account of its actions. In fact, in the 1980s a federal court explicitly found that the government had knowingly suppressed evidence and presented false information to the Supreme Court as to the basis of the army's wartime actions, and it thus overturned the convictions of Gordon Hirabayashi and Fred Korematsu for violating the military orders that the Supreme Court had upheld during the war. Whatever truth there is to McCloy's, Bowron's, and Lippmann's self-exculpatory explanations, the narrative ignores the disingenuousness that surrounds them, especially in view of McCloy's documented manipulation of court evidence, Bowron's patent political self-interest in pushing evacuation, and Lippmann's later insistence that he suggested evacuation only to protect Japanese Americans from mob violence.

Because the importance of wartime events has been so inflated and distorted by internment defenders, any argument about their role in Roosevelt's decision is suspect and is difficult to resolve fairly. In one sense, the entire evacuation was contingent on events: the President would not have had the same fears over security and Japanese-American disloyalty if tensions between the United States and Japan had not grown to the point of war, and if there had not been a wartime emergency Roosevelt would have lacked the authority to make such an order.

Nevertheless, it does not appear that the actual military situation on the West Coast was directly influential on Roosevelt, since his policy toward Japanese Americans did not evolve in response to it. Had Roosevelt acted in proportion to actual military conditions, his priorities and his timetable would have been different. Anti-Japanese-American action would have begun directly after Pearl Harbor and would have focused on Hawaii, where throughout early 1942 Roosevelt expected an imminent invasion. Rather, except to the extent that events such as Pearl Harbor, Japan's conquests in the Pacific, and the Roberts Commission Report helped engender military and political hysteria for evacuation, they had little intrinsic relation to Japanese Americans.

The only event that had a direct impact on Japanese Americans during this period, and that "should" have most directly and strongly influenced Roosevelt's decision, was the January 14, 1942, order by the Canadian government removing male Japanese nationals from British Columbia. (The Canadian government subsequently issued an order-in-council on February 27 removing all people of Japanese ancestry.) However, this event received hardly any attention in the United States, and there is no evidence that it appeared in any administration discussions of evacuation.

Similarly, the question of access to information is complex and delicate because of its role in subsequent challenges to the internment. Roosevelt was subjected to false information from numerous sources, both inside and outside the government. The military justified its call for control by spreading (demonstrably untrue) stories of Japanese-American communications with Japanese submarines. The President was also apparently led to believe, either by private sources or by hysterical newspaper accounts or letters, that Nisei saboteurs had actually been arrested on the West Coast. The President's visitors and Cabinet officers repeated stories of Japanese-American farmers poisoning vegetables. Most importantly, most discussions of espionage by the Japanese consulate, notably those by Knox and the Roberts Commission, failed to make the clear distinction between agents brought in from Japan and members of the Japanese-American community.

This tide of misinformation no doubt contributed to Roosevelt's belief that dramatic action had to be taken to curb Issei and Nisei subversives. Yet, at the same time, the President was willingly misled. He had access to reliable information, which he chose to ignore, from sources he trusted, notably the FBI, that the Japanese Americans did not represent a danger. Even before the war with Japan began, Roosevelt had received FBI reports about the nature of the local Japanese community in Hawaii, and he had his own secret intelligence network report on the loyalty of West Coast Japanese Americans. He was again assured by the FBI and his special investigators after Pearl Harbor that Japanese Americans were loyal and that there was no evidence of sabotage in Hawaii. However, he chose not to accept such findings.

In contrast, the President lent credence to the wildest and most unsubstantiated anti-Japanese rumors. A few weeks after Executive Order 9066 was signed, for example, Roosevelt told his Cabinet that "friends of his" who had explored the lower California region of Mexico some time previously had uncovered numerous secret Japanese air bases, which could be mobilized for work in concert with Japanese aircraft carriers on bombing raids into southern California.[91] Thus, if the President believed unsubstantiated reports of fifth column activity by Japanese Americans, it was not simply because he lacked hard information but also because he was prepared to believe the worst, and expected the worst, from them.

Bad counsel was undeniably crucial in bringing about the evacuation. Even such "defenders" of Japanese Americans as Carter, Munson, and Biddle failed to alert the President until after he authorized evacuation that there was no truth in the hysterical stories about Issei and Nisei subversives or to insist to him that evacuation was unconstitutional, morally wrong, and racist in its inspiration and support. Rather, they based their arguments against evacuation on the premise that it was unnecessary, and would lower morale and interrupt food production. While this may have been their only possible hope of appealing to the President, an intensely practical man who scorned abstractions, they did not have the evidence or the political clout to prevail on such issues against the evacuationists. Also, Biddle, Carter, and Munson fatally compromised their opposition by urging strict controls on the Issei, against whom there was no more evidence of disloyalty than against the Nisei, and by recommending suspension of the writ of habeas corpus if necessary. While they presumably hoped to negotiate a less stringent set of restrictions, they instead played into the hands of the anti-Japanese-American forces, who did not make any such effort to temper their demands. Once Biddle, Carter, and Munson confirmed for Roosevelt the idea that there *was* something to fear, they thereby established the validity of evacuation. The President was then content to leave the issue of whom to include in military hands.

An even more central figure in giving bad counsel was Secretary of War Stimson. As a former Republican secretary of war and secretary of state who had come out of retirement in his mid-seventies to devote himself to the strenuous task of directing the war effort, Stimson had enormous prestige. (In contrast, Biddle was in his mid-fifties and was new to the Cabinet.) Roosevelt and Stimson had a longstanding relationship of mutual admiration and trust, dating back to their agreement over the Stimson doctrine and Japan policy in 1933. Stimson recognized that evacuation of citizens was likely unconstitutional, but he allowed himself to be persuaded by his army subordinates and by Owen Roberts that the racial difference of Japanese Americans made it impossible to determine whether they could be trusted. So influential was Stimson that Biddle ascribed to him the largest share of responsibility for evacuation, stating in his memoirs, "If Stimson had stood firm, had insisted, as he seems to have suspected [may well have believed], that this wholesale evacuation was [wrong and] needless, the President would have followed his advice."[92]

This assessment overstates the reality. Stimson was the most prestigious advocate of evacuation, and he had strong elitist prejudices against racial minorities. Yet, paradoxically, of all the officials involved, he was also the most aware of the racial discrimination inherent in mass removal of the Japanese Americans. Stimson pondered the necessity of evacuation carefully, and he sought to arrange a meeting with the President to discuss these concerns before taking action. It is thus quite possible that if Roosevelt had questioned the necessity for internment, Stimson would have abandoned the idea. Biddle may also have had an interest in shifting blame for the evacuation from FDR, his patron, to Stimson. In his praise for Roosevelt's decision to veto East Coast evacuation, Biddle downgrades the influence of Stimson: "The President knew at once when mass evacuation simply would not do. He would have made the same decision irrespective of any recommendation of the Secretary of War." If Roosevelt was ready to ignore Stimson's judgment on East Coast evacuation, the secretary of war's influence on West Coast policy was surely not in itself decisive.

The political pressures on the President were enormous and must be assigned significant weight in explaining the final decision. For one thing, there were political considerations inherent in FDR's relationship with the War Department, as Stimson and McCloy were both prominent Republicans who helped assure bipartisan support for the war effort in Congress. Similarly, there was a strong political consensus in favor of evacuation in Congress and on the West Coast. Roosevelt was aware from government-sponsored polls and from the letters and lobbying he was receiving that a solid phalanx of West Coast opinion favored military control of Japanese Americans. The Leland Ford–Clarence Lea ad hoc committee, which claimed to represent the entire West Coast House delegation, lobbied for evacuation and even sent Roosevelt a plan. Several Pacific Coast senators, including Hiram Johnson and Mon Wallgren, also joined the call for "removal." Numerous Pacific Coast state governors and other elected officials, notably California Governor Culbert Olson and Attorney General Earl Warren, also spoke publicly in favor of evacuation. The opinion of Olson and Warren, two respected moderates, likely played a part in persuading Roosevelt of the necessity for evacuation.

In contrast, before Executive Order 9066 was signed there were only a handful of letters opposing evacuation, and no coordinated public protest by liberal or religious forces. Even the Japanese-American community did not offer united resistance. It had been weakened and divided by the incarceration of the Issei leadership in the ABC list raids after Pearl Harbor. While the young Nisei leaders opposed evacuation in principle, their newspapers and organizations (notably the Japanese American Citizens League) pledged total cooperation with the government as a means of proving their loyalty. In the face of such one-sided pressure, it did not require any great sense, let alone FDR's consummate political skills, to determine that some form of action against Japanese Americans was prudent.

However, even if we accept that the public outcry was a crucial element in the President's decision, it does not follow that Roosevelt ordered the evacuation out of simple political expediency. Rather, public support is the engine of democratic government, especially in wartime. Roosevelt was aware that white hysteria and racial tension over "the Japanese problem," even if popular fears of disloyalty were groundless, interfered with the production of food and essential goods and detracted from the fragile sense of national purpose that was crucial to the success of the war effort. In particular, he needed to keep up morale on the West Coast, where the main shipbuilding and port facilities for the defense of the Pacific were located, where a large sector of the war industry was concentrated, and where the lion's share of the nation's produce was grown. As Biddle summed up the situation, "Public opinion was on [the military's] side, so that there was no question of any substantial opposition [by the President], which might tend towards the disunity that at all costs he must avoid."[93]

In the weeks before Pearl Harbor the President asked his agents to work out a campaign to calm racial tensions and reduce the chance of anti-Japanese-American violence. He clearly determined at length that such tensions could not be cooled and that even a large-scale evacuation was less costly than paralysis due to low morale or race riots. Although some postwar writers rationalized the evacuation on the ground that the government sought to protect Japanese Americans from mob violence, there is no evidence that protection per se was ever a consideration in Roosevelt's final decision.

To take a similar case, after the Roberts Report on Pearl Harbor was released, Roosevelt faced the problem of how to handle the cases of Admiral Kimmel and General Short, the Hawaiian commanders whom the report had charged with dereliction of duty due to their failure to prepare for such an attack. While the President originally left matters to the military, which temporized, a month later he decided a court martial was necessary. Stimson commented in his diary that Roosevelt, a master of judging public opinion, realized there was no choice but to hold a trial, in light of the public clamor for punishment. Stimson added that the President agreed that the two officers were being made scapegoats for the country's general pre-war mood. Nevertheless, given the strength of public opinion, the best he could do was to devise some face-saving way to delay the trial until public passions cooled.[94]

All these factors, however important, do not suffice to explain why FDR signed Executive Order 9066. In the final analysis, to understand Roosevelt's decision we must also explore the question of individual character, or what Milton Eisenhower referred to as FDR's own "training, background, and personality." The psychological portrait of any individual, especially one of such a complex and enigmatic historical figure as Franklin Roosevelt, is bound to be oversimplified and distorted, and so judgments along these lines are necessarily speculative and imprecise. In relating a President's decisions to previous events in his life, particularly his inner life, one must be wary of the temptation to present a given action as an inevitable product of past experience and to ignore the contingent circumstances in which it took place. However, it *is* possible to discover continuing patterns of thought or conduct that may dispose an individual to behave or react in a certain way. By this standard, Roosevelt's past feelings toward the Japanese Americans must be considered to have significantly shaped his momentous decision to evacuate American citizens from their homes. FDR had a long and unvaried history of viewing Japanese Americans in racialized terms, that is, as essentially Japanese in their identity and emotional allegiance, and of expressing hostility toward them on that basis. In the years before World War I, Roosevelt considered immigration part of the Japanese threat to the West Coast. During the 1920s, when Roosevelt urged better relations with Japan, he supported immigration restriction and legal discrimination in order to deter Japanese-American settlement. His willingness to pander to popular prejudice against Japanese Americans in a time of peace anticipates his failure to defend the citizenship rights of a despised minority in the face of hysterical wartime demands for their incarceration. Several years before World War II started, Roosevelt became personally engaged in efforts to monitor Japanese Americans and to prepare plans for dealing with them as part of preparations for war with Japan, and he approved surveillance and tolerated racial discrimination in defense industries on the assumption that Nisei could not be trusted. In the months before the war began he enlisted his intelligence network to report to him on the threat of Japanese-American disloyalty, and he increased his efforts to identify and control "saboteurs" even after being reassured that no threat existed. In contrast, he made no such assumptions regarding Americans of German or Italian ancestry.

Roosevelt's view that the character of different ethnic and racial groups was biologically inherited, and the influence of such ideas on his policy decisions, expanded during the war years, even though such Social Darwinist racial theories had begun to be discredited by the anthropological writings of Franz Boas, Ruth Benedict, and others. In mid-1942 the President commissioned Dr. Ales Hrdlicka, an anthropologist at the Smithsonian Institution, Dr. Isiah Bowman, president of Johns Hopkins University, and Dr. Henry Field of the Field Museum of Natural History to direct a massive secret series of anthropological studies by experts on postwar migration and resettlement of Jews and other groups, with an emphasis on "problems arising out of racial admixtures and . . . the scientific principles involved in the process of miscegenation as contrasted with the opposing policies of so-called 'racialism.'"[95] The President stated that he wanted the scientists to determine the optimum racial mixture of postwar refugee populations: "The President wishes to be advised what will happen when various kinds of Europeans—Scandinavian, Germanic, French-Belgian, North Italian, etc.— are mixed with the South American base stock. The President specifically asked the [research] committee to consider such questions as the following: Is the South Italian stock—say, Sicilian—as good as the North Italian stock— say, Milanese—if given equal social and economic opportunity? Thus, in a given case, where 10,000 Italians were to be offered settlement facilities, what proportion of the 10,000 should be Northern Italians and what Southern Italians?"[96]

Similarly, Roosevelt commented at different times about the possibility of imposing eugenicist policies against troublesome groups. He joked in 1945 that Puerto Rico's high birthrate could be curbed through mass sterilization, using "the methods which Hitler used effectively." Similarly, in August 1944 the President discussed with his Cabinet "the advisability of sterilizing about 50,000 Junkers and officers of the German Army. [FDR] said that science had done wonderful things and that sterilization could now be accomplished by the use of rays which were practically painless." Although these remarks may also have been facetious, at least in part, Roosevelt told Treasury Secretary Morgenthau a few days earlier, "You either have to castrate the German people or you have got to treat them in such a manner so they can't go on reproducing people who want to continue the way they have in the past." Other administration officials, notably Navy Secretary Knox, discussed sterilizing Germans in earnest.[97]

Throughout the period of evacuation, Roosevelt's ideas about people of Japanese ancestry remained dominated by his belief in innate biological character. In spring 1942 FDR maintained a correspondence with Hrdlicka on the source of the nefarious and warlike Japanese character, which Hrdlicka attributed to the less developed skulls of the Japanese.[98] Roosevelt's view of the Japanese as inherently savage was likewise reflected in his private conversations. He stated in 1935 that aggression "was in the blood" of Japanese leaders. In January 1942 he told Quentin Reynolds that the Japanese were "treacherous people," and hissed through his teeth while quoting Japanese leaders in imitation of stereotypical Japanese speech patterns.[99] FDR's assistant, William Hassett, recounted in August 1942 that "the President related an old Chinese myth about the origin of the Japanese. A wayward daughter of an ancient Chinese emperor left her native land in a sampan and finally reached Japan, then inhabited by baboons. The inevitable happened and in due course the Japanese made their appearance."[100]

Roosevelt's words and actions both before and after Pearl Harbor, when taken in their entirety, point to his acceptance of the idea that Japanese Americans, whether citizens or longtime resident aliens, were still Japanese at the core. He regarded them as presumptively dangerous and disloyal on racial grounds. There might well be some loyal individuals: Roosevelt was willing to make exceptions for Japanese Americans of demonstrated loyalty once they were properly vouched for, and he had approved John Franklin Carter's plan during fall 1941 to organize protection for "the loyal Japanese" in case of war. However, in the absence (and sometimes in the presence) of evidence of loyalty, the presumption remained, and in an extreme situation it overshadowed all other considerations. When Carter's "Roosevelt" character is asked about the feelings of Japanese Americans who were deported "because they had slant eyes and yellow skins," he remarks coolly, "Their patriotism was suspect."[101]

Roosevelt's decision to approve the race-based exclusion of West Coast Japanese Americans followed logically from this view that they were incapable of being true Americans. Already in his 1920s articles, FDR justified discriminatory legislation by "Americans" toward a group he gratuitously referred to as "unassimilable aliens." His refusal to admit discriminatory intent in the race-based exclusion of Japanese immigrants during the 1920s logically precedes his willful blindness toward the role of racial bigotry in catalyzing Californians with longtime nativist grudges to press for the evacuation of Japanese Americans from the West Coast.

Roosevelt's inner attitudes may also have shaped his response to the constitutional issues involved in the evacuation. Admittedly, in addition to enormous political courage (which only a few prominent Americans showed), it would have required enormous commitment to the constitutional rights of all citizens to have overridden the initial clamor for action against the "Japs." FDR gave little evidence of such constitutional scruples. In his view, fortified by Biddle (who was in turn backed by the Cohen-Cox-Rauh memo), the President had authority under his wartime powers to take whatever action he deemed necessary for the defense of the country. On February 26, 1942, a week after signing Executive Order 9066, Roosevelt sent a memo to Navy Secretary Knox, who had renewed his advocacy of the evacuation of Japanese Americans in Hawaii but expressed concern over the constitutionality of the measure. "Like you, I have long felt that most of the Japanese should be removed from Oahu to one of the other islands," the President commented. "I do not worry about the constitutional question—first, because of my recent order and, second, because Hawaii is under martial law."[102] If the government could declare martial law in Hawaii, certainly it could take less disruptive steps where necessary to meet a crisis. Roosevelt was not visibly troubled by the violation of the internees' civil rights. Biddle felt he was actually wary of the entire concept of rights: "If anything, he was a little afraid that the civilians might be too soft in nurturing 'rights.' He disliked any theoretic approach and the word conveyed to him something that was visionary and impractical and had none of the urgency of the task ahead."[103]

Perhaps the most decisive part Roosevelt's anti-Japanese-American prejudice played in his decision to approve evacuation was in fostering a moral indifference. Although he may have been politically pressured and badly advised, the President was not ignorant or uninformed on the "Japanese problem." Indeed, he was kept well apprised of the situation. However, in the final analysis he did not care enough about Japanese Americans to intervene on their behalf or to become deeply involved in their concerns, especially if it meant opposing public opinion and the military. He refused Carter's and Munson's pleas that he issue a statement of support for loyal Japanese Americans, which would have defused at least some of the hysteria against them, and he declined to follow through on MacLeish's proposal for a speech urging calm on the West Coast. The President's failure to provide moral leadership allowed the situation to fester to the point where drastic action was demanded. As the government's own report on the evacuation reported, "Had the appropriate 'high' authority [made] a declaration of the Government's faith in the loyalty of the Nisei, there is reason to believe that the West Coast racists and superpatriots would at least have had harder going to achieve their objective of mass exclusion."[104] Similarly, as long as the army promised to be "reasonable" in dealing with the Japanese-American menace, Roosevelt was prepared to sign orders "so the army could handle the Japs," in Biddle's phrase, without making any effort to determine whether any necessity existed or if a less extreme policy could be designed.[105] He did not ask the tough questions that would have revealed the flimsy reasoning behind the military's policy and its failure to make a specific showing of necessity.

Roosevelt's unquestioning acceptance of evacuation was paralleled by his lack of interest in exploring the issue. Clearly the rights of Japanese-American citizens were a less-than-vital consideration to him. When Stimson asked to speak to Roosevelt in order to make the case for evacuation, FDR stated that he was too busy for a meeting (although he called Stimson in to discuss other issues the same day), and he instead told the secretary of war to do whatever he thought best. He silenced Eleanor Roosevelt when she lobbied against extreme measures. The President was equally casual about the practical considerations involved in removal. To be sure, none of the army or government officials involved in the evacuation seems to have foreseen that it would inevitably lead to mass incarceration. Nevertheless, Stimson complained after a Cabinet meeting a week after the order was signed that Roosevelt had "given very little attention to the principal task of the transportation and resettlement of the evacuees."[106]

In particular, FDR failed to respond to repeated requests from his advisors in the weeks before February 19 to appoint a powerful alien property custodian to protect Japanese-American property. In fact, Roosevelt had long been conscious of the need for a custodian to take care of alien property.[107] Several months before Pearl Harbor—and well before most of his advisors had even considered the subject—FDR stated that he intended to appoint a custodian in order to avoid the waste and looting of alien-owned property that had taken place during World War I (and had caused a major scandal within the Wilson administration).[108] However, Roosevelt failed to take any action on a property custodian after Pearl Harbor—much to the dismay of Carter and Munson, who asked that a custodian be appointed to aid the loyal Nisei in guarding Issei property—with the result that the evacuees lost millions of dollars of property through theft or fire sales.

What emerges from an examination of the various factors leading to Executive Order 9066 is a pragmatic decision, made by a practical-minded President in a time of crisis. The decision thus fits well into Roosevelt's leadership style, made famous by New Deal historians. Yet, FDR's pattern of conduct toward Japanese Americans highlights the negative face of such pragmatism. The President's attitude toward Japanese Americans was marked by what John Hersey termed a "grand offhandedness."[109] Unlike Stimson, who was tortured by doubts over the morality and constitutionality of making racial distinctions and removing American citizens, the President displayed no worry or hesitation over evacuation and its consequences. In Biddle's words, "I do not think he was much concerned with the gravity or implications of this step. He was never theoretical about things."[110]

Roosevelt's failure was a lack of compassion, or, more precisely, of empathy.[111] Although the President may have seen the evacuation as entirely a matter of military judgment, underlying his approval of that plan was a carelessness toward innocent people that was born of prejudice. Although he had genuine humanitarian instincts, his paramount concern was leading the country to victory in a conflict of global proportions and unprecedented destructiveness. The rights of American citizens, especially those of Japanese ancestry, paled in comparison. As James MacGregor Burns commented, FDR either did not consider the consequences of his order on Japanese Americans or he simply "wrote them off" as part of the price of winning the war. When John Franklin Carter's "Roosevelt" is challenged about his decision, he says, "When the war is over, they'll go back . . . It's a small matter compared to the war itself."[112] This insouciant remark, though fictionalized, appears to sum up the real Roosevelt's view. The sin that pervades the President's decision to approve evacuation was not one of malice but of indifference.

IMPLEMENTING AN
UNDEMOCRATIC POLICY

ROOSEVELT'S DIRECT participation in
the process of internment of the Japanese Americans
following their removal from the West Coast has
remained largely unexplored, even by those critical of
his signing of Executive Order 9066. However, FDR's
initial decision to approve evacuation cannot be separated from his subsequent involvement in the shaping of the internment. Though his interventions were
inconsistent and partial, he made important contributions to the policy as it emerged. Indeed, the
President's actions—and sometimes his failure to
act—were crucial in determining the nature and duration of the internment. The public announcement
of Executive Order 9066 and the military takeover of
the "Japanese problem" on February 20 was greeted
with joy and relief by West Coast newspapers and
groups that had pushed for evacuation. The clamor
for federal action immediately subsided, although it
was not clear what form of evacuation the military
intended, and individuals continued to write the President and other government officials to call for mass

imprisonment or deportation of Japanese Americans. Outside the West Coast, press reaction was generally nonexistent or mildly favorable. A number of liberal and church groups, such as the American Civil Liberties Union and the American Friends Service Committee, protested the order as unjust and unconstitutional. They made public statements, and sent the President letters and petitions asking him to rescind the order.

Apart from the West Coast delegation, which publicly expressed its strong approval, Congress paid little attention to the policy. In early March the War Department, with the backing of the President, had bills introduced in the House and Senate to provide for enforcement of Executive Order 9066 through the federal courts. Secretary Stimson wrote congressional leaders that expedited action was necessary for General DeWitt to protect national security interests. North Carolina Senator Robert Reynolds spoke in support of the bill, treating rumors of sabotage by Japanese Americans as fact. Although conservative Ohio Senator Robert Taft objected to the speed and sloppiness of the legislative process on the bill, which he claimed would obviously be improper in peacetime, there were no objections to the legislation, and it quickly passed.[1]

The nature of public reaction to the order can be gauged in part by the testimony before the Tolan committee. During the third week of February 1942, in response to the demands of the West Coast congressional delegation for evacuation (and allegedly with the personal encouragement of FDR), Congressman John Tolan announced that the House Select Committee on National Defense Migration, which he headed, would hold fact-finding hearings on "evacuation of enemy aliens and others from prohibited military zones."[2] Tolan, a liberal California Democrat, hoped to reduce the anxiety over the Japanese Americans and avoid mass evacuation. However, by the time the committee arrived on the West Coast, the President had already signed Executive Order 9066, so Tolan focused on hearing testimony and making recommendations on the conduct of the evacuation. From February 21 through March 12, Tolan held a series of hearings in San Francisco, Los Angeles, Portland, and Seattle. Dozens of city and state government officials, West Coast agricultural and nativist groups, and community leaders testified.[3] California Attorney General Earl Warren warned of the danger of Japanese-American saboteurs and maintained that the peril was too urgent for civil procedures. Warren admitted to the committee that there had been no reported cases of sabotage or espionage by Japanese Americans. However, that very fact, he insisted, was evidence of their guilt, since it clearly demonstrated that a concerted fifth column campaign had been organized for some future time. The California Joint Immigration Committee, the principal anti-Japanese pressure group, supported immediate action to restrict the Issei and Nisei. Some insight into the racist motivation of the Joint Immigration Committee's members can be gained from the report it issued to the Tolan committee, in which it stated, "The Founding Fathers of the Republic stipulated that citizenship should be granted only to free white persons. But a grave mistake was made when citizenship was granted to all born here, regardless of fitness or desire for such citizenship. Another grave mistake was the granting of citizenship to the Negroes after the Civil War."[4]

Most West Coast Japanese Americans, already reeling from the blows of economic hardships, social ostracism, and arrest of family and community leaders that the war had brought, were too shocked to protest Executive Order 9066. Stigmatized as disloyal and ordered out of their homes for no apparent reason, with no understanding of what their future would be or what was expected of them, the internees suffered from feelings of shame and depression and were vulnerable to family breakdown, alcoholism, and other social problems. Many community members, especially among the older Issei generation, reacted to events with resignation, using the phrase *shigata gan-ai* ("It can't be helped," or "Nothing can be done about it").

Reactions among the Nisei were more mixed. In their public statements and testimony before the Tolan committee, Nisei groups and individuals took different positions, although all strongly asserted their citizenship rights and deplored the racism and greed of the pressure groups trying to exclude them. One faction, led by the Japanese American Citizens League, argued that if evacuation was a military necessity, Japanese Americans should prove their loyalty by cooperating cheerfully. Another group, notably Mich Kunitani of the Nisei Democratic Club of Oakland, were prepared to relocate if required but doubted that any such necessity existed. A few Nisei, such as James Omura, Gordon Hirabayashi, Fred Korematsu, and Minoru Yasui, opposed exclusion on principle. The last three refused to be removed and challenged the government in court.

The President's signing of Executive Order 9066 led to the evacuation of over 110,000 people during spring 1942—the largest group migration in American history. Although Executive Order 9066 gave the army authority to exclude any civilians from a military area, the War Department and Justice

Department representatives who drafted it clearly understood that it was directed primarily against Japanese Americans. When General DeWitt subsequently sought permission to use his powers under the order to exclude all German and Italian aliens, the government declined to approve indiscriminate mass removal of any other group, although a number of aliens deemed suspicious were subjected to individual exclusion orders.

In accordance with the order, the army successively excluded all people of Japanese ancestry living in two military districts proclaimed by General DeWitt. This area ultimately encompassed the entire state of California, the western portions of Oregon and Washington, and the southern half of Arizona. (The boundary of the restricted area of Arizona was later redrawn further south at the behest of local farmers who did not wish to lose their Japanese American labor force.) Technically, Executive Order 9066 simply authorized the army to restrict or exclude civilians from military zones and to provide them with transportation and other aid. The order thus presupposed voluntary migration, at least in part. However, the practical difficulties of such voluntary evacuation soon became apparent. The evacuees were generally reluctant to liquidate their possessions and leave before they were forced to, and most did not have friends or family living in other parts of the country to sponsor them. Most Japanese Americans lacked the resources to afford moving and resettlement expenses, especially when Issei bank withdrawals were still limited to $100 per month by the Treasury Department, and the government did not step in to offer aid for resettlement. In addition, officials in the mountain states through which the migrants would have to travel made clear to the army that they were not welcome—if they were a danger to the Pacific Coast, they were a danger to other states—and warned of mob violence. Thus, on March 26, 1942, DeWitt formally revoked all travel permits for Japanese Americans in the excluded zone and ordered them to remain until they could be removed by the army. In the end, only 5,000–10,000 West Coast Japanese left the West Coast voluntarily, and many of those relocated to eastern California, where they were trapped when DeWitt decided to evacuate that area as well.

Once voluntary evacuation was halted, the restricted military area was divided into districts, which were successively emptied of their Japanese-American residents over the following weeks by a series of civilian exclusion orders. A special curfew was imposed on all people of Japanese ancestry. The "evacuees" were then notified by newspaper announcements and signs placed in public areas by the Western Defense Command that they were to be excluded. They were ordered to prepare for evacuation on a specific day, and a representative of each family was told to report to processing centers in the district for further instructions. The Japanese Americans were told to bring linens, utensils, plates, bowls, cups, toilet articles, extra clothing, and such other essential personal effects as they could carry. No pets, cameras, or automobiles were permitted. Everything else had to be sold, left with white friends, or abandoned. The government belatedly permitted Japanese Americans to store properly packaged household goods in government warehouses at their own risk.

On evacuation day, all Japanese Americans in a given district reported to the processing center, some escorted by groups of white friends or neighbors. From there they were sent by bus or train to a network of "assembly centers" established along the West Coast by the army's hastily created Wartime Civil Control Administration (WCCA), mostly in requisitioned race tracks and fairgrounds. There, the evacuees remained under guard, living in stables and animal pens, for weeks or months while the army began looking for sites to erect "reception centers" and planning the construction of these centers.

The WCCA was assisted, and eventually supplanted, in the task of caring for those evacuated by a new civilian agency created by Roosevelt, the War Relocation Authority (WRA). The President's advisors recognized from the beginning that the army's involvement was required only to provide the evacuation with a legal basis of wartime military necessity and to conduct the actual evacuation. Once Japanese Americans were removed, a civilian agency would need to take control of them. On February 26, 1942, Biddle met with the President and proposed that he appoint "Major Walker," who had previous experience in handling problems of migration from his work in the New Deal's Resettlement Administration, to coordinate assistance for Japanese Americans. FDR agreed to ask Harold Smith, director of the Bureau of the Budget, to assign Walker and provide sufficient funding for his operation by the following week.

At a Cabinet meeting the next day, Stimson explained that the army's purpose was to evacuate Japanese along the Pacific Coast, intern, and examine them. Those who could show that they had no connection to any "fifth column" would be permitted to return to their homes.[5] Stimson explained that any involuntary evacuation would necessarily be gradual because of limitations on the army's resources: the army simply could not evacuate and guard

100,000 people all at once. Roosevelt quickly "seized upon the idea" that the burden of the Japanese Americans should be lifted from the army's shoulders as soon as the evacuees were removed from the restricted areas. With Stimson's concurrence, Biddle proposed that a civilian be named to direct resettlement efforts, and he reminded Roosevelt of their conversation regarding Major Walker. The President readily accepted Biddle's propositions.[6]

The following week, McCloy, Biddle, and Harold Smith met and unanimously agreed to establish an independent civilian agency to "look after" the evacuees.[7] Smith, who was one of Roosevelt's most influential and trusted advisors, then met with the President to explain that the new agency would be set up in the Office of Emergency Management. Roosevelt had assumed that the WRA would be attached to an existing Cabinet department, but Smith persuaded him that only an independent agency could foster interdepartmental cooperation. "The President asked something to the effect of 'Do we have to have that in the executive office?' I pointed out the reasons and he acquiesced somewhat reluctantly, I think."[8] Although Roosevelt had previously agreed to appoint Biddle's candidate for director, he asked Smith to find him a head for the new agency.[9] Smith recommended Milton Eisenhower, an Agriculture Department staffer, to direct the new agency. With Smith's support and an endorsement from Milton Eisenhower's brother, Assistant Army Chief of Staff General Dwight Eisenhower, McCloy agreed to the appointment.[10] After a perfunctory meeting with Milton Eisenhower, on March 18 the President signed an executive order creating the WRA with Eisenhower at its head. Roosevelt's press secretary, Stephen Early, described the WRA as a voluntary "war work corps."[11]

As soon as the WRA was established, Eisenhower began to plan the resettlement of Japanese Americans. His first task was to continue the work that the army had begun of developing "reception centers" for the removed Japanese Americans. Using a mixture of army, civilian, and volunteer evacuee labor, the WRA began the construction of camp facilities. At first, these were intended as temporary facilities, as Eisenhower envisioned final resettlement either in terms of integrating refugees into scattered established communities or of building planned communities.[12] However, Eisenhower soon was forced to alter his proposal for immediate resettlement in the face of the overwhelming public hostility toward Japanese Americans. Ironically, although Executive Order 9066 was designed in part to quiet anti-Japanese hysteria on the West Coast, the evacuation stirred up enormous sentiment against Japanese Americans nationwide. By treating both Nisei and Issei as enemy aliens and foreigners, Roosevelt and the army had tacitly encouraged the widespread public identification of Japanese Americans with Japan, a problem that the government's own participation in the dissemination of wartime anti-Japanese propaganda only intensified.[13] Most Americans who followed the news of the evacuation naturally concluded that Japanese Americans had committed crimes sufficiently grave to merit mass exclusion, and the evacuees were stigmatized as traitors. Eisenhower was badly shaken after he attended a meeting of the Western Governor's Association in early April and saw how violently the governors—with the notable exception of Colorado's Ralph Carr, who was hostile to the evacuees but nevertheless pronounced himself ready to do his "patriotic" duty—opposed any Japanese Americans being allowed at liberty in their states.

The WRA director thus reluctantly established plans for the indefinite wartime incarceration of Japanese Americans. Ten such camps were soon established—eight camps in western states, in remote desert lands or Indian reservations, and two in Arkansas. The WRA arranged with the military for armed soldiers to patrol the camp's borders, and it hired its own security guards to keep order inside. It also planned schools and employment for the "residents." The WRA and the army agreed to refer to the camps under the euphemistic title "war-duration relocation centers" and to explicitly forbid the use of the term "concentration camps" as too negative and coercive.

Roosevelt did not actively participate in the progression from evacuation to internment, but he was kept closely informed. In March 1942, even before he appointed Eisenhower, Roosevelt discussed the disposition of Japanese evacuees with Thomas Campbell, a large Montana wheat producer and long-time unofficial advisor who hoped to be placed in charge of the "evacuees." The day after their conversation, Campbell sent the President a copy of a report he had prepared for McCloy, in which Campbell had advocated the creation of what he termed temporary concentration camps to hold the removed Japanese-American "foreigners" and the subsequent hiring of able-bodied laborers from among them, on the analogy of the military draft, to fill jobs on public or private irrigation, farm labor, and road-building projects.[14]

In mid-April, after the WRA had been created, Stimson sent the President an update on the West Coast evacuation. Stimson explained that voluntary evacuation had been abandoned due to the logistical difficulties and adverse public opinion, and he stated that Japanese Americans would remain under army control until the prejudice against them died down and they could be resettled. Once the hostility to Japanese Americans eased, it would be possible to let them out of camps in order to make use of the laboring power of these "potential assets of the country" to reduce the manpower shortage.[15] Roosevelt evidently continued to receive reports from other sources, since in early May he informed Stimson that he heard the West Coast evacuation was going well.[16]

At a Cabinet meeting on May 15, in response to Biddle's concerns about evacuation of Italian and German aliens on the East and West coasts, Stimson orally reviewed for Roosevelt the procedures the army had taken toward Japanese Americans on the West Coast and reported that they had gotten "pretty nearly to the end of the Japanese." Roosevelt expressed his satisfaction with the situation.[17] Two weeks later, Roosevelt's Chief of Staff General George Marshall gave the President a further update on the progress of internment and the numbers involved.[18]

In early June, Eisenhower decided to resign as WRA director. Although he publicly ascribed the decision to his interest in joining the Office of War Information, which he had helped design, he was also sickened and disheartened by the treatment and predicament of the Japanese-American evacuees. On June 5 the Cabinet discussed the matter of Eisenhower's successor. Interior Secretary Harold Ickes (who had privately opposed the evacuation but considered the policy beyond his area of responsibility)[19] sharply criticized Eisenhower's conduct of the camps and complained of the lack of progress in organizing facilities for the internees. When Ickes was asked to have the Interior Department take over the WRA, however, he replied firmly that he did not want it.[20] As soon as the meeting was over, Ickes reconsidered and wrote Roosevelt endorsing Vice President Henry Wallace's nomination of his deputy, Indian Affairs Director John Collier, to take over the WRA. Collier hoped to be given control over the WRA in order to implement an ambitious program of irrigation of desert lands, agricultural cooperatives, and model communities.[21] Following the meeting, Roosevelt began discussions of whom to appoint to the WRA. A week later, on the advice of Eisenhower and of Budget Director Harold Smith, who believed the WRA should be independent of existing agencies, Roosevelt passed over Collier and selected Dillon Myer, another Agriculture Department staffer, to head the WRA.[22]

On June 18 the departing Eisenhower sent Roosevelt a progress report, explaining in detail the actions the WRA had taken. Like Stimson, Eisenhower described at length the failure of immediate resettlement and the move to internment in camps because of the widespread public hostility toward Japanese Americans. Eisenhower explained that Japanese-Americans would be held in "war-length relocation centers" (where 20,000 had already arrived), at least until such time as a lessening of such bitterness made a genuine relocation program possible. He closed by estimating that 80 to 85 percent of the Nisei were loyal, while at least 50 percent of the Issei were passively loyal, and he suggested that Roosevelt recommend to Congress repatriation after the end of the war for those who "prefer the Japanese way of life" and a program of postwar rehabilitation and reintegration to bring the rest of the "displaced population" back into the mainstream.[23] The originally envisioned evacuation was shifting into a policy of indefinite internment.

It is difficult to determine whether Roosevelt perceived that the removal of Japanese Americans would lead to mass incarceration—he seems not to have anticipated the possible consequences of the policy when he signed Executive Order 9066. He may have recognized, as Thomas Campbell and other advisors rapidly did, that some form of incarceration would inevitably follow; or, like Stimson, he may have initially believed that Japanese Americans would be held only until their loyalty could be determined. However, the President did not protest when it became clear that the concentration camps (as Roosevelt himself referred to them later that year) would not be simply a temporary expedient but would likely last throughout the war.

FDR's failure to take charge of the situation reflected in part the enormous demands made on him by the war. During spring 1942 he planned military action against the Nazis, supervised the conversion of American industry to war production, suffered the conquest of the Philippines by Japan, and ordered a secret bombing raid on Tokyo. However, he was not unaware of what was transpiring. Every few weeks Stimson and others brought him up to date on developments in the evacuation, and he repeatedly approved the military's actions without requesting any modification. His only expressed concern was to accomplish the removal of Japanese Americans as quickly as possible in order to resolve the uncertain situation on the West Coast. He equally acquiesced in popular opposition to immediate resettlement. Roosevelt did not order the army and WRA to proceed with the insertion of evacuees into communities which protested such place-ment, and he did not seek to assuage local fears of "dangerous" Japanese Americans that his order had aroused among western state officials and pub-lic opinion. Roosevelt failed to make any statement during 1942 on behalf of evacuee loyalty and citizenship rights, or even to explain government policy.

On the contrary, Roosevelt displayed a shocking unconcern for the nega-tive effects and ramifications of the policy as it developed. He ignored the legal problems created by the institution of a policy of incarceration of citi-zens. Rather than declare martial law or endorse congressional efforts to leg-islate mass involuntary confinement of citizens without charge—a power *not* granted by the Constitution nor contained in Executive Order 9066—he presided over a joint army-WRA policy of denial and euphemism in which the indefinite incarceration of Japanese-American "evacuees" was termed "resettlement" and camps with armed guards and barbed wire were officially named "relocation centers."[24]

Furthermore, he refused to take steps to meet the practical needs created by such a drastic and unprecedented policy. Chief among these was the pro-tection and storage of evacuee property. Roosevelt was aware of the need for an alien property custodian even before Pearl Harbor. With the approval of Biddle, who had previously been given authority over alien property issues, Roosevelt decided in fall 1941 to appoint Federal Deposit Insurance Corpora-tion director Leo Crowley as alien property custodian once war was declared.[25] However, once the United States entered the war, the President was stymied by a tug-of-war between Crowley, Biddle, and Secretary of the Treasury Henry Morgenthau, Jr., over the custodianship, a disagreement over policy and turf that has been called "so bitter that it rocked the President's official family to the core."[26] Biddle and Morgenthau each believed that the alien property custodian's office should be placed within their respective departments. Biddle felt that the Treasury Department was too bureaucratic and inflexible to give proper attention to the multitude of small claims a cus-todian would be forced to deal with. On January 16 he noted, "After the Cabi-net I told the President I thought he should appoint an Alien Property Custodian immediately on account of the great confusion, that I thought responsibility should be centered in one individual" who should *not* be from the Treasury Department.[27] Conversely, Morgenthau believed that the Trea-sury Department's Foreign Funds Control Office was best able to supervise the running of large companies. Morgenthau was also aware, from the World

War I experience, of the political patronage such a custodian would wield. He was hostile toward Crowley, whom he considered a corrupt influence-peddler because Crowley, though a government official, also received a salary from a private corporation.[28] In addition, there was ideological dissension within the administration over the proper disposition of lucrative German-owned chemical and dye patents and businesses to U.S. corporations, and whether or not they should be restored to their owners after the war.

On January 21, through the mediation of then-Supreme Court Justice James Byrnes, FDR's longtime senatorial ally and political "fixer," Crowley was finally induced to accept the post and give up his private salary. However, Morgenthau continued to object to Crowley. Roosevelt then tried to goad the two men into an agreement by playing on their sensitivities as members of ethnic minority groups. A few days later, Crowley, who was Irish Catholic, related to the German Jewish Morgenthau that during a lunch meeting FDR had brought the conversation around to the question of control of alien property, and whether it would stay in Treasury or go to the Office of Emergency Management: "Then Leo said that for no apparent reason whatsoever the President proceeded to give him the following lecture. He said, 'Leo, you know this is a Protestant country, and the Catholics and Jews are here on sufferance,' and he said, 'It is up to both of you to go along with anything I want at this time.' Leo said he was never so shocked in his life."[29] Morgenthau sympathized with Crowley, and told him that Roosevelt had made a similar remark, "but not nearly as bad," at a Cabinet meeting the previous month. "I talked to the President afterwards, and he proceeded to give me a lecture and cited as an example how there were two Catholic judges in Nebraska, and he had refused to appoint a third."[30] FDR's heavy-handed attempt to bring the two rivals to an agreement offended both men, who saw his remarks as bigoted, without resolving their dispute.

While the President continued to favor Crowley as alien property custodian, during the following weeks he resisted making any final decision on delimiting responsibility. Instead, he fed Morgenthau's hopes that the Treasury's Foreign Funds Control Office would be given responsibility for alien property, and encouraged him to make further inroads on custodial responsibility. On February 16 he signed an executive order granting Treasury control of a 97 percent interest in General Aniline and Dye, a large German-owned chemical company. A week later, he stated at a press conference that the matter of a custodian was still under consideration, and no decision had been reached.[31]

During this time, pressure grew within the government for the appointment of a special custodian for Japanese-American property, a very different problem from that of control of the German-owned corporations operating in America. On February 13 the attorney general repeated his previous plea to the President for the immediate appointment of such a custodian. He added that aliens who had been ordered out of West Coast "military zones" were terrified at leaving their property. Roosevelt suggested appointing a custodian from the Treasury Department for the "Japanese." The attorney general, knowing that Morgenthau's chief interest was expropriating alien-owned property, quickly expressed his opposition.[32]

On February 21, 1942, two days after Roosevelt signed Executive Order 9066, Assistant Secretary of War John McCloy, the army officer chiefly responsible for evacuation, wrote to Harry Hopkins, Roosevelt's closest advisor, to enlist his intercession with the President in securing a custodian. McCloy explained to Hopkins that he hoped to encourage voluntary migration as much as possible in order to reduce the military's burden, but that the Japanese Americans' concerns over losing their property presented a great impediment to such relocation. If the government would undertake to take care of their property, they would be more likely to move. McCloy added that Biddle had infor̄ned him that the appointment of an alien property custodian had been considered but that no action had been taken. "Could you move it along?" he asked Hopkins.[33]

Two days later, Hopkins responded. He stated that the Treasury Department already had machinery to protect "alien" property, and so McCloy should contact Treasury in respect to the Issei. However, Hopkins pointed out that no laws then existed to permit the President to create a custodian for the citizen internees' property, and he suggested that McCloy should draw up legislation "in proper form" for the President to sign. "It seems to me it would be a very good idea," Hopkins concluded.[34] Implicit in Hopkins's suggestion that McCloy, rather than the Justice Department, design such legislation was a recognition of the extraordinary nature of the military's action toward American citizens and of the need to recognize that the situation could not be handled through normal procedures.

McCloy did not share Hopkins's view of the distinction between aliens and United States citizens, and he was opposed to asking for new legislation. Instead, McCloy devised a scheme to extend army authority over citizens in order to include control of their property. McCloy had General Allen Gullion (the major instigator of the evacuation) draft a proposal for Secretary of War Stimson's signature, according to which the secretary of the treasury would designate a civilian staffer to join General DeWitt's staff, at army expense, in order to take action in regard to property of "enemy aliens or persons assimilated to that status."[35] The constitutional weakness of the plan was reflected in the logical (and syntactical) gymnastics the army and McCloy went through to avoid mentioning that it was citizens whose property they envisioned taking over.

It is not clear whether McCloy ever shared his proposal with Morgenthau. As it happened, the treasury secretary was not enthusiastic about using his alien custodianship authority to guard even Issei-owned property, since it would mean appointing receivers for hundreds of small businesses. Already, in the days after Pearl Harbor, he had rejected the suggestion of Treasury's Foreign Funds Control Office that he assume control of thousands of small Japanese-owned businesses as "hysterical" and "impractical."[36]

On February 23, the same day that McCloy heard from Hopkins, Morgenthau received a telegram from California Congressman John Tolan, chair of the House Committee on National Defense Migration, which was then holding hearings on the West Coast to advise on policy toward the evacuees.[37] Tolan urged that a regional alien property custodian be appointed immediately to guard the evacuees' property, especially in order to avert the "sacrifice sales" that had already begun to occur on the West Coast. As Hopkins had done, Tolan distinguished between aliens and citizens, and he formally requested legislation to establish a separate custodian for the property of evacuated citizens. He further emphasized that such a custodian was only one part of a general need for advance planning and coordination by the civilian agencies that would have to assist the army in the evacuation and resettlement of evacuees.

Morgenthau wired back to Tolan three days later that he agreed that careful government planning was necessary in order to deal with the evacuation, but he made clear that he opposed the government's taking custody of Japanese-American property. Morgenthau drew an analogy between the Japanese-American evacuation and a hypothetical army decision to clear an area for use as a munitions dump or firing range. The people who were quickly resettled in such cases would have to "liquidate at forced sale their immovable property." He did not mention that people would normally receive government restitution for such property losses; for instance, when the army took over a boy's school at Los Alamos that year to house the atomic bomb project, the government compensated the owners. Sidestepping Tolan's suggestion for legislation to appoint a custodian for the property of citizens, Morgenthau instead used the evacuation of citizens as an excuse for ducking the entire issue, stating that the presence of citizen evacuees made the creation of an alien property custodian too complicated. In any event, the problems connected with "up-rooting" a large segment of the population and "transplanting it in a new location" were largely social in nature and not within Treasury's sphere of operations. He proposed that a new agency be created to deal with the needs created by "national defense migration."[38]

Morgenthau sent Hopkins a copy of his reply to Tolan for his advice, ostensibly because of Hopkins' experience in the areas of resettlement and employment, but more likely to assert his own control of alien property matters. Hopkins, after consulting with Biddle and Crowley (to Morgenthau's fury) on the status of a custodian, replied by strongly supporting Tolan.[39] Even more explicitly than he had to McCloy, Hopkins told his former Cabinet colleague that the federal government could not shirk its responsibility to care for people's property if it was disrupting their lives, especially as it was "undoubtedly the only agency which has the power to look after these houses." (Hopkins's advocacy of federal custodianship and his use of the word "houses" also indicates that he believed that such relocation would not be permanent.) Hopkins insisted that there was no time to form a new agency to deal with resettlement, as Morgenthau had advised Tolan, since it was a situation "that is immediately urgent."[40] Hopkins thus tactfully reminded Morgenthau, of whose ambitions to be alien property custodian he was no doubt aware, that he was the official who must act.

Morgenthau did not take the hint to step in. The evacuation, he insisted, was a domestic problem, not suited for agencies like the Treasury Department which were charged with waging economic warfare.[41] Existing agencies could coordinate efforts to handle such "welfare" problems. The Farm Security Administration would remove people from farm land, sell off the land, and buy new land in the interior, while the Federal Security Agency would obtain employment for refugees and sell their property and furniture. If they could not do the job, a new agency would become necessary.

Morgenthau's refusal to care for Japanese-American property did not stem simply from his own reluctance to shoulder what he knew would be an overwhelming and thankless "welfare" task. Rather, his opposition to Hopkins and Tolan also carried an ideological component. The treasury secretary clearly believed the government could not hold people's property, either movable or immovable. Indeed, Morgenthau's description of the tasks to be accomplished, such as buying land in the interior, left no doubt that he considered resettlement a permanent event, not a wartime expedient. Clearly, if people were intended never to return to their homes, holding their property might do more harm than good.

During the Cabinet meeting on February 27 at which the evacuation was first discussed, Stimson (who privately fumed that the President had not given any thought to the practical details involved) raised the subject of a custodian for evacuee property. Roosevelt told Morgenthau that responsibility for alien property would now probably include that of caring for the property of the imprisoned Japanese Americans. "If you were smart . . . I don't think you should take it."[42] Morgenthau agreed. He told the President that he was ready to handle big businesses such as General Aniline and Dye, but he was not interested in the small businesses and farms of Japanese Americans. Roosevelt then finally resolved the matter of a custodian by dividing responsibility. He granted Morgenthau continued control over large businesses such as General Aniline and over the alien bank accounts Treasury had previously frozen, leaving other alien property matters in Crowley's hands.[43]

Since there would be a time lag before an executive order could be drafted for the appointment of Crowley, Morgenthau provisionally retained control of alien property issues, including Japanese-American property. However, he still opposed having the government take custody of this property. Thus, he quietly joined forces with McCloy in the first days of March to consider other ways for the Treasury Department to act.[44] With McCloy's approval, Morgenthau drew up a "Suggested Program" for the Federal Reserve Bank in San Francisco to deal with evacuee property. The plan called for the bank to immediately open offices in cities with Japanese-American communities and to hire up to 100 agents to protect the evacuees against "fraud, forced sales, and unscrupulous creditors." Bank officers would arrange for the fair liquidation of their property, either by putting property owners in touch with buyers or lessors or by providing for them to grant powers of attorney to agents for such liquidation. Morgenthau recognized that Japanese Americans were being forced to move, but he made clear that the government would not or could not secure them or preserve them from the economic sacrifices involved. "Obviously the emergency will cause financial loss to the group involved."[45] The secretary of the treasury saw his plan as a means to assure them some reasonable compensation, consistent with the needs of the war effort.[46]

Morgenthau's program, while designed to be helpful, was set up with contradictory goals and was fundamentally flawed. The Federal Reserve Bank was simultaneously to protect the evacuees and assure them a fair price for their property, while also arranging for the speediest possible liquidation. Morgenthau clearly stated that the goal of the program was to "greatly expedite the departure on a voluntary basis of the evacuees from the military area."[47] The evacuees, who had only a short time to sell their property, would thus be forced to take whatever sums the buyers offered. The bank could not alter the market forces of supply and demand.

The emphasis on liquidation, as the Tolan committee later reported, also came at the expense of a rational storage policy. Morgenthau's plan stated explicitly that the bank would not store property. While the bank was empowered to help the evacuees arrange private storage, the plan limited such services to a few hypothetical cases where the real value of an evacuee's property could be realized only at a future date (Morgenthau gave the example of the sale of Japanese novelties). Japanese Americans were thus pressured to dispose of their property, even their household goods, any way they could.

Worst of all, since the Federal Reserve's assistance was designed as a voluntary program in order to get around the problem of jurisdiction over the property of American citizens, the bank had no legal enforcement power. Morgenthau warned that, should voluntary efforts fail, it might be necessary for the bank's representative to confiscate property in order to assure a "fair and reasonable liquidation," but this was clearly a hollow threat in the absence of actual legal authority.

Ironically, at the same time Morgenthau was drawing up his plans, there were calls for a property custodian from some of the same West Coast army and congressional forces that had most strongly demanded evacuation. On March 3 California's House delegation met to discuss the question of an alien property custodian to protect the property of the "dispossessed" aliens. Two days later, Representative Clarence Lea wrote the President directly in the name of the delegation to request the appointment of such a custodian. Lea warned Roosevelt that the evacuation of "aliens and others" would "remove many people from their properties, much of which will require active attention or else a great loss, including a productive loss to the nation." While the letter mentioned "liquidation" as an objective, Lea clearly envisaged federal administration and custody of the properties. Other West Coast political forces began to call for similar action. *The Los Angeles Times* commented a few days later, "The matter of custodianship of property and assets of the Japanese has been of great concern with the Japanese, alien born and native born. [The Tolan committee] some time ago dispatched word to Washington of the urgent need of setting up custodian machinery so that evacuated peoples of all nationalities are assured their assets will be preserved. Civic and church leaders also have stressed this point."[48]

Simultaneously, Assistant Attorney General Tom Clark, then in California as chief of civilian staff attached to General DeWitt's Western Defense Command, was assigned responsibility for coordinating efforts with civilian agencies. Clark hoped, within the framework of the expulsion of Japanese Americans from the West Coast, to encourage voluntary migration whenever possible. Indeed, in a regionwide radio address on March 7, 1942, Clark stated, "We cannot emphasize too strongly that it is neither the intention nor the desire of the army to order any mass evacuation." Clark advised that "those with either independent means or with friends or relatives living outside of Military Area No. 1 leave the prohibited areas now without waiting for the evacuation proclamations."[49]

Clark became absorbed in the alien property question during early March. He coordinated with the Farm Security Administration to provide assistance to evacuees and warned whites not to take unfair advantage of Japanese Americans. His motives were not completely altruistic. Like McCloy, Clark wished to assure a speedy and practical evacuation. Clark shared widespread views of both Issei and Nisei as foreigners despite their citizenship. "Our motive behind every procedure," he explained, "is to treat the Japanese in a manner in which we expect our nationals to be treated in Japan. This will be reflected in the manner we care for their property."[50] However, unlike Morgenthau, he thought federal administration of property was both the fairest and most practical policy. On March 4 Clark gave a press interview in which he publicly warned the Japanese Americans "not to sell their property unless they get fair prices."[51] He stated that custodians of alien property would be named soon, and these custodians would give full protection to the property of the evacuees. "There is no occasion for an alien facing ouster to sacrifice his property. The government will protect him."[52] Despite Clark's reference to "aliens," he specifically promised that all properties "whether owned by aliens or American-born will be returned to the original owners after the war."[53]

On March 5 Morgenthau brought to Roosevelt his plan to have the Federal Reserve assist in the liquidation of Japanese-American property. FDR was not receptive. The President stated that his only priority was getting the evacuees moved, and asked whether they could go to Texas. He then asked what was holding up the evacuation. Morgenthau explained McCloy's concern over the property question. Roosevelt responded, "Well, I am not concerned about that." Morgenthau explained to the President that the property problem was slowing down the evacuation, since evacuees were reluctant to relocate themselves while their property was insecure, and involuntary mass removal would be expensive and prolonged. He described his plan as a temporary gesture, "just a suggestion so that the Army can move these people out at once instead of waiting two weeks." Roosevelt once again made clear that speeding evacuation was his only concern, although he promised to get to Morgenthau's plan that afternoon.[54] Alarmed by the President's dismissive attitude, Morgenthau explained about the pressure for government custodianship. Presumably in hopes of winning the President's support for his own less radical plan, Morgenthau showed Roosevelt a summary of the press interview with Tom Clark that highlighted his promise that the government would hold and return all property owned by Japanese Americans. As Morgenthau intended, the President was taken aback by the idea of a federal guarantee. "He [Clark] is crazy. What is the matter with him?" Roosevelt snapped.[55]

Following the meeting, Morgenthau bluntly reported back to McCloy that Roosevelt had said that he was "interested in what happened to the Japanese after they get moved—not in what happened to their property."[56] McCloy must have feared that the entire Federal Reserve plan would be rejected, for he called Harold Smith, Roosevelt's influential director of the budget, to discuss with him the Federal Reserve plan, then followed up the call with an immediate memo. In both the call and the memo, he was careful to describe the Federal Reserve plan as "only a free banking service." That afternoon, no doubt with the encouragement of Smith, Roosevelt grudgingly granted authorization to Morgenthau and McCloy for the plan. He made no further inquiry concerning the property of Japanese Americans. Despite his green light to Morgenthau, the secretary's plan did not make much of an impression on him. In his response to Lea's and Tolan's earlier inquiries about an alien property custodian, the President made no mention of the Federal Reserve "banking service" but stated that he "hoped" that Crowley's imminent appointment would "solve the problem."[57]

By the time the Federal Reserve plan went into effect, the army was reconsidering its encouragement of voluntary migration, and so the government's chief motivation for encouraging the service was eliminated. Although the Japanese-American community trumpeted the arrival of alien property custodians from the Federal Reserve as a guarantee from the government, McCloy immediately explained to newspapers and community groups such as the Japanese American Citizens League that the Federal Reserve service was "not in any sense an alien property custodianship." In a very few cases, he stated, the government would take title to the property. However, the service was meant simply as a voluntary means of providing "financial aid and other advice" to help evacuees "gradually" dispose of their property.[58]

Although the Federal Reserve's employees were able in the end to offer some assistance to evacuees, the weaknesses of the plan immediately manifested themselves. The bank's representatives were rushed into service, ill-trained and in some cases hostile to the evacuees. Moreover, the branches were in urban areas and largely inaccessible to the heavily rural Issei and Nisei farm population. As a result, only about one out of ten of Japanese-American evacuees were able to use the Federal Reserve Bank or the Farm Security Administration.[59] Instead, the vast majority of the evacuees were forced to trust in white "friends" to hold their property for them, or to sell or lease their land to strangers.

Although the powers vested in the Federal Reserve included protection from "fraud, forced sales and unscrupulous creditors,"[60] the bank's representatives were extremely cautious in using any such powers. They did not annul any of the fire sales that had taken place in the weeks before the service began, and they failed to make any arrests for fraud or exploitation. Thus, for all practical purposes, the government encouraged forced sales by imposing a deadline for evacuation.

As the Tolan committee charged at the time, the Federal Reserve overemphasized disposal of goods, and it failed to make proper plans for storage.[61] When evacuees asked about storage, they were told by the Federal Reserve Bank to first dispose of whatever property they could.[62] Since the evacuees were allowed to take with them only what items they could carry, they were forced to abandon many household and personal goods or sell them for whatever they could get for them. The Federal Reserve (later the WRA) ultimately offered limited warehouse space for personal effects, at army expense.[63] However, the army took no responsibility for the items thus stored, and the Federal Reserve did not insure the warehouses. Many evacuees would not trust the warehouses. Their fears that their property would not be secure proved to be well-founded: an estimated 80 percent of the property stored in the warehouses was damaged by looting and vandalism by hostile whites, while local authorities looked the other way.[64]

The consequences of Roosevelt's decision not to protect Japanese-American property were staggering. The vast majority of evacuees were forced to leave their property behind, entrust it to white "friends"—many of whom never returned it—or sell it for a pittance. White scavengers and bargain-hunters went through Japanese-American neighborhoods buying refrigerators for one dollar or washing machines for a quarter. Using different methods, later researchers estimated that the Japanese-American community's losses amounted to somewhere between $67 million and $116 million in 1945 dollars, which comes to a figure in excess of $500 million in 2001 dollars.[65] Almost all families suffered economic loss, and many, perhaps most, lost their principal assets. Thousands of families were driven off the land they owned (or quasi-owned, because of legal curbs on alien land ownership) or were forced to sell at whatever price they could get. Almost all automobile owners sold or lost their cars, and many families were stripped of appliances and family heirlooms.

Roosevelt bears a heavy burden of guilt for his insensitivity to the needs and property of over 100,000 Americans. Having approved an unprecedented seizure of American citizens and created a situation uncovered by normal legal procedures, he had a responsibility as chief executive to make some special arrangement for securing evacuee property or providing compensation. However, when his advisers turned to him for guidance, he failed to provide political or moral leadership on how evacuee property should be protected. By refusing to focus on planning for the evacuation or even to resolve the appointment of a property custodian, Roosevelt allowed an emergency situation to arise with no means of dealing with it.

Ted Morgan contends that the President's statement that he did not care about the property of the evacuees showed an enmity toward Japanese Americans that grew out of the same racial animosity that he had expressed toward Japanese immigrants in his 1920s articles.[66] Morgan's position bears exploration. Certainly, FDR's indifference to the losses to be suffered by the evacuees reflects a disregard for Japanese-American property rights inherent in his earlier support for alien land legislation. Also, there was a brusqueness, even a nastiness, in Roosevelt's rejection of Clark's attempt to protect evacuee property values which suggests that FDR viewed Japanese Americans, if not quite as "potential enemies," in Morgan's terms, then at least as unworthy of his concern.

Yet Roosevelt's decision cannot be attributed entirely to racism. Rather, FDR's approval of the Federal Reserve plan, like his approval of the evacuation, was a blend of weak administration and deadly indifference, which was informed by racial hostility but was not synonymous with it. By failing to attend to the evacuee property situation, he blocked any meaningful solution. Morgenthau, who should have assumed responsibility for protecting evacuee property, took for granted that the evacuation would be permanent. In the absence of presidential leadership, he interpreted his own duties as narrowly as possible and used legalistic arguments to oppose federal custody even of Issei property, over which the government unquestionably had legal authority. Even Harry Hopkins, Roosevelt's deputy, was unable to push Morgenthau to act. His Federal Reserve plan, despite its humanitarian aims, was a means of passing the buck from the government and avoiding actual responsibility for safeguarding Japanese-American property. When he was presented with Morgenthau's plan, Roosevelt did not address the property issue or ask about alternatives. Rather, he clearly stated that the evacuation was the only matter that concerned him: he cared about what happened to the evacuees after they were moved, not before. Whatever Morgenthau's motives for telling Roosevelt about Clark's position, the President's rejection of government administration of the Japanese Americans' property was unmistakable.

The President's anxiety to speed evacuation was so consuming that even the political pressure for a custodian for Japanese-American property failed to engage his interest. Roosevelt waited several days before replying to Lea's and Tolan's requests for immediate action on a custodian. When he finally did reply, the President ignored the Federal Reserve service and instead referred vaguely to Crowley, who had no mandate or wish to handle Japanese-American property.

The fate of Japanese Americans in Hawaii presents a fascinating counterpoint to developments on the West Coast. In theory, Hawaii was a more logical site for mass evacuation than the West Coast states. Hawaii had actually been attacked by Japan, and in the minds of the President and his advisors there was a continuing threat of invasion, especially after Japanese forces took over the Philippines in March 1942. Following the Battle of Midway in June 1942, the tide of the Pacific War began to turn, and the U.S. Navy went on the offensive with an invasion of the Solomon Islands in November. However, the military was constantly on the alert for an imminent large-scale attack on Hawaii until at least mid-1943, and the territory remained under martial law until 1944. Hawaii had large military and naval bases, and its great military importance was augmented during the war by its status as command center and staging base for the war against Japan, while the territory's distant and isolated position made it less accessible to reinforcements in case of danger. Furthermore, the Japanese and Japanese-American population in Hawaii, while not appreciably larger than that on the mainland, was far more significant. People of Japanese ancestry comprised some 35 percent of the islands' population. The potential disloyalty of the "local Japanese" in case of conflict with Japan had been a subject of concern to the army and to Hawaii's politically dominant white minority population during the prewar years. Despite all these factors, there was no mass evacuation or internment of the "local Japanese" residents of Hawaii. The progression of events in the islands thus puts Roosevelt's decision to approve the internment in its proper perspective. In particular, it shows the limits of the President's control over policy and offers a useful reminder of the importance of the particular circumstances in shaping actions.

Pressure for action against the Japanese community in Hawaii started soon after Pearl Harbor. Hundreds of Japanese community members were arrested and interned following the attack. As early as December 19, 1941, Navy Secretary Frank Knox recommended at a Cabinet meeting that the War Department remove all Issei from Oahu to another island in Hawaii, while John Franklin Carter and Curtis Munson hotly protested that the "local Japanese" in Hawaii were overwhelmingly loyal. On January 10, 1942, the War Department asked the opinion of General Delos Emmons, the army commander appointed after Pearl Harbor to replace the disgraced General Short as Hawaii's military governor, regarding the sending of the Japanese Americans to relocation camps. Emmons responded that he favored evacuation eventually, but that the Japanese population, which made up much of Oahu's skilled and agricultural labor force, was first needed to rebuild the Pearl Harbor defenses. The general added that the construction and shipping facilities needed to erect camps for evacuees and transport them from island to island were not available. A week later, Emmons was granted permission to evacuate aliens deemed dangerous to the mainland, but he chose not to exercise that authority until February 20, when a group of 72 internees at Hawaii's Sand Island base who were classified as "troublemakers" were transferred to camps on the mainland.[67]

In early February, after Justice Roberts expressed concern over the Japanese Americans in Hawaii and the Roberts Report discussed spying by Japanese agents, Emmons was again asked for his recommendations regarding mass evacuation of Issei and Nisei. He agreed that evacuation was desirable, but he stated that the few Japanese who had been suspected of disloyalty were already in custody, and he added that the first priority must be the transportation of some 20,000 white civilians away from the danger zone. Emmons reported that if the War Department wished to eliminate any and all potentially disloyal Japanese, it would have to transport at least 100,000 people, as it was impossible to determine which Japanese Americans were potentially disloyal. Since Emmons must have known that this was a patently impossible task under the circumstances, it is reasonable to suppose that this excessive figure was meant to deter any mass evacuation.

Despite Emmons' opposition, the President received reports favoring evacuation during February from two influential advisers. On February 12 William J. Donovan, FDR's coordinator of information, sent Roosevelt a plan submitted by his colleague Atherton Richards. Richards viewed the "unpredictable activities and loyalties" of the local Japanese Americans as a threat to national security and favored their evacuation. Richards recommended against any large evacuation of Japanese Americans to the U.S. mainland, since it would strain transport facilities and bring about a hostile political reaction with "an accentuation of the problem as illustrated by the California Japanese situation." Rather, the Japanese residents should be sent underground to the big island of Hawaii or another area outside Oahu, where they could grow their own food and construct useful facilities.[68]

The same day, General George Marshall, the army chief of staff and a close Roosevelt advisor, circulated J.C.S. 11, a draft recommendation for the Joint Chiefs, concerning new military dispositions for the defense of Hawaii. In addition to the plans for external defense, Marshall stated that there was a problem of internal defense residing in the threat of "inimical action" from the 100,000 residents of Japanese origin. He added, without further explanation, that it was "probable" that all such residents would ultimately be placed in one location and put under continuous surveillance. Marshall further stated that, in the short term, plans must be made for the "essential" immediate evacuation of the most dangerous group of 20,000 persons:

> This can be effectuated either by
>
> (a) Instituting a *concentration camp* on one of the Hawaiian Islands, such as Molokai.
>
> (b) Transferring the Japanese population to a *concentration camp* located on the U.S. mainland. (emphasis in original)[69]

Unlike Richards, Marshall believed that establishing a camp in Hawaii would present a greater logistical problem than evacuating Japanese Americans to the U.S. mainland, since shipping would have to be diverted to bring to Hawaii the building materials and provisions for both the prisoners and the troops assigned to guard them. He therefore proposed that option (b) be adopted.

Despite its opening citation of the "short-term" problem caused by the 20,000 "most dangerous," Marshall's draft concluded by asking that the chiefs approve the deportation and incarceration of *all* 100,000 Japanese Americans from Hawaii: "The Joint U.S. Chiefs of Staff therefore unanimously recommend that: All Japanese residents of the Hawaiian Islands (whether U.S. citizens or aliens) be transported to the U.S. mainland and placed under guard at a concentration camp in such locality as is most suitable."[70] Not only was the sudden leap in Marshall's draft from action against 20,000 people to evacuation of over 100,000 startling, but the plan for indiscriminate evacuation indicates that Marshall was unwilling to distinguish, as both Munson and the FBI had done, between the loyalty or potential disloyalty of aliens and that of citizens (notwithstanding that there was no practical distinction between them while Hawaii remained under martial law). Similarly, the draft was specific in its plan for the disposition of those to be transported—there was no mention of resettlement, either voluntary or involuntary. Rather, the aftermath of proposed evacuation was explicitly described as confinement in concentration camps, presumably for the duration of the war.

Marshall's draft (issued two days before DeWitt made his final recommendations and one week before Executive Order 9066 was signed) powerfully suggests a consciousness, at least among some of FDR's advisors, that the likely end result of evacuation on the West Coast would also be concentration camps. In Hawaii, where the existence of martial law gave the army unchecked power over civilians, military planners recommended imprisonment in camps, which they took for granted was the logical end result of any evacuation. It is unknown whether Roosevelt was influenced by Marshall's recommendations when he approved the West Coast evacuation (in which the chief of staff played no direct role, although he knew of DeWitt's recommendations). However, it is reasonable to assume the President was aware of at least the outlines of Marshall's ideas, since he was in daily contact with the general on military matters and because Marshall's office sent the President a memorandum entitled "Notes on Evacuation of Japanese from Hawaiian Islands." Though undated, these "Notes" appear to have been written contemporaneously with the drafting of J.C.S. 11, whose provisions they summarized. The document explicitly stated under the heading of "evacuation" that "1. About 100,000 would be involved" and "2. It should be done." It also again explained why evacuation should be to the mainland rather than to a less populated Hawaiian island.[71]

Significantly, the "Notes" recommended that discretion be granted to local commanders in deciding who should be evacuated, in order to take account of local labor needs, and also to "get friendly but burdensome loyal people out of the way." In other words, Marshall intended to use the existence of martial law as a tool to transport all Japanese Americans, even those of unquestioned loyalty, whom the local army commanders considered somehow "burdensome." Even to minimize the drain on resources in a war situation, the creation of an arbitrary standard of utility for the freedom of Japanese Americans—Marshall did not sanction the forcible removal of "burdensome" whites—starkly reveals the racial animosity that underlay all debate on control of Japanese Americans.[72]

The next week, even as the Joint Chiefs deliberated on Marshall's recommendation, the President signed Executive Order 9066. On February 23, Knox sent a letter to Roosevelt stating that he had repeatedly brought up the question of evacuation within the islands but that the matter had always previously "bogged down" on the question of the constitutional rights of U.S. citizens. He asked whether Roosevelt's Executive Order dealing with the question on the mainland had resolved that problem so that the evacuation could now go forward. Knox recognized that it would be costly in terms of personnel and materials, but he declared that national security required the protection of Hawaii from a population with "predominantly enemy sympathies and affiliations" (based on what evidence, he did not reveal). The War Department, he believed, did not favor evacuation, and he stated that General Emmons, in particular, had sent him a long letter arguing against any "wholesale movement" of the Japanese population. Knox, however, was implacably committed to evacuation and forced labor. "Personally, I shall always feel dissatisfied with the situation until we get the Japanese out of Oahu and establish them on one of the other islands where they can be made to work for their living and produce much of their own food."[73]

Three days later, Roosevelt intervened directly. "Like you, I have long felt that most of the Japanese should be removed from Oahu to one of the other islands," he wrote Knox. "I do not worry about the constitutional question—first, because of my recent order and, second, because Hawaii is under martial law."[74] He told Knox to meet with Stimson and take care of arrangements. Although Knox must have wondered why the President had not previously acted more decisively on his "long felt" view, Roosevelt's memo did demonstrate a clear commitment to mass evacuation in Hawaii.

Nevertheless, it was not so easy to translate this warrant into action. The method and size of the evacuation still remained unresolved, and soon grew even thornier. On February 27 Stimson "staggered" the President by telling him that the plan he and Knox had approved for confinement of Hawaiian Japanese Americans under army guard in a "cantonment" on Molokai was impractical, and it would probably be necessary to send the evacuees to the United States, as Marshall had proposed.[75] Action was halted while the Budget Bureau, Justice Department, WRA, and the Joint Chiefs of Staff were consulted. On March 11 Admiral Stark, the navy chief of staff, informed the President that the Joint Chiefs had considered and approved J.C.S. 11 (Marshall's draft evacuation proposal), including the mass transportation of citizen and alien Japanese residents to the mainland and their placement under guard in concentration camps there. Even though the admiral blandly claimed that the final recommendations summarized those of J.C.S. 11, they differed from Marshall's total evacuation plan in one crucial detail: the memo prescribed evacuation only for those Japanese residents "as are considered by appropriate authority in the Hawaiian Islands to constitute a source of danger."[76] Thus, the choice of evacuees was left to Emmons' discretion. Stark's text cited Marshall's estimate of 20,000 Japanese as most dangerous. Two days later, on March 13, Roosevelt (and Stimson) approved the entire set of recommendations. When Stimson again explained that an evacuation within Hawaii was impractical, Roosevelt abandoned his plan for Hawaiian confinement and approved the transportation to the mainland by the War Department of the 20,000 "most dangerous" Japanese residents.[77]

Within two weeks of Roosevelt's order, Stimson and McCloy began to have doubts about Hawaiian evacuation. McCloy realized that any shipment of large numbers of Japanese Americans would inflame public opinion on the West Coast and imperil the orderly evacuation already taking place there. He traveled to Hawaii to see Emmons, who told McCloy that he now believed that there were only about 1,500 people who could be considered immediately dangerous. McCloy responded that Emmons had better come up with some plan that would satisfy the President and Knox.[78]

Meanwhile, Stimson and McCloy began to question the constitutionality of evacuation to the mainland. It was one thing, as Stimson wrote in his diary, to remove potentially dangerous people from a military zone. However, it was clearly illegal to imprison American citizens indefinitely without charge, at least in an area not under martial law. After being informed that civil liberties groups intended to introduce *habeas corpus* petitions for Japanese Hawaiians transported to the mainland, Stimson informed the President on April 15 that he was ordering all Nisei who had been sent to the mainland returned to Hawaii, where they could be summarily detained under martial law.[79] Stimson remained firmly convinced, however, that a Japanese attack on Hawaii was imminent and that Japanese Americans were potential saboteurs. Stimson stated directly to Roosevelt that not only did General Emmons think future evacuation might be important for Hawaii's safety but that "I, myself, have heard you mention the possible coming of a campaign of concerted sabotage made in connection with a simultaneous attack on our frontiers from without."[80] Stimson suggested suspension of *habeas corpus* on the mainland to imprison further evacuees and underlined the necessity for such evacuation.

Roosevelt did not contest Stimson's depiction of him as focused on the danger of sabotage in Hawaii, and in the face of the legal obstacles to imprisoning Hawaiian Nisei on the mainland he returned to his previous plan for imprisonment within the territory.

On April 20 Knox sent a memo reminding Roosevelt of his plan to evacuate the "Japs" from Oahu to a concentration camp on another island, and pressing for action.[81] The President agreed, and he wrote Stimson on April 23 to express impatience over the delay in evacuation and confinement. FDR added that he was concerned over the "large numbers of Japanese" on the other islands as well, which made him doubt that these islands, particularly the main island of Hawaii, were secure against attack and invasion.[82] The President repeated at Cabinet the following day that he shared Knox's concern over sabotage and wished the Japanese Hawaiians evacuated to one of the smaller islands. Stimson agreed to work with Knox on a new plan.[83]

The President's unhesitating readiness to evacuate Hawaii's Japanese Americans because of his strong fear of a Japanese invasion indicates his belief that neither Issei nor Nisei could be trusted to support the United States in the event of a conflict with Japan. The strength of his anxiety over Japanese Americans is further revealed by his contemporaneous reaction to a story, told to him by his old law partner Langdon Marvin, that a Japanese domestic servant in a Washington, D.C., household had been revealed to be a military officer attached to the Japanese embassy. The President was dissuaded from evacuating the 48 Japanese aliens residing in Washington, D.C., only by Biddle's promise on April 23 to have the FBI investigate each one.[84]

On April 28 Stimson and McCloy met with Knox and several admirals to devise some method of dealing with the Japanese Americans in Hawaii. The two secretaries agreed that internment within the islands, either on Oahu or elsewhere, was acceptable from a security viewpoint, but would be too limited in its scope by supply problems. Stimson thus resolved to devise a means of sending a group of "perhaps eight or ten or twelve thousand" evacuees to the mainland, despite the constitutional obstacles to internment. Although Stimson hoped to find some legal way to take such a group away from Hawaii, Knox believed that it would be impossible to resettle them in the United States other than in an internment camp. At a Cabinet meeting three days later, when Stimson brought up the question of moving the 12,000, explaining that there was insufficient food and water to hold them on any small Hawaiian island, Biddle suggested either declaring martial law in a small area on the mainland to which citizens could then be moved or putting the evacuation on a voluntary basis.[85] Roosevelt, who was leery of the whole idea of evacuation to the mainland, declared that he was unwilling to suspend *habeas corpus* anywhere on the U.S. mainland.[86] Although the President's basis for this refusal is not clear, it is reasonable to assume that he wished to avoid curtailing the civil rights of the general population any more than was absolutely necessary for national defense.

In hopes of satisfying the President, the War Department then asked Emmons once again to devise an evacuation plan. Emmons was not happy about evacuation, especially after he received a report from the Territorial Office of Defense affirming that there had been no sabotage by any Japanese Americans since Pearl Harbor and warning that any sizable evacuation would have enormous potential adverse consequences both on the islands' economy and on the morale of the remaining Japanese.[87] However, McCloy pressured Emmons to order at least some action, since Roosevelt and Knox were continuously calling for internment camps to be set up in the Hawaiian Islands. He suggested Emmons move 10,000 to 15,000 Japanese Americans from the smaller islands to the "Big Island" of Hawaii.[88]

Emmons thought the whole project "illogical," but in order to counter pressure for evacuation he designed a program of voluntary evacuation of up to 5,000 people to the U.S. mainland.[89] He targeted for "voluntary" transportation those who were potentially dangerous, such as interned Issei and their families, as well as what he later called "Japanese who are not essential to the war effort." These included the elderly, children, and individuals and families on relief.[90] On July 15 the Joint Chiefs adopted Emmons's ideas. The chiefs explained to the President that under their previous directive, any U.S. citizen transported to the U.S. mainland and interned in a concentration camp could free himself by a writ of *habeas corpus.* They therefore altered their recommendation from imprisonment of Hawaiian Nisei in concentration camps to their transportation to a "relocation canter" and "resettlement" by the WRA. Although the end result in both cases was indefinite incarceration, the Joint Chiefs disguised this fact by adopting the government's euphemistic terminology. On July 17 FDR authorized the transportation to the mainland and resettlement of up to 15,000 persons in family groups, to be made up of Japanese Americans considered "potentially dangerous to national security" and their immediate families.[91]

Roosevelt and Knox no doubt viewed Emmons's program as the first installment of a larger evacuation of Japanese Hawaiians. Over the following weeks, however, even as the WRA reserved space in the camps it was constructing for Japanese-American evacuees from Hawaii, Stimson became increasingly aware of the same fundamental problems of a Hawaiian evacuation that Emmons had already recognized. As early as the beginning of July, he privately expressed his doubts about the wisdom of such an evacuation and its economic impact, especially when all Hawaiian Japanese Americans considered actively dangerous were already in internment camps.[92]

In early October, as the War Department prepared to process the first shipments of evacuees from Hawaii, Emmons informed McCloy that the evacuation would consist of successive groups of up to 300 "volunteers" per ship who would be sent out over a six-month period. These "volunteers" were Nisei who agreed to accompany their Issei relatives to their new location. Emmons and McCloy estimated that the entire evacuation would not exceed 5,000 people.[93]

When Knox learned of the plan, he quickly protested to Roosevelt that Hawaii was still riddled with Japanese sympathizers and probably Japanese agents "who, in the event of an attack upon these islands, would unquestionably cooperate with our enemies."[94] An evacuation of only 5,000 people would not erase this threat. FDR was once again catalyzed into action by Knox's protest, and he asked Stimson's opinion about further evacuation. The secretary of war reminded the President that all Japanese Americans in Hawaii who were known to be hostile, as well as "many others suspected of subversive tendencies," had already been interned, either in the territory or on the mainland. Stimson stated that General Emmons had informed him that the removal of even those 5,000 people would greatly "simplify his problem" and, "considering the labor needs in the islands," that 5,000 added up to almost all the evacuees Emmons was "interested" in removing.[95] Stimson's remark about the labor situation irritated Roosevelt, who still shared Knox's suspicions of Japanese Americans in Hawaii. He immediately wrote Stimson and General Marshall that "General Emmons should be told that the only consideration is that of the safety of the Islands and that the labor situation is not only not a secondary matter but should not be given any consideration whatsoever."[96]

Although the President clearly indicated that he expected further action, Emmons was unwilling to order it. By November 1942, Japan was on the defensive in the Pacific War, and the chance of a Hawaiian invasion was remote. All local Japanese whom Emmons considered suspicious were in custody, and he had already implemented what the War Department privately admitted was a wasteful and unnecessary token evacuation plan in order to placate the President.[97] Emmons needed Japanese-American laborers for plantation labor and war industries, and he did not wish to reduce their numbers or morale by repressive action. On November 5, three days after Roosevelt's memo, Emmons publicly guaranteed that there would be no large-scale evacuation of Japanese Americans in Hawaii. He stated that only those not essential to the war effort would be moved. Stimson and McCloy were not interested in overruling Emmons.

By January 1943, as Biddle later commented, the idea of mass evacuation in Hawaii was dead.[98] In March 1943 Knox told the House Appropriations Committee that the problem of sabotage in Hawaii "is not being met head-on" and added that the evacuation program was not being followed to as great an extent as he would wish. He strongly suggested that he would welcome a large-scale evacuation.[99] Soon after, however, the secretary of the navy was forced to admit defeat.[100]

Between November 1942 and February 1943 (when the WRA asked that transportation of evacuees from Hawaii be suspended because it had no more room in its camps), a total of 1,037 Japanese Americans from Hawaii were transported to camps on the mainland. The majority of these people were citizens who "volunteered" to be evacuated with their previously interned alien family members in order to keep their family units intact.[101] A great injustice was practiced on these evacuees, who were the pawns in the chess game between the President, Emmons, and the War Department. The Japanese Americans who accepted transportation from Hawaii to the mainland did so in the belief, nourished by the military, that they would be released once they reached the mainland.[102] The army was careful to insist that it could simply *recommend* the release of the Issei aliens and their families but could not promise it. However, since the government had indiscriminately confined all West Coast Japanese Americans and no resettlement procedures had been set up, any pledge of support for release after transportation was either irresponsible or (more likely) duplicitous. Instead, the "resettlement" of Hawaiian Japanese Americans consisted of their being placed behind barbed wire in segregated sections of the established camps and forbidden to hold employment in them. Alongside the 1,037 Japanese Hawaiians transported to the camps, approximately 1,500 Japanese Americans remained interned without trial in Hawaii throughout the war, and 675 Hawaiian Issei were summarily transported to the U.S. mainland after Pearl

Harbor and held by the Justice Department in alien internment camps throughout the war. As unjust as this situation was, these figures nevertheless pale in comparison to the planned incarceration of 20,000–100,000 Japanese residents of Hawaii that Franklin Roosevelt ordered and which he and Frank Knox struggled repeatedly to achieve.

The events in Hawaii present an illuminating contrast to the West Coast. The President readily and unhesitatingly accepted the principle of mass transportation of Hawaiian Issei and Nisei to the U.S. mainland and their indefinite confinement in facilities expressly described by Marshall as concentration camps. While he had played a largely passive role in the decision to evacuate the West Coast Japanese, Roosevelt actively campaigned for mass removal in Hawaii. Although FDR justified his position by reference to the emergency military situation in Hawaii, he was unwilling—in notable contrast to the West Coast situation—to accept the strategic estimate of the local commander when he downplayed the necessity for mass removal. The President did not give consideration to the fact that the troops and materials needed for such an operation would cut drastically into urgently needed supplies and harm morale or that the Japanese-American population was necessary to the war effort. Rather, he dismissed those arguments as irrelevant when suspected sabotage was involved. Neither Roosevelt's nor Knox's demand for mass internment was appeased after the middle of June 1942, when the American victory at Midway turned the tide of battle in the Pacific and the threat of invasion receded.

Ironically, Hawaii's isolation and military importance—the very factors that led Roosevelt to press repeatedly for preventive custody of the local Japanese—represented the strongest deterrents to any mass evacuation in the islands. Hawaii's overwhelming military presence left it well defended against any internal subversion, and the fact that martial law was in effect after Pearl Harbor and that some 500 community leaders and consular officials who were considered dangerous had been rounded up and interned eased the fears of the military about combatting subversion. Furthermore, Hawaii's remote location made mass evacuation to the mainland all but impossible, due to the enormous drain on scarce resources involved in rounding up 135,000 people and shipping them over 2,500 miles away. FDR's plan to place Japanese Americans in concentration camps within the Hawaiian territory (such as on the famous "leper" island of Molokai) was equally impractical. The idea of housing and supplying 135,000 people and their guards on a tiny island distant from the mainland (which would be vulnerable in case of Japanese invasion) was absurd on its face.

In contrast to the West Coast, there was no outpouring of anti-Japanese hysteria in Hawaii driving the President to action. Whereas on the mainland Japanese Americans were a small, powerless, and hated minority, Japanese Hawaiians were integral to the local economy and society. Japanese Americans represented the largest portion of the plantation work force on which the islands' economy depended, and the territory's military rulers and the economic elite looked on them as indispensable laborers. The Japanese community was an important fraction of public opinion and political pressure—there were Nisei representatives, such as Senator Sanji Abe, in the territorial legislature, as well as numerous Japanese-American civil servants. Hawaiian political leaders such as Samuel King, the territorial delegate to Congress, defended the loyalty of the Japanese Americans, while the "Big Five" families of Hawaii's politically dominant white plantation aristocracy formed an influential barrier to evacuation. Indeed, Roosevelt was convinced that Emmons took his information from the "Big Five,"[103] and he remarked scornfully to the Cabinet after evacuation was defeated that the plan was stymied by the pineapple and sugar growers, who wished to retain their Japanese laborers.[104]

Most importantly, General Emmons did not support mass internment. Unlike General DeWitt, Emmons had no apparent predisposition against Japanese Americans and clearly felt that mass removal was unnecessary. He did not directly oppose evacuation, at least to the mainland, presumably because he understood that his superiors desired it and he did not want to take responsibility for opposing it in case anything went wrong. However, as the CWRIC Report put it, Emmons "effectively scuttled the Hawaiian evacuation" by attrition, continually emphasizing the practical and logistical difficulties and damage to the war effort that evacuation would entail.[105]

The abortion of the plan for Hawaiian evacuation reveals the limitations on the President's power to impose policy and suggests the essential role of the specific circumstances and political factors in the evacuation of the West Coast Japanese Americans. Roosevelt pushed strongly for evacuation in Hawaii—much more so than in the case of the West Coast—but failed to achieve it. Of course, the Hawaiian evacuation was stymied in large part by the enormous practical difficulties of supply and transport it would have entailed, which militated strongly against mass removal. FDR could not eliminate such barriers simply by issuing orders. The fact remains, nonetheless, that he had the theoretical power as commander-in-chief to push through an evacuation policy in Hawaii, even in the absence of united public and army sentiment, but was unwilling or unable to do so.

There are several distinct but related explanations for Roosevelt's failure to impose evacuation in Hawaii. One is the nature of presidential power.[106] FDR was unable to push through the policy because he could not persuade McCloy and Emmons, his subordinates, to execute the policy. It is unclear how much of their refusal to carry out the President's orders was conscious insubordination and how much was their recognition of the impossibility of their assignment. In any case, while neither Emmons nor McCloy was prepared to dispute the President's orders directly, and they labored to give the appearance of compliance, their joint policy of delay and evasion scuttled the program.

Roosevelt's particular administrative style also contributed to his failure. Although the President delighted in delegating responsibility for policy to opposing subordinates in order to keep final decision-making authority in his own hands, he disliked giving direct orders, especially when they would cause serious friction with important advisors. His decision-making power derived from consensus and was in a real sense subject to the moral and political influence of his official family. In the case of Hawaii, Roosevelt trusted Knox and Stimson to work out a policy. When the secretary of war turned against large-scale evacuation, the President refused to challenge or overrule him.

It could also be plausibly argued that FDR's failure to push through evacuation in Hawaii stemmed in part from the particular exigencies of the war. Pressed by military demands, Roosevelt did not (no doubt he could not) give the Hawaiian question consistent attention. Rather, he issued orders only in response to Knox's or Marshall's prodding and did not effectively follow through. Ironically, the vast powers FDR granted the military, which served as the underpinning for the West Coast evacuation, helped frustrate his designs in Hawaii. Emmons's position as military governor made him the sole source of power in Hawaii and allowed him great leeway to suspend execution of policies he opposed. His cool judgment and balancing of the needs of security against those of the war effort present a powerful contrast to General DeWitt's self-protective attitude.

Franklin Roosevelt's decision to maintain public silence on the internment policy was perhaps his most crucial and damaging act of injustice toward Japanese Americans during 1942. The mass evacuation and incarceration of the West Coast Japanese fanned racist sentiment and animosity toward them. Capitalizing on anti-Japanese sentiment, pressure groups and political leaders nationwide proposed measures to permanently restrict the rights of Japanese Americans. In March, Senator Stewart of Tennessee held hearings on his bill to authorize the secretary of war to detain indefinitely any citizen believed to have ties to an enemy country, and he clearly indicated it was directed at stripping Japanese Americans of citizenship, a position with which Justice Department representatives initially concurred.[107] The Senate Immigration Committee reported out the bill favorably in summer 1942. In May, the Native Sons of the Golden West unsuccessfully brought suit in Federal Court to strip the Nisei of their voting rights. Meanwhile, anti–Japanese-American newspaper columnists and officials sought to focus public anger over wartime shortages and restrictions by spreading stories about how the "Japs" were being "coddled" and given extra food and a life of comfortable idleness in the camps. Such ideas and attitudes would return to haunt the administration when it came time to end the internment.

This wave of public hostility had enormous consequences. The refusal of communities in the mountain states to permit the "dangerous" Japanese population to enter forced the government to shift its policy from immediate resettlement to indefinite internment. It also affected policy within the camps. For example, in order to deflect criticism, the WRA was forced to set pay scales for the internees below the minimum wage and army pay.

Throughout 1942, numerous people both inside and outside government encouraged Roosevelt to make a speech or statement praising and reassuring loyal Japanese Americans in order to curb anti-Japanese hysteria. They believed that the President's great communication skills, which he displayed in his press conferences and his famous radio "fireside chats," would improve morale, help educate public opinion, and reduce the possibility of violence against the evacuees. Barely a week after Pearl Harbor, Curtis Munson and John Franklin Carter had pressed the President to issue an immediate statement on behalf of the loyal Japanese Americans, and in early February 1942 Archibald MacLeish sent Roosevelt material for a speech against violence and hysteria on the West Coast. Biddle's February 17, 1942, memorandum opposing evacuation was couched in the form of suggested material for a press conference statement decrying the irresponsible actions of certain journalists. No such statement was forthcoming.

Pro–Japanese-American opinion, which had been all but silent during the weeks that preceded February 19, was energized by the news of the evacuation. Several individuals and organizations formed committees, signed petitions, and testified on behalf of Japanese Americans at the Tolan committee hearings. In addition, Roosevelt began to receive, in Milton Eisenhower's words, "quite a little mail" from liberal groups and others protesting the evacuation.[108] A few religious and progressive groups were completely opposed to the principle of evacuation. For example, the New York Conference of the Methodist Church deplored the concentration of American citizens as a violation of the Bill of Rights.[109] Socialist Party leader Norman Thomas repeatedly denounced the evacuation in the party press, and in April 1942 he organized the sending of a group letter to the President by the Post War World Council. The letter, signed by such liberal stalwarts as John Dewey, Oswald Garrison Villard, Harry Emerson Fosdick, and Reinhold Niebuhr, pressed for the immediate rescinding of Executive Order 9066 which, the writers asserted, "approximates the totalitarian theory of justice practiced by the Nazis in their treatment of the Jews."[110]

Other groups, including several West Coast "Fair Play" committees, acquiesced in evacuation but urged the President to protect the rights of Japanese Americans as much as possible.[111] The most important faction in the latter group was the American Civil Liberties Union (ACLU). In March 1942 a committee of the ACLU, made up of such notable figures as Roger Baldwin, Thurgood Marshall, and Arthur Garfield Hays, wrote a letter to Roosevelt denouncing the evacuation of citizens as well as aliens, which the signers claimed would "adversely affect our democratic practices and aims," lead to the demoralization of Japanese Americans, and feed mob violence and Axis propaganda. The letter urged the President to schedule speedy loyalty hearings for Japanese Americans. The signers argued that no Nisei should be removed from their homes without a hearing. They agreed that the Issei, as enemy aliens, could be indiscriminately removed but urged that after evacuation they be given trials before loyalty hearing boards, like other aliens.[112] Once the government had thus "separated the goats from the sheep" (as Churchill and others had also termed the process) on the British model, the loyal aliens should be allowed to return.[113]

Roosevelt seems not to have ever considered instituting hearings, either before or after signing Executive Order 9066. When New York Governor Herbert Lehman wrote the President in May 1942 expressing concern over possible evacuation of German and Italian aliens from the East Coast and proposing hearing boards for enemy aliens, the President's reply, drafted by the WRA, was noncommittal.[114] However, officers of the Western Defense Command discussed and rejected the idea of loyalty board hearings for Japanese Americans, at least for the foreseeable future. Not only would such hearings be too time-consuming but, as one military lawyer stated, they would undermine the basis of the evacuation—that it was impossible to distinguish between loyal and disloyal Japanese Americans.[115]

Even as the army rejected loyalty hearings, Roosevelt was beset by calls for him to endorse Japanese-American loyalty in other ways. In late April 1942 California Governor Culbert Olson wrote to Roosevelt about his fear that evacuation would interfere with the education of loyal Japanese American students in West Coast colleges. Olson asked the federal government to fund transportation costs in order to enable the students to be granted admission and relocated to other colleges outside the West Coast. Roosevelt responded (in a letter drafted by John Studebaker of the U.S. Office of Education), "I am deeply concerned that the American-born Japanese college students shall be impressed with the ability of the American people to distinguish between enemy aliens and staunch supporters of the American system who happen to have Japanese ancestry."[116] However, he took no steps to secure funding on the model suggested by Olson.

In May 1942 presidential aide Laughlin Currie (FDR's principal advisor and liaison with China) sent Roosevelt a memo explaining the concerns of Dr. Monroe Deutsch, a provost of the University of California, Berkeley, who had been a prime mover on behalf of Nisei students. Currie not only repeated Deutsch's proposals regarding aid for Nisei college education but also seconded his proposal that Roosevelt make a radio speech explaining the reasons for the evacuation and praising the cooperation of the internees. Currie enclosed a draft address written by Deutsch: "I deeply regret the necessity which prompted the removal of the Japanese nationals and their children from the Pacific Coast area; it seemed a wise precaution, and so the army asked that it be done. But remember that not a single one of those evacuated had been proved guilty of any crime—of any subversive act or espionage . . . The Japanese and Japanese Americans have cooperated loyally in this move, which entailed hardship, much financial loss to them, and a removal from their homes and a severance of ties."[117] Roosevelt seems not to have commented on Currie's memo or Deutsch's draft, but he evidently rejected them, since Currie's draft did not go into the "speech materials" file he maintained.

Roosevelt similarly ignored various pleas from the WRA for a statement. In particular, on June 18 Milton Eisenhower closed his memo to the President as departing WRA director with a series of recommendations. Significant among these was his wish that "at the appropriate time" Roosevelt would "issue a strong public statement in behalf of the loyal American citizens who are now bewildered and wonder what is in store for them."[118] Eisenhower's plea for an endorsement of Nisei loyalty was political as well as moral. Like his simultaneous request that FDR raise the wage scales in the camps, which had been set artificially low in response to public clamor, a statement championing Nisei loyalty would not only aid internee morale but also lessen the public hostility that interfered with the government's task of resettlement and use of Japanese-American labor. The President declined to take any action, although WRA staffers continued to prepare draft statements to this effect.[119]

During the summer, as the internment evolved, there were no public calls for a statement. However, in September, after Senator Stewart's bill to detain all Japanese Americans was reported out of committee, the American Civil Liberties Union wrote to expand on its members' previous protest letter. The ACLU (which had undergone a bitter internal struggle—and, ultimately, a member referendum—over its position on the internment) stated that it did not challenge the constitutionality of removing citizens found dangerous to security, but it added that "the wholesale indiscriminate evacuation of all persons of Japanese blood was obviously a measure taken in haste under the pressure of a strong public demand and without regard to individual loyalty."[120] Now that the evacuation had taken place, the ACLU asked the government to do all in its power to protect the personal safety and the citizenship rights of Japanese Americans, to release them as soon as possible from the camps to outside work, and to promise that all restrictions against them would be lifted after the end of the war.[121] Most importantly, since the evacuation had led the public to conclude that all Japanese Americans were disloyal, the letter urged Roosevelt to make a public statement explaining the government's policy, both to reassure Japanese Americans and their supporters and to counter "Axis propaganda which has capitalized on what is conceived to be racial discrimination." Such a statement would include a recognition that the "vast majority" of Americans of Japanese descent were loyal citizens who had willingly cooperated in evacuation, and that "no charge of sabotage or espionage has been made, as far as we are aware, against any persons of Japanese blood." Roosevelt did not respond.

On October 2, 1942, Elmer Davis, Director of the Office of War Information (OWI), and Milton Eisenhower, who had joined the OWI after leaving the WRA, wrote to warn Roosevelt that the bills pending in Congress to confine the Nisei for the duration of the war and strip them of citizenship had lowered Japanese-American morale and had stirred up public feeling that "this may after all be a racial war" in which all Japanese Americans were enemies. Davis and Eisenhower suggested that the President therefore make a brief public statement on behalf of loyal American citizens. They commented: "This matter is of great interest to the OWI. Japanese propaganda . . . insists that this is a racial war. We can combat this with counter propaganda only if our deeds permit us to tell the truth. Moreover, as citizens ourselves who believe deeply in the things for which we fight, we cannot help but be disturbed by the insistent public understanding of the Nisei; competent authorities, including Naval Intelligence people, say that fully 85 percent of the Nisei are loyal to this country and that it *is* possible to distinguish the sheep from the goats." As a sign of his trust, Davis and Eisenhower proposed that the President permit loyal American citizens of Japanese descent "after individual test" to enlist in the army and navy. It would be unfair, Davis pointed out, to draft people after evacuating them, but voluntary enlistment could be encouraged.

The idea of Japanese-American soldiers was not completely new. As early as April, the President had asked his military aides for data on the eligibility of aliens for military service.[122] In June 1942 FDR received a letter from a Hawaiian Nisei asking him to permit Nisei discharged from service after Pearl Harbor to show their loyalty to the United States by volunteering for military service.[123] In July 1942 the Army General Staff conducted an inquiry into possible military use of the Nisei and the effect of the military restrictions on their citizenship rights.

Roosevelt did not commit himself to make any statement on Nisei loyalty. However, he expressed cautious interest in Davis's and Eisenhower's proposal for opening the military by sending their letter on to Stimson and Knox for their comments. A few days later, he met with Davis and stated tentatively that he would be willing to have Nisei enlist in the army for restricted duty doing noncombat tasks. If the program went well, the Nisei would be assigned more normal military duties.[124]

Two weeks later, Knox responded with a discouraging letter. He decisively rejected Nisei enlistment in the navy, based on adverse feeling in the Navy Department, and suggested that the only possible use of "people of this character" could be as civilian intelligence staffers. Knox dismissed the whole question of Japanese American morale as a minor matter compared to the far more pressing subject of Hawaiian evacuation.[125] Interpreting Davis's request for a presidential statement in favor of "Japanese who are American citizens" as simply a response to the bills pending in Congress, Knox told Roosevelt that any such statement was "unwise and unnecessary" because the bills had no chance of passage.

At first, the army was equally hostile. Army commanders had discharged many Japanese-American soldiers in the months that followed Pearl Harbor, and selective service regulations barred further enlistment by Nisei.[126] Hawaiian Nisei who had joined the Territorial Guards before Pearl Harbor were discharged, while Nisei troops from the regular army were placed into the segregated 100th Infantry Battalion and sent for training in Wisconsin, far away from the islands. Only the personal intervention of General Marshall, the army chief of staff, prevented the transformation of the 100th into a labor battalion.[127]

When the General Staff asked General DeWitt his opinion during its July 1942 inquiry into the military utilization of Nisei troops, his reply made clear his overpowering suspicion of all Japanese Americans. DeWitt advised the committee of inquiry that the Nisei's high potential for disloyalty restricted their usefulness in combat to deployment in all-Nisei labor brigades in the European theater, and he urged that all Kibei (American-born citizens of Japanese ancestry educated in Japan) be automatically excluded from military service as presumptively disloyal. DeWitt further recommended that if the army decided not to use Nisei, every Japanese American already in the army should be discharged and placed in the "relocation centers." DeWitt asserted that if the Nisei were not accepted for military service, it would surely leave such a stigma that the Nisei would no longer be able to function as useful citizens, necessitating their expulsion from the nation. "If this condition arises and the United States then has within its borders a group of persons whose loyalties have been thus alienated, the solution of the problem must rest with Congress, because of the social-political aspects of the problem."[128]

In September 1942, following DeWitt's response, a board of officers led by Deputy Army Chief of Staff General McNarney formally recommended against any Nisei enlistment in view of the universal distrust in which Japanese Americans were held. At the time of Davis and Eisenhower's letter, the Military Intelligence Service's Language School had contacted the WRA to permit them to recruit Nisei volunteers to enlist as noncommissioned officers and serve as Japanese language teachers and specialists at Camp Savage and Fort Snelling in Minnesota.[129] However, this was understood to be an exceptional case.

Ironically, the army's opposition to Nisei soldiers was overruled by the decisive intervention of Assistant Secretary of War John McCloy, the main architect of the internment. McCloy had long believed that the Nisei would make good soldiers, and he argued that the propaganda value of such a unit would be enormous. McCloy strongly endorsed the proposal that Roosevelt make a public statement. As he expressed to Stimson, "I am firmly convinced that large numbers of [Nisei] are loyal, and they are suffering because they are classed indiscriminately with the 'goats.'"[130] Stimson, who was still haunted by the racial aspects of the evacuation, was inclined to agree. He wrote General Marshall, "I don't think you can permanently proscribe a lot of American citizens because of their racial origin."[131] Marshall shared this view and readily consented to the creation of a Nisei combat unit. Stimson then prepared a draft recommendation for the President. Although it is not clear that the memo was actually sent, Stimson would in any case have communicated its essence to Roosevelt in conference. The secretary of war stated that, while there was wide divergence within the army on the Nisei, he and General Marshall agreed that the army could raise an infantry regiment of Japanese-American volunteers, serving under white officers and using as cadres the Hawaiian "Japs" (that is, the 100th Infantry Battalion) already in training on the mainland. Such enlistment would provide extra manpower, and the Nisei would make excellent fighters.

Stimson also highlighted the psychological advantages of Nisei enlistment. Externally, enemy propaganda about American racial discrimination would be neutralized, and it would demonstrate the success of democracy. "The effect on India and elsewhere, of the yellow man voluntarily fighting for the white, would be substantial."[132] Meanwhile, internally, it would slow the deterioration in loyalty within the "relocation centers" and raise the morale of both the soldiers and their relatives.[133] Stimson readily admitted that there were risks of internal friction and disloyal conduct in such a plan, but he believed these were minor (provided the Nisei served outside the Far East), and he concluded that "the 'ayes' should have it" as far as the army was concerned. Aware of Roosevelt's proposal that the Nisei at first be confined to stateside duty, Stimson warned that such an arrangement would be a "faint-hearted compromise" that would defeat the purpose of enlisting Nisei soldiers, and he stated firmly that they should be sent for combat duty, even if they were assigned at first to nonvital sectors.

What Stimson's words reveal most strongly is his great feeling of responsibility for Japanese Americans. The man who had written in his diary eight months earlier that the Nisei were even more dangerous and untrustworthy than the Issei now tacitly confessed the government's and his own guilt: "After completion of the mass evacuation the indications were that the great majority of the evacuees, whether citizen or alien, remained completely loyal to the United States." Moreover, even at this early date, Stimson's analysis featured a marked sensitivity to the political factors that would be involved in postwar reintegration of the internees into American life: "[The soldiers] would return with pride in their hearts that they had done their bit, instead of being released like lepers to find their places in a world all too eager to reject them. There is no question in my mind that the Japanese problem in this country after the war would admit of far easier solution if voluntary enlistment were permitted. It would also tend to conciliate those who believe that the evacuees are having it too easy."[134]

Roosevelt does not seem to have reacted immediately to Stimson's proposal. The President may have indicated that he preferred to wait for the army to reach a consensus on Nisei enlistment, because McCloy immediately began collecting endorsements for the plan. In early November McCloy obtained General Emmons's statement that the Nisei would make "grand soldiers" based on the good showing made by the Nisei in the 100th Infantry Battalion while in training in Hawaii.[135] With McCloy's encouragement, the Japanese American Citizens League petitioned the President and the War Department to reinstate selective service for Japanese Americans.[136]

At the same time, Roosevelt did not abandon interest in the plan. Presumably, he was receptive to the idea of increasing military strength and using manpower more efficiently. In addition, he was very aware of the propaganda element. Indeed, when WRA head Dillon Myer (a longtime proponent of drafting Japanese Americans as a mark of equality) met with Roosevelt's assistant Harry Hopkins in early November in order to get the President's consent to the Nisei combat unit and to push for speedy resettlement of the internees, he discovered that the propaganda angle was the main ground on which Roosevelt could be reached: "I met Harry Hopkins yesterday morning about twenty minutes on the whole question of Japanese-American relocation, and leading up particularly, of course, to the matter of use in the army. I will frankly admit I was a little disappointed in what I thought I accomplished in the way of social point of view, but the outcome was all right in the sense that he is very much interested in the propaganda value, and said he would talk with the President about that angle but not bring up the other angle. He assured us he would try to keep it open."[137]

Roosevelt's focus on propaganda is further suggested by his attitude toward "national" units. In October 1942, shortly before the President met with Stimson regarding army personnel policies, he suggested to John Franklin Carter that it might be useful to create various small combat units composed of resident aliens, including Germans and Italians. After conferring with Stimson, Carter began making inquiries within the War Department.[138] In early November, however, he received a stinging rebuke from Stimson. The secretary wrote Carter that he considered it unwise to form any units with enemy nationals, whether German, Italian, or Japanese. The army was not yet even prepared to approve "small racial units" of resident aliens from allied countries such as Norway, Poland, or Czechoslovakia.[139]

Carter quickly advised Roosevelt of Stimson's position, and the President sent the secretary a memo on November 17. FDR expressed his sympathy with Stimson's desire to encourage "Americanization" within the army, and he agreed there should be no German or Italian units. However, FDR asserted that the idea of enlisting aliens from allied countries had merit. First, he pointed out, the formation of small units of resident aliens would not set a precedent. "We already have a Norwegian Battalion, Filipino Units and a Japanese Battalion."[140] Furthermore, a Danish or Czech or Polish unit, even one as small as a company, would have distinct political advantages. Roosevelt stressed, however, that the *"formation of such Battalions should be strictly limited to cases where political advantages are to be gained.* That is why the matter will be kept open and, of course, I must be the one to determine the political advantages if any."[141]

Although not directly related to the issue of Nisei volunteers, this memo nevertheless illuminates some of the paradoxes of Roosevelt's thinking about Japanese Americans. Roosevelt made clear that his primary interest in special units was the propaganda advantage to be gained from them, rather than military effectiveness or consistency. The formation of any such unit was a political matter which he alone would decide. More importantly, while Roosevelt agreed that there should be no unit made up of German or Italian "enemy aliens," he stated that there was already a Japanese Battalion among the "alien" units. The President could only have been referring to the Japanese-Hawaiian troops of the 100th Infantry Battalion, which was indeed a special unit formed of soldiers of a single ethnicity. This unit, however, was made up entirely of Nisei American citizens. There were no Japanese alien troops of any kind in the army at the time (and, indeed, few Issei of military age in the United States by 1942), and Roosevelt explicitly rejected the formation of *any* units of enemy aliens. From this evidence, one can only infer that the President considered the Nisei to be foreigners—not quite equivalent to German or Italian (or Japanese) enemy aliens but on a level with Filipino nationals and resident aliens from allied nations occupied by the Axis powers. He was willing to use the Nisei for propaganda purposes, since he did not suggest disbanding the existing battalion, but only as a symbolic gesture.

Moreover, Roosevelt was still not yet willing to speak publicly on behalf of the internees. At a Cabinet meeting on November 20, Interior Secretary Harold Ickes discussed the violent protests and letters of criticism he had received after he and Agriculture Secretary Claude Wickard had publicly expressed interest in hiring "interned Japanese" to do yard work on their farms in order to augment agricultural production. "I suggested that it would be helpful if a statement were given out by the President urging that Japanese who were known to be all right be given jobs." Once more, Roosevelt took no such action.[142] In December, when the President was informed that the influential Institute for Pacific Relations had publicly called for "more humane treatment" of people of Japanese ancestry in the United States and Canada, he made no comment.[143]

On January 1, 1943, the army's McNarney committee, which had recommended against enlisting Nisei the previous September, formally reversed that recommendation at McCloy's urging. Stimson and Marshall then decided to open up the army to Nisei volunteers, both to increase military strength and to provide the Nisei an opportunity to demonstrate their loyalty. The WRA opened the camps to army recruiters and propagandized on behalf of the new all-Nisei unit. The end result was a paradoxical success. The recruitment effort was a failure, in that only approximately 1,200 Nisei internees volunteered, about one third of the planned total. The vast majority of Nisei saw no reason to fight for the nation that had imprisoned them and their families. Yet, the 442nd Regimental Combat Team, which was formed out of the union of these internee troops with Nisei troops from Hawaii (including the existing 100th Infantry Battalion) fought valiantly and sustained heavy casualties in Italy and France, becoming the most highly decorated unit in the entire army.

The McNarney committee's report outlined a procedure for testing the loyalty of Nisei volunteers. All candidates would have to fill out a loyalty questionnaire dealing with their background and beliefs. Military Intelligence and FBI officers would then evaluate the loyalty of each applicant for release, and a military Joint Board would rule. This procedure was quickly approved (over the vehement protest of General DeWitt, who insisted that it was impossible to tell loyal "Japanese" from disloyal ones). In order to quell the concerns of the internees that they were being let into the army merely for use as cannon fodder, the committee further recommended that once the Nisei military unit was created, those internees whose loyalty was certified should also be made eligible for "leave" outside the camps to accept jobs in war industries or other employment. The loyalty investigations would permit the army to balance manpower needs against security concerns.

WRA officials seized on the military's proposed loyalty boards as a means of streamlining the release of loyal internees. After the WRA abandoned its initial plans for prompt resettlement of the evacuees of the excluded zone during spring 1942, it began developing policies for "leave clearance" of loyal Nisei. During summer and fall 1942, several thousand evacuees were recruited for temporary agricultural labor outside the camps, especially harvesting sugar beets. State officials undertook to transport and guard the internees and to pay them prevailing wages. In mid-1942 Dillon Myer proposed a policy of individual leaves whereby internees who had outside sponsors and had been investigated by the FBI could petition project directors for a "leave permit." However, concerns over army opposition had slowed implementation of the project. Myer realized that clearance by the new military loyalty board would reassure Americans concerned over security and make mass resettlement acceptable to anti-Japanese public opinion. He thus successfully lobbied the War Department to extend its loyalty examinations to all Issei and Nisei of both sexes over 17.[144]

Roosevelt was absorbed during most of January 1943 with preparations for the wartime Casablanca Conference. He doubtless gave his consent at some point to the Nisei enlistment plan, but he was not visibly involved in designing either the combat unit or the leave clearance program. Indeed, despite the repeated requests of Ickes and Biddle, he took no action to speed up release of internees for farm work.[145] However, his approval of Nisei soldiers left the door open for action on Elmer Davis's plea for a statement in support of loyal Nisei. Myer, believing that the announcement of the Nisei combat unit might be a propitious opportunity, drafted a presidential statement approving a program to permit loyal Americans of Japanese ancestry to serve their country in the army, war industries, and agriculture. Elmer Davis made some additions, then sent the statement to FDR. On February 1, 1943, three days after Stimson issued an official statement announcing that Nisei volunteers would be welcomed into the army and praising Japanese-American loyalty as "a voice that must be heard," Roosevelt issued the statement written by Myer. One section of the statement stood out boldly: "No loyal citizen of the United States should be denied the democratic right to exercise his citizenship, regardless of his ancestry. The principle on which this country was founded and by which it has always been governed is that Americanism is a matter of the mind and heart; Americanism is not, and never was, a matter of race or ancestry. A good American is one who is loyal to this country and to our creed of liberty and democracy."[146]

These eloquent remarks made a deep impression. The WRA and OWI accorded them enormous publicity. The WRA quickly printed up a pro-internee pamphlet, "A Voice That Must Be Heard," with the President's letter as its centerpiece. In addition, liberals both inside and outside the government immediately took it as sanction for a pro-Japanese-American attitude. When the Arizona legislature passed a resolution protesting the granting of leave permits for Nisei and denouncing the "favoritism" shown in permitting them to transfer to colleges east of the Rockies, Myer prepared a sharp public reply which was issued by FDR's secretary Marvin McIntyre: "It should be pointed out that these citizens of Japanese ancestry are no more enemy aliens than are citizens of Italian or German parentage, and that already they have borne with considerable sacrifice the demands put upon them by their removal from the west coast of the United States."[147]

How should we interpret Roosevelt's February 1 statement, and how does it fit against his previous refusal to speak? Some insight can be gained from the correspondence of the photographer Dorothea Lange, who was employed by the WRA. In May 1942 Lange and a colleague sent a proposed statement of support and an explanation of the evacuation for the President to sign. WRA officials returned her statement, saying the chances of persuading Roosevelt to make any statement were "exceedingly remote." Lange's correspondent suggested that she try another path but warned her that, based on their own discussions with FDR's advisors, "the consensus of those around here who should know seems to be that a statement of broad sympathy for the enemy alien groups is not feasible in view of the widespread popular bitterness toward the Axis countries."[148] When ACLU leaders met with Dillon Myer and Justice Department officials in September 1942, the WRA officials stated that "it would be unwise for them or the President to make any general statement of policy because it would stir up more opposition."[149]

This explanation, although revealing, is not altogether satisfying. In early January 1942 Roosevelt spoke publicly on behalf of loyal aliens without reference to their nationality, and he denounced employment discrimination against them. Also, other administration officials and Roosevelt insiders continued to make statements in support of Japanese Americans in spring 1942, even after Executive Order 9066 was signed. Stimson publicly promised to limit interference with Japanese-American civil rights, and he stated that "We are not unmindful of the fact that a majority of those evacuated are American citizens."[150] Attorney General Biddle called for fair play in several interviews and press conferences. In late March he publicly expressed opposition to Senator Stewart's bill to detain American citizens believed to have ties with enemy nations.[151] (Biddle was not totally immune from the feelings of suspicion and hostility toward the internees. In October, he expressed public doubts about Japanese-American loyalty, stating that "the Jap is in a class of his own . . . No one seems to understand the operations of his mind, and he becomes an imponderable quantity.")[152] Eleanor Roosevelt, though she did not publicly oppose the internment during 1942, pledged in April that the government would protect the evacuees from violence during the evacuation. In addition, on July 5, she wrote in her syndicated newspaper column a positive story on an evacuee. "This should remind us," she noted pointedly, "that among the group are really good and loyal Americans and we must build up their loyalty and not tear it down."[153] Milton Eisenhower and Dillon Myer issued multiple statements during the period reminding Americans that the evacuees were not dangerous and were loyally cooperating with evacuation. In June, Eisenhower told a congressional committee that the government had "a moral responsibility to aid the evacuees, many of whom are perfectly loyal American citizens." He expressed a "personal" wish that Japanese Americans, once removed from the West Coast, could have been let free to move or settle elsewhere, and he deplored the threat of violence that had made resettlement impossible.[154]

In view of these facts, it would be more accurate to say that Roosevelt's conduct, both in his initial refusal to issue a statement about Japanese Americans and then in the statement he did issue, stemmed from a combination of political expediency and ideological principle. Roosevelt had genuine humanitarian interests, but he was not fundamentally concerned with the needs of Japanese Americans and was indeed suspicious of them. When it was not in his political interest to do so, Roosevelt refused to help the internees or to make a public statement on their behalf. Roosevelt was ready to make exceptions and lend his support to groups or individual Japanese Americans when appropriate, as in the case of the Nisei college students whose loyalty had been previously approved by the army and guaranteed by California Governor Olson. Milton Eisenhower contends that Roosevelt's May 1942 letter to Olson on the importance of Americans being able to distinguish enemy aliens from loyal Americans of Japanese ancestry shows that he had gained a "human insight" into the plight of the internees which he lacked when he ordered the evacuation.[155] It is true that FDR signed the letter, but its importance is easily overstated. The words in the letter were not Roosevelt's own, and the contrast it made between "enemy aliens" and "supporters" implied that all Issei were *ipso facto* disloyal. More important, despite his statement of support, Roosevelt made no effort to provide the government aid to the transferring students that underlay Olson's letter.

Roosevelt's actions in regard to the Nisei volunteers follow the same pattern. Unlike Stimson and McCloy, who were concerned about the scapegoating of loyal Americans and the problem of morale in the camps, the

President was avowedly focused only on war propaganda. When Davis and Eisenhower suggested a volunteer Nisei battalion, Roosevelt was interested but cautious and would no doubt have scuttled the plan if the army had not been ready to accept responsibility for it. (FDR did not press the navy to enlist Nisei, and it remained closed to Japanese Americans until 1947.) While the army debated whether to create a Nisei unit and how to guarantee the loyalty of volunteers, Roosevelt made no effort to act on Davis's request (or any of the others) for a statement in support of internee loyalty. His February 1943 statement came only after the army agreed on a leave clearance program and Stimson had made his own public statement about Nisei loyalty. By then, there was little political risk for FDR in speaking on behalf of Japanese Americans. In fact, there were considerable potential benefits. American democracy would be enhanced in the eyes of world opinion, while liberal criticism of the internment and right-wing charges that the internees were being coddled would be simultaneously rebutted.

Ironically, the February 1 statement is still universally cited as Roosevelt's principal contribution to the internment. His supporters point to it as the President's expression of his true credo and a demonstration that the internment was not racially based. His critics also accept these words as FDR's own but interpret them either as proof of his blindness to the racial prejudice historically embedded in American life or as evidence of his hypocrisy in covering up the incarceration and dispossession of loyal Americans. In fact, Roosevelt approved verbatim a text written by others and had little to do with it. It is true that FDR, like other Presidents, often issued statements that had been prepared by aides but which he and others treated as his own. As the speechwriter and journalist Emmet John Hughes has stated, "The only politically meaningful fact is not what the aide writes but what the President says . . . Whatever he publicly declares is profoundly his."[156]

Nevertheless, an official statement, while definitive in setting policy, need not be taken as a transcendent picture of a President's views, especially when, as here, it conflicts with comments made in private. Even as he publicly praised Nisei Americans, Roosevelt privately placed the Nisei on a par with foreigners, and he continued to doubt their loyalty. Further, the form and purpose of an official statement is significant in determining its "authenticity." Despite its eloquent affirmation of equality, FDR's declaration of Japanese American loyalty was both limited in scope and specifically designed to process the Nisei more quickly into war production and military service. It did not affirm that most Nisei were loyal or explain why they were in camps. Nor, indeed, did it even mention the Issei and their loyalty. The proposition that Americanism was never a matter of race was clearly rhetorical rather than historical. To that extent, it was less a demonstration of Roosevelt's hypocrisy than an expedient means of justifying the shift in policy.

It is clear, in hindsight, that the President should have followed his critics' suggestion for speedy loyalty hearings. His refusal to even consider such hearings was costly in suffering and loss to the internees and cannot be justified in hindsight. It is easy to see, however, why Roosevelt did not do so. To have instituted hearings would have undercut the entire asserted basis for the military's actions on the West Coast during the spring of 1942, namely, that it was impossible to distinguish a loyal Japanese American from a disloyal one. It would thus have meant admitting that the evacuation the President had just approved and the army had carried out was wrong. It would have required immediately reversing the entire operation—an utterly unrealistic position to expect any leader to take.

Far more difficult to understand is Roosevelt's refusal during 1942 to respond to the repeated requests of leading Americans both inside and outside the government that he issue a public statement explaining the government's policy and reassuring the internees. He could have announced that he was evacuating Japanese Americans on an emergency basis and would inquire into their loyalty as soon as the immediate crisis passed. A speech defending the loyalty of Japanese Americans, or at least reminding Americans that the internees had not been convicted of any crime, would not have seriously embarrassed the administration or interfered with the evacuation. His failure to act is thus especially damning. Although the cost of his silence to Japanese Americans and the country generally is impossible to determine, it certainly inflicted psychological harm on its victims on top of the physical travails imposed on them. Roosevelt's eloquent, though careful, statement of February 1943, and the wide dissemination it received, may have repaired some of the damage caused by his earlier refusal to speak, but it does not excuse his neglectful and dismissive attitude during 1942.

The President's actions and policy decisions regarding Japanese Americans during 1942 reflect the same attitudes that led him to approve the original evacuation: an ideological predisposition to mistrust Japanese Americans, mixed with pragmatism gone awry. The President's anxiety about sabotage and his readiness to believe the worst of the local Japanese population fueled his repeated attempts to evacuate Japanese Americans in Hawaii, despite the impractical (if not utterly impossible) nature of the operation. FDR's casual pragmatism colored his ready acceptance of a policy of indefinite internment of the evacuees, for which no legal authority existed. His callous indifference to the basic rights and well-being of the victims is apparent in his refusal to safeguard evacuee property and his silence about the patriotic sacrifices of the Japanese Americans in the face of nationwide attacks on them. In addition, the President's failure to appoint a powerful property custodian and the abandonment of Hawaiian evacuation point up, in very different ways, the weakness of his decision-making process. Roosevelt's inability to plan or to foresee the consequences of events, coupled with his reliance on reluctant advisors to take initiative without presidential guidance, left him powerless to accomplish complicated tasks, whether positive or negative.

The pivotal element in the President's policy toward Japanese Americans was his handling of the legal and moral questions of Nisei citizenship raised by his signing of Executive Order 9066. He approved the internment of the Nisei, which violated the constitutional privileges of due process, equal protection of the laws, and *habeas corpus* ordinarily afforded citizens. At the same time, the President did not take the position that the Nisei were equivalent to the Issei—that they were "persons assimilated to the status" of enemy aliens, in the language of McCloy's memo on care of Japanese-American property. The administration did not endorse or acquiesce in the attempts of Senator Stewart and others to "legalize" detention of Nisei or strip them of citizenship, and it did not ban internee Nisei from voting. On the contrary, Roosevelt endorsed the relocation of college students for the (at least ostensible) reason that he wished to assure that Americans could differentiate between loyal citizens and enemy aliens. Moreover, he approved the formation of a Nisei combat unit, though he explicitly barred recruitment of German or Italian enemy aliens, and when he declared that Americanism was not a matter of race, his endorsement of Japanese-American loyalty was restricted to citizens.

Roosevelt clearly understood that Nisei were citizens. However, because of their racial difference, he did not regard them as "American" in some undefinable yet nonetheless real sense, but as "foreign." As a result, he treated their citizenship to some extent strategically, as it suited his purposes. For instance, in order to overcome legal objections to evacuation of Hawaiian Nisei, the President was ready to agree with Knox that Executive Order

9066 had erased all constitutional bars to their transportation and confinement on the U.S. mainland. Yet in the debate over custody of internee property, it served Roosevelt's goals in speeding evacuation to follow Morgenthau's dictum that Nisei citizenship prevented government action, and to allow the internees to be despoiled of their property. In the case of Nisei soldiers, where the balance between citizenship, morale, and security was the most subtle, FDR simultaneously proclaimed that military service was a right of citizenship and privately indicated that his endorsement of a special combat unit was based on its propaganda value rather than a recognition of Nisei citizenship rights. He imposed a special loyalty test on internee volunteers for military service.

In sum, the President attempted to decouple the Nisei's citizenship status, which he recognized as absolute, from their civil rights, which he considered contingent. Just as General Marshall advocated evacuation of those who were loyal but "burdensome" from Hawaii, Roosevelt was prepared to recognize Nisei civil rights only when they did not hinder his larger objectives of winning the war and maintaining public unity. Perhaps FDR failed to consider instituting immediate loyalty hearings for Nisei not only because such a process would have damaged the army's and government's defense of the evacuation but also because in his view individual loyalty was largely beside the point. The President's standard for recognition of citizenship rights was not loyalty but utility—a serious subversion of the meaning of citizenship.

The President's decisions regarding Japanese Americans during 1942 demonstrate that the internment, however unprecedented in its scope and effects, was not fundamentally inconsistent with his overall political philosophy and world view (a fact which may explain his relative lack of interest in the policy as it developed). Rather, Roosevelt's actions highlight the complex relationship between his conception of citizenship and his attitude toward racial difference. FDR did not hate Japanese Americans or seek to punish them. He asked that they be treated as reasonably and humanely as possible. However, he refused on racial grounds to accept them on equal terms as Americans—legally in the case of the Nisei and morally in the case of the Issei. This refusal blinded him to the invidious and undemocratic character of the repressive actions he and the government undertook, and led him to abdicate responsibility for the treatment of the internees. FDR's failure to provide leadership would become increasingly pivotal during 1943 and 1944 as the administration struggled over how to dismantle the internment.

COVERING A RETREAT

THE PRESIDENT'S FEBRUARY 1943 announcement marked a turning point in the trajectory of the internment. Up to that time, the government's central concern had been the removal and control of Japanese Americans and the establishment of camps with sufficient facilities to meet their basic needs. The return of the mass of internees to the larger society was spoken of, if at all, as a distant (and probably postwar) phenomenon. Once the President approved the employment of "loyal" Nisei in the military and defense industries, the method and timing of releasing the internees became the focus of government attention.

The matter of release caught administration leaders on the horns of a dilemma. On the one hand, they hoped to wind up the internment and solve the "Japanese problem" by closing the camps and fostering the speedy mass resettlement of internees in small groups throughout the country. The camps wasted scarce manpower and military resources and left the United States open to enemy propaganda. In addition, the camp experience had a scarring effect on Japanese Americans. The internees' anger and frustration at their unjust treatment broke out in several protests and work strikes during 1942, culminating in the Manzanar Riot. On December 7, 1942, the arrest of a popular internee at Manzanar who had accused Caucasian kitchen staff members of theft led to a mass demonstration. When a mob marched on the camp stockade, guards dispersed it with bullets and tear gas, killing two people and wounding several others. As a result of this unrest, several administration advisors, notably Dillon Myer, warned that the continued confinement of the internees in camps would lead to another "Indian problem" in the form of chronic alienation and welfare dependency.[1]

The internment was also vulnerable on constitutional grounds. In early 1943, the U.S. Supreme Court agreed to hear a challenge to the army's race-based registration and curfew restrictions on Japanese Americans, while legal challenges to the evacuation made their way in the lower courts. Once the army had conceded that it was possible to separate loyal from disloyal internees, continued incarceration of loyal Japanese Americans was hard to justify.

On the other hand, the administration believed it could not simply release internees, much less permit them to return to their homes on the West Coast. The evacuation had created facts on the ground. The internees had been stripped of their jobs and, in many cases, their land. The government had invested in the creation of an extensive (and expensive) network of camps and had organized farms for the internees to grow essential food supplies. Few internees had resources to support themselves without government help, and the War Relocation Authority faced the daunting task of finding jobs for tens of thousands of people who were willing to be re-settled, plus arranging transportation and housing for them amid wartime shortages.

Even more important, from the White House point of view, the release of internees presented legal and political problems. General DeWitt, who remained as Western Defense Commander until late 1943, continued to insist that Japanese Americans posed a significant danger to security, and he refused to abandon or alter his exclusion order. The West Coast economic interests and nativist groups that had achieved their longtime aim of removing Japanese Americans, and had profited from their absence, strenuously objected to allowing the internees to return or do business in their states, and they exerted enormous pressure on the military and on political leaders to maintain exclusion. Even outside the West Coast, mass resettlement was fraught with difficulties. By evacuating and interning West Coast Japanese Americans, the government had impressed deeply on the public mind that they were disloyal and a menace to national security. Neither Roosevelt nor his advisors could convincingly explain how Japanese Americans who were so dangerous that they had had to be rounded up and confined had now become completely harmless and loyal—except, of course, on the West Coast, where they remained excluded. The President's long refusal to issue a statement praising Japanese-American loyalty bore bitter fruit. Anti-Japanese-American newspapers throughout the country filled the vacuum of official silence with invented stories of internee treachery and luxurious conditions in the camps. Congressmen and West Coast state legislators continued to exploit popular hostility toward Japanese Americans by moving to strip them of citizenship rights.

Furthermore, any moves toward opening the camps or ending West Coast exclusion threatened to undermine the legal basis for continued dispersion of internees throughout the country. The White House and the War Department feared that an adverse Supreme Court ruling in the evacuation cases would discredit the government in the middle of a war. Worse, they took for granted that if the Court declared Executive Order 9066 unconstitutional, the government's authority to bring about the controlled resettlement of Japanese Americans outside the West Coast would end. Chaos would quickly result as floods of internees left the camps and returned to the West Coast, straining overtaxed housing and welfare resources and inviting violent opposition from the hostile white population.

The pressure of this dilemma sparked conflict within the administration and between the administration and Congress during 1943. The President and the War Department moved to defend the internment against pressure from the WRA and liberals inside the White House to speed up resettlement and close the camps, even as they opposed efforts by anti-Japanese-American forces in the government and on the West Coast to forestall the release of any internees and permanently bar their return. Roosevelt's failure to resolve the divisions within the administration over the treatment of Japanese Americans resulted in the evolution of a policy that combined the conditional release of selected internees with harsh and arbitrary action against the entire group.

In spring 1943 the WRA began implementing the "leave clearance" program it had designed to make possible the exit of Japanese Americans from the camps. The leave process was slow, cumbersome, and tailored less to meeting security needs than to deflecting popular hostility and suspicion toward Japanese Americans. In order to determine their eligibility for "leave clearance," all internees aged 17 and over were given "loyalty" examinations by the Joint Board which the army had originally established to screen Nisei combat volunteers. An internee's loyalty could be established on the basis of either outside endorsements (preferably from Caucasians) or a positive score on the "loyalty questionnaire" that the WRA required internees to complete. Points were given or withheld based on a constantly shifting list of such arbitrary and irrelevant factors as whether the individual had bank accounts in Japan. This process took up to several months. If found loyal, an internee (at first only Nisei, later Issei as well) could apply for a "leave permit" to resettle in areas east of the Rocky Mountains. In order to obtain a leave permit, the internee had to obtain an offer of employment or education from a sponsor.

The political nature of the process was underlined by the additional requirement that the sponsor's community not oppose the internee's presence. Once resettled, the internees were subject to FBI supervision and had to report regularly to local WRA offices. The release of citizens from confinement on probationary leaves that could be revoked at any time was clearly unconstitutional (as Dillon Myer privately admitted). The Justice Department, citing the doubtful legality of the process, refused WRA requests to help return paroled internees whose leaves had expired.[2]

The WRA's loyalty process was tragically flawed and led to great misery. The loyalty questionnaire was sprung suddenly on internees, many of whom received no advice or guidance on why they were required to complete the forms or how the information they contained would be used. The requirement that all adults fill out the forms also caused resentment. Many internees, notably elderly Issei, were not permitted to leave the camps or were unwilling to resettle outside in the face of white hostility and uncertain economic prospects. They objected to a procedure they feared was designed to push them out of the camps and cast them adrift.

Moreover, the text of the questionnaire had been drafted hastily, with no consideration of its implications, and it contained intrusive, unclear, and irrelevant questions. The two questions the government considered most important were particularly confusing and damaging. Question 27, which asked "Are you willing to serve in the Armed Forces of the United States on combat duty, wherever ordered?" (or, in the case of women, the Women's Army Corps), was widely interpreted as a trick to get internees to volunteer for military service. Even more troubling was question 28, which asked the internees to "swear unqualified allegiance to the United States of America . . . and foreswear any form of allegiance or obedience to the Japanese emperor, or any other foreign government, power, or organization." The Nisei, particularly those interested in volunteering for the army, naturally resented having to swear a loyalty oath to the country that had imprisoned them, and they worried that the provision asking them to "foreswear" allegiance to the Japanese emperor meant admitting that they had ever had such allegiance. For the Issei, who were barred from American citizenship, question 28 required them to renounce the only citizenship they had, thus violating international law, and surrender their only protection in case of deportation (a not inconsiderable possibility, given the hostility against them). In response to complaints, the WRA subsequently changed the text of the question to ask Issei if they would "abide" by the laws of the United States. Conditional responses were not permitted. These two questions and the proper response to them provoked considerable soul-searching among the internees. Fifty years later, Nisei communities remained divided by tension between those who answered yes and those who answered no on the loyalty questionnaire.

Despite these obstacles, 85–90 percent of the internees answered yes to questions 27 and 28. These "loyal" internees then either applied for a leave permit to resettle east of the Rockies and waited weeks or months for their release to be processed, or they rejected resettlement and remained in camp. For various reasons—ignorance, confusion, fear of abandonment, protest, loyalty to Japan, or family / community pressure—about 10–15 percent of the internees answered no or qualified their answers to questions 27 and 28. These internees, dubbed "no-no boys," were certified as "disloyal" and barred from release.

The problem of dealing with the no-no boys led to a tug-of-war over policy between the War Department, the WRA, and members of Congress. The War Department was distressed by the number of no-no responses, especially among draft age Nisei men, and saw the leave clearance program as a way to isolate and neutralize the disloyal internees. The army had long been interested in a segregation policy. As early as May 1942 Kenneth Ringle (the former opponent of internment) had proposed to both General DeWitt and the WRA that the Kibei who did not declare their loyalty to the United States be segregated, along with their families, from other internees. By neutralizing the Kibei (whom he considered the most disloyal group of American citizens because they had been educated in Japan), Ringle hoped to lessen public hostility against the other Nisei and foster their release.[3] The WRA immediately opposed the idea. WRA leaders considered Ringle's proposal administratively unfeasible, and they objected to determining loyalty solely on the basis of such invidious categorization.

As if to confirm the WRA's fears, General DeWitt then seized on the Ringle proposal and took it as his own, adding a recommendation for separating out all Issei as well. DeWitt had no interest in aiding resettlement of loyal Japanese Americans or reaffirming their loyalty. Rather, he argued to Marshall and Stimson that all Kibei were *ipso facto* loyal to Japan and should be interned for the duration of the war, then stripped of their citizenship and deported to Japan.[4] McCloy expressed his assent to segregation, but he warned DeWitt that the question was for the WRA to decide, not the War Department.

The pressure for segregation increased as a result of the December 7, 1942, uprising at Manzanar, which heightened War Department fears of "troublemakers." On December 17 DeWitt submitted a detailed plan for the arrest of some 5,600 "undesirable" internees, including those who had been arrested by WRA security guards in camp and those who had requested repatriation to Japan, and their removal to a separate high security camp. Stimson was clearly impressed by DeWitt's proposal, and on December 30 (as he prepared to accept Nisei volunteers into the army), he sent it on to Dillon Myer. Myer firmly opposed DeWitt's scheme as needlessly punitive. Although the WRA director established a special "holding center" at Leupp, Arizona, where he placed the "troublemakers" arrested at Manzanar, he saw no need for segregation.

West Coast elected officials, taking advantage of sensational newspaper stories of the Manzanar Riot, used the army's proposal for segregation as a club to beat the WRA and forestall any resettlement of internees. In January 1943 Senator Mon Wallgren of Washington—a leading instigator of the original evacuation—introduced a bill in Congress to abolish the WRA and institute military control of Japanese Americans. Shortly afterward, the Senate Military Affairs Subcommittee, chaired by Kentucky Senator Albert B. "Happy" Chandler, opened a series of hearings designed to investigate widespread charges that the WRA was "coddling" the internees. Chandler told reporters he favored segregation of "disloyal" individuals so that loyal ones could be resettled into the army and defense industries, but the hearings highlighted the actions of the "disloyal" and the case for segregation. McCloy testified in favor of separating loyal and disloyal evacuees, as did officials of the Japanese American Citizens League, who hoped segregation would speed resettlement of loyal Nisei.[5]

In March 1943 the dispute between the WRA and the army came to a head. Myer wrote Stimson warning that the continued operation of the camps was causing a deterioration of internee loyalty and morale. He outlined three possible future scenarios for the future. Plan A was to continue existing leave procedures, which Myer complained were too slow and unjust. Plan B involved closing the camps, extending the military draft to the internees, and immediately reopening the West Coast to all those not found disloyal by the Joint Board. Myer felt this course was the best way to encourage Japanese-American loyalty, although he recognized that it would provoke great conflict with hostile whites on the West Coast and hinder the WRA's aim of resettlement of Japanese Americans throughout the country. Plan C (which Myer considered a fair compromise) provided for keeping the West Coast restricted but gradually allowing selected categories of Nisei to return, while closing the camps and ending all other restrictions.[6] Myer insisted that segregation was not the answer to the loyalty problem. As he told McCloy, "Segregation of the disloyal without offering compensatory benefits to the loyal would result in something close to disaster."[7] Rather, he pressed for massive relocation of loyal internees and the rapid closing of the camps.

Myer's proposals put the War Department in a delicate position. How could exclusion be justified once internees were found loyal? At the same time, Stimson and McCloy were well aware that both the Western Defense Command and West Coast public opinion strongly opposed lifting exclusion. Indeed, in April 1943 DeWitt, defying both the War Department and the President, told a House Subcommittee that Japanese Americans were dangerous and that there was no way to establish individual loyalty. He therefore absolutely opposed the return of any internees, whether Issei or Nisei, to the West Coast. After the hearings, in a widely publicized (although apparently off the record) remark to reporters, DeWitt added, "A Jap's a Jap."[8] McCloy did not feel that the War Department could overrule the judgment of the commanding general on a matter of military security.[9]

Beyond the problem of public opposition to closing the camps, Stimson and McCloy did not want to approve any policy that would weaken the legal basis for West Coast exclusion, especially after the Supreme Court agreed in late March 1943 to hear *Hirabayashi v. United States* and *Yasui v. United States*. In early 1942 Gordon Hirabayashi, a Nisei student at the University of Washington, declined to register for evacuation as a Japanese American under Executive Order 9066, claiming it violated his rights as an American citizen. Meanwhile, Minoru Yasui, a young lawyer from Oregon, protested the special curfew imposed on Japanese Americans by volunteering to be arrested as a test case. In the lower courts, Hirabayashi was found guilty of violating the laws enforcing Executive Order 9066. The judge in the Yasui case found the curfew law unconstitutional as applied to citizens but ruled that Yasui had forfeited his citizenship through his prewar employment in the Japanese consulate in Chicago. The Supreme Court agreed to decide whether Executive Order 9066 was an unconstitutional assertion of power by the federal government.

Although these cases did not explicitly address the constitutionality of the evacuation, they called into question the army's power to single out Japanese Americans for separate treatment, which formed the basis of the internment. The War Department placed enormous importance on winning these cases. The prestige of the army and the government were at stake. In addition, the War Department feared that if the orders were found unconstitutional, the government would be forced to open the camps immediately, and chaos would ensue. The War Department was so intent on prevailing in court that McCloy, who was a lawyer himself, engaged in egregious manipulation of evidence. Government lawyers, in order to present the best possible case for evacuation, had taken the position in lower court hearings that the army had been forced to act because it did not have sufficient time in an emergency situation to distinguish loyal Japanese Americans from disloyal. This post-hoc defense was specious—the army did not attempt to set up loyalty hearings and in fact rejected any such idea at the time of evacuation—but it allowed the government to rationalize its imposition of loyalty hearings and resettlement on the grounds that it now had time to make such determinations. However, in April 1943 General DeWitt sent McCloy a copy of the *Final Report* he had prepared on the evacuation, which stated flatly that he had ordered racially based evacuation because it was impossible to distinguish loyal from disloyal Japanese Americans and that lack of time for hearings had not been a factor in his decision. McCloy immediately ordered all copies of the report confiscated and destroyed, and he forced DeWitt to write a revised version adopting the more defensible position. McCloy refused the request of Justice Department lawyers for a copy of the *Final Report*, even though those lawyers were responsible for arguing the case before the Court, since he considered the Justice Department insufficiently committed to the defense of the policy. However, he arranged for the California attorney general's office, which was anxious to bolster the case for evacuation, to receive a copy of the report in order to draft an *amicus curiae* brief based on its contents.[10]

For two months Stimson did not reply to Myer's letter suggesting the end of exclusion. On May 10, 1943 (the same day that the *Hirabayashi* case was argued in the Supreme Court), the secretary of war sent the WRA director a letter insisting that the institution of a policy of segregation, which he contended the War Department had long recommended, must precede any change of policy and that the army would not consider removing the restrictions on the West Coast or extending selective service to internees until it was carried out. Stimson agreed that internee morale and loyalty were deteriorating, but he asserted that the principal cause was a pro-Japan minority group that the WRA had allowed to seize control in the camps and to use intimidation and violence to discourage cooperation. Stimson refused to address the question of opening the camps, which he claimed disingenuously was not under his jurisdiction, except to argue that once the disloyal had been put under close confinement, the resettlement process would be considerably simplified.[11]

Stimson's letter was extremely clever and politically astute. By fixing on segregation, he was able to put Myer, who had already been bloodied by the Chandler committee hearings, on the defensive and to divert attention from the continuing exclusion of concededly loyal internees. Similarly, by holding the end of exclusion hostage to the segregation of disloyal internees, he was able both to override Myer's objections to the plan and postpone consideration of any changes in policy.

Stimson's intervention was decisive, not only because the army held the key to opening the West Coast but because the support of the military was patently a political necessity for the beleaguered WRA. Infuriated by the War Department's pressure tactics, Myer retorted bitterly that segregation without relocation of the loyal would do nothing to improve evacuee morale and that if segregation had been as easy and desirable as Stimson suggested, the army could have attended to it at the time of the original evacuation or in the assembly centers.[12] Nevertheless, he gave in and announced that the WRA would begin separating out disloyal internees. Myer selected the Tule Lake camp as the segregation center. Some 12,000 "disloyals" were transferred over the following months.[13] These "segregees" were treated as enemies by the Tule Lake administration, and there were numerous cases of beatings of inmates by guards. The overcrowded and restrictive conditions, as well as the conflict between internee factions, turned Tule Lake into a tense and forbidding place.

Stimson's refusal to consider ending West Coast exclusion until after segregation was accomplished stagnated the relocation effort. On the one hand, mass resettlement was impossible to achieve through the cumbersome leave process. On the other hand, in spite of Stimson's statement that the War Department had no objection to the WRA's opening the camps and releasing internees outside the excluded areas, unconditional release was plainly impossible as long as the army's exclusion stigmatized Japanese Americans nationwide. The fact that Japanese Americans remained barred from the West Coast indicated to most Americans that they were somehow untrustworthy. Most communities felt that Japanese Americans were the government's problem and not theirs. As Myer explained to reporters, if the government closed the camps and set all loyal internees free outside the West Coast, it would add to the internees' problems. "It is not fair to them. The country doesn't know them well enough. It wouldn't be accepted generally." He added condescendingly that if the camps were opened, groups of internees would end up wandering around looking for jobs and getting into trouble with the police.[14]

Even as Stimson and Myer debated ending exclusion, President Roosevelt became involved in defending the internment status quo against both liberal and conservative critics. The most significant liberal thrust came from Secretary of the Interior Harold Ickes. Ickes had strong racial biases against Japan—he commented privately that he had no use at all for the Japanese as a race.[15] However, he silently deplored the evacuation and internment as an unnecessary and cruel policy. Ickes pushed vainly for control of the WRA in early 1942 in order to help the internees, and he campaigned against evacuation in Hawaii, over which the Interior Department had formal authority. During fall 1942 Ickes became interested in hiring resettled internee workers for his Maryland farm, and he attempted without success to persuade the

President to make a public statement endorsing the use of Japanese-American labor.

Ickes grew increasingly outraged during early 1943 when he experienced a several-month delay in obtaining the release of internees he had requested, and he embarked on further efforts to push the President to expedite the resettlement process. If a Cabinet secretary had such troubles obtaining internee labor, he reasoned, ordinary people must find it impossible, and in the meantime the government was making enemies out of loyal citizens by continuing to confine them. In January 1943 Ickes met with Attorney General Biddle to discuss ways to persuade the President to facilitate resettlement.[16] Ickes then brought up the problem of farm labor shortages at a Cabinet meeting in late February, despite FDR's evident lack of interest:

> I had gone to Cabinet determined to make the President listen to me on farm labor . . . As usual, the President tried to kiss the thing off but I hung on. I came back at him two or three times and although at first he was annoyed, I finally forced the Cabinet to consider what most of us regard as a very serious situation . . . I referred to the Japanese interned in internment camps, who are available, saying we would be willing to take some Japanese but the President ought to issue a proclamation to the country saying it was in the interest of the country to employ the Japanese as farm labor. It would help the Japanese too.[17]

When Roosevelt failed to acknowledge Ickes's concerns or to issue any proclamation, the secretary of the interior continued to pester him. Ickes and Biddle met with the President after another Cabinet meeting in mid-March. They warned Roosevelt that the incarceration of Japanese Americans was having a negative effect on their loyalty, and the internees' state of mind was rapidly deteriorating. Ickes urged the President once more to make a public statement asking employers to hire loyal Japanese Americans. Roosevelt again failed to make any such statement.[18]

In April 1943 Ickes wrote the President a formal letter to call for action. Ickes reported that he had learned that the situation in the camps was bad and getting rapidly worse, and he added that even the minimum plans that had been adopted to deal with the evacuees had not been carried out. As a result of their continued incarceration, Ickes continued, the "Native-born Japanese" who had at first accepted the evacuation were turning into angry prisoners. Striking at the heart of Roosevelt's attitude toward Japanese Americans, Ickes warned the President, "I do not think that we can disregard, as of no official concern, the unnecessary creating of a hostile group right in our own territory."[19] The administration could and must do better.

The President paid little visible attention to Ickes's comments or to his letter, which he may have regarded as one of the splenetic secretary's frequent attacks on his administration colleagues. Instead, FDR routinely sent the letter on to Milton Eisenhower for reply, forgetting that Eisenhower had resigned from the WRA ten months before and that his successor was also pushing for resettlement. Eisenhower enclosed a draft reply letter, but he also took the opportunity to write the President that he shared Ickes's concerns about bitterness among the internees, particularly the Nisei, which he felt was understandable in response to their situation: "Persons in this group find themselves living in a situation for which their public school and democratic teachings have not prepared them. It is hard for them to escape a conviction that their plight is due more to racial discrimination, economic motivations and wartime prejudices than to any real necessity from the military point of view for evacuation from the West Coast."[20]

Eisenhower graphically described the plight of the internees and the causes of their bitterness—they had been stripped of their jobs and property, imprisoned in barren camps surrounded by barbed wire and armed sentries, denied equal work opportunities, and victimized by anti-Japanese legislation and public opinion. He pointedly called Roosevelt's attention to General DeWitt's racist public pronouncements: "Some of the military leaders responsible for evacuation were motivated by a conviction that all persons of Japanese blood in this country cannot be trusted."[21] He urged the President to consult with Dillon Myer over ways to foster the reabsorption of "loyal Japanese Americans" into American life, a process which he believed would have to occur before the war ended.

Roosevelt did not respond directly to Eisenhower, but he signed without change the reply Eisenhower had drafted to Ickes's letter. While Eisenhower toned down this response considerably from his own letter to the President, it nonetheless expressed a great deal of compassion and sensitivity to the problems of Japanese Americans. Thus, Roosevelt's reply to Ickes stated that he shared Ickes's "regret" that military necessity had forced "the burdens of evacuation and detention" on Japanese Americans and he recognized that "some measure of bitterness is the inevitable consequence of a program

involving direct loss of property and detention on grounds which the evacuees consider to be racial discrimination." However, the letter continued, his
approval of the opening of military service and war industries to loyal citizens of Japanese ancestry proved that there was no discrimination involved.
Since "normal American life" was impossible under such "detention," the
best hope for the future lay in encouraging the relocation of Japanese Americans throughout the country as much as possible. He praised Ickes's own
example in hiring "evacuee" laborers.[22] The letter to Ickes remained private,
however, and the President did not make any statement of the kind Ickes had
urged.

During this same period, Roosevelt faced challenges to the internment by
two unofficial advisors. One was the First Lady. Eleanor Roosevelt did not
directly challenge the government's policy during 1942. She may have
believed there was some foundation for the charges of fifth-column activity
by Japanese Americans. She nonetheless deplored the fact that, as she told a
friend, "innocent people suffer for a few guilty ones,"[23] and she made numerous behind-the-scenes efforts to assist the internees: she approved the transfer of money from the special projects fund that she maintained with the
American Friends Service Committee to pay for emergency programs during evacuation; she corresponded with internees and outside sympathizers;
she planned a visit to the camps (until she was advised by the War Department to forego such a visit); she promoted the formation of the National
Japanese American Student Relocation Council to help Nisei students transfer to colleges outside the West Coast and continue their education; she sent
FDR a memo, which he ignored, enclosing a proposal for government loans
to resettled internees to purchase land; and she met with Dillon Myer to discuss conditions in the camps and remained in frequent contact with him
thereafter.[24]

In March 1943 Eleanor Roosevelt learned from Congressman John Tolan
that no acts of sabotage or espionage had been committed by Japanese
Americans, as she had previously been led to believe. She then threw herself
into championing the cause of resettlement with FDR. In particular, Mrs.
Roosevelt asked FDR for permission to inspect one of the camps, which he
granted, and she arranged for him to meet with Hung Wai Chung, a Chinese
Hawaiian who briefed the President on the condition of Japanese Hawaiians
and the problems of Hawaiian Nisei soldiers. She also pleaded with her
husband to show his trust in Japanese Americans by bringing an internee

family to live in the White House. That request he declined, telling her that the Secret Service would never allow it.[25] On April 22, 1943, with no advance notice or security, the First Lady visited the Gila River camp. By her presence and her interest, she made clear to the inmates her sympathy for their plight. Following the visit, she devoted her syndicated daily newspaper column to praising the efforts of the internees to grow their own food, ameliorate the harsh desert climate and the ugliness of the hastily constructed camps, and police and educate themselves. In an interview published in the *Los Angeles Times* a few days later, Eleanor Roosevelt publicly supported resettlement. Emphasizing the importance of immediate release of the Nisei, she stated that "the sooner we get the young Japanese out of the camps the better. Otherwise if we don't look out we will create another Indian problem. I think it is bad to institutionalize anybody." She stated that "of course, the citizen Japanese in the camps should be checked carefully" before release, but she made clear that the internment should end as soon as possible.[26]

Meanwhile, on April 15, 1943, the civil liberties lawyer Morris L. Ernst, a Roosevelt crony who delighted in sending FDR memos of political news and gossip he called "tidbits," wrote the President to apprise him of the fact that the U.S. Supreme Court was about to take up the *Hirabayashi* case.[27] Ernst had written earlier that year to Chief Justice Harlan Stone, proposing that a joint Anglo-American statement on protection of civil liberties be drafted.[28] Stone had replied that as a member of the court he could not take an active part in any political statement, and he was uncertain how any document about the government's treatment of civil liberties could properly address "the internment of our Japanese citizens."[29] Ernst interpreted the chief justice's comments as a sign of opposition to the internment. Without mentioning the letter, he warned FDR that he was certain that the Court would overturn Executive Order 9066, at least in regard to the Nisei. He therefore suggested that Roosevelt prepare a new program for "the day when the Supreme Court declares unconstitutional—as it will and should—our treatment of Japanese citizens."[30]

Ernst recommended that Roosevelt order the military to separate "citizen and non-citizen Japs" before the Court's ruling, in order to avoid administrative chaos afterward. Ernst offered to secure "fortuitous evidence" in the form of a letter from Stone stating the Court's probable ruling (presumably the letter he had already received from the chief justice) in order to help Roosevelt persuade the army to act.[31] Ernst volunteered to help craft a new executive order, and he proposed that FDR alert the Farm Security Administration to be prepared to use current funds to finance those citizens "now in concentration camps" who were farmers, in order to obtain or recover land.

The President quickly dictated a confidential reply to Ernst, agreeing that he should work on a new program designed to deal with the "Japanese citizens": FDR did not specify the form the new program should take or respond to any of Ernst's specific proposals for action. Instead, his closing sentence indicated that he meant to continue the internment irrespective of the Supreme Court's decision: "I hate the thought of martial law—but that, of course, would solve the problem—a limited, local martial law which could be made to stick anywhere we wanted."[32] Roosevelt's terse request that Ernst prepare a declaration of martial law in order to circumvent an adverse Court ruling demonstrates that, in spite of his previous statement praising internee loyalty, the President had not fundamentally altered either his private views of Japanese Americans or his political assessment of their situation. His readiness to suggest martial law indicates that, like General DeWitt, he continued to believe that all internees, including Nisei, posed a threat to security which overshadowed their civil rights. Roosevelt's proposal for "limited local martial law," though clearly intended as a pragmatic solution to avert full-scale military rule, would have represented a stunning assertion of arbitrary and patently extraconstitutional power had it ever been implemented. As the President must have known, martial law is the emergency absence of all civil power. A "limited local martial law" is thus a contradiction in terms.

It is instructive to compare Roosevelt's response to Ernst with that to Ickes and Eisenhower. Although Ernst briefly mentioned the wrongness of applying Executive Order 9066 to citizens, he did not complain or chastise the President about the situation of the internees. Rather, he confidentially offered practical help with specific tasks to fix the situation. He did not challenge the continued incarceration of the Issei or plan aid for them. Roosevelt replied in kind, directly and succinctly. Unlike Ickes, Ernst the political operator did not require an official letter expressing regrets over the policy. Indeed, the President's mind was so fixed on practical details that he mistook or ignored Ernst's stated opposition to the internment in accepting his help.

On June 21, 1943, the Supreme Court announced its ruling in *Hirabayashi v. United States*. Despite Ernst's prediction, Chief Justice Stone's opinion unanimously upheld the initial race-based curfew and evacuation order as a wartime emergency measure. Although nativist groups hailed the decision as confirmation of their efforts to remove the "dangerous" Japanese Americans, the ruling did not attract a great deal of public attention. The Court's opinion contained language which offered some support for the government's evacuation, but the administration understood that the West Coast exclusion order and the internment had still not survived judicial scrutiny. Indeed, Justice Frank Murphy's concurrence (originally drafted as a dissent) stated that the army had gone "to the very brink of Constitutional power" with the curfew, a comment which suggested that the government would have an even harder task justifying itself in case of a direct attack on the internment.[33]

Even as the government defended the internment policy against those who wanted to end it, Roosevelt moved to contain the growing political attacks on the WRA for being too "soft" on Japanese Americans. These charges varied in their source and motivation. Some of these attacks came from West Coast nativist and commercial pressure groups and their elected representatives or from Republicans eager to discredit the New Deal administration, including Wyoming Senator Edward V. Robertson, who alleged that internees at Heart Mountain were living in luxurious conditions.[34] However, a large fraction of these attacks were launched by opportunistic politicians and newspaper editors of varying regions and political tendencies looking for popular issues to raise. In April, following the end of his committee's hearings on the WRA, Senator "Happy" Chandler went on a series of "investigations" of the camps. While the senator ceased his accusations that the WRA was "coddling" the internees after his lightning visits (he could have seen little evidence of luxury in the six camps he visited, or much of anything else—he spent a total of only six hours in them), he began work on an anti-WRA, pro-segregation resolution.

Soon after, following a raid of the Japanese American Citizens League's Washington office, a subcommittee of the House Un-American Activities Committee (the Dies committee), known for its politically conservative members and for its headline-grabbing investigations of subversion, began its own slanted "investigation" into the "collusion" between the WRA and the JACL.[35] During summer 1943, the committee held a series of hearings, which were closely covered in the Hearst press and other tabloids. In the course of these hearings, anti-WRA witnesses aired unfounded and absurd charges that the agency had collaborated with pro-Axis groups, that disloyal internees had been released, and that missing dynamite at government projects had been stolen by internee saboteurs at the Poston camp in order to blow up Arizona's Parker Dam.[36] Edwin Best and Harold Townshend, two disgruntled ex-WRA employees, testified at length regarding laxness and luxurious conditions in the camps, where they alleged the internees had abundant stores of whiskey and prime beef.[37] Townshend charged that the Poston camp was overrun by pro-Japanese mobs who stole supplies and hid them in the desert for the use of Japanese paratroopers and that within the camp "a Japanese unit of 1,000 officers and men openly train in tactical problems." Townshend stated that "camp inmates" admitted to him that the unit "was organized at Terminal Island to fight with invading Japanese formations."[38]

Dillon Myer's point-by-point rebuttal revealed that Townshend's charges were completely baseless and fantastic. (Myer testified before the Dies Committee that Townshend's testimony contained 41 separate errors and distortions, whereupon a committee member objected that there were in fact only 37!) However, the committee refused to issue a retraction and the sensational charges remained current in the public mind. A Dies subcommittee also held a set of hearings in Los Angeles that offered an opportunity for nativist and church groups such as the American Legion to air race-based hostility toward the "Japs" and clamor for the permanent exclusion of Japanese Americans from the state. Subcommittee Chair John Costello, a conservative Los Angeles congressman who had been an early advocate of evacuation, took advantage of the surroundings to whip up hysteria against resettlement, stating that Japanese Americans were not safe as unrestricted residents anywhere in the nation. California Governor Earl Warren, who had stated at a governor's conference shortly before that "we don't propose to have the Japs back in California during this war if there is any lawful means of preventing it,"[39] told the committee, "If the Japs are released no one will be able to tell a saboteur from any other Jap." He urged that strict detention and exclusion of Japanese Americans be maintained in order to avoid "an American Pearl Harbor."[40] Committee member J. Parnell Thomas, a New Jersey Republican, issued a press release repeating Townshend's charge that the Japanese army had had an armed combat battalion in the city's Terminal Island before the war.[41] The continuing hostile testimony from the Dies committee hearings and the public attention they attracted kept Myer and the WRA on the defensive during spring 1943 and caused serious problems in arranging any constructive programs for the internees. For example, Aubrey

Williams, Director of the National Youth administration (NYA) and a prominent administration liberal, was forced to pull out of a planned joint NYA-WRA youth training program in order to preserve the NYA from being gutted by congressional critics.[42]

Roosevelt treated the congressional committee charges of "coddling" as political attacks on the administration and moved quickly to affirm his support for the WRA. In April 1943 FDR asked Eleanor Roosevelt, who was accompanying him to a meeting on the border with the president of Mexico, to visit one of the camps on her return trip and report to him on conditions there, thus prompting her visit to Gila River. In interviews afterward, the First Lady described the conditions in the camps as not indecent but "certainly not luxurious," and she noted, "I wouldn't like to live that way." Her comments were widely reported and effectively rebutted the "coddling" charges.[43] At Eleanor Roosevelt's behest, on May 23, 1943, the President invited Myer to lunch—the only time FDR ever met with the WRA director—and they informally discussed the agency's policies. Myer was unwilling to press Roosevelt to rescind the exclusion order. Instead, he focused on his political difficulties with Congress. "The President and I had an excellent discussion about [our] problems. When I told the President about the 'Happy' Chandler Committee and the fact that they were doing things not helpful, he said 'I think I can help you with this.'"[44] According to Myer, Roosevelt followed through on his promise of support by calling on Senator Joseph O'Mahoney of Wyoming to intervene with Chandler and tone down the Chandler committee report.

Administration allies also helped kill the Wallgren bill to abolish the WRA and institute military control of the camps before it got to the Senate floor.[45] The War Department, closing ranks behind Myer, issued a public statement praising the WRA and announcing that it had no interest in taking over the camps. In early May, McCloy told a California audience that "there is a place in California and elsewhere for loyal Japanese."[46] When a banker in Oregon wrote the secretary of war to suggest deporting all Japanese Americans, Stimson responded by praising Japanese-American soldiers and added that such a move "would not only be inappropriate but contrary to our experience and traditions as a nation."[47] In the wake of warnings by Arizona Governor Sidney Osborn and Congressman Carl Hayden that the release of internees in Arizona would lead to bloodshed, the War Department, acting "on President Roosevelt's authority," sent U.S. Army Inspector General Virgil Peterson to tour the area and plead for tolerance.[48]

On July 6, 1943, Senate Resolution 166, which embodied the toned-down Chandler committee recommendations, was introduced by the liberal California Senator Sheridan Downey and unanimously adopted. It "requested" the President to order the WRA to segregate disloyal persons and persons of questionable loyalty from the assuredly loyal. It also requested that "an appropriate agency of the government" (that is, not the WRA) issue an authoritative statement on conditions in the relocation centers and plans for the future operation of the centers and "the movement of persons of Japanese ancestry interned therein."[49] Downey's resolution was clearly an administration "set-up," at least in part. Although it supported segregation, it avoided attacking the WRA by name and merely "requested" that the President take action. The provision for a report on resettlement was a ploy to put pressure on the administration to speed up the closing of the camps. The WRA nevertheless stood condemned by implication, and Myer was left on shaky political ground. Francis Biddle told his staff that Myer would undoubtedly have to be sacrificed to mollify congressional pressure, and he proposed that, for the sake of public relations, Myer be replaced by a military figure.[50] Once again demonstrating his support for Myer, Roosevelt sent the congressional resolution on to the WRA director for his advice. Myer replied that the segregation policy had already begun, so that the first recommendation could be ignored, and that he enthusiastically approved the making of an "independent" report. Downey arranged with his former Senate colleague James Byrnes, now director of the Office of War Mobilization (OWM), McCloy, and White House Press Secretary Steve Early for the preparation of an immediate preliminary response.[51] An official statement (originally described as a presidential announcement) was hurriedly drafted by the WRA and the War Department and issued in Byrnes's name on July 17.

Although ostensibly responding to Senate Resolution 166, the Byrnes statement concentrated on rebutting the Dies committee's sensational charges about luxurious and disorderly conditions in the camps, and it strongly supported the WRA. It stated that the evacuation had been a "precautionary measure [which] carried no implication of individual disloyalty" and explained that the leave procedures and segregation policy had been formulated by the WRA in cooperation with the War Department in order to assure that only loyal evacuees were released. In its description of the camps, it noted that the WRA obeyed rationing requirements and added that "in general, the food is nourishing but definitely below army standards." Responding to charges that prime beef was served in the camps, it pointedly described the beef served as "third grade." The text concluded by announcing that the West Coast exclusion would remain in force as long as the military situation required, and it praised the contribution of Japanese-American soldiers.

It is not clear how closely the President was involved in the details of the Byrnes statement, but he was familiar with its general outline and the strategy behind it, and he was directly responsible for one significant change. The original text (drafted by the Western Defense Command) read that because of the military conditions on the West Coast, "it is not the intention of the Federal Government to permit the return to the West Coast for residence of Japanese, whether American or foreign born." According to McCloy, Roosevelt let it be known that he would not accept any statement "that would imply in any way either that none of the people that have been evacuated were ever going to go back or that they were not going back for the duration."[52] Therefore, the text was altered to state that there was no "present intention" to alter or relax the restrictions. Whether Roosevelt's amendment reflected a humanitarian interest in the future of Japanese Americans or a pragmatic decision not to close off future options is not certain, but the effect was to put the Western Defense Command on notice that exclusion could not be sustained indefinitely.

On September 14, 1943, Byrnes issued a full report to the Senate on segregation and on future plans for Japanese Americans. The report included a letter of transmittal signed by Roosevelt—which had presumably been drafted, like the report itself, by the War Department with help from the WRA. The letter described the WRA's segregation program and the restraints placed on the "segregants" (who the President emphasized were a small minority of the "evacuees") at Tule Lake. In particular, the letter stated that all segregants would remain under guard and would be automatically ineligible for release for the duration of the war with Japan.

In the final paragraph of the letter, Roosevelt addressed the future of the camps. He announced that, with the successful completion of segregation, the WRA could now redouble its efforts to relocate loyal Japanese Americans to homes and jobs in communities outside the evacuated zone. Paying public tribute to these internees, "whose loyalty to this country has remained unshaken through the hardships of the evacuation which military necessity made unavoidable," the President promised them an expedited return to the West Coast: "We shall restore to the loyal evacuees the right to return to the evacuated areas as soon as the military situation will make such restoration feasible. Americans of Japanese ancestry, like those of many other ancestries, have shown that they can, and want to, accept our institutions and work loyally with the rest of us, making their own valuable contribution to the national health and well-being. In vindication of the very ideals for which we are fighting this war it is important to us to maintain a high standard of fair, considerate, and equal treatment for the people of this minority as of all other minorities."[53]

Roosevelt's letter was publicized in liberal and Japanese-American media as proof that the government believed in the internees' loyalty and as a sign that the internment was almost over. The *Pacific Citizen,* the JACL organ, pointed to Roosevelt's words as proof that the internment was not race-based and hailed his pledge to expedite the reopening of the West Coast as "a promise of rectification of the injustices resulting from evacuation" that the Nisei "have long waited to hear."[54] However, mainstream media coverage of the Byrnes report and the letter, especially on the West Coast, focused on the segregation policy and the transfer of "loyal" and "disloyal" evacuees between Tule Lake and the other camps. These reports passed over or ignored the President's pledge to expedite the opening of the West Coast. Presumably either the reporters involved did not absorb FDR's promise or they decided that once the public was satisfied that potentially disloyal internees would be confined, it would not be threatening to allow the loyal to return.

Despite the lack of attention paid, the President's letter represented a striking change in policy. Although FDR was silent on the continued confinement of the internees in camps, for the first time he publicly affirmed that the vast majority of Japanese Americans were loyal and had been subjected to hardship at the hands of the government. More importantly, the letter represented the first authoritative notice that the internees would be permitted to return to the West Coast before the end of the war, irrespective of local political opposition.

The reasons for the President's shift and his pledge to expedite the end of West Coast exclusion are not clear. He was not active in the policy during the month preceding the issuance of his letter, during which time he was heavily engaged in discussing wartime strategy with British Prime Minister Churchill at the first Quebec Conference and subsequently in Washington. His attention was also absorbed by the Allied invasion of Italy at Salerno on September 9. As with his February statement opening military service to the loyal Nisei, the President signed without alteration or recorded comment a letter drafted by his advisors.

The text of the letter nevertheless offers clues to Roosevelt's motives. The appeal to Americans to respect the rights of Japanese Americans and "all other minorities" suggests that Roosevelt's policy was in part a reaction to the racial unrest that had erupted in the United States during the summer of 1943. In the first week of June, white Anglo servicemen enraged by false rumors of attacks on white women rampaged through Mexican-American neighborhoods of Los Angeles, beating up and stripping Chicanos and African Americans wearing "zoot-suits." In late June, fights between blacks and whites at Detroit's Belle Isle resort touched off a massive three-day riot across the city in which 34 people died. The President was ultimately forced to call in army troops to quell the disorder. Meanwhile, smaller race riots between whites and African Americans broke out in locations as diverse as Beaumont, Texas, and New York City's Harlem. The President's reference to fair treatment may also have been related to the administration's support for China and its campaign to repeal the Chinese Exclusion Act as a sign of America's friendship for its wartime ally, which had begun in early spring but had been stalled in Congress. On October 11, shortly after he issued his letter on Japanese Americans, Roosevelt wrote an official letter to Congress supporting repeal as a war measure. He referred to the Chinese Exclusion Act as an "anachronism" which gave rise to Japanese racial propaganda and asserted that it stood in the way of the U.S.-Chinese partnership for peace. "Nations like individuals make mistakes," FDR commented. "We must be big enough to acknowledge our mistakes of the past and to correct them."[55]

Another influential element in the change in policy was the departure of General DeWitt and Colonel Bendetsen in mid-September 1943. DeWitt's insubordinate (and intemperate) public criticism of the loyalty board, combined with his inflexible opposition to lifting West Coast exclusion (he repeatedly refused even to permit Nisei soldiers to enter the excluded zone) made him expendable as Western Defense Commander. Although DeWitt's dismissal was couched as a promotion to the staff of the Army-Navy War

College in Washington, and Roosevelt presented the General with the Distinguished Service Medal in part for the "conspicuous dispatch and efficiency" with which DeWitt had handled the evacuation of the West Coast Japanese Americans, his removal signaled an unmistakable change in direction by his War Department superiors.[56] Significantly, his place at the Presidio was taken by General Delos Emmons, who had forestalled mass internment of the local Japanese in Hawaii. DeWitt's departure and the President's promise to open the West Coast to loyal evacuees as soon as the military situation warranted led to increased pressure within the administration to end exclusion. In early October 1943 Dillon Myer met at the Pentagon with John McCloy and with General Emmons to discuss the situation. On October 16 Myer wrote McCloy informing him that segregation was complete and asking when it would be militarily possible to end exclusion. Myer reminded McCloy that the Supreme Court would shortly be hearing a case on the evacuation and added that he believed that continued detention and exclusion could not be defended. He thus suggested that the War Department lift exclusion before the Court ruled. Since the army's prestige, he admitted, was such that it could do things the WRA could not, he asked the War Department to have representatives consult with the WRA to formulate a joint policy.[57]

Although McCloy quickly told Myer that he did not foresee any imminent change in the exclusion policy, he knew that the situation could not persist indefinitely. American victories at Guadalcanal and the Gilbert Islands and the U.S. thrust toward the Philippines had demonstrated the superiority of American arms in the Pacific theater and eliminated the threat of Japanese invasion of the United States. As a result of these victories, on November 1, 1943, the West Coast was officially removed from designation as a military theater of operations. Four days later, McCloy wrote Emmons confidentially that the army would soon have to open the West Coast, and he asked the General's advice on the political aspects of such an operation. Emmons agreed that the legal position for exclusion was weak, but he stated that there might still be security concerns over sabotage, and certainly a risk of espionage. The main problem, though, was obviously public opposition, which could nullify any program, no matter how safe, for ending exclusion. Emmons was hostile to Myer's plan for consultation as a scheme to drag the army into supporting an unpopular move. The fact that the army had conducted the initial evacuation failed to move Emmons, who said the army had stepped in because nobody else could. Instead, he recommended to McCloy that the army treat the return as a civilian matter and remain aloof.[58]

While McCloy and Emmons debated their response to Myer, conflict erupted at the dismal and overcrowded "segregation center" at Tule Lake. In the last week of October 1943, following the death of an internee laborer in a traffic accident, a group of agricultural workers at the camp organized a work stoppage (threatening the imminent harvest) and formed a negotiating committee to obtain better living and working conditions from the camp's director, Raymond Best. On November 1 Dillon Myer visited Tule Lake. Before a restive crowd numbering several thousand, he promised a redress of grievances. Although the crowd dispersed peacefully, local white laborers hired by the WRA spread rumors that a riot had taken place. Three days later, a group of militant internees, provoked by rumors that the vegetables being grown at Tule Lake were being sent to other camps, attempted to stop a convoy of trucks from leaving the center and ran into a group of WRA internal security officers. One officer was beaten by the internees, and several internees were beaten in return by security officers. Although the fight was short-lived and minor, Best called in reinforcements from the army troops patrolling the camp perimeter, who arrived the following day with rifles and tanks. Military police took over the camp and arrested 350 segregants. Tule Lake remained under martial law until mid-January 1944.[59]

The Hearst press and other anti-Japanese-American newspapers, whose editors hoped to forestall the return of the internees to California, immediately ran lurid and distorted front-page stories playing up the Tule Lake "riot" and reporting that the inmates had run rampant and had held the WRA director hostage. Even more prestigious commentators insisted that the "riot" was proof that Japanese Americans were still dangerous. *The New York Times* editorialized that the existence of loyal Nisei should not blind Americans to the danger posed by the disloyal. "This is no occasion for sentimentality. We can't give leeway to possible spies and saboteurs simply because we want to believe that human nature, including that which is wrapped in a saffron-colored skin, is inherently good."[60]

Public reaction to the news of the disturbances was intense and hostile. Although Tule Lake contained only "disloyal" internees, the unrest set off a new wave of racial animosity toward all Japanese Americans. On December 7, 1943, a month after the "riot," *The Los Angeles Times* printed the results of a public poll called the "Jap Questionnaire," timed for the anniversary of Pearl

Harbor and made up of a series of tendentiously phrased questions such as "Would you favor 'trading' Japanese now here for American war prisoners held in Japan if it could be arranged?" The 11,000 readers who responded "voted" by a ten-to-one margin to exclude Japanese Americans permanently from the West Coast, to ban future immigration from Japan, and to deport all Japanese Americans, including Nisei, to Japan after the end of the war. The *Times* editorialized that the poll and the Tule Lake "riot" would now convince Congress that Californians had been right all along in their hostility to the internees and their criticism of the "inept, New Dealish" WRA.[61]

Unsurprisingly, West Coast congressional and lobbying groups also seized on the events at Tule Lake to bolster their demand for further restrictions on the internees. Nativist groups organized a widespread letter-writing campaign to the President for the firing of Myer and an army takeover of the camps.[62] A group of West Coast congressmen organized a resolution calling for Myer's resignation and an overhaul of the WRA, although one representative expressed doubt that FDR would willingly overhaul an agency which he said reflected the ideas "of Mrs. Roosevelt and Assistant Secretary of War McCloy" (an odd ideological couple indeed!).[63] Liberal and Japanese-American groups launched a defensive campaign urging Myer's retention.[64]

Reaction inside the government to the Tule Lake incident was no less furious. McCloy and Emmons swiftly agreed that lifting exclusion amid the public furor over Tule Lake was unthinkable, despite the admitted absence of any military threat to the West Coast from loyal internees. Although Emmons had previously commented that the army should remain aloof from the political side of release, he now suggested that Myer coordinate plans for release with California Governor Earl Warren and other West Coast officials before proceeding, in order to assure their support and nullify opposition to return.[65] Meanwhile, Biddle, relying only on early (and distorted) West Coast press accounts, rushed Roosevelt an initial report on the events at Tule Lake. "Five Hundred Japanese internees armed with knives and clubs shut up Dillon Myer and some of his administrative officers . . . for several days. The army moved in to restore order. The feeling on the West Coast is bitter against the administration for what they think is weak policy towards the Japanese."[66]

With the President away at the wartime Teheran Conference, Biddle quickly initiated the administration's damage-control efforts. The attorney general commissioned an FBI investigation of the "riot" and began gearing up for prosecution of suspects under federal law.[67] At the same time, with the encouragement of OWM Director James Byrnes, he made a series of public statements asserting that Japanese Americans were overwhelmingly loyal and that the cause of their troubles was not disloyalty but public intolerance. He also defended the WRA against charges of laxness, even though this meant adopting the fiction that the camps were a voluntary "social service" and "refuge" for the evacuees. "The War Relocation Authority has no power to intern American citizens; and constitutionally it is difficult to believe that such authority could be granted to the government."[68]

Biddle also met with the West Coast congressional delegation to head off new proposals for "firmer" treatment of the evacuees, such as a military takeover of the WRA. Explaining that the army opposed such a takeover, Biddle warned that it might make things harder for Americans being held as prisoners of war in Japanese prison camps. He suggested instead that laws be drafted to ease renunciation of citizenship by disloyal internees. The idea was to eliminate the obstacle to indefinite incarceration of disloyal Nisei, who were assumed to favor Japan. Once these American citizens "voluntarily" renounced citizenship, they could be held as enemy aliens. With Biddle's support, a renunciation bill quickly passed Congress. It was signed into law by FDR in July 1944, becoming the first denationalization law of its kind in U.S. history. This law would ultimately cause enormous trouble for many internees.[69]

By early December 1943, after consulting with his political advisors, Biddle became convinced that the Tule Lake incident had fatally discredited Dillon Myer, and he began lobbying privately for a Justice Department takeover of Tule Lake. He privately commented that the WRA had done a good job, but its terrible public relations had now rendered it ineffective.[70] When Byrnes, a close presidential advisor, told Biddle that Roosevelt was considering handing him responsibility for administering the entire WRA, the attorney general was tempted to accept in order to assure that resettlement of internees would continue. Although Biddle was not anxious to oppose Interior Secretary Harold Ickes, who he worried might still be interested in the WRA, he did not believe that a switch to Interior would appear to be the kind of significant change in the WRA that was required to appease public anger after Tule Lake.[71] Meanwhile, Ickes, after discussing the subject with his advisors, passed the word to Biddle that he did not wish to take over the WRA.[72]

On December 17, 1943, following Roosevelt's return from Teheran, the future of the WRA became the subject of an elaborate diplomatic ballet at a Cabinet meeting. Byrnes, who may have been acting as the President's surrogate, stated that the WRA should be taken from Myer, who was not "strong enough," and transferred to Justice. Biddle tactfully stated that the WRA should go to Ickes, who remarked in turn that he no longer wanted it.[73] Byrnes added that he also did not want it in the Office of War Mobilization, and the matter was left for the President to resolve. Roosevelt did not express his preference at the Cabinet meeting, but he clearly leaned toward Biddle, no doubt because of the attorney general's actions in regard to Tule Lake. He did, however, make eminently clear his feelings about the Tule Lake internees. Vice President Henry Wallace's notes on the meeting reveal FDR's punitive and hostile attitude toward the inmates, as well as his conception of them as connected to Japan: "Byrnes mentioned about the various misdeeds of the Japs at Tule Lake. The President suggested that a strong hand be used and it did not make any difference what the Japs in Japan thought about it. I spoke up at once and said, 'Wait a minute, Mr. President. It makes a lot of difference to the Americans whom the Japs have in the camps in the Philippine Islands.' Jimmie Byrnes took my side . . . and the President backed away."[74]

Although willing to assume control over Tule Lake, Biddle evidently had second thoughts about taking over the entire WRA. On December 26 he suggested to Ickes and Byrnes that the WRA be added to the Interior Department. At Byrnes's suggestion, Biddle sent the President a memo reviewing the situation of the internees, praising the WRA's handling of the resettlement issue, and urging that the government close the camps as soon as possible. As Biddle stated bluntly, "The current practice of keeping loyal American citizens in concentration camps on the basis of race for longer than is absolutely necessary is dangerous and repugnant to the principles of our government."[75]

According to Biddle, the greatest problem the WRA faced in resettlement was political. The Hearst press and influential groups in California opposed a "successful" relocation program, in hopes that the internees could be forced to go to Japan, or at least remain permanently excluded from California. Members of Congress and local officials had a political interest in exploiting this prejudice by proposing harsh anti-Japanese legislation. Biddle argued that the WRA had been weakened by the "grossly exaggerated" press reports of the events at Tule Lake and was too weak to survive as an independent agency. It needed to be absorbed by a permanent Cabinet department, in part so it would benefit from greater administrative efficiency, but primarily for reasons of public relations and political "cover." He concluded that the bulk of the WRA should go into the Interior Department, while Tule Lake should be turned over to Justice. Although such a division of the WRA might invite administrative trouble, it was wiser from a political point of view to separate responsibility for the "loyal" from that for the "disloyal" internees. Biddle underlined the importance of the transfer being accomplished in such a way as to avoid giving the public any impression that the WRA had been discredited or impugning the loyalty of the internees.[76]

After receiving Biddle's memo, Roosevelt took the matter up with Byrnes and Harold Smith. Both men proposed that the entire WRA, including Tule Lake, should be transferred to Interior. Roosevelt then ordered Smith and presidential advisor Samuel Rosenman to make the necessary arrangements. The President's order led to a dispute over Myer. Based on talks with Senator Downey and California congressmen, Byrnes contended that Myer was too unpopular to keep and proposed that he be retained, if at all, only as a figurehead. Smith, who had been Myer's main contact and chief advocate within the White House, argued vociferously for retaining him and maneuvered to rescue him.[77]

In the ensuing weeks, while Roosevelt resisted any decision on Myer's future, the budget director stage-managed the transfer. He talked Biddle into agreeing to let the Interior Department take over the entire WRA, joined with Byrnes to induce Myer to agree to the transfer to Interior, persuaded Ickes (over the objection of his advisors) to retain Myer provisionally as WRA director, and got Roosevelt to agree to meet with Ickes so that the interior secretary could vent his complaints about being stuck with the WRA.[78] So involved was Smith with the WRA (and so uncertain was Myer's future) that when the President received a letter at the end of January from a group of Pacific Coast congressmen urging him to ship the "disloyal" internees to Japan and to exclude all Japanese Americans from the West Coast for the duration of the war, he sent the letter on to Smith for reply.[79]

During the third week of January 1944, Ickes conferred with Roosevelt about the WRA. Ickes reminded Roosevelt that he had lobbied to take over the WRA before but that the President had turned him down then. He did not want it now, but if Roosevelt gave it to him anyway, Ickes stated, he would do his best. Having thus won Ickes's reluctant consent to take over the WRA, Roosevelt placated him by promising to work toward giving him jurisdiction over the Forestry Service, which had once been in the Interior Department but had been switched to the Agriculture Department.[80] On February 16, 1944, Smith brought the President a copy of an executive order authorizing the transfer of WRA to Interior. FDR signed the order and edited a draft press release explaining the transfer as part of a general policy of "administrative simplification." Smith was gratified when Roosevelt expressed concern for the beleaguered WRA director: "The President asked what was going to happen to Dillon Myer. I explained that Ickes was going to use Myer to head the Organization. The President seemed to be pleased about this."[81] The move was announced the following day. Public reaction was generally positive, although several congressmen deplored Myer's retention.

The transfer to Interior came almost precisely one year after Roosevelt's February 1, 1943, statement opening military and defense employment to loyal Japanese Americans. In the wake of that statement, the President and his advisors were faced with a dilemma of their own creation. Having undertaken a drastic evacuation policy and spent millions of dollars establishing a network of camps, the White House and the army could not simply admit that they had made a mistake and that the internment had been unnecessary. They recognized that the policy was destructive and probably legally indefensible, but they believed that the only solution to the problems it had created was the gradual dismantling of the camps and scattering of the internees. Yet, each step they took in order to disentangle themselves from the internment created additional problems.

In order to escape from the paradoxical situation it had created, the administration followed a strategy of secrecy and deception during 1943. With Roosevelt's blessing, the army and the WRA made resettlement as politically palatable as possible by terming all relocation of internees "conditional leaves" and coupling the release program with confinement of "disloyal" internees. Meanwhile, in order to defend the internment against legal challenge and buy time for relocation outside the West Coast, the War Department manipulated evidence regarding the original "necessity" for the evacuation, and the Justice Department and WRA cooperated in fabricating the fiction that internment was benign and voluntary.

Throughout these months, as Roosevelt and his advisors debated how to wind down the internment on their own terms, they continually, and often unthinkingly, subordinated the basic rights of the internees to the political demands involved. Although a number of administration figures, notably Harold Ickes and Eleanor Roosevelt, plus such outside figures as Morris Ernst, pressed on the President the urgency of ending the internment and suggested practical steps for him to take in order to do so, Roosevelt rejected consideration even of the most reasonable alternatives to the government's destructive policy and adhered to a strategy of "staying one step ahead of the sheriff" in order to preserve it.

Ironically, Roosevelt's most positive action in regard to Japanese Americans during this period came about largely by accident. The President approved the Interior Department takeover of the WRA primarily as a cosmetic gesture to provide the agency some protection against its critics. However, the move to Interior tilted the balance of political forces decisively in favor of the internees. Interior Department staffers had long-established contacts with news media, and they were experienced at drafting press releases. As a result, they were much more effective than the WRA had been at disseminating positive news about Japanese Americans, especially the achievements of Nisei soldiers, and in neutralizing opposition to resettlement. The department also boasted able political tacticians such as Undersecretary of the Interior Abe Fortas, who was skilled in building support for liberal policies in Congress and within the administration. Roosevelt deserves special credit for handing principal authority over the WRA to Interior Secretary Harold Ickes, who had proved himself a stalwart defender of the citizenship rights of Japanese Americans. By selecting Ickes, the former gadfly on the internment, as supervisor of the WRA, Roosevelt demonstrated concern for the interests of the internees and assured them a persistent and sympathetic voice in administration policy circles. Ickes would take the leading role on behalf of Japanese Americans during 1944, when the final battle over closing the camps and ending exclusion took place.

EQUAL JUSTICE DELAYED

ON APRIL 13, 1944, Secretary of the Interior Harold Ickes made his first public statement about Japanese Americans following the transfer of the WRA to his department. Ickes emphasized the rights of Japanese-American citizens and loyal aliens and asserted that they should not be confined any longer than the necessities of war demanded. He denounced nativist groups on the West Coast as "professional race-mongers" who hoped to resolve the situation of Japanese Americans "on the basis of prejudice and hate" and accused them of opposing the WRA "for not engaging in this sort of lynching party." Ickes pledged not to let the WRA be "stampeded into undemocratic, bestial, inhuman action . . . or racial warfare."[1]

Ickes's outspoken public support of the rights of Japanese Americans was matched by his department's efforts within the administration to end the internment. As soon as the WRA was officially under their supervision, Ickes and his deputy, Undersecretary of the Interior Abe Fortas, began to assemble a coalition within the government to support the lifting of exclusion and the closing of the camps. Fortas, a brilliant New Deal lawyer, shared Ickes's views on ending exclusion. In a letter, he described the whole internment as a "terrific mistake" but recognized that there was nothing he could do about it. Rather, his task was "to ameliorate the evils which resulted from it."[2] Fortas saw as his first mission improving the WRA's public image. At the end of February he conferred with Biddle, who agreed to the end of exclusion and promised to take over Tule Lake if necessary, thus freeing the WRA to deal "only with the right kind" of internees. Shortly afterward, Fortas met with McCloy's deputy, Captain John Hall, to sound him out on the end of exclusion. While Fortas disclaimed interest in any immediate change in the exclusion policy, he suggested certain steps, such as the formation of a new loyalty board to clear those targeted for a return to the West Coast, in order to secure army assistance in enhancing public confidence in such steps.[3]

In early March Fortas forwarded to Ickes a memo from Myer urging him to secure the War Department's agreement to end exclusion within 90 days. Myer stated flatly that there was no longer any conceivable military justification for exclusion, and he played up the economic benefits to the war effort of opening the camps, as well as its utility in raising morale and neutralizing enemy propaganda. He also noted that the internee property which the WRA had assumed responsibility for storing in government warehouses on the West Coast would be increasingly difficult to handle until its owners returned to care for it. Although Myer's analysis ignored the thorny question of pending challenges to the constitutionality of confinement before the Supreme Court, it did cover the progress of resettlement outside the Pacific Coast, a question that would soon become contentious. Myer insisted that the end of exclusion would encourage further relocation outside the West Coast by calming public hostility and easing fears of discrimination among the internees. Fortas's cover memo agreed that exclusion should end soon, but Fortas suggested that the government prepare public opinion for return by first restricting return to selected categories of Japanese Americans, such as veterans and their families. He pressed Ickes to raise the issue at Cabinet.[4]

Ickes decided to concentrate on securing the aid of McCloy. The assistant secretary of war was receptive to proposals for closing the camps, since he did not consider security a problem. Emmons had already stated that there was no real danger from Japanese Americans apart from espionage, and McCloy realized that such threats could not justify exclusion of individuals whom the army had already investigated and agreed were loyal. In addition, on January 31, 1944, in response to a vigorous lobbying campaign by Myer and the JACL, the army reimposed selective service on Japanese Americans. The contradiction between drafting Nisei and confining them was too glaring for the army to ignore. Nevertheless, McCloy remained constrained in his willingness to act by his interest in maintaining the government's legal position in the courts, in order to assure that the army would be able to screen internees leaving the camps and control the process of return. He was aware that *Korematsu v. United States* had been appealed to the Supreme Court (the Court agreed on March 27 to hear the case). Fred Korematsu, a young Nisei, had refused to evacuate the West Coast and had been arrested for violating DeWitt's exclusion orders. He had challenged his arrest as a violation of his citizenship rights. A lower court had upheld his conviction. McCloy believed the government could prevail under the doctrine of military emergency which the Court had approved in the *Hirabayashi* case, and he warned Justice Department lawyers not to take any action that might cast doubt on the connection between the two cases.[5]

There were also increasingly hostile expressions of public opinion on the West Coast to contend with. The Tule Lake "riot" had served to rally anti-Japanese forces. The California State Senate's Committee on Japanese Resettlement warned of riots and bloodshed if Japanese Americans returned to the West Coast. Pressure groups such as the California Joint Immigration Committee, once deprived of the fig leaf of military security to justify excluding Japanese-American residents, resorted to nakedly racist appeals, arguing that the "Japanese" could not be trusted. Reports of Japanese atrocities against American prisoners in the Philippines which appeared in late January 1944 further incited public against all "Japanese," whether citizens or aliens.[6]

McCloy himself contributed to arousing hardline opposition to Japanese Americans following the New Year. Hoping to defend the evacuation from legal challenge, he ordered (or at least authorized) the public release of General DeWitt's rewritten *Final Report,* which he had previously withheld. The report's contents were rife with misrepresentations and false information. In particular, it alleged that the signaling of Japanese ships by West Coast Japanese Americans had led to the sinking of American ships. In fact, not a single American ship in the Pacific was sunk by Japanese submarines in the first part of 1942 (in contrast to German submarines off the Atlantic Coast, which had sunk significant numbers of ships and had made incursions ashore on Long Island in New York). Furthermore, Federal Communications Commission Chair James Fly informed Justice Department lawyers, as he had previously informed DeWitt, that there was no evidence of radio signaling by Japanese Americans and that the army's intelligence stations were staffed by untrained monitors with primitive equipment. Upon receiving this information, a group of Justice Department lawyers who had been assigned to prepare the *Korematsu* case before the Supreme Court drafted a detailed disclaimer for insertion in the government's brief in accordance with their duty to inform the Court of false evidence. However, following intense pressure from McCloy and Solicitor General Charles Fahy, who were focused on presenting the best possible case, the disclaimer was softened into a single vague footnote in the final brief.[7] Since the report carried the prestige of the War Department (Stimson had even signed the preface praising both DeWitt and the report)[8] and no forces either inside or outside the government publicly refuted its conclusions, it weighed heavily in West Coast public debate against Japanese Americans.

At the same time that McCloy supervised preparation of the Supreme Court brief, he prepared a memorandum on Japanese Americans for Stimson's review, along with a draft statement for him to make at the March 17 Cabinet meeting. These two documents provide an interesting picture of War Department thinking in early 1944. The memo was a detailed confidential report to the secretary on the "military aspects" of return. After opening with a brief defense of the "military necessity" of the original evacuation, the memo went on to explain that the question of military necessity had to be reexamined in light of later developments. As American forces pushed back the Japanese military, the West Coast ceased to be in imminent danger of invasion and the return of loyal Japanese Americans would not pose any threat beyond the power of regular law enforcement authorities to handle. Thus, "before the end of hostilities with Japan" the War Department would no longer be able to justify wholesale exclusion on the grounds of military necessity.

Once that was the case, the question ceased to be a military one but became rather a question of national policy, to be handled by civilian agencies. However, the army would still have to take a certain amount of public responsibility for return, "at least to the extent of announcing that the return is consistent with military requirements," in order to assure military security.

Despite Emmons's arguments that the army should remain aloof from the process, McCloy stated that it would have to involve itself in the return in order to retain control of the screening out of disloyal individuals. In addition, given the violent public opposition on the West Coast to Japanese Americans, the army was concerned to arrange return in such a fashion as to avoid any "riot or disorder" that might provoke Japanese authorities into reprisals against American prisoners of war.[9]

McCloy's draft Cabinet statement took much of its language from the confidential memo for Stimson (although the statement read that military necessity for exclusion would end "soon," rather than "before the end of hostilities with Japan," as the confidential memo had more urgently termed it), but it was much more focused on the need for action on the political problems of return, which McCloy believed the army was not prepared to handle. McCloy had Stimson explain that the army's involvement would be limited to stating that return was consistent with military requirements. Thus, "other government agencies will have to be prepared to take firm steps, in the face of bitter political opposition, to assure that these people are not denied their civil rights and are given a square deal economically."[10] The internees had lost their businesses and farms and would need outside financial help to reestablish themselves. However, the return would be "a political football," and local welfare and police agencies would be more likely to oppose the returnees' presence than to promote their safety and economic well-being.

In short, the memo was designed to list the political problems inherent in lifting exclusion and to push the government's civilian agencies to coordinate all efforts. McCloy rightly believed that local opposition could not be permitted to override the rights of Japanese Americans to return to their homes, and he agreed that the government had a responsibility to make up for the hardships and losses it had brought to Japanese Americans by taking a leading role in aiding and protecting them. Curiously, however, McCloy foresaw only a minimal role for the army in this process, even though the army had been responsible for the original evacuation. McCloy considered the army ill-equipped to carry out the locally based social welfare and police tasks required. On a deeper level, McCloy's plan demonstrated the emphasis he placed on preserving the army's public image, which might be damaged if it undertook the thankless and politically unpopular tasks involved in aiding return. McCloy may have feared that if the military was connected too closely with the return of Japanese Americans, it would constitute an admission that the army had been wrong and the original evacuation order had been unnecessary or unjust.

In any case, Stimson declined to make the statement drafted by McCloy, presumably because he thought the time was not yet ripe for action. The army as a whole remained hostile to ending exclusion. The G-1 (Administration), G-2 (Intelligence), and Operations Division staff units all unanimously interpreted Emmons's statement about the residual danger of sabotage and espionage to require prohibitive increases in guards for strategic installations in case of return. They also strongly argued that public hostility militated against any change in policy. As a result, all recommended against ending exclusion. The navy, which still excluded Japanese Americans, also protested lifting exclusion.[11]

Even more than the army staff, McCloy was consumed by the problem of public opinion, and it paralyzed him. Pro-internee activist Herbert Nicholson, who had helped persuade McCloy to support a Nisei combat unit, met with him on March 20, 1944. According to Nicholson, the assistant secretary of war was disgusted by the countless badly written and hateful letters that the War Department had received from West Coast residents urging them not to let "the Japs" back. "It's just because of public opinion we have them there [in the camps], and because of public opinion we can't send them back to the West Coast," he lamented. McCloy asked Nicholson to organize a letter-writing campaign by pro-internee residents of the West Coast for the return of their Japanese friends, telling him, "We'll open the camps as soon as we're sure that public opinion is not one hundred percent against it."[12] Nicholson's efforts were not widely successful.

Like McCloy, Ickes clearly believed more time was needed to coordinate the public response to ending exclusion, since he did not raise the matter of return at Cabinet, in spite of Myer's and Fortas's urging. Instead, the secretary of the interior decided to travel to the West Coast to evaluate the situation and meet with liberal groups before making any decisions on a plan for ending exclusion.[13] However, he commissioned Fortas to draft a strong statement in support of Japanese Americans for him to deliver during the trip. Ickes's April 13 statement promised a speedy return of the evacuees and denounced "race-mongers." The text did not directly address ending exclusion, although Fortas warned that Ickes's comments "probably would be so construed" and feared that they might affect the upcoming California primary elections.[14] However, WRA officials regarded the speech as the "opening gun" in the campaign to win public support for the internees and carefully tallied the letters they received concerning the speech. They totaled the results as 115 pro (including 67 from California) and 56 anti (including 45 in California). The largely positive reception encouraged Ickes to begin working in earnest with Fortas on making contingency plans for the lifting of the ban.[15] (The interior secretary also fired off characteristically trenchant answers to the protest letters, accusing his critics of trying to scuttle the constitutional guarantees of equal rights to U.S. citizens and denouncing anti-Nisei public officials for having foresworn their oath to uphold and defend the Constitution of the United States.)[16]

In late April 1944, following his return from the West Coast, Ickes held a series of discussions with McCloy to persuade him to secure War Department support for ending exclusion. Ickes's hand was strengthened by the Supreme Court, which on April 25 agreed to hear the *habeas corpus* petition filed by Mitsuye Endo, an internee at Topaz, challenging her confinement. Endo argued that the government had no right to prevent her, as a concededly loyal citizen, from returning home to California. The government had long recognized that it had little hope of prevailing in such a case, and both Ickes and McCloy believed that an adverse decision would force the immediate opening of the West Coast and end government control over the return process.

The secretary of the interior also had an unwitting ally in New York City Mayor Fiorello LaGuardia. When WRA officials announced in early April 1944 that a hostel would be opened in the city for resettled internees, LaGuardia, who had a long record of enmity toward Japanese Americans, officially protested the relocation of internees from western states to New York, saying that the transfer would endanger the city's defense plants and military installations and cause rioting among New York's Chinese population.[17] Ickes responded by publicly accusing LaGuardia (as well as Republican Governors Walter Edge of New Jersey and John Bricker of Ohio, who had also opposed resettlement) of racial discrimination.[18] Privately, he used the controversy to persuade McCloy that unless the West Coast ban was lifted, bipartisan forces on the East Coast could plausibly object to accepting internees, and "we might just as well abandon our whole resettlement plan."[19]

McCloy was uneasy about continued exclusion, especially when there was no longer any conceivable military threat to the West Coast, and he had warned his colleagues that it could not be sustained indefinitely. However, because he knew that public opinion remained strongly hostile to Japanese Americans and that many factions in the military still considered Japanese Americans to be inherently dangerous on racial grounds, he had withheld his own support. Now he feared the breakdown of relocation nationwide and its effect on Japanese Americans still in the camps, and he promised Ickes his full aid in gaining military consent. On April 27 McCloy reported to Ickes that the people in the War Department who were principally concerned with Japanese Americans agreed that the ban should be lifted.[20]

As soon as Ickes learned of the War Department's positive attitude, he had WRA officials quickly begin work on a detailed plan for ending exclusion. By the time this plan was submitted to Ickes in early May 1944, Stimson had also given his assent to the end of exclusion.[21] Soon after, in response to McCloy's pleas, General Marshall overrode the army staff's recommendations in favor of maintaining exclusion and stated on behalf of the army that there was no military objection to return except for the potentially harmful consequences of violence against the returnees on the treatment of American prisoners of war in Japanese hands.[22] McCloy assured Marshall in return that he had obtained the promise of California Attorney General Robert Kenney that local authorities would protect the returnees against assaults as long as the army would testify to their loyalty and ask that they not be molested.[23]

Once the consensus on ending exclusion was cemented, the chief problem was stage-managing the request to win Roosevelt's approval. Fortas, whose careful diplomacy had helped build the coalition for return, agreed with McCloy that Stimson should present the matter at the Cabinet meeting on May 18, 1944. When McCloy warned that the navy might oppose the lifting of the ban and asked (following Marshall's recommendation) whether the naval staff officers responsible for the West Coast should be consulted beforehand, Fortas convinced him that it would be sufficient simply to inform the new secretary of the navy, James Forrestal (who had just been appointed, following Frank Knox's death), that the subject of lifting the ban would be discussed at Cabinet.[24]

The President and his staff had been largely removed from the internal debate over ending exclusion during early 1944, although several White House figures had involved themselves in the "Japanese problem" during and after its transfer to Interior. Budget Director Harold Smith continued to communicate with Dillon Myer, and OWM Director James Byrnes kept in touch with congressional opinion on WRA leadership. Meanwhile, in mid-January 1944, presidential aide Jonathan Daniels commissioned a report from the WRA on resettlement and public opinion.[25] Eleanor Roosevelt (who had published an extended article in *Collier's* magazine in fall 1943 lauding the contributions of the internees to the war effort) continued to correspond with Japanese Americans and speak publicly on behalf of their citizenship rights. In addition, the President's daughter, Anna Roosevelt Boettiger, who moved into the White House as an unofficial hostess in February 1944 and quickly became a close advisor, interested herself in the WRA. She lobbied Harold Ickes to replace Dillon Myer, whom she viewed as a poor administrator and political liability. She shared with Ickes confidential material critical of Myer which she received from her friend Edward Joyce, a WRA employee.[26]

Nevertheless, Roosevelt himself was not active in shaping administration policy in regard to the internment during these months. Following his return from the Teheran Conference, Roosevelt was absorbed with preparations for the cross-channel invasion of Europe planned for spring 1944, and with fighting in Italy and the Pacific. He was also forced to contend with resistance in Congress to his proposed budget and to a war profits tax. The President's health began to fail, and he suffered repeated colds. His only recorded comment on the subject of Japanese Americans during early 1944 was a reply to Hawaiian Governor Ingram Stainback, who wrote the President in December 1943, following the repeal of the Chinese Exclusion Act, to complain of the discriminatory naturalization laws. Stainback complained that these laws prevented members of other nonwhite immigrant groups, including Japanese, who were contributing to the war effort from becoming citizens. Roosevelt responded in early January 1944 that he had "the highest regard for those Polynesians, Samoans, Japanese, Koreans, Maoris, Filipinos, and members of other Pacific races" who were demonstrating "in a positive way" their loyalty and attachment to the United States, but that the question of removing racial requirements of naturalization would require careful study before any plan could be proposed, and he took no further action.[27]

By early spring 1944, Roosevelt had become a part-time President. He was already terminally ill with congestive heart failure and other ailments. FDR had a chronic fever during late March and was tortured by painful daily sinus treatments. He spent approximately a month from April to early May recuperating at Hobcaw, financier Bernard Baruch's home in South Carolina.[28]

After his return to the White House, he drastically limited his work day and increasingly delegated responsibility for all but essential war decisions.[29] Nevertheless, his health did not improve, and he suffered from weight loss, palsied hands, and a chronic cough. Roosevelt was psychologically and physically worn out. He had been President for over a decade, and the excruciating burden of the presidency in wartime had taken an enormous toll on him. Although he was still able to pull himself together for important visitors or appearances, he had trouble concentrating on ordinary business, and his mind often wandered during conversation. He was also terribly isolated. Confined by polio to a wheelchair, he had little opportunity for physical diversion or escape from his surroundings, and most of his former close companions were dead or absent. The President's advisors and White House assistants, accustomed to a dynamic and decisive Roosevelt, were largely unwilling or unable to face the reality of his deterioration or deal with the leadership vacuum it left.

Under the circumstances, FDR's intervention was not sought. When Myer and the WRA drew up their plans for implementing the end of exclusion, they took for granted that the President, who had promised the Senate to permit loyal evacuees to return as soon as it was militarily possible, would approve lifting the ban once the War Department agreed. Ickes and Stimson clearly did not feel it necessary to raise the subject with Roosevelt until then.

On May 17 (the day after the California primary), Stimson casually brought up lifting exclusion during a private conference with Roosevelt. The secretary of war explained that the army was satisfied that there was no longer a reason to keep loyal Japanese in what he called "internment camps," but since their release would cause a "row" on the California coast, he wanted to inform the President beforehand. To Stimson's surprise, Roosevelt immediately seized on the political problems involved in lifting exclusion. "The President said, 'Well, why not call Governor [Earl] Warren here to talk it over?' He said he thought he was a fair man and would take it on the right side."[30] The secretary of war was taken aback by Roosevelt's request that he consult the California governor, a leading contender for the Republican nomination in that year's presidential race, to gain his political support for lifting exclusion. Although Stimson was himself a prominent Republican, he had been guaranteed freedom from involvement with politics as a condition for joining the Cabinet four years earlier.

Stimson reluctantly promised the President that he would talk to Warren, but he changed his mind by the time he spoke to Fortas and Biddle immediately before Cabinet the following day. Fortas reported to the absent Ickes that Stimson had been troubled by the President's attitude. Despite Roosevelt's letter promising to permit return once the military situation warranted, his chief concern now seemed to be finding ways to limit the political fallout by associating prominent Republicans with return. Although FDR considered Warren "not a bad fellow," his advisors recognized that inviting him to Washington would mean holding the end of exclusion hostage to Warren's (doubtful) approval. Fortas reminded the others that Warren had been a leading instigator of the original evacuation, and even though he might have moderated his views since then, the governor would probably either object if consulted or refuse to present a view.[31] As Fortas and the others were well aware, Warren had no incentive to take the political heat for supporting return: he had won election as California governor in fall 1942 largely on the basis of his opposition to Japanese Americans, he had publicly opposed return during 1943, and he needed the backing of the anti-Japanese Hearst press if he wished to be a contender for the presidency.

Fortas told Ickes that Stimson had expressed concern during their pre-Cabinet discussion over the deprivation of the internees' civil liberties and had indicated that he was still willing to add his agreement if Fortas recommended ending the ban during the meeting. However, Fortas decided not to raise the question at Cabinet in order to avoid a repetition of Roosevelt's request for consultation with Warren. He hoped instead to arrange for Ickes, Stimson, and Biddle to call jointly for a special conference with the President and together persuade him to support lifting exclusion. No conference could be held during the following week since Roosevelt was away at Hyde Park, so the question of lifting the exclusion did not come up again until the Cabinet meeting on May 26, 1944, the day after the President's return.

By this time, however, Stimson's views had shifted somewhat, as his fears for the safety of American POWs in the Pacific overshadowed his concern for civil liberties. Before the meeting, he showed Ickes and Biddle confidential pictures he had received of Japanese soldiers beheading American prisoners, to remind them how violent the opposition to return would likely be. Once the meeting started, the secretary of war reported that his department favored opening the camps since there was no military reason for confining the internees, but he warned of the danger that riots against the returnees on the West Coast would bring on reprisals by Japan against American prisoners. He thus recommended careful planning and timing of release.[32]

Biddle then spoke up in support of return and announced that the Supreme Court was likely to rule against detention of loyal evacuees. However, he too was uneasy about opening the West Coast, despite his long opposition to the internment. His political advisors (as well as J. Edgar Hoover, a theoretically nonpartisan official) had counseled him against recommending return before the election in order to avoid trouble in California.[33] Shaken by Stimson's pictures, Biddle remarked that it would be wiser to postpone release until after the November election, especially since the Supreme Court would not even hear the internment cases until its fall term.

Ickes quickly stepped in to rebut Stimson and Biddle. He argued that since there was no military reason why the ban should not be lifted, as Stimson agreed, there would be less danger in opening the camps with their 90,000 inmates right away—the sooner the better—than in delaying, unless the President decided as a matter of deliberate policy to wait until after the election. The secretary of the interior reminded the others that 23,000 Japanese Americans had already been resettled without difficulty in areas outside the West Coast in the preceding 18 months through the WRA's "leave clearance" program, so that the problem was smaller than the others believed. Nevertheless, he added firmly, there was no possibility of further resettlement until the ban was lifted: LaGuardia and others in the East were willing to accept resettlement of internees, but not if they were barred from the West Coast.

Roosevelt stated that he agreed with Ickes in principle but thought piecemeal relocation would be better than having evacuees "dumped" on California. He proposed instead a gradual release program designed to scatter the internees. FDR had evidently had various discussions on the subject with his Dutchess County neighbors during his week at Hyde Park, and he used them as a basis to refute Ickes's warnings about the impossibility of East Coast relocation. "He stated that by personal inquiry he had reached the conclusion that quite a few [internees] could be distributed in Dutchess County and that if the same could be done all over the country it would take care of all."[34] The President avoided making any final determination about lifting exclusion. Instead, he asked Ickes to first inquire further about resettlement outside the West Coast.

The President's refusal to take a stand on lifting the West Coast ban is noteworthy. Even when asked to make a clearcut choice, Roosevelt was unprepared, and perhaps unable, to provide leadership or to make a definite decision. Whatever the sincerity of his interest in resettling Japanese Americans in Dutchess County and similar regions, it also evaded the nub of the problem. Roosevelt was beginning to concentrate on his 1944 reelection campaign at this time. Given Biddle's comment about the political wisdom of delay and his own previous request that Stimson consult Earl Warren, FDR was obviously aware of the political factors involved in return. By concentrating on the feasibility of East Coast relocation, he may well have been attempting to find a more expedient solution and save himself the trouble of making a formal decision based on sheer political advantage by turning Ickes (and Stimson) away from the explosive topic of lifting West Coast exclusion.

Ickes, however, was impatient with the President's temporizing on West Coast exclusion, which he thought was more destructive than an outright negative. He was also concerned that if the Supreme Court granted Mitsuye Endo's *habeas corpus* petition, the administration would be in the position of acting illegally on the eve of the election. This would be politically disastrous and would end all government control over the resettlement process. Ickes explained to Anna Roosevelt Boettiger that he hoped to get permission from the President to resettle at least some internees on the West Coast. This would dilute East Coast opposition to relocation and lessen the chance that an adverse Supreme Court ruling would result in chaos.[35]

On June 2, after a conference during which he was unable to speak privately with the President, Ickes decided on a frontal assault, and he wrote Roosevelt to ask him to make a firm decision on revoking the exclusion orders. He explained that in the absence of military necessity there was "no basis in law or equity" for maintaining the West Coast ban, and he repeated for Roosevelt the arguments that had been presented at Cabinet: that the War Department found no justification for exclusion in terms of military security; that the Justice Department considered exclusion of Japanese Americans from the West Coast to be clearly unconstitutional; that the Supreme Court would be hearing cases on the exclusion that fall; and that the exclusion made resettlement elsewhere difficult. Ickes added that continued confinement in the "centers" was harming Japanese Americans psychologically, particularly the children cut off from contact with the outside world, and hampering efforts to aid American POWs in Japanese hands by giving Japan a ready response to State Department complaints about mis-treatment. He closed by exhorting the President to end exclusion and release the internees, warning that their further "retention" in the camps would be "a blot upon the history of this country."[36]

Ickes did not bring up in his letter the President's September 1943 promise to the Senate to expedite the return of the loyal internees as a reason for lift-ing exclusion. Ickes's silence is curious. Perhaps he was unaware of the com-mitment or had forgotten about it, although Myer had reminded him of it not long before.[37] More likely, Ickes recognized that the President had put his name to the letter, despite its official status as part of a state paper, purely as political window-dressing. The promise was designed to meet the needs of a particular situation and was not intended to be legally or morally binding.

Roosevelt, absorbed by the D-Day invasion of Normandy and meetings with the prime minister of Poland, did not attend immediately to Ickes's letter. Meanwhile, General Emmons (who may or may not have known of Roosevelt's statements at Cabinet) responded to Fortas's previous suggestion by submitting a plan for a "Selective Exemption Program" that would permit gradual opening of the West Coast. The program provided for the ban to be immediately lifted from Military Area #2 (the eastern or noncoastal half of California) and for the holding of a new set of loyalty hearings and clear-ances to permit selective reentry of internees into Military Area #1 (the Pacific Coast zone). Emmons's plan was intended to build public confidence by permitting return initially only to a select group of model internees and by making the army fully responsible for clearances. Myer was firmly opposed, and remarked scornfully that the plan resembled the Plan C he had suggested in March 1943. To implement it now, he complained, would dis-credit the entire leave clearance system the WRA had worked so diligently and painfully to put together and would cast doubt on the loyalty of the 23,000 internees whom the WRA had relocated from the camps. The process of arranging new loyalty examinations would further traumatize the internees and would protract and complicate the return process.[38] Although Fortas remained interested in associating the army with the return process as a way of improving WRA public relations, he privately expressed his doubts about this policy, as did Ickes.[39] McCloy nevertheless took up Emmons's plan as a workable compromise.

On June 8 Roosevelt sent Ickes's June 2 letter to Undersecretary of State Edward Stettinius, who was then heavily involved with him in the conferences with Polish officials, and asked him to consult with Stimson, and then Ickes, on the situation.[40] It is not clear why Roosevelt assigned this task to Stettinius. Although Stettinius expressed support for lifting exclusion, he had little connection with or interest in Japanese Americans (unless his unfamiliarity with the situation *was* the reason).[41] It may be that the President, too occupied to give his attention to what he considered minor matters and always chary of confrontations, simply handed off the responsibility to the nearest advisor. In any case, Stettinius reported to the President the following day that he had reached McCloy, who confirmed that the army agreed with Ickes that exclusion was not a military necessity. He then added, "The question appears to be largely a political one, the reaction in California, on which I am sure you will probably wish to reach your own decision."[42] It was clear even to Stettinius, a former businessman and Lend-Lease administrator who had little political experience, that the President could not evade or obscure the political nature of the decision that he alone could make.

On June 12 Roosevelt sent a responsive memo to Ickes and Stettinius which sidestepped both the constitutional problems posed by exclusion and Ickes's moral strictures over continuing the imprisonment of innocent Americans. Rather, "for the sake of internal quiet," the President recommended that nothing be done that was "drastic or sudden." He proposed a gradual approach which would involve:

> (a) Seeing, with great discretion, how many Japanese families would be acceptable to public opinion in definite localities on the West Coast.
> (b) Seeking to extend greatly the distribution of other families in many parts of the United States. I have been talking to a number of people from the Coast and they are all in agreement that the Coast would be willing to receive back a portion of the Japanese who were formerly there—nothing sudden and not in too great quantities at any one time.

Roosevelt concluded that internees, "one or two families to each county as a start," should be "distributed" around the rest of the country, and added, "Dissemination and distribution constitute a great method of avoiding public outcry."[43] He asked Ickes to proceed with that plan "for a while at least."

Roosevelt's memo demonstrated unmistakably that his chief concern was the political ramifications of return. Since he knew from Ickes that continued West Coast exclusion stiffened opposition to relocation elsewhere, his reference to "internal quiet" could only have referred to the Pacific Coast. Further, while FDR's concern about whether returning internees would be "acceptable" was legitimate, his exclusive focus on placating West Coast opinion and his order that the internees be "disseminated" betray a cavalier disregard for the concerns of Japanese Americans, whom the President saw only as a problem, and to their right to choose where they lived.

The War Department was not privy to Roosevelt's memo. The following day, June 13, Stimson wrote an official letter to California Congressman John Z. Anderson. Although he denied that the restrictions on Japanese Americans had been lifted and refused to predict when they would be, his statement that the exclusion policy was under "constant study and surveillance" by the War Department and the Western Defense Command and his reference to "forthcoming changes" in policy based on developments in the military situation implied that the end was approaching.[44]

That same day, McCloy visited the White House to confer about Emmons's plan for gradual resettlement. Since McCloy considered military policy entirely a national security matter, he was shocked (and disgusted) to find the President surrounded by political advisors such as David Niles and Tommy Corcoran.[45] "The President smilingly said that [Emmons's plan] could not be done for political reasons, and he went on to suggest that there ought to be some sort of activity about the placement of Japs where they would be acceptable and he talked about Dutchess County. He knew they could be placed on many farms there."[46] Although FDR advocated scattering the internees in small numbers throughout the nation, and he repeated the homey description of welcoming Dutchess County neighbors that he had used at Cabinet, he was less circumspect with McCloy about the roots of his opposition than he had been with Ickes. As Roosevelt intended, McCloy got the message to avoid any visible change in policy. Upon returning to his office, McCloy called Emmons over the telephone and told him to forget the whole business of lifting exclusion until November, noting, "I just came from the President a while ago. He put his thumbs down on this scheme. He was surrounded by his political advisors and they were harping hard that this would stir up the boys in California and California, I guess, is an important state."[47]

Word of the President's position quickly spread (likely via Eleanor Roosevelt) to Clarence Pickett, secretary of the American Friends Service Committee and a sponsor of the JACL, and to Walter White, the executive secretary of the National Association for the Advancement of Colored People (NAACP). Knowing that Roosevelt relied on African-American votes for reelection, Pickett and White hit on the idea of exerting black political pressure to counter West Coast nativists. They brought up with Eleanor Roosevelt the possibility of an NAACP protest campaign to have the President take "a bold and decisive step . . . with regard to the Japanese-American citizens now that the West Coast is no longer a theatre of operations."[48] On June 17, 1944, five days after FDR sent his memo on "dissemination" to Ickes, the First Lady approached him with White and Pickett's idea. Roosevelt disingenuously told his wife that the question of ending the internment and having the internees return to California was in the hands of the military, and he further advised her that a public protest campaign by one racial minority on behalf of another would probably backfire and might provoke "unpleasantness."[49] As Eleanor Roosevelt thereafter informed White, "The President feels that you should not make a point of coming out as a minority group for the Japanese, but as each case arises in a community, the colored people should take their stand with the forces in the community that are for proper and kindly treatment."[50] FDR also moved successfully to defuse the threatened protest by offering White an off-the-record meeting to discuss the policy (which White was unable, despite repeated efforts, to arrange with the President's secretaries). A few days later, Pickett reported to White that it was too late. "The President finally decided to take no action with regard to Japanese Americans now. It is quite evident that his political advisors said a firm 'no.'" White and Pickett realized that they could do nothing until after the election.[51]

Even though Roosevelt had spoken vaguely to Ickes and McCloy about permitting gradual return of some internees to the West Coast, his statements about "dissemination" of internees at Cabinet and in his June 12 memo effectively stalled resettlement both inside and outside the excluded area. The secretary of the interior protested in vain to Anna Roosevelt Boettiger, who responded by arguing strenuously in favor of delaying the end of exclusion until after the election.[52]

Fortas had no more success with McCloy. In mid-June, he proposed that the army announce that it was altering the exclusion orders and instituting a permit system to allow small numbers of evacuees, such as families of soldiers, to return gradually to the excluded area, and he enclosed a proposed statement for Emmons. Fortas explained that he recognized that the President wanted the WRA to concentrate its efforts on relocation outside the West Coast, but he hoped to announce the easing of West Coast restrictions in order to diminish opposition to relocation in the rest of the country.[53] To Fortas's fury, McCloy interpreted Roosevelt's position as meaning only a few carefully screened returns, such as the families of soldiers, would be permitted. More importantly, no announcement and no publicity would be accorded any change.[54]

Aside from his understanding of Roosevelt's wishes, McCloy may also have been playing to his constituency. Although the Western Defense Command continued to make plans for the end of exclusion and the navy finally gave its consent to lifting exclusion in September, the armed forces were, to say the least, not uniformly supportive of return. In fact, Ickes repeatedly complained to Stimson and Forrestal during the summer about public comments by army and navy officers opposing return and advocating deportation of Japanese Americans.[55] Although the army ultimately did provide exemption certificates to a few categories of internees, such as families of soldiers, to enable them to return to the West Coast over the following months, its policy of mass exclusion and its ban on public announcement that returns were taking place forced the WRA to continue its efforts to resettle internees outside the West Coast, amid local opposition. As Ickes trenchantly commented, "It is the President himself who has insisted that the ban not be lifted until after the election and in the meantime we are having the devil's own time trying to persuade people in the Middle West and in the East that the Japanese are perfectly safe in those areas when they cannot be trusted in California."[56] By September 1, 1944, 850 internees had been resettled in Washington and 485 in Oregon (almost all outside the excluded zone), 76 in Arizona, and only 37 in California. In contrast, there were 23,000 outside the restricted area, including 453 in Nebraska, 2,047 in Utah, and 3,213 in Colorado. Some 65,000 people were still confined in camps.[57]

During the summer and early fall of 1944, Roosevelt was once again absorbed by the demands of wartime strategy and alliance diplomacy. Roosevelt was faced with decisions over whether to concentrate military efforts on breaking German resistance in northern France following the D-Day invasion or on advancing through Italy or the Balkans, as Churchill recommended. Roosevelt was forced to resolve rancorous disputes over the composition of new governments in France and Poland and to consider the postwar fate of Germany. In the Pacific Theater, the President supervised preparations for the invasion of the Philippines, which took place in mid-October, and he engaged in an extended and fruitless attempt to push Chiang Kai-Shek to join in a united front with the Chinese Communists against Japan.

Roosevelt was also burdened with domestic affairs, including labor strikes and racial tensions. During July and August, he made a demanding inspection tour of the West Coast, Alaska, and Hawaii. The President's health remained poor during these months. He was frequently listless, his hands shook, and he had difficulty concentrating on ordinary matters. The excitement of the election campaign raised his spirits temporarily, and in September and October he threw himself into the presidential race, making a round of campaign speeches and statements and riding through New York and Boston.

Despite this strenuous agenda, the President kept himself informed on the issue of resettlement and on the legal challenges to the evacuation and internment. His efforts were chiefly devoted to preserving the status quo of West Coast exclusion and gradual resettlement of internees throughout the rest of the country. On July 1 FDR signed Biddle's bill providing for "voluntary" renunciation of citizenship by Nisei into law. Biddle advised him that the bill would eliminate legal challenges to the confinement of the "disloyal" internees at Tule Lake. A few weeks later, during his tour of the Pacific Coast, the President met in San Diego for a lengthy discussion with General Charles H. Bonesteel, Emmons's new successor as western defense commander. General Bonesteel, who had affirmed to McCloy that there was no military necessity for exclusion, provided the President with the army's analysis of the legal challenges to the exclusion policy then pending in lower courts. FDR ignored the issue of lifting the West Coast exclusion order and recycled the arguments he had used with Ickes and McCloy in favor of "dissemination" of internees throughout the country. Bonesteel remarked later that Roosevelt "seemed to feel that there should be no difficulty in accomplishing a solution of the problem whereby one or two Japanese families would be placed in each of several thousand small communities throughout the nation. He went into detail in showing how the plan would work in his own county." Bonesteel was unimpressed and informed McCloy that he considered the idea of scattering more than a few thousand Japanese Americans unrealistic. Not only did the internees oppose such a solution, but they would encounter insurmountable economic discrimination once isolated in white communities.[58] On September 1 the President asked Fortas at Cabinet what success the WRA had had in placing internees throughout the country. The undersecretary of the interior immediately sent him a map showing the number of internees in each state.[59] Meanwhile, sometime during this period, Solicitor General Charles Fahy briefed the President on the details of the *Korematsu* and *Endo* cases, which he was preparing for argument before the Supreme Court. Roosevelt, Fahy later stated, showed an intelligent understanding of the issues involved but made no suggestions as to their presentation.[60]

Roosevelt made no public statements in support of internee resettlement during these months. On the contrary, he may have made a difficult situation more tense by fanning the flames of racist sentiment in a series of wartime morale-boosting speeches he made during his July 1944 West Coast trip. In his speeches in Washington state and Alaska, Roosevelt focused on the past invasion threat from Japan and praised the American response. Unlike in the case of Germany and Italy, where he maintained a rhetorical separation between the dictatorial rulers, who were the "enemy," and their enslaved populations, he spoke of the Japanese people as equally guilty for their rulers' actions: "Whether or not the people of Japan itself know and approve of what their war lords and their home lords have done for nearly a century, the fact remains that they seem to be giving hearty approval to the Japanese policy of acquisition of their neighbors and their neighbors' lands and a military and economic control of as many other nations as they can lay their hands on." Although the President did not specifically mention Japanese Americans during these speeches, he publicly denounced all Japanese as hostile and untrustworthy. "In the days to come," he told his audiences, "I won't trust the Japs around the corner."[61] Many of his West Coast listeners, unwilling or unable to separate between "Japs" in Japan and the United States, were undoubtedly fortified in their opposition to the return of the internees.

Perhaps in atonement for such remarks, Roosevelt included praise of Japanese Americans in a Columbus Day radio address to "American Republics." Hoping to rally support from Latin Americans for the war effort, the President extolled the contributions of American soldiers of different backgrounds who were providing an answer to false Nazi assertions about "Nordic superiority." Among these groups were the "combat teams composed of Americans of Japanese ancestry who came from Hawaii."[62] Although the

President's tribute was undoubtedly sincere, his description ignored both the Nisei soldiers from the West Coast in the 442nd and their families who remained confined in the camps.

On November 7, 1944, Roosevelt was elected to a record fourth term. Three days later, Attorney General Biddle brought up at Cabinet the *Korematsu* and *Endo* cases, which had been argued before the Supreme Court the previous month. Biddle told the President that the Court would almost certainly soon overturn the detention and exclusion policy. With support from Ickes and Stimson, Biddle suggested that it would be wiser to open up the camps voluntarily before the Court's decision was issued and to immediately begin gradual resettlement using the army's plan, "it having been held up until after election."[63] Roosevelt did not dispute Biddle's characterization of the delay. Rather, he consented to release and asked Stimson to send him a plan, along with a letter affirming that there was no longer any military necessity for "internment of Americans of Japanese descent" and justifying release by "giving as a second point their good war record as soldiers."[64]

On November 13, 1944, Biddle, Ickes, and Stimson met to discuss plans for lifting exclusion, and an interdepartmental committee was formed under Dillon Myer's leadership to draft a program and the letter to the President. The plan they worked out provided that all internees who had not been denied leave clearance would be eligible for immediate release, while those who were cleared by the army could return to the West Coast. Above and beyond the inmates at Tule Lake, who were already ineligible for resettlement, the Western Defense Command proposed increasing security and public confidence by issuing individual exclusion orders to some 4,000 to 5,000 internees whom it found ineligible for return to the West Coast.[65] McCloy prepared a draft announcement of the new policy which Stimson rejected as overly "outspoken." In deference to the secretary of war's fear of "exciting the radicals" and causing riots on the West Coast, the committee ultimately decided against making any major public announcement of the end of exclusion.[66]

In order to lessen popular opposition, the committee also devised provisions to steer as many internees as possible away from the West Coast. Although the government had no legal right to prevent internees from returning, as Myer admitted to Ickes, the WRA planned to use transportation vouchers and financial assistance as weapons of persuasion.[67] Financial support would be granted as a matter of course to internees who relocated outside the West Coast, but the WRA would assist only those West Coast returnees whose relocation plans they approved—a number Myer intended to limit as much as possible. For those who did not seek government aid, the inevitable administrative delays in obtaining army clearance would assure a gradual and orderly process of return to the West Coast.

While the committee conferred on details, the departments involved agreed to maintain silence regarding exclusion, in order to avoid giving local white resistance a chance to organize before the returns actually began. However, rumors of a change quickly broke out, especially after California Governor Earl Warren (who had been passed over for a place on the Republican presidential ticket) announced publicly that California could not bar the return of citizens of Japanese ancestry and would protect their legal and constitutional rights.[68] McCloy wrote Biddle an irritated note on the 17th, complaining that he had already received three phone calls asking about the rumors. The attorney general immediately sent around a memo urging secrecy, a plea which Stimson repeated at Cabinet.[69] It was Roosevelt who managed, either adroitly or unwittingly, to defuse the situation. When he was asked at his November 21 press conference about rumors that Japanese Americans would soon be returning, FDR publicly renewed his previous disquisition on nationwide scattering of internees and stated that he knew nothing about any shift in policy. Roosevelt's comments were widely interpreted as a sign that no change was at hand.[70] Since the President in fact knew that the government was planning to lift exclusion, his response was less than truthful, but his canny evasion of the question avoided the negative effects that would have ensued from a premature announcement. When a committee of California congressmen passed a resolution asking the secretary of war for an official statement on the lifting of exclusion, McCloy responded that it was strictly a military matter and that "no assurances as to time [of lifting exclusion] can be given."[71]

On December 13, 1944, Stimson sent the President a formal letter the committee had drafted which outlined the agreed-upon machinery for implementing return. As FDR had requested, the letter affirmed that the internment was no longer required by the military situation and stated that the "progress of litigation" in the courts made the end of mass exclusion both desirable and necessary. The letter conspicuously downplayed the opposition to return as the reason for both gradual resettlement and the government's encouragement of relocation outside the Pacific Coast, as well as for the continued confinement of the internees at Tule Lake. Instead, it was careful to cite military factors such as the need to protect defense plants from sabotage as the sole underlying rationale for those provisions. While Stimson did note that "some initial opposition to return" was anticipated, he also declared that this was not expected to cause any "serious incidents or disorders." Significantly, in light of Roosevelt's past temporizing, Stimson did not send the letter directly to the President but directed it to Roosevelt's longtime confidential secretary, Grace Tully, along with a separate cover letter explaining to her that the President did not have to decide whether or not to approve the plan, since Stimson was taking full responsibility for it upon himself. Stimson only wanted assurance that the President had no difficulties with the text of the letter he had requested.[72] Roosevelt did not volunteer to associate himself with the decision or endorse the end of the internment, but the White House immediately informed Stimson that the President had no objections to his letter.[73]

The Supreme Court's decisions in the cases of *Korematsu v. United States* and *Ex part Endo* were announced on December 18. In *Korematsu* the Court ruled 6–3 that the government had acted constitutionally in February 1942 in ordering the emergency exclusion of Japanese Americans from West Coast areas. The majority opinion, written by Justice Hugo Black, found that the army had reason to believe that Japanese Americans posed a danger to national security. In a blistering dissent, Justice Frank Murphy called the decision a "legalization of racism."

Korematsu has since become a historic case in American law, not only for its purported upholding of the internment—which it did not explicitly do—but for its declaration that classifications based on race were inherently suspect under the Constitution. The ruling thus helped pave the way for the postwar struggle for civil rights by African Americans. Ironically, however, *Korematsu* had little or no effect on the immediate situation of Japanese Americans. Rather, it was the now generally forgotten *Endo* ruling, in which the Court unanimously held that the government had no right to detain any concededly loyal citizen without charge, that both shaped and complicated the resettlement process, because the government could no longer legally confine any loyal Nisei. As a result, the army rushed to produce some 5,000 individual exclusion orders (themselves of doubtful legal validity), most of which were for internees at Tule Lake.[74] To add to the irony, the government's fears that an adverse Supreme Court decision would lead to the immediate and uncontrolled mass migration of internees, which had led the War Department to hide and distort evidence regarding the evacuation, were not realized. Neither the ACLU nor any individual among the excluded internees brought a legal challenge to the new leave clearance regulations, and the camps remained open without hindrance as the WRA wound down the internment—a process which lasted for over a year.

The government was tipped off in advance about the *Korematsu* and *Endo* rulings (presumably by Justice Felix Frankfurter, who was a close friend of McCloy and an admirer and past disciple of Stimson) a day early, on December 17. In order to anticipate the decision and keep the army from appearing to breach the law, the War Department immediately announced that it was rescinding DeWitt's exclusion orders as of January 2, 1945. General Henry Pratt, the new western defense commander, issued a proclamation allowing all Japanese Americans, except those who were found to have a "pro-Japanese attitude," to return as of that date. The WRA then issued bulletins to the internees and to camp staff explaining its plans. WRA project directors would direct their attention to facilitating the departure of residents, and all services except for schools and essential food and medical care would immediately be curtailed. All camps except for Tule Lake would close by the end of 1945.

The internees reacted to the news of the end of the internment with disbelief mixed with concern. Although most of the Nisei who had not already resettled were eager to be released, many Issei were unhappy at the idea of being forced out of the camps, where at least their basic needs were met, and left with no resources in a hostile outside society.

The WRA began implementing its new policy in earnest after the beginning of January 1945, and within a few weeks many areas of the camps had been emptied and dismantled. The JACL, along with a number of liberal and Fair Play groups that had originally opposed the internment, petitioned Ickes, Fortas, and Myer to postpone closing the camps in order to prepare better facilities on the West Coast for returning internees. Myer refused, and he toured each of the camps in order to persuade reluctant inmates to resettle. By early summer 1945, as the school term ended and the camps were stripped of their amenities, most of the inmates departed. Finally, on August 1, 1945, the WRA issued regulations ordering project directors to remove the small number of internees who had not previously scheduled their departure from camp and to transport them to the point from which they had been evacuated.

Although a significant fraction of the internees leaving the camps during the first part of 1945 accepted resettlement east of the Rockies, most residents chose to return to the Pacific Coast, as did a substantial percentage of those who had initially been resettled elsewhere. By the end of the war, some 50 percent of the formerly interned population was residing in the three West Coast states. The returnees suffered great hardship. The majority were unable to acquire or regain their farm property and were forced to seek employment as tenant farmers or as laborers in urban areas. Even those who did regain their land were harassed by enforcement of state alien land acts. The California state legislature provided funding for a series of "escheat" actions, legal proceedings to absorb "vacant" land illegally owned by Japanese Americans. Meanwhile, the Oregon legislature passed a harsh new Alien Land Act (these laws remained in effect until 1948, when the U.S. Supreme Court declared their enforcement unconstitutional). Housing was difficult to secure—much of the living space in the prewar Little Tokyos had been taken by African Americans and other war workers—and the returning internees had little money to spend on rent or other necessary living expenses. The federal government, which still hoped to discourage resettlement on the Pacific Coast, provided scant financial aid. State governments, already ill-equipped for the task of absorption and heavily influenced by anti-Japanese sentiment, offered only limited monetary support.

West Coast whites, who had formed numerous anti-Japanese organizations and demonstrated in favor of permanent exclusion, made return especially troubled. The returnees were confronted with outbreaks of racial violence in addition to the daily hostility and prejudice to which they were subjected. The WRA reported 34 separate incidents of violence against Japanese Americans by West Coast whites during the first part of 1945, notably in farm areas such as the San Joaquin and Imperial valleys in California and the Columbia River Gorge in Oregon. White mobs beat and fired bullets into the houses of Japanese Americans, and arsonists destroyed their property. In May 1945 a group of whites in Auburn, California, who confessed to dynamiting the barn of a Nisei farmer were nonetheless acquitted after their defense attorney told the jury, "This is a white man's country."[75] Ickes publicly decried the "pattern of planned terrorism" and called for the suppression of "storm-trooper tactics" and arrest of the "hoodlums" responsible, following which the terrorist attacks subsided.[76]

The closing of the other camps worsened the already hostile atmosphere at Tule Lake, where the "disloyal" internees continued to be confined. During the first months of 1945, the Justice Department began carrying out the procedures for renunciation of citizenship contained in the bill Roosevelt had signed in July 1944. Many of the Tule Lake Nisei were there because they refused to be separated from their "disloyal" Issei parents. Resentful over their continued imprisonment and believing that their parents would be deported, they were driven to renounce their citizenship in order to remain with them. In addition, a militant pro-Japanese minority that had grown up amid the harsh and joyless conditions of the camp exerted pressure on other Nisei to file renunciation requests. These "resegregants," who championed Japanese culture and sought to separate from America, organized beatings of internees considered too pro-American. Five thousand Nisei were ultimately physically or psychologically coerced into renouncing their citizenship before the regulations governing renunciation changed in mid-1945. After the end of the war, the government refused to permit these renunciants to recant, and they and their attorney, Wayne Collins, were forced into a legal struggle that lasted in some cases for over twenty years before they were finally able to regain their citizenship.

FDR remained aloof from the complex process of release and return during the beginning months of 1945, and he made no speeches or public statements during this period concerning Japanese Americans or the violence against them, although the White House awarded a Presidential Distinguished Unit Citation to the all-Nisei 442nd Combat Team in March 1945.[77] The President's health, which had noticeably improved during his reelection campaign, deteriorated markedly after Election Day, and he remained preoccupied with war and diplomatic matters, notably the Yalta Conference. A number of people both inside and outside the administration tried vainly to interest him in the situation of the returnees. Around Christmastime Ickes sent him an autographed copy of *Born Free and Equal*, photographer Ansel Adams's volume on loyal Japanese Americans, for which the secretary of the interior had written an introduction. Adams called for political leaders to act bravely in addressing the human problems of resettlement through government support of equal rights and education in tolerance.[78] Roosevelt ignored Adams's ideas and had the book placed unread alongside other gifts in his library.[79] In March 1945 Eleanor Roosevelt forwarded to her husband a letter on the problems of returnees in Puget Sound. Roosevelt passed the memo on to Ickes without taking any action.[80] FDR made no further comments on issues relating to the internment before he died on April 12, 1945.

Franklin Roosevelt's behavior in regard to Japanese Americans during 1943 and 1944 does not form a consistent pattern and appears to have been at times completely contradictory. The April 1943 letter the President sent to Harold Ickes spoke of his regret over the internment and his goal of resettlement of evacuees throughout the country; yet he simultaneously expressed to Morris Ernst his readiness to override the constitutional rights of Japanese Americans in order to keep them under guard. Less than two months later, Roosevelt specifically instructed John McCloy to avoid any suggestion that evacuees would be barred from the West Coast for the duration, and the following September FDR publicly promised to reopen the evacuated areas to the internees as soon as it was militarily possible. However, by mid-1944 he reversed himself in the face of West Coast opposition and refused to permit the internees to return to their homes, even though he was aware that there was no military necessity for exclusion.

The most likely explanation for FDR's contradictory position during these years is that he was too busy, too sick, and too indifferent to the plight of Japanese Americans to interest himself closely in the workings of the internment, with the result that he acted only when specifically called upon to do so. Roosevelt was so detached from the policy that he sent Ickes's April 1943 letter on to Milton Eisenhower for a response, forgetting that Eisenhower had long since left the WRA. He likewise routinely approved important statements on the internment drafted by his advisors, including the letter to the Senate that contained a major policy shift, without any change or evident discussion. Roosevelt was so apathetic about domestic policy matters that in mid-1944, at the same time that he delayed ending exclusion (and thus the release of the internees) until after the election, he allowed his political advisors to dictate the selection of his vice presidential candidate in the upcoming election. Although FDR must have known that he would likely not survive for another full term of office and that whoever he selected would thus become the next President, he had limited energy to devote to the matter. Roosevelt had virtually no contact with Harry Truman, his running mate, during the next months, and he made virtually no effort to involve Truman in policy, or brief him on it, either before or after the election.

Because of Roosevelt's impersonal approach to the internment, the motivation behind his actions during 1943 and 1944 is difficult to determine. What is clear is that Roosevelt acted primarily in response to the political problems created by the policy, particularly in the matter of his decision to delay opening the camps until after the 1944 election, despite his previous promise to open the West Coast as soon as militarily possible. Neither FDR nor any of his advisors considered ending the internment a strictly military question, and all were conscious of the political givens. Roosevelt suggested bringing in Earl Warren, a popular West Coast Republican, to endorse any decision to end exclusion, and he told McCloy frankly that Emmons's plan to end exclusion in summer 1944 was impossible on political grounds after consulting with his advisors on the issue. Biddle, Stettinius, and Hoover each explicitly referred to the issue of permitting internees to return to the West Coast as a political question and assumed Roosevelt would decide the question on that basis, while Fortas worried that Ickes's comments defending Japanese Americans would lead to electoral losses. Ickes himself, though he pleaded with the President to end the internment on constitutional and moral grounds, viewed the decision to do so as political and accepted the President's prerogative in the matter.

The timing of FDR's final decision likewise reveals the importance of political concerns over any other. The fact that the President finally agreed to open the camps three days after the election had taken place and that he never protested Biddle's characterization of the delay as prompted by that election is especially telling. As a much later government commission commented after a review of the matter, "The inescapable conclusion . . . is that the delay in closing the camps until after the [election] was motivated by political considerations."[81]

However, the real question is what is meant by "political considerations." The delay was not simply a matter of Roosevelt's wish to win votes in California, and it defies credulity that Stimson and McCloy, strong-minded Republicans who had joined the administration upon the express condition that they would not be involved in partisan politics, would have supported such a nakedly self-serving policy. On the contrary, as the War Department officials were the first to recognize, the success of return was, at its core, a matter of public support rather than the Japanese-American security risk. Ironically, the chief obstacle to such support was the political process itself.[82] Was Roosevelt inspired to delay resettlement, at least in part, by the fear that the resettlement program would be nullified by becoming a campaign issue, and did he thus make a decision to delay return in order to avoid politicization? The evidence is mixed. On the one hand, given the hysteria against Japanese Americans on the West Coast, the President had good reason to believe that the return of Japanese Americans to the West Coast would become even more of a "political football" (in Stimson's and McCloy's term) than it already was if it took place during the 1944 campaign season. Even more than in 1942, California media and politicians would have been likely to have engaged in anti-internee rhetoric, and the risk of anti-Japanese violence would have correspondingly increased. As it was, California Lieutenant Governor Frederick F. Houser, running for U.S. Senate on the Republican ticket, made a number of campaign speeches in which he affirmed his opposition to "turn[ing] the Japs loose" and accused the "New Deal administration" of planning to permit the evacuees to return to the West Coast and to restore their civil rights as soon as the election was over, a charge that the War Department publicly denied.[83] Although Republican presidential candidate Thomas E. Dewey dodged requests that he state his views on the question of return, his running mate, Ohio Governor John Bricker, announced that he favored allowing each community to decide whether or not to permit Japanese Americans to resettle in the area.[84] Roosevelt believed that racial barriers could be surmounted only by winning community support and avoiding confrontation. His advice to Walter White to avoid pro-internee protest campaigns in favor of local activism, whatever his other motivations for it might have been, exemplifies his belief that the success of resettlement was dependant on local acceptance, while organized protest or coercion would only exacerbate racist opposition.

On the other hand, Roosevelt did not accept the military's plans for a very gradual return to begin in summer of 1944, which he admitted that the West Coast was prepared to accept, and he did virtually nothing to assure that return would be successful. After his initial proposal to consult Earl Warren, the President did not contact any state governors or offer federal aid for resettlement. He made no speeches supporting Japanese Americans nor other efforts to educate local opinion. To the contrary, during his trip to the West Coast, he denounced Japanese people in undifferentiated and racially charged terms.

Probably Roosevelt's decision to delay return was prompted in part by his genuine interest in "dissemination and distribution" of internees throughout the country, which, though calculated to maximize "internal quiet," was more than an attempt to mask electoral expediency. Franklin Roosevelt had a long history of advocating the Americanization of minority groups as a way of relieving racial and ethnic tension. What he wanted to achieve, by whatever means, was assimilation. As the "Roosevelt" character in *The Catoctin Conversation* explains when speaking about anti-Semitism, "It's only human nature for people to want others to conform to their standards. The Jews are a race apart, a religion apart . . . a special group inside every other nation. Such separations have always caused suspicion and trouble."[85]

The vehicle which the President favored for bringing minority groups into the mainstream was the destruction of ethnic enclaves and the scattering of their residents in small numbers to undeveloped and predominantly rural areas. As early as 1920, Roosevelt, then the Democratic candidate for vice president, had laid out in an interview a conscious program of incentives for dispersion of immigrants: "We have permitted the foreign elements to segregate in colonies. They have crowded into one district and they have brought congestion and racial prejudices to our large cities. The result is that they do not easily conform to the manners and the customs and the requirements of their new home. Now, the remedy for this should be the distribution of aliens in various parts of the country."[86]

Roosevelt's interest in dispersing minority populations was also evident in his commissioning of the anthropological studies on migration and settlement which made up the "M Project." The President planned to use these studies as a basis for postwar distribution of refugees and displaced persons to less-settled regions. In connection with that project, he made inquiries at Hyde Park and at Warm Springs during early 1943 regarding postwar immigration of Jewish refugees. In July 1943 the President remarked privately that he had been informed by leaders in both communities that they would be each willing to accept about five Jewish families but no more. He thus stated that he intended to settle the refugee problem by distributing equivalent numbers of Jews to communities throughout the country.[87] This plan served as the precursor, and no doubt the model, for his plan to disperse Japanese Americans.

Roosevelt was not alone in his views on dispersion and assimilation of minorities. Rather, they reflected the prevailing sociological wisdom of the time. Many Japanese-American leaders, such as *Pacific Citizen* editor Larry Tajiri and journalist Togo Tanaka, spoke of the breaking up of the Little

Tokyos as a positive aspect of the evacuation.[88] Eleanor Roosevelt commented publicly that the United States should plan immigration policy more carefully in the future to avoid repeating the mistake of "concentrating" Japanese Americans.[89] The dispersion of the internees was also a primary goal of the WRA. Indeed, so fixed was the agency on the importance of relocation that after the war ended Myer expressed his opinion that the internment, however unnecessary, had actually been beneficial, because it was the vehicle for nationwide resettlement. "The Nisei, over the long pull, are better off as a result of the evacuation because of their dispersion over the country and the better understanding that the country as a whole has of their problem and of the problems on the West Coast."[90]

Ickes likewise publicly endorsed resettlement outside the West Coast as better for the internees and the country and was chagrined in early 1945 when his comments were cited as evidence that he opposed the internees' return to California.[91] The War Department also favored dispersion as a matter of policy. On July 7, 1942, Stimson wrote Roosevelt to warn him against possible efforts by California Governor Culbert Olson to lobby for the release of internees from the military-run Assembly Centers to help with the autumn harvest. The secretary of war objected that such release would hinder "our permanent relocation of the evacuees," which he termed "the permanent settlement of a great national problem."[92]

The fact that so many administration leaders held such ideas does not mean that the internment represented a deliberate strategy by the government to remake American society under a cloak of military necessity. However, once the evacuation had been ordered, many administration leaders came to believe that the removal of the evacuees was not simply a necessary wartime policy but an opportunity for social progress.[93] There were also practical factors in favor of dispersion. In Canada, for example, residents of Japanese ancestry were "assigned" to farms and dispersed to abandoned mining towns and settlements in the interior of the country to revive the local economy.

Nevertheless, even within administration circles the President's attitude was extreme, since he not only believed in the desirability of scattering the internees across the country but placed great faith in the feasibility of placing one or two internee families on farms in each county in the United States. The fact that Roosevelt continued to bring the plan up even after Ickes and Bonesteel had expressed opposition to it, and that he publicly endorsed the project in a press conference after the election when he no longer needed a pretext for opposing return to the West Coast, indicates the sincerity of these beliefs.

Yet, the dispersion plan was plainly unworkable on simple logistical grounds. The government would have had to transport Japanese Americans to scattered locations throughout the country and then collaborate with local forces to ensure that they were absorbed into the resident population. There is no evidence that Roosevelt or his advisors (with the exception of General Bonesteel) ever considered the financing of such a resettlement scheme, but its cost in money and effort would have been staggering. Even had the program been economically feasible, its adoption would have necessarily been tyrannical. In order to prevent ethnic conflict, the army would have to effect the involuntary transfer and geographical distribution of an internee population composed predominantly of American citizens, without any conceivable excuse of military necessity. The government would then presumably have to compel the resettled internees to remain within their assigned location, isolated from other Japanese Americans, in order to assure their absorption into white communities and the disappearance of their racial and cultural "difference."

Even though no such involuntary redistribution program was ever put into practice, the President's embrace of the idea is extremely revealing. What it shows above all else is the essential continuity in Franklin Roosevelt's perception of Japanese Americans as inherently foreign. In the 1920s, Roosevelt had referred to Japanese Americans as "unassimilable" and had defended legal discrimination against them on that basis. In the 1930s he had approved employment discrimination against citizens of alien extraction in Hawaii because of their questionable loyalty. In 1944, even after he had publicly praised the loyalty of Japanese Americans, he considered the Nikkei community such a foreign presence in the American body politic that he conceived a policy of enforced geographical and cultural assimilation as the only way to transform them into true Americans. He did not consider or question the inhumane implications of such a policy.

The President and his advisors were confronted during 1943 and 1944 with the problem of gradually dismantling the internment and opening the camps without weakening their political and legal position by admitting that they had ever made a mistake in creating them. To defend against a Supreme Court challenge that it feared would torpedo the policy of resettlement they had built up and open the floodgates of uncontrolled migration, the War Department presented a mendacious account of the necessity for evacuation and opposed any move to open the West Coast to the returning internees (thereby forestalling, for all practical purposes, the closing of the camps) for more than a year after the government had devised procedures for ensuring the release of individuals whom it conceded were loyal. Finally, after the War Department informed the President in spring 1944 that there was no longer any conceivable military reason for exclusion, Roosevelt delayed ending exclusion and opening the camps for six additional months, until after the November election.

Even if we accept that the administration tried to atone for its previous policy and steer a reasonable course out of the internment, Roosevelt bears considerable responsibility for the delays in freeing Japanese Americans, since his predicament was in large part one of his own creation. The hazards he faced in resolving his political dilemma over ending the internment were in large measure the natural consequences of policies that he undertook without sufficient thought at the beginning, and that should not have been permitted to take precedence over the constitutional rights of American citizens. As it turned out, the administration's fears of court-ordered release of the internees and violent opposition to their return proved to be greatly exaggerated. The Supreme Court avoided ruling on the internment until December 1944, and even then its decision in the *Endo* case did not alter the progress of the government's plans for closing the camps. Despite isolated outbreaks of racial violence, the return of the internees to the Pacific Coast was accomplished without rioting or significant trouble, even though the President made no effort to ensure its success. Thus, the internment could have been ended earlier without widespread bloodshed, especially if President Roosevelt had been willing to use his great prestige on behalf of Japanese Americans. His refusal to commit himself to defending the rights of American citizens and loyal aliens, whether it sprang from his wish to be reelected or from a belief that the internees were not really Americans, was costly.

THE PRESIDENT OF
ALL THE PEOPLE?

FRANKLIN ROOSEVELT'S signing of Executive Order
9066 and his direction of the ensuing internment of
the West Coast Japanese Americans came about as the
result of a complex interplay of circumstances and
motives. The Japanese bombing of Pearl Harbor did
more than sink ships and kill soldiers; it left a deep
wound in the American psyche. The surprise attack
provoked nationwide anger and a desire for revenge
against Japan which far surpassed American bitterness
against Germany or Italy. This hatred did not translate
immediately or directly into attacks or restrictions on
Japanese Americans, although a few people, notably
Navy Secretary Frank Knox, favored immediate repressive action against them. During December 1941
the community was left largely alone. Even in Hawaii,
which remained vulnerable to invasion and where
martial law was in effect, the local Japanese were not
subjected as a group to special restrictions.

However, as the Japanese army raced through Asia
and the Pacific in early 1942, overrunning Southeast
Asia and the Philippines, the nation's rage over Pearl

Harbor became overlaid with fear and anxiety. Most people in the United States, whether in the government, in the military, or on the street, knew very little about Japan. They were accustomed to viewing the Japanese in stereotypical terms as a small and distant race whose industry and military produced inferior imitations of Western models. Japan's military victories overturned their most basic ideas about the world and gave rise to feelings of enormous physical and emotional insecurity.

These intertwined feelings of rage and insecurity were magnified on the West Coast. First, the West Coast was at the border of the Pacific and would be the staging ground for an invasion of the United States. Japan had confounded so many people's expectations that American military and civilian leaders seriously considered the possibility of a Japanese invasion—and continued to believe in it and fear it long after it had proven to be a chimera. More importantly, the region was home to 120,000 Japanese Americans with the "face of the enemy," on whom West Coast whites could project their hostility toward Japan. Moreover, just as Japan's shocking success had confounded the expectations of Americans in regard to the Japanese, West Coast whites began to perceive Japanese Americans, whom they were used to thinking of as essentially Japanese, as an unpredictable and thus dangerous element. With the aid of opportunistic politicians and commercial and nativist groups that had long resented the Nikkei's presence and economic success, these fears gave birth to rumors of fifth column activity. The feeling of being surrounded by potential enemies which engulfed the West Coast population also plagued local army commanders (and, through them, War Department leaders). To military leaders such as General DeWitt, Japanese Americans were a faceless mass whose feelings and loyalties were unknowable. As popular anti-Japanese sentiment escalated and rumors of subversion became more frequent, army staffers became convinced that there must be some foundation for them. Since the army's fear was based on ignorance, it resisted evidence or rational arguments to the contrary, while every step the Justice Department took to meet or moderate demands to ensure security led DeWitt to escalate his demands for repression of Japanese Americans. The extent of General DeWitt's hysteria about the Japanese-American threat can be seen in his refusal, once he issued his exclusion order, to approve any exceptions even for orphaned Nisei babies or young children.

Franklin Roosevelt, like most Americans, was outraged by the Pearl Harbor attack. He immediately devoted himself to the task of winning the war and engrossed himself in cementing relations among the Allies, planning military strategy for conflict with the Axis powers on multiple fronts, and guiding conversion of American industry to a war economy. In contrast with his active leadership of the war effort, he remained a passive and distracted figure in the conflict over Japanese Americans. He did not immediately connect Japanese Americans with the Japanese danger. On the contrary, he rejected Knox's pleas for action against Japanese Americans during mid-December, and he expressed interest in Curtis Munson's scheme to support the loyal Nisei. The demise of that plan after the beginning of January 1942 revealed, however, the narrow limits of the President's interest in the matter. When the War Department and West Coast political officials began to press for mass removal in early February, the President chose to go along. He was unwilling to devote sufficient attention to the matter to see the weakness of the case for evacuation and the bias and opportunism that underlay it.

Two closely interrelated elements stand out strongly as determinative in the President's decision and his subsequent actions. One of these was undoubtedly Roosevelt's own negative beliefs about Japanese Americans, while the other was a failure of political and moral leadership that resulted from weaknesses in his presidential style and administrative organization. FDR's hostile attitude toward Japanese Americans had deep roots in his past. As early as 1913, when legal discrimination against Japanese aliens in California brought Japan and the United States close to war, the young FDR, then at the outset of his career in public service, began to regard both the Issei immigrants and their American-born Nisei children as a menace—a foreign and racially "unassimilable" population whose presence was a source of both chronic irritation to their white "American" neighbors and conflict with Japan. During the 1920s, even as he praised the Japanese government and called for closer relations between the two countries, Roosevelt publicly opposed any further immigration of the Japanese into the United States. He justified discriminatory legislation against Japanese aliens on the West Coast as a means of preserving white "racial purity." Although FDR did not consider people of Japanese ancestry racially inferior, in his view they were a biologically distinct people who were innately incapable of adapting to American society or becoming true Americans. He argued that they needed to be kept apart, and he considered anti-Japanese nativist sentiment reasonable and just.

FDR's suspicious attitude toward the Nikkei community became crucial during the long period of deteriorating relations between Japan and the United States that preceded Pearl Harbor. The President assumed that Japanese Americans, whom he considered innately Japanese, would identify with their mother country and act as fifth columnists in the war to come. His view of people of Japanese descent as a discrete, unified group irrespective of nationality, age, or experience shaped his policy toward them. Once Japan launched its successful surprise attack, FDR was prepared to believe the various rumors and reports of espionage by Japanese Americans in Hawaii and on the West Coast. Ignoring the fact that the reports were proven to be false and that credible sources vouched for the loyalty of Japanese Americans, he ordered the mass removal and internment of Japanese Americans living on the West Coast, and he pushed for a similar evacuation in Hawaii, although he was unable to carry out the project due to logistical difficulties and local resistance.

The President's inability to conceive of people of Japanese ancestry as true Americans contributed to his failure to intervene to protect their liberty and property rights in the face of public hysteria. As late as the November 1944 press conference, Roosevelt was still referring to the Nisei as "Japanese people from Japan who are citizens" despite the fact that there was no such category of person during his lifetime (apart from a handful of World War I veterans naturalized in the 1930s). Although he realized that the Nisei were United States citizens, Roosevelt was unwilling to recognize that they had the same inalienable rights to due process and equal protection of the laws as other citizens. Rather, he spoke vaguely about their citizenship as giving them certain legal "privileges," which could by implication be sacrificed to an overriding public interest in security or the exigencies of speedy evacuation. This could be sanctioned, he believed, as a more lenient alternative to declaration of martial law or suspension of the writ of *habeas corpus*.

Even after the internees' "loyalty" was favorably reviewed by a joint military board, Roosevelt continued to view Japanese Americans as a foreign element that had to be isolated and contained. He had virtually no contact with Japanese-American communities, and he showed no interest in or appreciation of their contributions to the nation's culture and society. On the contrary, he sought to solve the "Japanese problem" by developing a plan to break up these communities and "scatter" the ethnic Japanese population throughout the country, distributing one or two families to each locality. Roosevelt's forced scattering policy was not seriously considered by his advisors, even those who favored such resettlement on a voluntary basis, and the plan was never implemented. Not only did the President fail to consider the expense and effort such a policy would entail, but his conception revealed a total disregard for the needs and desires of the Japanese-American individuals whose family ties and community life he sought to destroy. Though FDR's plan was meant to reduce anti-Japanese-American prejudice by eliminating Japanese Americans as a distinct community, it was so extreme and coercive as to constitute a classic example of blaming the victims of racism for the discrimination against them.

It is instructive to compare Roosevelt's attitude in regard to Japanese Americans with that of his secretary of war, Henry Stimson. Stimson had strongly negative feelings toward racial minorities, and his personal diary is laced with offhand comments that reveal a racist streak (such as a reference to the president of Liberia as an "irresponsible coon").[1] Stimson's racial feelings helped make him the administration's primary advocate of evacuation. He firmly believed that the racial characteristics of Japanese Americans made it impossible to trust them as a group or to distinguish loyal individuals from disloyal ones.[2] Yet, Stimson was conscious of the racist nature of such a position, and he strongly pushed his subordinates to present a compelling case for military necessity in order to justify "blow[ing] a tremendous hole in our Constitutional system" by an evacuation based only on racial factors.

Stimson continued to agonize over the internment once it was set into motion. He publicly defended the army's actions, but he privately expressed his regrets. As he stated in his postwar memoirs, he was well aware that whatever the government's reasons, "it remained a fact that to loyal citizens this forced evacuation was a personal injustice, and Stimson fully appreciated their feelings."[3] Both during and after the initial evacuation, Stimson stressed the citizenship rights of the Nisei and opposed discriminatory legislation. Partly in the hope of easing the internees' future reintegration into society, in late 1942 he wrote a memo supporting the recruitment of Japanese-American soldiers. After the all-Nisei 442nd Combat Infantry Unit was mobilized, Stimson trumpeted its excellent record in combat, which he considered conclusive proof of the good citizenship of the Nisei and "a splendid example of true Americanism."[4] While the secretary of war remained suspicious of "disloyal" internees and campaigned for their isolation, once he became convinced that no military danger to the West Coast existed, he pushed vainly to end the internment as an urgent matter of civil liberties. After Japanese Americans began returning to the West Coast, Stimson spoke out in favor of their patriotism and civil rights. In 1945 he referred to an act of violence against a returning Nisei veteran as "an inexcusable and dastardly outrage."[5]

In contrast, Roosevelt never revealed any hesitation over the racist implications or the possible constitutional violations of evacuation. His paramount object was to win the war. He feared that Japanese Americans presented a danger to security and to West Coast morale, and he believed that he was empowered to approve a policy that represented the most expeditious and least intrusive means of removing that danger. Compared to winning the war, the legal and moral questions involved in evacuation were, in FDR's view, trivial. As he stated in another context, "The President has the power, under the Constitution and under Congressional acts, to take measures necessary to avert a disaster which would interfere with the winning of the war."[6]

Even more strikingly, throughout the internment Roosevelt evinced a remarkable lack of interest in the consequences of his policies. Although FDR expressed his desire that the evacuation process be "reasonable" and not unduly punitive, he showed virtually no concern for the extraordinary needs it created among its victims. Instead, he told his advisors that he was not concerned about the internees' property, and he apparently never considered compensating them for their losses. Further, despite repeated calls from both inside and outside the administration for a presidential statement explaining the internment policy and praising the loyalty of the majority of Japanese Americans, he declined to issue any such message until after almost a year had passed and widespread public hostility toward the internees had become entrenched. He took little interest in conditions in the camps, and he met only once with WRA Director Dillon Myer. In the months after the West Coast was finally reopened to Japanese Americans and the internees began to return home from the camps, he provided no verbal support or government initiatives to aid them in their readjustment to normal life.

Roosevelt's conduct of public policy was not designed to consciously punish Japanese Americans or exact revenge on them for Japanese atrocities. In fact, he expressed a desire that the evacuation be carried out humanely, and he created a civilian agency, the WRA, to provide essential services to the internees in the camps. But FDR's negative—one might even say hostile—

attitude toward Americans of Japanese descent revealed itself in a malign indifference to the rights and interests of Japanese Americans. His failure to conceive of them in essential terms as Americans entitled to equal treatment meant that he did not offer the internees his support, public or private, nor provide leadership for efforts to limit or compensate them for the physical and financial sacrifices they were forced to make.

Whatever role Roosevelt's personal biases and blind spots may have played in his decisions, his direction of the internment was equally the result of a failure of his presidential leadership. Roosevelt has often been celebrated as a model of presidential achievement, and the successful reforms of the New Deal have been attributed largely to his pragmatic administrative style. Historians have extolled FDR's advocacy of "bold, persistent experimentation" with creative and unorthodox programs to revive the national economy, his willingness to compromise and accept half-measures in support of his goals, and his readiness to alter or jettison programs that did not work.[7]

These historians found a corollary to the programmatic flexibility of the New Deal in the President's organization of the expanded White House bureaucracy that the New Deal programs brought into being. They are particularly admiring of Roosevelt's habit of dividing authority between competing advisors and delegating responsibility to agencies with overlapping mandates in order to mediate between factions and concentrate ultimate power in his own hands. Arthur Schlesinger, Jr., remarked that Roosevelt's fuzzy administrative methods "often provided a testing of initiative, competence, and imagination which produced far better results than playing by the book."[8]

Frank Freidel added that the genius of this system was that it permitted FDR to keep himself informed of developments: "On the whole the [advisors] presented vigorously their alternative views from which the President could choose, more often than not complemented each other in their thinking, and their competitiveness to achieve was of benefit to Roosevelt."[9]

In contrast, the unfolding of the President's decision to approve evacuation and his subsequent conduct of the internment highlight the negative side of Roosevelt's pragmatic philosophy and decision-making process: the disregard of formal legal process; the sudden shifts of policy in response to immediate political currents; the failure to plan for contingencies; and the overreliance on FDR's own initiative.

Roosevelt's dislike of theoretical considerations and his devotion to compromise and achievable ends often resulted in a more realistic and useful assessment of what action to take. However, these same factors tended to make him overly sensitive to immediate conditions and political considerations in setting policy, particularly in areas where he did not have an overriding objective or strong inner motivation. In the case of the decision to evacuate, Roosevelt was prepared to leave most Japanese Americans alone until a strong movement arose among the military and public on the West Coast for evacuation. In the face of political pressure from West Coast governors and congressmen, the President quickly assented to taking drastic action against the Japanese-American community. Once the evacuation began, the President and his advisors almost immediately abandoned their initial idea of voluntary relocation or individual resettlement because of the nationwide opposition to having Japanese Americans, who were considered sufficiently dangerous to be removed from the West Coast, settle in their own cities and states. The government thus confined the internees in camps for an indefinite period of time, despite the fact that Executive Order 9066 did not provide for such incarceration and government officials admitted that such confinement was a violation of constitutional rights.

The conduct of the internment was reshaped constantly to serve the administration's political interests, and the President's direct involvement in internment policy after 1942 was restricted in large part to its political defense. With Roosevelt's approval, administration advisors designed a cumbersome and avowedly unconstitutional parole system in order to make the release of internees politically acceptable to public opinion. They combined the parole system with a punitive and questionable policy of segregating and confining those internees whom the government considered "disloyal" based on their scores on the loyalty exam. By spring 1944, as the tide of the Pacific War had decisively turned, Roosevelt was informed by his advisors that there was no longer any possible military justification for internment. Nevertheless, he refused to absorb the political responsibility for release—despite his own previous public promise to expedite the return of loyal Japanese Americans to their homes. Concerned with election-year politics, FDR eventually ordered all action on ending exclusion from the West Coast halted until after the November election. Meanwhile, as the internees remained confined, Roosevelt explored various politically palatable alternatives to opening the

West Coast. Even after the election was over, he finally agreed to release the internees only because he knew that the Supreme Court was about to over-turn their confinement in any case, leaving the government with no control over the release process. His agreement to release was smoothed after Secretary of War Stimson, a prominent Republican, offered to take upon himself the full burden of responsibility for such action.

While the President's emphasis on improvisation generally meant he could meet a crisis situation quickly and imaginatively, it also meant that he neglected at times to think through the implications of his programs, a fault for which he was often criticized by his detractors during his lifetime. In the case of Japanese Americans, Roosevelt decided on evacuation with little or no thought about its possible unintended consequences. Even Stimson was surprised by the casualness of the President's approval and irritated by his failure to devote any attention to the practical details involved in the her-culean task of removal. Roosevelt did not consider that evacuation would lead to the long-term incarceration of Japanese Americans, who would have no means of support once they were removed from their homes and jobs. Nor did he consider their need for protection against the widespread hostility generated by the government's decision to eject them from their homes. Also, he did not anticipate that the internees would be stigmatized as disloyal by their removal, and that the issue of their eventual release would cause dif-ficulties even after the perceived security crisis passed.

The decision to evacuate also reflected flaws in Roosevelt's administrative organization. In his policy-making process, the President depended largely on his ability to keep himself informed of developments and to balance his advisors' contrasting reports and competing viewpoints. Yet, any President is only as effective as the advice he receives, and FDR's ability to make a well-informed decision was especially dependent on the skill and assiduousness with which rival factions were able to reach him. In the case of the evacua-tion, Roosevelt was either overly preoccupied with his duties as war leader or unprepared to seek out fully the nature and ramifications of the opposing views. On the contrary, because of the war situation he was especially sus-ceptible to influence from his military advisors, who were able to set the terms of the debate over removal. In the end, he accepted the need for evacu-ation on the largely unsupported recommendation of Secretary of War Stimson, a prestigious advisor who had daily access to the Oval Office. FDR overruled the well-founded objections of Attorney General Biddle, a newcomer to the Cabinet who was not a close advisor. His dependence on advisors in this instance led to an unbalanced presentation of information and an ill-conceived policy.

At the same time, the internment revealed the flaws inherent in the President's insistence on controlling policy, which made government action dependent on his constant approval. James MacGregor Burns commented that "by establishing in an agency one power center that counteracted another, [Roosevelt] made each official more dependent on White House support; the President in effect became the necessary ally and partner of both."[10] Although designed to counteract chaos and bureaucratic inertia, the President's refusal to delegate policy-making authority all too often led to stagnation when he was unable or unwilling to devote sufficient attention to a matter. This was especially true in the case of Roosevelt's failure to make provision for the care of internees' property during the first months of 1942. His refusal to resolve the competing claims of Leo Crowley and Henry Morgenthau to custodianship of alien property meant that no policy could be put in place to protect the internees. Consequently, thousands of Japanese Americans were deprived of their possessions by being cheated out of them by the "friends" who held them, or forced to dispose of them cheaply to scavengers and speculators, or left with no alternative but to abandon them. This great tragedy could have been minimized had Roosevelt taken steps to order the establishment of an efficient agency to administer and hold the internees' property. Roosevelt's failure to delegate such authority not only cost the internees millions of dollars in property losses, but the loss of personal and family possessions inflicted untold psychological harm on them.

On the afternoon of April 12, 1945, Franklin Roosevelt died of a cerebral hemorrhage at Warm Springs, Georgia. Word of the President's death spread rapidly across the United States. Millions of Americans would be able to recall in later years exactly what they were doing when they heard the news. All through the country, people sat in stunned silence or wept openly in the streets. As the day passed, word of FDR's demise reached the world's leaders. Winston Churchill later stated that when he received the bulletin in England, he felt the news like a body blow. In Moscow, Stalin sent Foreign Minister Molotov to the American Embassy to express his regrets. In Tokyo, Premier Suzuki made an official announcement of Japan's profound sympathy—a chivalrous gesture widely reported in the enemy American press.

The collective sense of loss was deep and personal. Franklin Roosevelt had been in office for over twelve years and his administration had transformed the country. Most young Americans, including countless soldiers, could not remember any other President. The sorrow was compounded by the knowledge that, as the most bitter and destructive war in history drew to a close, the man who had been the chief architect of the victorious alliance had not lived to see the peace.[11]

When FDR died, the internment had not yet ended. On April 12, 1945, approximately 18,000 people remained imprisoned at Tule Lake, and some 55,000 internees were confined in the eight remaining camps (only the camp at Jerome had been emptied and closed). In February 1945 the WRA had announced its intention of closing all camps other than Tule Lake within a year, but many internees refused to be relocated amid the hostile and potentially dangerous conditions prevailing outside. As the war drew to a close and anti–Japanese-American tensions eased, the pace of resettlement accelerated. Nevertheless, the WRA was ultimately forced to evict a number of internees in order to finally shut down the camps. By December 1945 all the "relocation centers" were empty; the Tule Lake "detention center" closed its gates in March 1946.

The internment left its mark on the Japanese-American community. The internees had been excluded from the wartime economic boom and generally lacked resources. They were forced, especially on the West Coast, to accept substandard housing and low-status employment. The Issei, stripped of their property and mentally and physically shattered by their confinement, were generally unable to start again from scratch and rebuild their businesses or farms. The Nisei struggled bravely to overcome the effects of their incarceration. During the postwar years they entered institutions of higher education in accelerating numbers and concentrated on building successful careers. By the 1970s, Japanese-American educational and family income levels ranked above national averages. These achievements, however, not only obscured the continuing discrimination against Nisei and significant numbers of families living in poverty, but they masked the psychological stress the Nisei community experienced, which expressed itself in family dysfunction and substance abuse.

The federal government was slow to recognize the injustice of the internment. Congress passed a law in 1948 granting token reparations for actual property losses by evacuees, but the Justice Department took several years to settle cases and those compensated were required to waive all other claims against the government. In 1976 President Gerald Ford formally revoked Executive Order 9066 and praised the contributions of Japanese Americans. During the 1970s Japanese-American activists formed a network of organizations to press the government for an official apology and financial reparations for the internment. In response to this "Redress Movement," in 1980 the Commission on Wartime Relocation and Internment of Civilians (CWRIC) was created by Congress to gather information and recommend action. In 1983, following eighteen months of public hearings and evidentiary review, the commission released its report, *Personal Justice Denied,* which contained an official finding that the internment had been unnecessary and unjust and which recommended that a redress payment be made to the victims of Executive Order 9066. The commission stated: "Executive Order 9066 was not justified by military necessity, and the decisions that followed from it—exclusion, detention, the ending of detention and the ending of exclusion were not founded upon military considerations. The broad historical causes that shaped these decisions were race prejudice, war hysteria, and a failure of political leadership."[12]

Following release of the report, a bill based on the commission's recommendations was introduced in Congress, but it stalled. Opponents of the redress bill, led by the aged John McCloy, insisted that the evacuation had been reasonable and humane and asserted that President Roosevelt, in particular, had not been influenced in his decision by racism because he did not have "a shred of racial prejudice" in him.[13] It was not until five years later that a redress bill finally passed Congress and was signed into law by President Ronald Reagan. It provided for an official apology and a tax-free payment of $20,000 to each person who had been evacuated. Meanwhile, teams of lawyers led by Peter Irons, Rod Kawakami, Dale Minami, and Peggy Nagae brought a series of actions under the seldom-used writ of error *coram nobis* to overturn the convictions of Gordon Hirabayashi, Minoru Yasui, and Fred Korematsu, Japanese Americans who had challenged Executive Order 9066 and the evacuation, on the grounds that their trials had been tainted by government misconduct. The lawyers presented newly discovered proof of the War Department's knowing presentation of false information and its suppression and manipulation of relevant evidence in the wartime Supreme Court cases. Following legal hearings, in the mid-1980s Federal District Court judges vacated the convictions of the three defendants.

Of course, the granting of redress and the legal victories, although important symbolically, did not and could not compensate for the irrevocable loss
of freedom, jobs, property, and dignity which the internment imposed on
Japanese Americans. However, these achievements capped the long struggle
of Japanese Americans to come to terms with their internment experience
and to achieve closure. As decades passed and the wartime events grew more
distant, Japanese Americans became absorbed in studying the internment in
order to understand what happened and to assess its lessons. In the process,
their feelings about the President who had directed the policy began to shift.
Although the available evidence of Japanese-American views of Roosevelt is
fragmentary and anecdotal, it suggests that a dramatic reversal in sentiment
took place among the former internees after FDR's death.

Before the internment, Roosevelt was a genuine hero to many Japanese
Americans, especially the young Nisei, as he was to most Americans, and the
community responded to news of the war by offering him a very personal
expression of allegiance. In the wake of Pearl Harbor, the JACL and other
Nisei groups rushed to send telegrams to the President expressing their support for him. The JACL's telegram read, "In this solemn hour we pledge our
fullest cooperation to you, Mr. President, and to our country. There cannot
be any question, there must be no doubt. We, in our hearts, know we are
Americans—loyal to America. We must prove that to all of you."[14] A Buddhist church held special prayers for the President's health and safety.[15]

As war hysteria accelerated and the pressure for removal of Japanese
Americans on the West Coast grew, the Nisei latched even more firmly onto
the President's shadow in the hope of warding off danger. In mid-February,
the *Rafu Shimpo* newspaper (which devoted the front page of its January 1,
1942, issue to a portrait of Roosevelt) told its readers, "Are you a loyal American? TO EVERY LOYAL NISEI: Speak up now! Write or wire your stand to
the President."[16] At a public meeting on February 19—the day Executive
Order 9066 was signed—one JACL activist referred to FDR as "that great
American President and statesman." Another added that "our greatest friend
is a man who is probably the greatest living man, Franklin Delano Roosevelt"
and urged the entire audience to write the President and their congressmen
to apprise them of the situation.[17]

Although the signing of Executive Order 9066 and the subsequent evacuation dimmed some of the ardor of the Nisei for Roosevelt, and their admiring references to him ceased, many Japanese Americans continued to rely on

him. The old attachment to Roosevelt was not easily broken. A number of Japanese Americans assumed that the President must have been badly advised or uninformed and would soon correct his mistake. Indeed, for many Japanese Americans, especially Issei, the fact that the esteemed President had ordered them to evacuate may have foreclosed any thought of resistance.[18] Many Nisei felt that expressions of faith in the President demonstrated their steadfast loyalty to America. At the beginning of March, when activist Yone Sakai designed a proposed loyalty exam for journalists, he included a question which put the issue of allegiance in starkly personal terms: "Whom do you respect, Franklin Roosevelt or the Japanese Emperor?"[19] The internees, both Issei and Nisei, wrote FDR to express their support for the war effort, to offer themselves for military duty, and to ask him to improve conditions in the camps: one Nisei boy even asked the President to send him money for a model airplane![20]

Japanese-American newspapers reported favorably on the President's policies and eagerly construed his statements regarding Japanese Americans as evidence of his support and sympathy. Frank Hijikata reported in *The Tulean Dispatch* that FDR's February 1943 announcement in favor of Nisei enlistment meant that the "word of President Roosevelt" now stood against the ill-informed opinion of anti–Japanese-American demagogues.[21] Similarly, *The Pacific Citizen* seized on Roosevelt's September 1943 letter to the Senate praising the loyal evacuees and promising them an expedited return to the West Coast as proof that the internment had never been racially motivated.[22] FDR continued to enjoy electoral support from many Nisei, especially those outside the evacuated zone. In 1944 Nisei organizations such as the Independent Nisei Voters Committee of Chicago and the New York-based Japanese American Committee for Democracy, which were made up of local residents who had never been interned plus resettled internees, endorsed Roosevelt's candidacy, praising the liberal humanitarian reforms of the New Deal and the antidiscrimination efforts of the President's Fair Employment Practices Committee. Two hundred Nisei in New York attended a rally in support of FDR's reelection.[23] A number of Nisei in the camps marked absentee ballots for Roosevelt in the November 1944 election.[24]

Admiring feelings were not unanimous, however. Internees included the President by implication in their complaints about the government, and even some of the Nisei who voted for him did so merely as a "known evil" who was better than an unknown one. Furthermore, while some internees censored their expressions of opposition to the President or the administration for fear of being labeled disloyal, a few singled out Roosevelt for censure in their writings. Kiyoshi Okamoto, who founded the Heart Mountain Fair Play Committee to protest the conscription of Japanese Americans deprived of citizenship rights, denounced the President in a letter for his invasion of constitutional rights.[25] A striking example of internee disillusionment with Roosevelt is contained in the diary of Kasen Noda, an internee at Rohwer and Tule Lake. In mid-1943 Noda referred to the President in his diary as a "great" man. However, he became offended soon after when he heard a radio address in which Roosevelt referred to the Japanese several times as "Japs." On Lincoln's birthday 1945, he commented, "I wonder if we will ever have another great president like Lincoln. If he is like him, then he will see the Japanese problem. He will say, 'Don't call them Japs. They are good citizens like the rest of us Americans.'"[26] Still, such sentiments, at least in written form, were rare among internees.

The Japanese Americans, internees as well as others, were stricken by FDR's death. In Hawaii and on the mainland outside the camps, large numbers of people attended remembrances for the President in churches, Buddhist temples, and schools.[27] The JACL sent telegrams of condolence to Washington, and the league's newspaper, *The Pacific Citizen,* recorded Roosevelt's passing with a black-bordered front-page editorial eulogy. "He believed in democracy and his humanitarianism knew no political or geographical boundaries, no limitations fixed by race or color or creed."[28] The English-language section of the independent Denver Japanese newspaper *Rocky Shimpo,* which the administration had accused of disloyalty because of its opposition to drafting internees, echoed its readers' grief. "To the multitude of evacuees, the President, and Mrs. Roosevelt, have been . . . sympathetic and understanding friends."[29] Nisei soldiers felt a particular sense of loss. Frank "Foo" Fujita, a Japanese-American Texan being held by the Japanese as a prisoner of war, recorded that the news was a "terrible shock" for him, as Roosevelt was "not only my beloved Commander-in-Chief, but one of America's great Presidents."[30] In Europe, the members of the 442nd Regimental Combat Team chipped in funds for a memorial to Roosevelt. A delegation of soldiers subsequently delivered $4,315.53 in donations to President Truman in a ceremony in September 1945.

Within the camps, where the WRA ordered the flags to be flown at half-mast in honor of FDR, there was an outpouring of emotion. The staff of the

Heart Mountain Sentinel sent a telegram to Eleanor Roosevelt on behalf of the camp's inhabitants, expressing profound sorrow and paying tribute to the "fundamental honesty, integrity, and belief of the world's greatest leader against intolerance, bigotry, and fascism."[31] Entertainment events were cancelled and special memorial services were held at all the camps, including Tule Lake.[32] *The New York Times* reported that 3,000 people attended the memorial at Manzanar, where Catholic, Protestant, and Buddhist clergymen collectively led an English-Japanese service.[33]

The sorrow that Japanese Americans felt at Roosevelt's death was unquestionably genuine. Still, the tributes could not efface the pain and bitterness the internment had caused, and Roosevelt's stature in the Japanese-American community began to diminish gradually after the war. During the postwar years, some former internees reportedly refused to speak FDR's name, and a number of voters switched their registration from Democrat to Republican. Others who remained Democrats distanced themselves from Roosevelt. The actor George Takei recalled that his Issei father, who was working for Adlai Stevenson at the 1960 Democratic National Convention, refused to meet Eleanor Roosevelt because of her connection to FDR.[34] In spite of such evidence of discontent, the former internees' resentment toward Roosevelt remained largely dormant or concealed during the early postwar years. As late as 1969, two white critics of the internment reported that Japanese Americans did not generally hold Roosevelt responsible for their incarceration.[35]

By the mid-1960s, however, former internees began to express increasingly negative attitudes toward FDR. Histories by former internees referred to Roosevelt's wartime actions in words such as "political expediency," "culpable," and "motivated by racial bias."[36] As one Nisei summed up the revised assessment of Roosevelt: "FDR—a worldly person, he was not; a constitutional president, he was not; a strong willed president, he was not. All of these shortcomings are exhibited in his decision to sign Executive Order 9066."[37] Democratic U.S. Congressman Norman Mineta, a California Nisei who had been interned as a child, publicly decried the "wrong" that Roosevelt and the others responsible for the internment had committed.[38]

In part this new attitude was a product of the slow simmering of the internees' anger over their experience, which had previously been repressed by the shock and shame the internment had instilled. Once Japanese Americans absorbed the fact that the government which they had so fervently supported had wantonly violated their constitutional rights, they began to feel pain and resentment toward the chief executive who had ordered their confinement. Presumably for much the same reasons, WRA Director Dillon Myer, who had been celebrated by Japanese Americans in the years during and after the war as "the great white father" for his humane administration of the camps and defense of the internees against anti–Japanese-American bigots, came under concentrated attack during the 1980s as the deceitful and paternalistic "jailer" of the internees. Throughout the twelve-plus years of his presidency, Franklin Roosevelt had been the living, visible symbol of a benevolent federal government. His portrait hung in iconic glory in homes and businesses throughout the nation, including Japanese ones. The fact that Roosevelt signed Executive Order 9066 thus triggered a particular feeling of betrayal and outrage among Japanese Americans.

The shift in attitude toward FDR reflected the adoption of a more militant self-consciousness within the Japanese-American community as a whole. As the Issei and older Nisei who had been community leaders aged and died off, a new generation of younger Nisei and of Sansei—third-generation Americans who had been born after the war—rose to prominence in the Nikkei community. These younger leaders resented the ethos of conformity and silence that the older generations had imposed on the Japanese-American community, and they lacked the sense of personal shame and stigma over the internment that their elders had felt. With the aid and encouragement of the Sansei activists, a group of former internees inaugurated the "Redress Movement" of the 1970s and 1980s, holding remembrances and attending public hearings in which many of them spoke publicly for the first time about their traumatic wartime experience. Once the lid on their rage and resentment had been removed, it poured forth freely, and it covered FDR as the leader of the country that had betrayed its promise of equality to them.

The change in Roosevelt's stature among Japanese Americans after the 1960s is an extreme case of the gradual shift in opinion on Roosevelt that was simultaneously taking place among other Americans, particularly African Americans and Jewish Americans. As he was for Japanese Americans, FDR was a beloved figure among these groups during his lifetime. Black and Jewish advisors were more visible in the Roosevelt White House than in previous administrations, and government programs were administered more fairly and less discriminatorily than before. In a period of widespread racist and anti-Semitic hostility the President was able (with considerable help from his wife, Eleanor) to convey to individual minority group members the feeling that he understood their concerns. With increased distance from the events and greater ethnic awareness and self-confidence, as well as open access to archives and historical records of the period, members of younger generations held the President to a higher standard in judging his interventions in regard to minority rights. Many Jews have questioned whether Roosevelt did enough to save European Jews during the Holocaust, and some have accused him of being anti-Semitic. Similarly, as African Americans have grown more assertive in demanding equal justice, they became increasingly critical of Roosevelt's poor record on civil rights legislation.

The President did not conduct the internment alone, and he should not be saddled with the entire burden of guilt for it. Nevertheless, Roosevelt failed to transcend the prejudice around him in his direction of public policy. Because of his early training and experiences, FDR was ready to believe that Japanese Americans posed an indiscriminate threat to national security, and he persisted in this belief without ever attempting to check the credible information to the contrary. He also deserves censure for not providing moral and constitutional leadership. Although his duty as President of the United States was to protect the constitutional rights of all citizens, he repeatedly subverted the rights of those of Japanese descent. His decision to sign Executive Order 9066 was made casually, with no consideration or weighing of the racial or constitutional implications of that action. After he ordered the evacuation, Roosevelt effectively stripped the internees of their property and possessions, but he did not offer any restitution or just compensation for their financial losses. He did not consider instituting immediate loyalty hearings, even though the government later took the position in Court that the loyalty of Japanese Americans could be so determined. He refused to take steps to permit internees to return immediately to their homes even after the government endorsed their loyalty. On the contrary, he prolonged the internees' confinement for several months after he knew there was no military justification for it.

And finally, Roosevelt bears a special measure of guilt for his inability to project any real sympathy or consideration for the concerns and interests of the interned Japanese Americans. FDR made little effort to defend the internees from the stigma of disloyalty in the months after Executive Order 9066 was signed, and he took no recorded steps to improve conditions in the camps. He refused his advisors' pleas that he demonstrate his faith in the internees or publicly declare resettlement to be in the national interest. Once

Japanese Americans were released from the camps, FDR made no effort to assist them in the difficult task of reintegrating into mainstream society. In contrast, Roosevelt's successor as President, Harry Truman, was a notable defender, both privately and publicly, of the rights of Japanese Americans. When Truman learned in December 1945 of the discrimination and violent resistance facing returning internees in California, he was outraged, and he immediately ordered his attorney general to investigate whether there was any way that the federal government could either legally intervene or pressure state authorities into doing their duty to enforce the law. The disgraceful conduct of the Californians, he snapped, "almost make[s] you believe that a lot of our Americans have a streak of Nazi in them."[39] In 1946 Truman invited the 442nd Regimental Combat Team to the White House and told the Nisei soldiers, "You fought not only the enemy, but you fought prejudice—and you have won."[40] He also privately lobbied congressional leaders during 1946 to pass a bill to compensate the internees for losses. When Congress failed to act, Truman made a public appeal for evacuation claims legislation as part of the civil rights program he submitted to Congress in 1948, and he signed the bill into law that August. Roosevelt's unwillingness to demonstrate a similar commitment to the rights and well-being of Japanese Americans is glaring, and the wanton indiference he displayed to the human dimensions of a public policy sets forth more clearly and powerfully the injustice of his actions.

NOTE ON TERMINOLOGY

THERE IS NO agreed-upon set of terms to describe either the government's wartime policy toward Japanese Americans or its components. On the contrary, the highly charged debates over terminology reflect the intense passions aroused by the events.

In the government's official terminology, the army operation was called an "evacuation" and those affected were "evacuees." The army also devised the term "non-alien" to describe the citizens affected. The facilities where the "evacuees" remained after being transported from the West Coast were given the name "relocation centers." Their inmates were referred to as "residents."

In conversation, government officials used a variety of terms, as did contemporary media accounts. The word "relocation" was sometimes employed to describe the initial mass removal, and at other times to denote the government policy of voluntary individual resettlement outside the West Coast. In addition, some government officials (including Secretary of War Stimson) described the government's action as one of "internment" of Japanese Americans, and referred to the "relocation centers" as "internment camps." When the Joint Chiefs of Staff discussed the mass removal of Japanese Americans from Hawaii in early 1942, the proposal described the action to be taken as internment in "concentration camps." President Roosevelt twice publicly used the term "concentration camps" to describe these facilities.

More recently, historians and Japanese-American activists have described the government's treatment of Japanese Americans using words such as "imprisonment," "detention," or "incarceration." Moreover, they have insisted on the use of "concentration camps" (a phrase coined during the Boer War to describe a camp in which a mass of people is held) for the institutions involved. They argue that the camps were not properly "relocation centers": rather, they were prison barracks surrounded by barbed wire and armed guards, who shot at and in some cases killed inmates who went too far.

I use the word "internment" to describe the government's wartime policy toward the West Coast Japanese Americans as a whole as well as their placement in confinement in the interior following their removal from the coast. The facilities in which the "internees" were held I call "camps." I have elected not to use the phrase "concentration camp." As a result of its association with the Holocaust and the sites of mass murder set up by Nazi Germany, the term "concentration camp" evokes such powerful and emotional responses that its use obscures rather than clarifies the nature of the Japanese-American camps. I have therefore decided to use the word "camp" without further qualifier.

I employ the word "internment" to describe the government's policy and the experience of the Japanese Americans. Although the word "internment" usually connotes treatment of enemy aliens, it is readily grasped and has been commonly employed in reference to the government's policy. "Relocation" is inaccurate since the mass removal from the West Coast during 1942 was involuntary and custodial. I use "evacuation" to describe the forced expulsion of these people, the "evacuees." I use the terms "relocation" and "resettlement" more or less interchangeably to describe the voluntary movement of internees, with government assistance, from the camps to locations outside the West Coast.

ABBREVIATIONS

ACLU	American Civil Liberties Union
AF	FDR, Authorship File, FDRL
BL	Bancroft Library, University of California, Berkeley
CF	Confidential File, President's Secretary File, FDRL
CWRIC Papers	*Documents of the Committee on Wartime Relocation and Internment of Civilians,* microfilm, 35 reels (Frederick, MD: University Publications of America, 1983)
ERP	Eleanor Roosevelt Papers, 1884–1945, FDRL
FBP	Francis Biddle Papers, FDRL
FDRL	Franklin Delano Roosevelt Library, Hyde Park
HIP	Harold Ickes Papers, LC
HLSP	Henry L. Stimson Papers, Stirling Library, Yale University (microfilm copy in FDRL)
HMP	Henry Morgenthau Papers, FDRL
HSTL	Harry S. Truman Library
JACL	Japanese American Citizens League
JERS	Japanese Evacuation and Relocation Study Papers, BL
JFCF	John Franklin Carter File, CF, PSF, FDRL
LC	Library of Congress
NA	National Archives
NAACP	National Association for the Advancement of Colored People
OF	FDR, Official File, FDRL
PASN	FDR, Papers as Assistant Secretary of the Navy, FDRL

PFBF   FDR, Personal, Family, and Business File
PPF   FDR, President's Personal File, FDRL
PSF   FDR, President's Secretary File, FDRL
TRP   Theodore Roosevelt Papers, LC
WRA   War Relocation Authority

NOTES

1. FDR, Press Conference Number 982, November 21, 1944, in Franklin D. Roosevelt, *Complete Press Conferences of FDR,* introduction by Jonathan Daniels, vol. 24 (New York: Da Capo Press, 1973), pp. 247–248.
2. There were two other groups of people of Japanese ancestry incarcerated by the U.S. government. Approximately 150 people of Japanese ancestry, including people of mixed Japanese, Native American, and Inuit ancestry, were removed from Alaska by the War Department and confined during the war years. Also, as a result of an agreement between the U.S. State Department and several Latin American governments, approximately 2,300 people of Japanese ancestry from Latin America, about 80 percent of whom were residents of Peru, were rounded up in their countries during the war and transported to the United States, where they were imprisoned in internment camps run by the Justice Department. C. Harvey Gardiner, *Pawns in a Triangle of Hate* (Seattle, University of Washington Press, 1981).

3. Glen Kitayama, "Franklin Delano Roosevelt," in Brian Niiya, ed., *Japanese-American History: An A to Z from 1868 to the Present* (New York: Facts on File, 1983), p. 298.

1. A Racial Fear Emerges

1. On the "yellow peril," see Roger Daniels, *Concentration Camps, U.S.A.* (New York: Holt, Rinehart, and Winston, 1971), p. 30; William L. Neumann, *America Encounters Japan* (Baltimore: Johns Hopkins Press, 1963), p. 161 *passim*.

2. For the role of material culture in shaping Western views of Asia, see John Kuo Wei Tchen, *New York before Chinatown: Orientalism and the Shaping of American Culture, 1776–1882* (Baltimore: Johns Hopkins University Press, 1999).

3. On the Delano side, for example, FDR's cousin Jane Delano, a pioneer nurse, worked in Japan and was decorated by the Japanese Red Cross. Daniel W. Delano, Jr., *Franklin Roosevelt and the Delano Influence* (Pittsburgh: J. S. Nudi Publications, 1946). According to Roosevelt family folklore, FDR's friend and cousin Laura "Polly" Delano became enamored of a Japanese man while on a trip to the Far East and was immediately sent home. There is a somewhat twisted account in Elliott Roosevelt and James Brough, *A Rendezvous with Destiny: The Roosevelts of the White House* (New York: Putnam's, 1975), p. 302. Theodore Roosevelt's children shared his attachment to Japan. TR's daughter Alice visited Japan during her father's presidency, and Theodore Roosevelt, Jr., did so during the 1920s. Archie and Kermit Roosevelt were both involved with Japanese businessmen during the 1920s. See Kermit Roosevelt Papers, Library of Congress (henceforth LC), Washington, D.C.

4. Haru Matsukata Reischauer, *Samurai and Silk* (Cambridge: Belknap Press of Harvard, 1986), pp. 267–273; see also Letter, Hall Roosevelt to Eleanor Roosevelt, June 1911, with his comment: "I'm bringing up the Jap," Hall Roosevelt Correspondence, Eleanor Roosevelt Papers, 1884–1945 (henceforth ERP), Franklin Delano Roosevelt Library, Hyde Park (henceforth FDRL).

5. Letter, Otohiko Matsukata to FDR, August 1, 1919, FDR, Papers as Assistant Secretary of the Navy (henceforth PASN), FDRL; telegram, Otohiko Matsukata to FDR, July 15, 1920, FDR, Papers as Vice Presidential Candidate, FDRL.

6. See Otohiko Matsukata Correspondence, President's Personal File (henceforth PPF), FDRL; President's Secretary File (henceforth PSF) (Otohiko Matsukata), President's Confidential File (henceforth PCF), FDRL; Ryozo Asano Correspondence, PPF.

7. Letter, FDR to Kichisaburo Nomura, April 6, 1937, PCF (Japan). Roosevelt's account of the embassy dinner is in a letter to his mother of November 14, 1915, in Elliott Roosevelt, ed., *F.D.R.: His Personal Letters, 1905–1928* (New York: Duell, Sloan, and Pearce, 1949), p. 298. Nomura regularly sent FDR election-year congratulations, and he so treasured the letters Roosevelt sent him that he reproduced Roosevelt's letters from 1929, 1933, and 1937 as frontispieces to his memoirs, *Beikoku ni Tsukai Shite Nichibei Kosho no Kaito [Envoy to the United States: Reminiscences of the Japanese American Negotiations]* (Tokyo: Iwanami Shoten, 1946), cited in John K. Emmerson, *The Japanese Thread: A Life in the U.S. Foreign Service* (New York: Holt, Rinehart, 1978), p. 105.

8. Letter, FDR to his mother and father, May 16, 1899, in Elliott Roosevelt, ed., *F.D.R.: His Personal Letters: Early Days–1905* (New York: Duell, Sloan, and Pearce, 1947), p. 310.

9. FDR, "Shall We Trust Japan?" *Asia* 23 (July 1923): 478.

10. Alfred Thayer Mahan, *The Influence of Sea Power upon History, 1660–1783* (Boston: Little, Brown, 1890); Alfred Thayer Mahan, *The Interest of America in Sea Power, Past and Present* (Boston: Little, Brown, 1897).

11. Joseph P. Lash, *Roosevelt and Churchill, 1939–1941: The Partnership That Saved the West* (New York: Norton, 1976), p. 37; Mrs. James Roosevelt, as told to Isabella Leighton and Gabrielle Forbush, *My Boy Franklin* (New York: Ray Long and Richard Smith, 1933), p. 15.

12. William Neumann, "Franklin D. Roosevelt: A Disciple of Admiral Mahan," *U.S. Naval Institute Proceedings*, September 1952. FDR's citation of Mahan came in support of his argument that America's interest lay in avoiding formal annexation of distant colonies that were expensive to maintain and defend, provided the navy could maintain coaling stations. Japan, he noted, had disclaimed any desire to annex Hawaii, which would in any event be a "foolish enterprise" for Japan to undertake since Hawaii lay "entirely out of the Japan-American sailing route." FDR, Notes from Groton Debate, Speeches File, Box 1, FDRL.

13. Letter, George Marvin to FDR, November 17, 1922; Letter, FDR to George Marvin, June 30, 1923, FDR, Personal, Family, and Business File (henceforth PFBF), FDRL. For FDR's admiration of Mahan generally, see also Edward J. Renehan, Jr., *The Lion's Pride: Theodore Roosevelt and His Family in Peace and War* (New York: Oxford University Press, 1998), p. 232.

14. See, for example, Geoffrey C. Ward, ed., *Closest Companion* (Boston: Houghton Mifflin, 1995), p. 10; Henry L. Stimson diary, April 10, 1934, Henry L. Stimson Papers, Stirling Library, Yale University (microfilm copy in FDRL) (hereafter HLSP).

15. Joseph P. Lash, *Eleanor and Franklin* (New York: Norton, 1971), p. 182. Since Eleanor Roosevelt later disposed of her husband's courtship letters, his response is unknown.

16. *F.D.R.: His Personal Letters: 1905–1928*, pp. 7, 9.

17. Letter, Franklin and Eleanor Roosevelt to Sara Delano Roosevelt, August 30, 1905, ibid., p. 122.

18. Alden D. Hatch, *Citizen of the World: Franklin D. Roosevelt* (London: Skeffington & Son, 1946), pp. 43–44. Eleanor and Franklin's mutual interest in the Russo-Japanese war can also be inferred from their joint reading of Ian Hamilton's "ponderous" two-volume account of the war in 1907. See William Neumann, "Franklin D. Roosevelt and Japan, 1913–1933," *Pacific Historical Review* 22 (May 1953): 144.

19. See Alfred Thayer Mahan, "Retrospect upon the War between Japan and Russia," in Alfred Thayer Mahan, *Naval Administration and Warfare* (Boston: Little, Brown, 1908), pp. 133–173.

20. Perhaps out of loyalty, FDR remained sympathetic to Theodore Roosevelt's actions in the Philippines even after he shifted to opposing imperialism. Franklin D. Roosevelt, "Our Foreign Policy: A Democratic View," *Foreign Affairs*, Summer 1928, p. 574.

21. Asahi Shimbun, *The Pacific Rivals* (New York, Tokyo: John Weatherhill, 1972), pp. 62–63.

22. Theodore Roosevelt to Sir Cecil Spring-Rice, June 16, 1905, quoted in Outten Jones Clinard, *Japan's Influence on American Naval Power* (Berkeley: University of California Press, 1947), p. 170.

23. A. Whitney Griswold, *The Foreign Policy of the United States* (New York: Harcourt Brace, 1938), pp. 124–132.

24. Clinard, *Japan's Influence on American Naval Power, 1897–1917*, p. 43. The Root-Takeshira Agreement was widely seen as Theodore Roosevelt's acquiescence in Japanese occupation of Korea and penetration of Manchuria.

25. George Sinclair, *The Racial Attitudes of American Presidents* (New York: Doubleday, 1971), pp. 320–323. The quote is from TR's letter to Arthur Balfour of December 18, 1906.

26. Robert Seagar, *Alfred Thayer Mahan: The Man and His Letters*, vol 5 (Annapolis, MD: Naval Institute Press, 1977), p. 479.

27. Richard W. Turk, *The Ambiguous Relationship: Theodore Roosevelt and Alfred Thayer Mahan* (Westport, CT: Greenwood Press, 1987), pp. 90–91. In addition to his private warning, Mahan wrote a series of articles for *Collier's* and the *National Review*, as well as letters and editorials, on the perils of dividing the fleet in wartime, in which he used Russia's mistake against Japan as a prime illustration. Seagar, *Alfred Thayer Mahan*, p. 677, n. 10.

28. Raymond A. Esthus, *Theodore Roosevelt and Japan* (Seattle: University of Washington, 1966).

29. Theodore Roosevelt, Letter to Baron Kentaro Kaneko, May 23, 1907; Theodore Roosevelt, "Japanese Immigration," *The Outlook*, May 8, 1909, rpt. in Albert Bushnell Hart and Herbert Ronald Ferleger, eds., *Theodore Roosevelt Cyclopedia*, 2nd ed. (New York: Theodore Roosevelt Assoc. and Meckler Pub., 1989), pp. 274–275.

30. Seagar, *Alfred Thayer Mahan*, p. 479.

31. Clare Boothe, "Introduction," in Homer Lea, *The Valor of Ignorance* (rpt. New York: Harper and Bros., 1942), pp. xvi–xxx.

32. Homer Lea, *The Valor of Ignorance* (New York: Harper's, 1909), pp. 88–89.

33. Ibid., book 3.

34. Ibid., pp. 122–127.

35. Ibid., pp. 109–110.

36. Richard O'Connor, *Pacific Destiny* (Boston: Little, Brown, 1969), pp. 320–321. See also Boothe, "Introduction," pp. xxx–xxxi.

37. Sir Valentine Chirol, "Japan among the Nations: The Bar of Race, a Grave International Issue," *London Times*, May 19, 1913, p. 7f; Admiral Alfred Thayer Mahan, Letter, *London Times*, June 23, 1913, p. 9c; "Admiral Mahan Extols Japanese," *New York Times*, June 23, 1913, p. 6.

38. Alfred Thayer Mahan, "Japan among the Nations," *Living Age*, August 2, 1913, pp. 312–315.

39. Ibid.

40. Ibid.

41. Ibid. Mahan's conclusions were immediately cited and strenuously rebutted by Sidney Gulick in *The American Japanese Problem* (New York: Scribner's, 1914), pp. 223–224.

42. Josephus Daniels, *The Wilson Era: Years of Peace, 1910–1917* (Chapel Hill: University of North Carolina Press, 1946), p. 124.

43. Wilson and Secretary of State William Jennings Bryan at first disingenuously stated that the act implied no racial bias. In response to mounting diplomatic protests from Japan, Wilson belatedly sent Bryan to California to plead with the governor not to embarrass the government by signing the act. Johnson, who had been Theodore Roosevelt's running mate on the Progressive Party ticket against Wilson, saw no reason to appease an unfriendly administration in Washington. See Thomas A. Bailey, "California, Japan, and the Alien Land Legislation of 1913," *Pacific Historical Review* 1 (March 1932): 37; Herbert Patrick LeFlore, "Exclusion by Prejudice," unpub. diss., Brigham Young University, 1973, pp. 80–97.

44. Milton R. Konvitz, *The Alien and Asiatic in American Law* (Ithaca: Cornell University Press, 1946), chs. 1, 2, 5, 7; Ronald Takaki, *Strangers from a Different Shore: A History of Asian Americans* (Boston: Little, Brown, 1989), p. 204.

45. Jonathan Daniels, *The End of Innocence* (Philadelphia, Lippincott, 1954), p. 108.

46. Lash, *Roosevelt and Churchill*, p. 40.

47. Letter, Theodore Roosevelt to FDR, May 10, 1913, Theodore Roosevelt Papers (hereafter TRP), LC.

48. Daniels, *The Wilson Era*, pp. 164–67; Bailey, "California, Japan and the Alien Land Legislation of 1913," pp. 36–59; Robert Louis Burke, "Franklin Roosevelt and the Far East, 1913–1941" (unpub. Ph.D. diss., University of Michigan, 1969), pp. 21–23. Lash, *Roosevelt and Churchill*, pp. 40–41.

49. Letter, FDR to Theodore Roosevelt, May 18, 1913, TRP. FDR noted that he was writing by hand "as I do not yet entirely trust all my office force!" Ibid.

50. FDR, undated memorandum, PASN, 1913, FDRL, summarized in Burke, "Franklin D. Roosevelt and the Far East, 1913–1941," pp. 24–25.

51. *San Francisco Examiner,* May 26, 1913; *Boston Herald,* May 20, 1913; FDR, Extemporaneous Statements to the Press, Watertown, NY, May 29, 1913, *Daily Standard,* May 30, 1913, 1:1.

52. FDR, Extemporaneous Statements to the Press, May 25, 1913, reported in *Washington Times,* May 26, 1913, p. 2.

53. Jonathan Daniels, "Franklin Delano Roosevelt and Books," in *Three Presidents and Their Books* (Urbana: University of Illinois Press, 1963), p. 49. Roosevelt received his copy of the book from a Los Angeles physician on April 11, 1914. Frank Freidel, *Franklin Roosevelt: The Apprenticeship* (Boston: Little, Brown, 1955), p. 232.

54. Homer Lea, *The Day of the Saxon* (New York: Harper's, 1912), p. 92.

55. *New York Times,* January 18, 1914, p. 7.

56. Carey McWilliams, *Prejudice: Japanese Americans, Symbol of Racial Intolerance* (Boston: Little, Brown, 1944), p. 42. The connection between immigration and defense of the West Coast also impressed statesmen such as the former secretary of war, Henry L. Stimson. At the time of the debate over evacuation of the West Coast Japanese Americans thirty-two years later, Stimson, by then once more secretary of war, referred in his diary to Lea's writing as prophetic. Henry Stimson Diary, February 5, 1942, HLSP.

57. Letter, FDR to Alfred Thayer Mahan, May 28, 1914; Letter, FDR to Alfred Thayer Mahan, July 17, 1914, PASN.

58. In accordance with his promise to FDR, Mahan wrote an article in *North American Review*, "The Panama Canal and the Distribution of the Fleet," but President Wilson's neutrality directive of August 1914 which prohibited military officers from public comment on policy and Mahan's death in December prevented further action on his part.

59. Alfred Thayer Mahan to FDR, June 2, 1914, PASN. Mahan privately wrote TR that he feared Japan would try to force the United States to make a "concession" and authorize Japanese land ownership on the West Coast, which the nation could not safely permit "with our less than twenty to the square mile population on the Pacific Coast." Alfred Thayer Mahan to Theodore Roosevelt, July 19, 1913, TRP.

60. FDR to Alfred Thayer Mahan, July 17, 1914, PASN.

61. FDR, Speech, "The Future of the Navy," at the Republican Club's Weekly Luncheon, New York, NY, January 30, 1915, Master File of Speeches, FDRL.

62. These reports ranged from a series of studies by the Office of Naval Intelligence (marked "secret—to be destroyed") on "Evidence of Japan's Preparation for War," which contained large quantities of useful information regarding Japan's postwar naval buildup and preparations for war, to more sensational intelligence reports which echoed the hysteria over German-Japanese-Mexican entente that had been aroused by the Zimmermann telegram in 1917. There is no sign that Roosevelt gave any of these wild reports much credence. Japan Folder, PASN.

63. FDR, Interview with Frederick Boyd Stevenson, *Brooklyn Eagle*, July 18, 1920, p. 6.

64. Geoffrey C. Ward, *A First Class Temperament* (New York: Harper Perennial, 1989), p. 559. For American foreign policy in the 1920s, see Joan Hoff-Wilson, *American Business and Foreign Policy* (Boston: Beacon Press, 1973; University of Kentucky Press, 1971), p. 44 *passim*.

65. FDR, Letter to Mabel Caldwell Willard, Pro-League Independents Committee, May 12, 1921, FDR Correspondence, 1920–1928, FDRL.

66. Raymond L. Buell, *The Washington Naval Conference* (New York: Appleton and Co., 1922).

67. Ibid., pp. 317, 319, 328–330.

68. Ibid., pp. 325–27, 367–368.

69. For the impact of popular anti-Japanese-American sentiment on the State Department, see, for example, Akira Iriye, *Across The Pacific: An Inner History of American-East Asian Relations* (New York: Harcourt Brace Jovanovich, 1967), pp. 139–143.

70. Alan Cranston, *The Killing of the Peace* (New York: Viking, 1945), pp. 89, 113.

71. Roger Daniels, *The Politics of Prejudice* (New York: Atheneum, 1968), p. 85.

72. For the nativist movement generally, see John Higham, *Strangers in the Land* (New Brunswick: Rutgers University Press, 1955).

73. Madison Grant, *The Passing of the Great Race* (New York: Scribner's, 1916), p. 175.

74. Ibid., cited in Oscar Handlin, *Race and Nationality in American Life* (Boston: Little, Brown, 1957), p. 77.

75. Ibid., p. 74.

76. In the years after Lea wrote his book, several other books, such as James F. Abbot, *Japanese Expansion and American Policies,* and Carl Crow, *Japan and America,* proposed that the Japanese Americans had been deliberately placed in California by Japan to secure a foothold for a Japanese invasion. For a fuller discussion of hysteria about a Japanese invasion, see also O'Connor, *Pacific Destiny,* pp. 430–433.

77. Lothrop Stoddard, *The Rising Tide of Color against White World-Supremacy* (New York: Scribner's, 1920), pp. 252–301.

78. Letter, Cornelius Vanderbilt, Jr., to FDR, March 11, 1921, PFBF.

79. Cornelius Vanderbilt, Jr., *The Verdict of Public Opinion on the Japanese American Question: A Symposium Instituted by Cornelius Vanderbilt, Jr., and Founded on Peter B. Kyne's Novel "The Pride of Palomar"* (privately printed by Cornelius Vanderbilt, Jr., 1921).

80. Ibid., pp. 11, 14, 19.

81. Ibid. In the Western states 49 correspondents favored total exclusion of Japanese immigrants, 12 opposed, and 4 expressed no definite opinion. In the "North Atlantic States," 53 favored exclusion, 13 opposed, and 7 expressed no definite opinion. Twelve New England correspondents favored exclusion, while 3 opposed. The percentages favoring exclusion in the Midwest, Southeastern, and Southwestern states were even more lopsided.

82. Takaki, *Strangers from a Different Shore,* pp. 191, 206.

83. Yuji Ichioka, *The Issei: The World of the First Generation Japanese Immigrants, 1885–1924* (New York: Free Press, 1988), pp. 217–232.

84. McWilliams, *Prejudice,* p. 66.

85. Elliott Roosevelt and James Brough, *Mother R: Eleanor Roosevelt's Untold Story* (New York: Putnam, 1977), p. 219.

86. FDR's reference to America as "aryan" came in a speech in Troy, NY, in 1912. "If we go back through history . . . we are struck by the fact that as a general proposition the aryan races have been struggling to maintain individual freedom . . . in almost every European and American country this has been the great and fundamental question in the economic life of the

people." FDR, Speech before People's Forum, Troy, NY, March 3, 1912, rpt. in Basil Rauch, ed., *The Roosevelt Reader: Selected Speeches, Messages, Press Conferences and Letters of Franklin Delano Roosevelt* (New York: Holt, Rinehart, 1957), p. 10.

87. Frank Freidel, *Franklin Roosevelt: The Ordeal* (Boston: Little, Brown, 1954), pp. 108–109.

88. FDR, Interview, *Brooklyn Eagle*, July 18, 1920, p. 6. This argument foreshadows FDR's famous comment in a presidential speech to the Daughters of the American Revolution: "Remember always that all of us, and you and I especially, are descended from immigrants and revolutionists." Dr. Laurence J. Peter, *Peter's Quotations: Ideas for Our Time* (Bantam, New York, 1977), p. 453.

89. FDR, Interview, *Brooklyn Eagle*.

90. FDR, "Roosevelt Says," April 23, 1925, rpt. in Donald Scott Carmichael, ed., *F.D.R. Columnist* (Chicago: Pellegrini & Cudahy, 1947), pp. 36–40.

91. A rare clue to Roosevelt's attitude toward Chinese immigration can be found in a story he often told about how he and his Groton roommate, Lathrop Brown, while at Campobello in 1897, had discovered a ship smuggling "Chinese potatoes" (that is, illegal Chinese immigrants) because of the peculiar smell of the cargo. Versions of this story can be found in William Hassett, *Off the Record with F.D.R., 1942–1945* (New Brunswick, NJ: Rutgers University Press, 1958), pp. 101–2, and in Mrs. James Roosevelt, *My Boy Franklin*, p. 54.

92. Letter, FDR to Cornelius Vanderbilt, Jr., March 17, 1921, PFBF.

93. Letter, George Marvin to FDR, September 3, 1922, FDR, Authorship File (hereafter AF), FDRL.

94. Although he began and abandoned several projects, Roosevelt published only a handful of works, mostly undistinguished, during the 1920s. His writings include two short-lived newspaper columns and a pair of books—*Whither Bound?* a slim volume of a 1926 speech on progress, and *The Happy Warrior,* an extended Al Smith campaign pamphlet. FDR also wrote a book review in the *New York Evening World* and articles in well-known journals such as the *National Business Review* and *American Review of Reviews,* as well as editing two volumes of historical documents.

95. Letter, FDR to George Marvin, September 12, 1922, AF.

96. Letter, FDR to George Marvin, October 12, 1922, AF.

97. The typescript of Roosevelt's draft is housed in AF. The presence of the word "Jap" in the title is curious, since it had some derogatory connotations even then. Roosevelt clearly did not mean to offend in his use of the

word, if he chose it, since it was a longtime habit (as, for example, his and Eleanor's honeymoon letters about the "Jap officers").

98. Roosevelt, "Shall We Trust Japan?" p. 485.

99. Ibid., p. 475.

100. Roosevelt's strategic views contain a fair sampling of historical irony, since within twenty years he would lead the United States in a successful trans-Pacific conquest of Japan following a Japanese attack on Pearl Harbor. Roosevelt nevertheless insisted that the article had been prescient in foreseeing the difficulty and long duration of such a campaign. See Henry Wallace Diary, March 31, 1942, Henry Wallace Papers, University of Iowa (microfilm copy in LC).

101. Ibid., p. 478.

102. Ibid., p. 526.

103. Ibid., p. 526.

104. Ibid.

105. Letter, Archie Roosevelt to FDR (undated 1924), PFBF; Letter, Akira Fukami to Kermit Roosevelt, November 8, 1924, Kermit Roosevelt Papers, LC. Since the Japan Society no longer retains its membership rolls from the 1920s, it is impossible to determine whether Roosevelt ever joined, but the absence of the society from his correspondence indicates that he did not.

106. Letter, FDR to George Foster Peabody, September 26, 1923, AF. Roosevelt's exchange with Peabody was responsible for inaugurating a friendship between the two men that would lead Roosevelt to a central project in his life. Nine months later, Peabody told Roosevelt about the healing powers of the water at a resort he owned in Georgia called Warm Springs. FDR bought Warm Springs from Peabody in 1926, turning it into a major center for paralytics.

107. Hector C. Bywater, Letter to the Editor, *Baltimore Sun*, August 5, 1923. For Bywater and Roosevelt's debate, see William C. Honan, *Visions of Infamy* (New York: St. Martin's Press, 1991), pp. 97–104 *passim*.

108. FDR, Letter to the Editor, *Baltimore Sun*, August 13, 1923, AF.

109. FDR, "Roosevelt Says," April 30, 1925, rpt. in Carmichael, *FDR Columnist*, pp. 56–57.

110. Ibid., pp. 57–58. In fact, as Vanderbilt's survey demonstrates, racial factors and not economics were in fact the (ostensible) grounds used by the proponents of immigration restriction.

111. Ibid., p. 58.

112. Daniels, "Three Presidents and Their Books," p. 49.

113. For the relation between Southern racism and Western nativism, see Higham, *Strangers in the Land*, pp. 166–167.

114. The year before FDR published his article, Walter Lippmann commented acidly on the stirring up of fears of intermarriage to promote economic exclusion. "The Japanese ask the right to settle in California. Clearly it makes a whole lot of difference whether you conceive the demand as a desire to grow fruit or to marry the white man's daughter." Walter Lippmann, *Public Opinion* (1922), excerpted in Clinton Rossiter and James Coe, *The Essential Lippmann* (Cambridge: Harvard University Press, 1956), p. 138.

2. War Abroad, Suspicion at Home

1. FDR, "Our Foreign Policy: A Democratic View," *Foreign Affairs*, July 1928, p. 582.

2. See, for example, George Alexander Lensen, *The Damned Inheritance* (Tallahassee: Diplomatic Press, 1974), pp. 487–489; Raymond L. Buell, "Our Policy on the Sino-Japanese Dispute," *Foreign Affairs Reports*, February 1933, pp. 789–795.

3. Henry Stimson Diary, January 9, 1933, HLSP.

4. Rexford Tugwell, *The Democratic Roosevelt* (Garden City, NY: Doubleday, 1957), p. 257; Steven Pelz, *Background to War: The Failure of the Second London Naval Conference* (New York: Oxford University Press, 1986), pp. 67–68.

5. Sir Ronald Lindsay to Sir John Simon, January 30, 1933, quoted in Frank Freidel, *FDR: Launching the New Deal* (Boston: Little, Brown, 1973), p. 105.

6. Raymond Moley Diary, January 19, 1933, cited in Freidel, *FDR: Launching the New Deal*, p. 121.

7. FDR went so far as to reprimand William E. Dodd, his ambassador to Germany, for suggesting that recognition of the USSR implied an effort to coerce Japan on the Manchurian question. Herbert Feis, *1933: Characters in Crisis* (Boston: Little Brown, 1966), pp. 329–330.

8. In one of three first Cabinet meetings, FDR spoke of the possibility of war with Japan. James A. Farley, *Jim Farley's Story: The Roosevelt Years* (New York: Whittlesey House / McGraw Hill, 1948), p. 39.

9. FDR to Malcolm Peabody, 1933, PPF, cited in Burke, "Franklin Roosevelt and the Far East," p. 67.

10. Geoffrey Ward, ed., *Closest Companion* (Boston: Houghton Mifflin, 1995), p. 10.

11. Clarence E. Pickett, *For More than Bread* (Boston: Little Brown, 1953), pp. 392–393.

12. Rexford Tugwell, cited in Nathan Miller, *FDR: An Intimate History* (Garden City, NY: Doubleday, 1983), p. 418.

13. Pelz, *Background to War*, pp. 139–140.

14. Burke, "Franklin Roosevelt and the Far East," p. 76.

15. Dorothy Detzer, *Appointment on the Hill* (New York: Henry Holt, 1947), p. 184.

16. Letter, Josephus Daniels to FDR, June 20, 1933, FDR Correspondence, Josephus Daniels Papers, LC; see also Bob Matsumoto, "The Search for Spies: American Counterintelligence and Japanese Americans, 1933–1942," *Amerasia Journal* 6, no. 2 (1979): 45–75.

17. Detzer, *Appointment on the Hill*, p. 184.

18. Sumner Welles, *The Time for Decision* (New York: Harper's, 1944), pp. 209–210.

19. *Pacific Citizen*, April 1933, p. 1.

20. Letter, Rep. Clarence F. Lea to FDR, January 22, 1934; Letter, Cordell Hull to FDR, January 31, 1934; Letter, William Phillips to FDR, February 24, 1934; Memo, FDR to "MAC" (Marvin MacIntyre), undated, February 1934; Folder 1933–1935, Official File (hereafter OF) 133 (Immigration).

21. William Phillips, Memorandum for the President, April 10, 1934, Box 197, PSF (Japan).

22. A. Whitney Griswold, *The Far Eastern Policy of the United States* (New York: Harcourt Brace, 1938), pp. 450–452; Lawrence H. Battistini, *The United States and Asia* (Tokyo: Kenkusa, 1955), pp. 43–44.

23. Bill Hosokawa, *JACL: In Quest of Justice* (New York: William Morrow, 1982), pp. 53–55.

24. Robert F. Rogers, *Destiny's Landfall: A History of Guam* (Honolulu: University of Hawaii Press, 1995), p. 152. While assistant secretary of the navy, FDR himself declared in 1915 that the Navy Department did not consider discussion of citizenship rights for Chamorros to be in the public interest. Ibid., p. 134.

25. Gary Y. Okihiro, *Cane Fires: The Anti-Japanese Movement in Hawaii 1865–1945* (Philadelphia: Temple University Press, 1991), pp. 165–167. For pro-Japanese sentiments among Japanese Americans in Hawaii, see John J. Stephan, *Hawaii under the Rising Sun* (Honolulu: University of Hawaii Press, 1984).

26. FDR, Memorandum for Chief of Naval Operations, PSF 197 (Japan).

27. See, for example, Peter Irons, *Justice at War* (New York: Oxford University Press, 1983), p. 20; Okihiro, *Cane Fires*, pp. 173–174. See especially Ronald Takaki, *Strangers from a Different Shore* (Boston: Little, Brown, 1989),

p. 390, and Ronald Takaki, *Democracy and Race* (New York: Chelsea House, 1995), p. 14.

28. Letter, Harry Woodring and Claude Swanson to FDR, October 22, 1936, RG 80, Box 216, Folder A 8–5, National Archives (hereafter NA), rpt. in *Documents of the Committee on Wartime Relocation and Iinternment of Civilians*, microfilm, 37 reels (Frederick, MD: University Publications of America, 1983) (hereinafter referred to as CWRIC Papers and listed by page number for the original documents and by reel and page number for microfilm), p. 33122 (reel 34, p. 222).

29. Ibid.

30. Ibid.

31. Copy, Letter, Secretary of War to the President, November 17, 1937; Memo, Secretary of War to Secretary of the Navy, December 1, 1937, NA, RG 80, Box 216, Folder A 8–5, rpt. in CWRIC Papers, pp. 33126–33130, (reel 34, pp. 137–141).

32. FDR to Admiral William Leahy, August 22, 1937, DEC, Box 78, PSF (Navy); cited in Michael A. Barnhart, *Japan Prepares for Total War: The Search for Economic Security 1919–1941* (Ithaca: Cornell University Press, 1987), p. 123.

33. President, Memo for the Secretary of War, May 22, 1937, PSF (War Department).

34. Letter, Secretary of War to the President, September 8, 1937, PSF (Woodring).

35. Sumner Welles, *Seven Decisions That Shaped History* (New York: Harper's, 1951), p. 75.

36. FDR to Joseph Grew, November 30, 1939, in Elliott Roosevelt, ed., *F.D.R.: His Personal Letters 1933–1945*, Vol. 2 (New York: Duell, Sloan, and Pearce, 1950), p. 694.

37. Elliott Roosevelt, *As He Saw It* (New York: Duell, Sloan & Pearce, 1946), p. 12.

38. Memorandum, Secretary of the Navy to the President, October 9, 1940, PSF (Safe File: Navy Department), rpt. in CWRIC Papers, pp. 3602, 3603 (reel 3, pp. 596–597).

39. United States Navy, Office of Intelligence, "United States Naval Administration in World War II," pamphlet, not dated, pp. 66–69.

40. Federal Bureau of Investigation, Memorandum, November 15, 1940, FBI Records 65–286–61, rpt. in CWRIC Papers, p. 19456 (reel 17, p. 9).

41. Ibid.

42. See Robert J. C. Butow, *Tojo and the Coming of War* (Princeton: Princeton University Press, 1961), p. 279n; David Bergamini, *Japan's Imperial Conspiracy* (New York: William Morrow, 1971), pp. 291, 741.

43. The MAGIC excerpts do not reveal conclusive evidence of any espionage activities by Japanese Americans. See testimony of David Lowman, John A. Herzig, and Peter Irons, U.S. Congress, *Japanese-American and Aleutian Wartime Relocation Hearings before the Subcommittee on Administrative Law and Governmental Relations of the Committee on the Judiciary House of Representatives Ninety-Eighth Congress Second Session on H.R. 3387, H.R. 4110 and H.R. 4322*, June 20, 21, 27 and September 12, 1984 (Washington, DC: Government Printing Office, 1985), pp. 439, 801–841, 922–936.

44. Letter, FDR to Harold Ickes, July 1, 1941, FDR Correspondence Folder, HIP.

45. Robert Dallek, *Franklin D. Roosevelt and American Foreign Policy, 1932–1945* (New York: Oxford University Press, 1979), pp. 271–272.

46. Letter, FDR to Harold Ickes, July 1, 1941, FDR Correspondence Folder, HIP.

47. FDR clearly felt confident enough about the journey to inform Eleanor Roosevelt, who wrote their daughter Anna in Seattle that she and the President would be stopping there on the way to "meet with the Japs." Bernard Asbell, ed., *Mother and Daughter: The Letters of Eleanor and Anna Roosevelt* (New York: Coward McCann Geohagen, 1982), p. 126.

48. See Office of Naval Intelligence, "Japanese Organizations and Societies Engaged in Propaganda, Espionage, and Cultural Work," ONI File A-8/EF37, ONI Records, NA, cited in Peter Irons, ed., *Justice Delayed: The Record of the Japanese American Internment Cases* (Middletown, CT: Wesleyan University Press, 1989), p. 175. See also Lt. Col. George Bicknell, Memo, "Seizure and Detention Plan (Aliens)," in CWRIC Papers, pp. 33224–33230 (reel 34, pp. 236–242).

49. Committee on Wartime Relocation and Internment of Civilians, *Personal Justice Denied* (Washington, DC: Civil Liberties Public Education Fund, and Seattle: University of Washington Press, 1997 [1982]), p. 54.

50. "Biddle Takes Firm Stand against Any Repression of Alien Groups in U.S.," *Japanese American Review*, October 18, 1941, p. 1.; "Attorney-General Defends Aliens," *Rafu Shimpo*, November 12, 1941, p. 1.

51. Jordan A. Schwartz, *Liberal: Adolf A. Berle and the Vision of an American Era* (New York: Free Press, 1987), p. 171.

52. Wayne S. Cole, *Roosevelt and the Isolationists 1932–1945* (Lincoln: University of Nebraska Press, 1983), p. 461. Roosevelt appreciated Curtis B. Munson's August 1941 assessment of the political situation in Martinique and Guadeloupe so much that he sent Munson a rare private letter of gratitude. Letter, FDR to Curtis Munson, August 23, 1941, John Franklin Carter File, CF, PSF (hereafter JFCF).

53. Letter, John D. Dingell to FDR, August 18, 1941, OF 197, cited in Roger Daniels, *The Decision to Relocate the Japanese Americans* (Philadelphia: Lippincott, 1975), p. 8.

54. Letter, Curtis Munson to John Franklin Carter, October 19, 1941, June–October 1941 Folder, JFCF. In order to buttress his conclusions, Munson (one hopes facetiously) added these chilling lines: "In the first place there are not so many people of Japanese descent in the United States that in an emergency they could not all be thrown into a concentration camp in 48 hours. Of course you might get a few Chinamen too because they sort of look alike. But the looks are a great aid to rounding them up and in keeping them away from sabotage or other troublesome pastimes." Ibid.

55. Ibid.

56. Memo, John Franklin Carter to FDR, October 22, 1941, June–October 1941 Folder, JFCF.

57. Memo, John Franklin Carter to FDR, October 27, 1941, June–October 1941 Folder, JFCF.

58. Francis Biddle, Cabinet Notes, November 7, 1941, Francis Biddle Papers (hereafter FBP), Box 1, FDRL.

59. C. B. Munson, "Japanese on the West Coast," November 7, 1941, 17 pages, RG 210, Box 573, NA, rpt. in CWRIC Papers, pp. 3664–3681 (reel 3, pp. 639–655).

60. Memo, John Franklin Carter to FDR, November 7, 1941, RG 210, Box 573, NA, rpt. in CWRIC Papers, p. 3663 (reel 3, p. 638).

61. Letter, FDR to Henry Stimson, RG 210, Box 573, NA, rpt. in CWRIC Papers, p. 3682 (reel 3, p. 656). Stimson did not reply until February 5, 1942, by which time the memo was out of date.

62. Memo, FDR to John Franklin Carter, November 11, 1941, November–December 1941 Folder, JFCF.

63. Memo, John Franklin Carter to FDR, November 17, 1941, November–December 1941 Folder, JFCF.

64. Federal Bureau of Investigation, Memorandum re: Japanese Activities, November 13, 1941, rpt. in CWRIC Papers, pp. 19463–194367 (reel 17, pp. 16–20).

65. Ibid.

66. See Henry Field, Memorandum, "Japanese in the United States, 1941," October 16, 1963, Japanese-American Population Folder, Henry Field Papers, FDRL; Henry Field, *The Track of Man: Adventures of an Anthropologist,* vol. 2: *The White House Years* (Miami: Banyan Books, 1982), pp. 54–55. When Field's story was made public in 1981, the Census Bureau issued a

statement denying Field's story and insisting that such a project would have been not only illegal but impossible, using the technology of the day, to complete in such a short time. CWRIC Papers, pp. 1729–1741 (reel 2, pp. 453–464). Field's papers in the FDRL contain requests by Field for population statistics (not individual addresses) from November 1941; the reply is dated December 17, ten days *after* Pearl Harbor.

67. Memorandum, John Franklin Carter to FDR, November 18, 1941; Letter, Curtis B. Munson to John Franklin Carter, attached to Memo, John Franklin Carter to FDR, December 24, 1941, November-December 1941 Folder, JFCF.

68. Memorandum, FDR to John Franklin Carter, November 12, 1941; Memo, FDR to John Franklin Carter, November 14, 1941, November-December 1941, JFCF.

69. Memorandum, FDR to John Franklin Carter, November 12, 1941; Memo, FDR to John Franklin Carter, November 14, 1941; Memo, John Franklin Carter to FDR, November 18, 1941, November-December 1941 Folder, JFCF. See also Ted Lyons, "Lancer's Column," *Rafu Shimpo*, December 7, 1941, p. 3.

70. John Franklin Carter, *Power and Persuasion* (New York: Duell, Sloan and Pearce, 1960), p. 73.

71. Ibid.

72. Stephan, *Hawaii under the Rising Sun;* Haru Matsui, *Restless Wave* (New York: Modern Library, 1940), p. 210.

3. FDR's Decision to Intern

1. See, for example, Edwin T. Layton et al., *"And I Was There": Pearl Harbor and Midway—Breaking the Secrets* (New York: Quill, 1985), pp. 54, 74–75.

2. Ibid., pp. 211, 216–217.

3. "Gov. Poindexter's Martial Law," *Pacific Citizen*, October 16, 1948, p. 2.

4. Conversation, Treasury Department, December 12, 1941, Henry Morgenthau Diaries, Henry Morgenthau Papers (hereafter HMP), FDRL.

5. Curtis B. Munson, "Report on Hawaiian Islands," p. 17, attached to Memo, John Franklin Carter to FDR, December 8, 1941, JFCF.

6. Ibid.

7. FDR, Memo to Captain Beardall, December 9, 1941, JFCF.

8. Claude Wickard, Cabinet Notes, December 19, 1941, Secretary of Agriculture Files, Box 8, Claude Wickard Papers, FDRL.

9. Francis Biddle, Cabinet Notes, December 19, 1941, Box 1, FBP.

10. William L. Neumann, *America Encounters Japan: From Perry to MacArthur* (New York: Harper Colophon, 1965 [1963]), p. 209.

11. Francis Biddle, Cabinet Notes, December 19, 1941, Box 1, FBP.

12. Hoover later publicly repeated these denials of sabotage. "Pearl Harbor Sabotage Rumors Checked, Proved False, Says Hoover, National FBI Director," *Pacific Citizen*, August 26, 1944, 1:4–5.

13. Memo, John Franklin Carter to FDR, December 16, 1941, JFCF.

14. Curtis Munson, "Update on the West Coast Situation," December 20, 1941, attached to Memo, John Franklin Carter to FDR, December 22, 1941, JFCF.

15. Ibid.

16. Memo, John Franklin Carter to FDR, December 19, 1942, JFCF.

17. Ibid.

18. Memo to the File, GCT (Grace C. Tully), December 20, 1941, JCFC.

19. Memo, William Donovan, December 15, 1941, OSS, Donovan Reports, PSF, PCF. See Cliff Lewis, "John Steinbeck's Alternative to Internment Camps: A Policy for the President, December 15, 1941," *Journal of the West* 34 (January 1995): 55–61.

20. Memo, John Franklin Carter to FDR, December 22, 1941. Carter noted that he was passing the memo on to the Department of State, Army Intelligence, the "C.O.I." [William Donovan], and the attorney general, the group that had been responsible for organizing propaganda and averting anti–Japanese-American violence before Pearl Harbor.

21. Memo, John Franklin Carter to FDR, January 28, 1942, JFCF.

22. FBI Analysis of Munson Report, January 16, 1942, cited in Peter Irons, *Justice Delayed: The Record of the Japanese American Internment Cases* p. 323.

23. Memo, John Franklin Carter to FDR, December 24, 1942; Letter, Curtis B. Munson to John Franklin Carter, undated; Curtis B. Munson, "Progress Report on Axis Fifth Column Activities," January 9, 1942; Memo, John Franklin Carter to FDR, January 12, 1942, JFCF.

24. Letter, Francis Biddle to Stephen Early, December 30, 1941, OF 133 (Immigration); *Rafu Shimpo*, January 11, 1942; *Pacific Citizen*, February 1942.

25. The story of the military and popular movement has been told in detail in numerous works, including Stetson Conn, "The Decision to Relocate the Japanese Americans," in Stetson Conn, Rose C. Engelman, and Byron Fairchild, *The United States Army in World War II, the Western Hemisphere: Guarding the Unitd States and Its Outposts* (Washington, DC: Office of the Chief of Military History, Department of the Army, 1964); Roger Daniels, *Concentration Camps USA: Japanese Americans and World War II* (New York: Holt, Rinehart, 1971); Michi Nishiura Weglyn, *Years of Infamy* (Seattle: University of Washington Press, 1996 [1976]); and Peter Irons, *Justice at War* (New York: Oxford University Press, 1983).

26. The army's apparatus and ability to detect signaling, according to the FBI, were extremely faulty. There were ships attacked by submarines, but not with the deadly accuracy of the German submarines patrolling the East Coast. Although DeWitt and Bendetsen assumed that the sinkings automatically meant that the ships' positions were being radioed to the enemy, in 1944 FCC Chairman James Fly reported to the Justice Department that there had been no actual incidence of radio-signaling of ships. See Memorandum, James Fly, March 1944, CWRIC Papers, pp. 8701–8706 (reel 8, pp. 258–263).

27. Telephone Conversation, General John DeWitt and Colonel Karl Bendetsen, January 24, 1942, Provost Marshal General, Record Group 389, NA, cited in Daniels, *Concentration Camps USA*, p. 49.

28. *Personal Justice Denied*, p. 65.

29. John Hersey, "Commentary," in John Armor and Peter Wright, *Manzanar* (New York: Times Books, 1988), p. 31.

30. "Nisei: California Casts an Anxious Eye upon the Japanese Americans in its Midst," *Life*, October 14, 1940, pp. 75–80. See also "Between Two Flags," *Saturday Evening Post*, September 30, 1939, pp. 14–15; "The Emperor's Stray Children," *New Yorker*, April 6, 1940, pp. 40–46.

31. "Japanese in U.S.," *Newsweek*, October 14, 1940, pp. 42, 44.

32. "Japanese Assured on U.S. Residence," *Japanese American Review*, August 23, 1941, p. 1.

33. "Biddle Takes Firm Stand against Any Repression of Alien Groups in U.S.," *Japanese American Review*, October 18, 1941, p. 1.

34. Jim Marshall, "West Coast Japanese," *Collier's*, October 11, 1941, pp. 14–15, cited in Caleb Foote, "Outcasts: The Story of America's Treatment of Her Japanese American Minority," Pamphlet, Fellowship of Reconciliation, 1944, pp. 4–5.

35. Ernest O. Hauser, "America's 150,000 Japanese," *American Mercury* 53 (December 1941): 689–697.

36. Ibid.

37. "Let's Not Get Rattled," *Los Angeles Times*, December 10, 1941, p. 7.

38. *Personal Justice Denied*, p. 71.

39. "Race and Patriotism," *Rafu Shimpo*, January 2, 1942, p. 1.

40. Dennis M. Ogawa, *From Jap to Japanese: An Evolution of Japanese American Stereotypes* (Berkeley: McCutchon Publishing, 1971), pp. 11, 17–21; Stanley High, "Japanese Saboteurs in Our Midst," *Reader's Digest*, January 1942, pp. 11–15. For reasons that remain unknown, *Reader's Digest* removed the article from its second printing and from future editions and microfilm.

41. "Bad News," *Rafu Shimpo,* January 11, 1942, p. 1.
42. *Personal Justice Denied,* p. 69.
43. "Bad News," *Rafu Shimpo,* January 11, 1942, p. 1; Morton Grodzins, *Americans Betrayed* (Chicago: University of Chicago Press, 1949).
44. U.S. Department of the Interior, War Relocation Authority (hereafter WRA), *Wartime Exile: The Exclusion of the Japanese Americans from the Pacific Coast* (Washington DC: Government Printing Office, 1946), p. 104.
45. Letters to the President from the Public, Japanese Evacuation and Relocation Study Papers (hereafter JERS), microfilm reel 6, Bancroft Library, University of California, Berkeley (hereafter BL).
46. Irons, *Justice at War,* p. 38.
47. Letter, Francis Biddle to Leland Ford, January 24, 1942; Letter, Francis Biddle to Leland Ford, January 27, 1942, rpt. in CWRIC Papers, pp. 5739, 5740 (reel 5, pp. 417–418).
48. "Warn of Japanese Submarine Menace," *San Francisco Examiner,* January 25, 1942, cited in WRA, *Wartime Exile,* p. 107.
49. See correspondence regarding coordination of activities between the Western Defense Command and the Canadian authorities. Office of Commanding General, Western Defense Command to Chief of Staff, United States Army, May 10, 1942, RG 59, 014.311 (G-2), NA, rpt. in CWRIC Papers, pp. 13049–13065 (reel 11, pp. 873–889). But see also Dillon Myer's ambiguous comment during a congressional hearing: "Senator [Mon] Wallgren: Do you know of any other country outside of this that is permitting a [relocation] program? Myer: I don't think there is any country doing what we are doing." "U.S. Senate, Subcommittee of Committee on Military Affairs," *Hearings on S.444, Jan 20, 1943* (Washington DC: Government Printing Office, 1943), p. 45.
50. Louis Adamic, *Dinner at the White House* (New York: Harper & Brothers, 1946), p. 41.
51. Ibid.
52. Ibid.
53. President's Appointment Diary, 1942, FDRL. The Roberts commission, despite its "independent" character, was actually composed (apart from its chairman) entirely of military officers, who were handpicked to produce a speedy report that would reassure the public of the military's effectiveness and shield the President and the chief military officials from blame for Pearl Harbor.
54. Henry Stimson, Diary, January 20, 1942, p. 3, HLSP.
55. Report of Roberts Commission, January 23, 1942; *New York Times,* January 25, 1942, pp. 1, 5.

56. "Army Fearful of Stirring Up Enemy Aliens Prevented Arrest of 200 Tokyo Consular Spies," *Philadelphia Inquirer,* January 25, 1942, p. 1; "Hawaii a Warning On Coddling Spies," *Philadelphia Inquirer,* January 28, 1942, p. 10.

57. John M. McCullough, "Jap Autos Jammed Hawaii Base Roads," *Philadelphia Inquirer,* January 27, 1942, p. 5. These reports were later authoritatively discredited by Hawaiian delegate Sam King and Honolulu Chief of Police W. A. Gabrielson. U.S. Congress, House Select Committee Investigating National Defense Migration, *National Defense Migration: Report of the Select Committee Investigating National Defense Migration, House of Representatives: Preliminary Report and Recommendations on Problems of Evacuation of Citizens and Aliens from Military Areas March 19, 1942* (Washington, DC: Government Printing Office, 1942), p. 31.

58. Morton Grodzins, Interview with James C. Ingebretsen, October 14, 1942, Report 14, p. 3, A7.02, JERS, BL.

59. Cited in Daniel Stephen Bozik, "Rhetorical Decision-Making: The Japanese-American Relocation Decision, 1941–1945," unpub. diss., Northwestern University, 1976, p. 113.

60. Harold Ickes Diary, February 1, 1942, pp. 6302–6303, HIP. Roosevelt's comments about a "movie star" presumably referred to members of a delegation from Hollywood, including actresses Dorothy Lamour and Rosalind Russell, that had visited him earlier that day.

61. Memo, Attorney General to the President, January 30, 1942, JERS, reel 7, BL.

62. Morton Grodzins, Interview with A. G. Biddle, February 14, 1945, JERS, A7.03, BL.

63. John Hersey, "Commentary," pp. 40–41.

64. Office of Facts and Figures, "Survey of Public Opinion on the West Coast Japanese," February 4, 1942, Main Office Files, WRA Files, RG 210, NA, rpt. in CWRIC Papers, pp. 10743–10749 (reel 9, pp. 844–851).

65. Robert Bendiner, "Cool Heads or Martial Law"; Howard Costigan, "The Plight of the Nisei," *The Nation,* February 14, 1942, pp. 183–185.

66. Alan Cranston, Monthly Report, Office of Facts and Figures, February 1942, OWI file, Alan Cranston Papers, BL; Alan Cranston interview, January 21, 1999. See also generally "Japanese Aliens" folder, Subject file, Papers of the Director, Office of Facts and Figures, Section 7, Office of War Information Papers, RG 208, NA.

67. Daniels, *Concentration Camps USA,* pp. 67–68.

68. Doris Kearns Goodwin, *No Ordinary Time: Franklin and Eleanor Roosevelt: The Home Front during World War II* (New York: Simon & Schuster, 1994), p. 323.

69. James Rowe, Jr., Confidential Memorandum for Grace Tully, February 2, 1942, OF 133 (Aliens).

70. Benjamin Cohen, Joseph L. Rauh, Jr., and Oscar Cox, "The Japanese Situation on the West Coast," undated memorandum [February 1942], attachment to letter, Joseph L. Rauh, Jr., to Joan Z. Bernstein, May 21, 1982, OF 197 (Japan).

71. Memo, J. Romagna to Roberta, February 4, 1942, OF 197 (Japan).

72. Francis Biddle, Memo of Luncheon Conference with the President, February 7, 1942, Box 2, FBP.

73. See Bozik, "Rhetorical Decision-Making: The Japanese-American Relocation Decision, 1941–1945," p. 100 *passim*.

74. Memo, FDR to the Secretary of War, February 16, 1942, 1942 File, OF 133 (Immigration).

75. Page Smith, *Democracy on Trial* (New York: Simon & Schuster, 1995), pp. 131–133.

76. Conn, "The Decision to Relocate the Japanese"; Biddle, *In Brief Authority*, p. 218.

77. Henry Stimson Diary, February 17, 1942, HLSP.

78. Francis Biddle, Memorandum to the President, February 17, 1942, CF, PSF, Box 10, 7, rpt. in CWRIC papers, pp. 5754–5755 (reel 5, pp. 432–433).

79. Morton Grodzins, interview with A. G. Biddle, February 14, 1945, JERS, A7.03, BL.

80. Numerous studies have been made of the legal and constitutional issues involved in the internment, including Irons, *Justice at War*; Eugene Rostow, "Our Worst Wartime Mistake," *Harper's* 191 (1945): 193–201; Jacobus tenBroek, Edward N. Barnhart, and Floyd W. Matson, *Prejudice, War, and the Constitution* (Berkeley: University of California Press, 1954); and, most recently, William H. Rehnquist, *All the Laws But One: Civil Liberties in Wartime* (New York: Knopf, 1998).

81. Biddle, *In Brief Authority*, p. 219.

82. Jay Franklin (John Franklin Carter), *The Catoctin Conversation* (New York: Scribner's, 1947), pp. 195–196.

83. Irons, *Justice at War*, p. 61. See also testimony of Mike Masaoka in *Hearings before the Subcommittee on Administrative Law and Governmental Relations of the Committee on the Judiciary, House of Representatives Ninety-Eighth Congress, Second Session on H.R. 3387, H.R. 4110, and H.R. 4322, Japanese-American and Aleutian Wartime Relocation*, pp. 232, 245.

84. See testimony of John Herzig, in ibid., pp. 832, 930–931.

85. Forrest C. Pogue and Gordon Harrison, eds., *George C. Marshall*, Vol. 1: *Education of a General, 1880–1939* (New York, Viking 1963).

86. Biddle, *In Brief Authority*, p. 207.

87. Roosevelt's inquiry evidently did not turn up any results. See Memo from the President, February 18, 1942, OF 133 (Immigration).

88. Memo, The President to the Secretary of War, May 5, 1942, OF 197; Henry L. Stimson, Cabinet Meeting Notes, May 15, 1942, Henry Stimson Diary, HLSP; Secretary of War, Memorandum for the President, May 14, 1942, RG 107, NA, rpt. in CWRIC Papers, p. 311 (reel 1, p. 311).

89. Francis Biddle, "Attorney General" manuscript, pp. 394–396, Box 4, FBP.

90. Milton S. Eisenhower, *The President Is Calling* (Garden City, NY: Doubleday, 1974), p. 126.

91. Cabinet meeting, March 13, 1942, described in Harold Ickes Diary, March 15, 1942, p. 6432, HIP.

92. Bracketed words in manuscript text. Biddle, *In Brief Authority*, p. 220; Biddle, "Attorney General" manuscript, p. 418.

93. Biddle, *In Brief Authority*, p. 218.

94. Henry Stimson Diary, January 26, February 25, 1942, HLSP.

95. John Franklin Carter, Memorandum for Dr. Ales Hrdlicka, July 30, 1942, JFCF. See also Henry Field, "'M' Project for F.D.R: Studies on Migration and Settlement (Ann Arbor: Edwards Brothers, 1962), p. x.

96. John Franklin Carter, Memorandum for Dr. Ales Hrdlicka: Presidential Directive, August 7, 1942, Attachment to John Franklin Carter, Memorandum for Miss [Grace] Tully, August 7, 1942, JFCF.

97. Abe Fortas, Memorandum of Cabinet Meeting, August 25, 1944. Interior Department Folder #1, Abe Fortas Papers, Yale University, CT; Henry Wallace Diary, October 21, 1942, Henry Wallace Papers, University of Iowa (microfilm copy in LC).

98. Christopher Thorne, *Allies of a Kind: The United States, Britain, and the War against Japan, 1941–1945* (New York: Oxford University Press, 1978), pp. 158, 167–168. Thorne points out that Roosevelt discussed the racial character of other groups, claiming to Churchill that he had always "disliked the Burmese" but that the Vietnamese were no threat because they were a small, pacific race.

99. Quentin Reynolds, *Quentin Reynolds by Quentin Reynolds* (New York: McGraw-Hill, 1963), pp. 266–267.

100. Entry for August 18, 1942, William D. Hassett, *Off The Record with F.D.R.* (New Brunswick, NJ: Rutgers University Press, 1958), p. 104.

101. Although in the published version of *The Catoctin Conversation* (p. 195)

"Roosevelt" answers that the Japanese Americans "have shown superb patriotism," an examination of Carter's original manuscript at the Argosy Book Store in New York reveals that the original line was "Their patriotism was suspect," a more logical statement in context. (If the Japanese Americans' patriotism was "superb," why approve evacuation?) Internal evidence suggests that the mistake was the result of an unchecked editorial misreading.

102. Memorandum, President to the Secretary of the Navy, February 26, 1942, rpt. in Rogers Daniels, ed., *American Concentration Camps*, Vol. 3: *February 20, 1942–March 31, 1942* (New York: Garland Publications, 1989), Section 1: "Archival Documents, February 20, 1942–March 19, 1942."

103. Biddle, "Attorney General" manuscript, p. 396.

104. WRA, *Wartime Exile*, p. 152.

105. Michi Nishiura Weglyn, *Years of Infamy*, p. 73.

106. Notes of Cabinet Meeting, February 26, 1942, Henry Stimson Diary, HLSP.

107. Indeed, as early as 1938, Roosevelt had discussed the taking of "Japanese owned property" in the United States into escrow under the Alien Property Custodian Act, in response to the Japanese military's looting of American-held property in Nanking, China, during the Japanese invasion. FDR, Memorandum for the Secretary of State, January 28, 1938, in Elliott Roosevelt, ed., *F.D.R.: His Personal Letters*, Vol. 3: *1928–1945* (New York: Duell, Sloan, and Pearce, 1950), p. 753.

108. Memorandum from the President, July 21, 1941, CF, PSF, Box 9 (Justice).

109. Hersey, "Commentary," pp. 53–54.

110. Biddle, *In Brief Authority*, p. 235.

111. James MacGregor Burns, *Roosevelt: The Soldier of Freedom*, p. 267.

112. Franklin (Carter), *The Catoctin Conversation*, p. 194.

4. Implementing an Undemocratic Policy

1. Jacobus tenBroek, Edward N. Barnhart, and Floyd W. Matson, *Prejudice, War, and the Constitution*, pp. 113–116.

2. U.S. Congress, House, Select Committee Investigating National Defense Migration, *National Defense Migration: Report of the Select Committee Investigating National Defense Migration, House of Representatives: Preliminary Report and Recommendations on Problems of Evacuation of Citizens and Aliens from Military Areas, March 19, 1942* (Washington, DC: Government Printing Office, 1942), p. iv.

3. Neither General DeWitt nor the staff of the Western Defense Command testified before the Tolan committee, but they made public statements highlighting the threat represented by the internees. In particular, Karl Bendetsen made a widely publicized address, "The Story of Evacuation," to San Francisco's Commonwealth Club in May 1942, during which he defended evacuation and repeated his previous charges of Japanese-American disloyalty. In particular, Bendetsen repeated the charge, which (according to Kenneth Ringle) he knew to be false, that no Japanese American had ever reported suspicious conduct by another. See letter, E. G. Ferguson to Philip Glick, July 7, 1942, WRA Files, BL.

4. California Joint Immigration Committee, Report to Tolan Committee, Spring 1942, cited in Allen R. Bosworth, *America's Concentration Camps* (New York: Norton, 1967), pp. 77–78.

5. Harold Ickes Diary, March 1, 1942, p. 6388, HIP.

6. Henry L. Stimson, Notes after Cabinet Meeting, February 27, 1942, HLSP; Francis Biddle, Cabinet Notes, February 27, 1942, Box 1, FBP.

7. Letter, Biddle to Stimson, March 5, 1942, War Department Files, AG 014.311, rpt. in Roger Daniels, ed., *American Concentration Camps*, Vol. 3: *February 20, 1942–March 31, 1942* (New York: Garland Press, 1989).

8. Harold Smith, Memorandum of Meeting with President, March 4, 1942, Box 3, Harold Smith Papers, FDRL.

9. WRA, *Wartime Exile*, p. 132.

10. Kai Bird, *The Chairman: John J. McCloy and the Making of the American Establishment* (New York: Simon & Schuster, 1982), p. 157.

11. Milton Eisenhower, *The President Is Calling*, pp. 94–95. "President Issues Proclamation," *Rafu Shimpo*, March 18, 1942, p. 1.

12. Eisenhower, *The President Is Calling*, p. 230. Eisenhower's hopes for resettlement were shared by many of FDR's civilian advisors, including Indian Affairs Secretary John Collier. See John Collier, Letter to Mr. A. L. Walker, March 5, 1942, Assistant Secretary of War Files, RG 210, NA, rpt. in Daniels, ed., *American Concentration Camps*, Vol. 3.

13. For American anti-Japanese propaganda and its effect on Japanese Americans, see John Dower, *War without Mercy: Race and Power in the Pacific War* (New York: Pantheon, 1986), pp. 82ff.

14. Letter, Thomas D. Campbell to FDR, March 12, 1942, including enclosure of Thomas Campbell, Memorandum for the Assistant Secretary of War, Subject: Japanese in the United States, February 25, 1942, CF, PSF (Thomas Campbell), FDRL.

15. Secretary of War, Memorandum for the President, In re Evacuees and the

Attorney General's Memorandum to the President of April 9, 1942, April 15, 1942, RG 210, NA, rpt. in Daniels, ed., *American Concentration Camps*, Vol. 4: *April 1942*.

16. FDR, Memorandum for the Secretary of War, May 5, 1942, War Department File, CF, PSF.

17. Henry Stimson Diary, May 15, 1942, HLSP.

18. John McCloy Diary, May 28, 1942, p. 30, rpt. in CWRIC Papers, p. 29600 (reel 28, p. 621).

19. See Harold Ickes Diary, March 1, 1942, HIP.

20. John Morton Blum, ed., *The Price of Vision: The Diary of Henry Wallace, 1942–1946* (Boston: Houghton Mifflin, 1973), p. 88.

21. Letter, Harold Ickes to FDR, June 15, 1942, FDR Correspondence, HIP.

22. Harold Ickes Diary, p. 6694, June 7, 1942, pp. 6728–6729, June 21, 1942, HIP.

23. Letter, Milton Eisenhower to FDR, June 18, 1942, OF 4849 (WRA).

24. Government lawyers agreed that incarceration of American citizens outside the excluded area was no doubt unconstitutional but proposed that either the camp areas themselves be made restricted areas or that the matter be left for the courts to decide. Memo, Solicitor General, Department of the Interior to Undersecretary of the Interior, August 1942, WRA File #1, Papers of the Undersecretary of the Interior Abe Fortas, RG 48 337, NA.

25. Ibid.

26. Stuart L. Weiss, *The President's Man: Leo Crowley and Franklin Roosevelt in Peace and War* (Carbondale: Southern Illinois University Press, 1996), p. 114.

27. Francis Biddle, Cabinet Notes, January 16, 1942, Box 1, FBP.

28. Memorandum for the President from Harry Hopkins, January 2, 1942, PSF (Harry Hopkins), FDRL.

29. Henry Morgenthau Diaries, January 27, 1942, p. 1034, HMP.

30. Ibid.

31. Francis Biddle, Cabinet Notes, February 27, 1942, p. 4, Box 1, FBP.

32. Note of Conference with President, February 13, 1942, Francis Biddle, Cabinet Notes, FBP.

33. Letter, John McCloy to Harry Hopkins, February 21, 1942, Papers of the Assistant Secretary of War, rpt. in CWRIC Papers, p. 91 (reel 1, p. 91).

34. Harry L. Hopkins, Memorandum to Mr. McCloy, February 23, 1942, Assistant Secretary's Office, War Department, NA, rpt. in Daniels, ed., *American Concentration Camps*, Vol. 3: *February 19, 1942–March 31, 1942*.

35. Draft letter from the Secretary of War to the Secretary of the Treasury, enclosed in Memorandum, General Allen Gullion to Mr. McCloy, Febru-

ary 26, 1942, Papers of the Assistant Secretary of War, RG 210, NA, rpt. in CWRIC Papers, pp. 93–94 (reel 1, pp. 93–94).

36. John Morton Blum, *From the Morgenthau Diaries: Years of War, 1941–1945* (Little, Brown: Boston, 1967), p. 6.

37. Telegram, John H. Tolan to Francis Biddle, February 28, 1942, Justice Department Papers, RG 107, Box 2, NA, rpt. in CWRIC Papers, p. 96 (reel 1, p. 96).

38. Letter, Henry Morgenthau to John Tolan, February 26, 1942, OF 77 (Alien Property Custodian).

39. Francis Biddle, Cabinet Notes, February 27, 1942, p. 2, Box 2, FBP.

40. Harry Hopkins, Telephone Message to Miss Klotz for Secretary Morgenthau, February 26, 1942, OF 77 (Alien Property Custodian).

41. Letter, Secretary of the Treasury to Harry Hopkins, February 27, 1942, OF 77 (Alien Property Custodian).

42. Blum, *From the Morgenthau Diaries,* pp. 8–9; Francis Biddle, Notes of Cabinet Meeting, February 27, 1942, Box 1, FBP.

43. Ibid.

44. John McCloy Diary, March 3, 1942, rpt. in CWRIC Papers, p. 29583 (reel 28, p. 605).

45. Henry Morgenthau, "Suggested Program for the Federal Reserve Bank of San Francisco and Other Public Agencies to Deal with Property of Evacuees from Pacific Coast Military Areas," March 4, 1942, Henry Morgenthau Diaries, March 5, 1942, pp. 74–76, HMP.

46. Morgenthau's plan was released to the Tolan committee on March 9 and subsequently made public. U.S. Congress, House, Select Committee Investigating National Defense Migration, *National Defense Migration,* pp. 6–8.

47. Morgenthau, "Suggested Program for the Federal Reserve Bank," p. 2.

48. "Alien Property Custodians on Way to Coast," *Los Angeles Times,* March 8, 1942, p. 1.

49. "Coordinator Clark in Advice on Evacuation," *Rafu Shimpo,* March 8, 1942, p. 1.

50. Quotation, Newspaper Interview with Tom Clark, *San Francisco Chronicle,* March 5, 1942, p. 6. Henry Morgenthau Diaries, March 5, 1942, HMP.

51. Ibid.

52. "Japs May Go to Owens Valley," *Los Angeles Times,* March 5, 1942, pp. 1, 6.

53. Note containing quotation, Interview with Tom Clark, *San Francisco Chronicle,* March 5, 1942, p. 6. Henry Morgenthau Diaries, March 5, 1942, HMP. This last passage is underlined in the diary, though not in the original.

54. Henry Morgenthau, Jr., "General Aniline and Film," conversation with Mr. Foley, Mrs. Klotz, and Mrs. Morgenthau, March 5, 1942. Henry Morgenthau Diaries, March 5, 1942, HMP.

55. Ibid., p. 74.

56. Henry L. Morgenthau, Jr., Memo to John McCloy, March 5, 1942. Henry Morgenthau Diaries, March 5, 1942, p. 77, HMP.

57. Clarence Lea to FDR, March 5, 1942; FDR to Clarence Lea, March 17, 1942, OF 77 (Alien Property Custodian).

58. John McCloy, Address, Afternoon Session, March 8, 1942. See "Proceedings, Special Emergency Meetings, Japanese American Citizens League, San Francisco, California, March 8, 9, 10 1942," Pamphlet, Ethnic Studies Library, University of California, Berkeley.

59. Dillon Myer, "Press Conference," May 14, 1943, p. 27, Director Public Statements File, WRA Papers, BL.

60. "Custodians to Protect Evacuees' Property: Federal Reserve Bank to Establish Offices," *Rafu Shimpo*, March 11, 1942, p. 1.

61. Sandra C. Taylor, "The Federal Reserve Bank and the Relocation of the Japanese in 1942," *Public Historian* 5, no. 1 (Winter 1983): 9–30.

62. "Promise Storage Space for Japanese Evacuees," *Rafu Shimpo*, March 30, 1942, p. 1.

63. "What to Do with Our Furniture"; "Storage Place Provided for First Volunteer Group," *Rafu Shimpo*, March 19, 1942, p. 1.

64. Taylor, "The Federal Reserve Bank and the Relocation of the Japanese in 1942," p. 25.

65. Frank S. Arnold, Michael C. Barth, and Gilah Langer, "Economic Losses of Ethnic Japanese as a Result of Exclusion and Detention, 1942–1946," Unpublished Report Prepared for Commission on Wartime Relocation and Internment of Civilians, June 1983, WRA Papers, RG 210, NA. See especially the section on "Property Losses," pp. 39ff. This figure does not include the $25 million in compensation paid for property by the government after passage of the Japanese American Evacuation Claims Act of 1948.

66. Ted Morgan, *FDR: A Biography* (New York: Simon and Schuster, 1985), pp. 628–629.

67. Gary Okihiro, *Cane Fires*, p. 224.

68. Atherton Richards, "A Proposed Solution for the Japanese Question in Hawaii," contained in William J. Donovan, Memorandum for the President, February 12, 1942, OSS Reports, February 5–February 12, 1942, CF, (Donovan).

69. Joint U.S. Chiefs of Staff, Hawaiian Defense Forces, JCS 11, February 12,

1942, PSF, PCF (Hawaii), rpt. in CWRIC Papers, pp. 3664–3665 (reel 3, pp. 639–640).

70. Ibid. It is impossible to determine from the document whether the army chief of staff was presenting his colleagues with fresh information or whether there was already informal accord on principles and he was circulating the draft to obtain agreement on the form of the recommendation. The confident use of the word "unanimously" in the draft strongly suggests the latter.

71. War Department, Office of the Chief of Staff, Notes on Evacuation of Japanese from Hawaiian Islands, Undated Memorandum, PSF, PCF (Hawaii), rpt. in Roger Daniels, ed., *American Concentration Camps* Vol. 3, *February 20, 1942–March 31, 1942.*

72. Captain Frank O. Blake, Memorandum to the Officer in Charge, December 1, 1942, File 5034, Evacuation of Hawaii, NA, rpt. in CWRIC papers, pp. 29548–53 (reel 28, pp. 569–574).

73. Memorandum for the President from the Secretary of the Navy, February 25, 1942, rpt. in Weglyn, *Years of Infamy,* p. 174. Knox was evidently unaware that the Japanese-Hawaiian population was already fully employed in production of agricultural products such as pineapples and sugar, although admittedly these were cash crops, not food for their own tables.

74. Memorandum, President to the Secretary of the Navy, February 26, 1942, rpt. in Roger Daniels, ed. *American Concentration Camps,* Vol. 3: *February 20, 1942–March 31, 1942.*

75. Henry Stimson, Notes after Cabinet Meeting, February 27, 1942, Henry Stimson Diary, HLSP.

76. Letter, Admiral Stark to FDR, March 11, 1942, CF, PSF (Hawaii), rpt. in CWRIC Papers, pp. 4489–4490 (reel 4, pp. 266–267). General Dwight Eisenhower later reported to General Marshall that, as the latter had understood, the President had in fact approved the text of JCS 11, but only on the basis that the initial evacuation would be limited to 20,000 potentially dangerous Japanese. Memorandum, Assistant Chief of Staff to Chief of Staff, March 27, 1942, Papers of the Chief of Staff, U.S. Army, rpt. in CWRIC Papers, p. 26438 (reel 25, p. 252).

77. Stetson Conn, Rose C. Engelman, and Byron Fairchild, *The United States Army in World War II, the Western Hemisphere: Guarding the United States and Its Outposts,* p. 199.

78. Ibid., p. 211.

79. Henry Stimson Diary, April 15, 1942, HLSP.

80. Memorandum for the President from the Secretary of War, In re Evacuees and the Attorney General's Memorandum to the President of April 9, 1942, April 15, 1942, RG 210, NA, rpt. in Daniels, ed. *American Concentration Camps*, Vol. 4, *April 1942*. As late as May, FDR referred to Hawaii as "under definite strain in fear of momentary Japanese attack." Presidential Memo for the Postmaster General, May 19, 1942, OF 197-A (Japan).

81. Memorandum for the President, Secretary of the Navy, April 20, 1942, RG 107–47–8, ASW 014.311 (Hawaii), NA, rpt. in CWRIC Papers, p. 580 (reel 1, p. 488). It is not clear whether Knox was unaware that FDR had approved the Joint Chiefs' plan for mainland evacuation or whether he was reviving the abandoned plan for Hawaiian evacuation in order to avoid the constitutional difficulties it entailed.

82. Presidential Memorandum for the Secretary of War and the Secretary of the Navy, April 23, 1942, RG 107–47–8, ASW 014.311 (Hawaii), NA, rpt. in CWRIC Papers, p. 581 (reel 1, p. 489).

83. Notes after Cabinet Meeting, April 24, 1942, Henry Stimson Diary, HLSP; Harold Ickes Diary, April 26, 1942, p. 6576, HIP.

84. Francis Biddle, Notes of Conference with the President, April 22, 1942; Francis Biddle, Memorandum for the President, April 23, 1942, Box 1, FBP.

85. Francis Biddle, Cabinet Notes, May 1, 1942, Box 1, FBP.

86. Biddle, *In Brief Authority*, p. 225.

87. Territorial Office of Defense, The Japanese Population of the Territory of Hawaii—Its Relationship the War Effort, Report, May 21, 1942, RG 210 39.034, WRA Papers, NA.

88. Letter, John McCloy to General Delos Emmons, May 18, 1942, rpt. in Daniels, *American Concentration Camps*, Vol. 8, *1944–1945*.

89. Letter, General Delos Emmons to John McCloy, June 16, 1942, RG 107, ASW 014.311 (Hawaii), NA, rpt. in Daniels, *American Concentration Camps*, Vol. 8, *1944–1945*.

90. Delos Emmons, Interview with *New York Times*, cited in Letter, Miss Rosamond H. Clark to The Editor, *New York Times*, November 8, 1942, rpt. in Daniels, ed., *American Concentration Camps*, Vol. 8, *1944–1945*. See also Capt. David J. McFadden, Memorandum to Col. Karl R. Bendetsen, Hawaiian-Japanese Evacuation Program, rpt. in CWRIC papers, pp. 25978–255979 (reel 24, pp. 891–892).

91. *Personal Justice Denied*, p. 273.

92. Letter, Henry L. Stimson to John W. McCormack, July 8, 1942, RG 107–47–8, ASW 014.311 (Hawaii), NA, rpt. in CWRIC Papers, p. 12792 (reel 11, p. 673).

93. Letter, John McCloy to Dillon Myer, October 4, 1942; Letter, John McCloy to Dillon Myer, October 14, 1942, WRA Files, RG 210 39.034, NA.

94. Letter, Secretary of the Navy to the President, October 17, 1942, CF (Navy).

95. Letter, Henry Stimson to FDR, October 28, 1942, CF (Navy).

96. Memorandum from the President to the Secretary of War and the U.S. Army Chief of Staff, November 1942, CF (Navy).

97. Capt. David J. McFadden, Memorandum to Col. Karl R. Bendetsen, Hawaiian-Japanese Evacuation Program, rpt. in CWRIC papers, pp. 25978–25979 (reel 24, pp. 891–892).

98. Biddle, *In Brief Authority*, p. 223.

99. "Secretary Knox Hints Desire for Evacuation," *Pacific Citizen*, March 11, 1943, p. 1.

100. See Enclosure, stating Secretary of the Navy's acceptance of suspension of evacuation program, in Letter, Col. William P. Scobey to Dillon Myer, April 2, 1943, RG 210 39.034, WRA Papers, NA.

101. Irene Matyas puts the figure at 1,875. Irene Matyas, *Die Internierung Japanisch-Stämmiger Amerikaner Während des Zweite Weltkrieges* (Vienna and Cologne: Böhlou Verlag, 1990), p. 43. Matyas's interpretation is open to question, however, because she states, without evidence, that Knox and the other Cabinet secretaries became resigned to the status quo in Hawaii after mid-July 1942, once the Japanese invasion threat had eased and the American armed forces were on the offensive in Guadalcanal and New Guinea. Ibid.

102. Weglyn, *Years of Infamy*, pp. 88–89; Captain Frank O. Blake, Memorandum to the Officer in Charge, December 1, 1942, File 5034, Evacuation of Hawaii, NA, rpt. in CWRIC papers, pp. 29548–53 (reel 28, pp. 569–574).

103. Memorandum from the President to the Attorney General, December 18, 1942, Box 1, FBP.

104. Harold Ickes Diary, November 8, 1942, p. 7177, HIP.

105. *Personal Justice Denied*, p. 269.

106. The classic exponent of this theory is Richard E. Neustadt, *Presidential Power* (Cambridge: Harvard University Press, 1960).

107. See testimony of Edward Ennis, *Hearings before the Subcommittee of the Committee on Immigration, United Sates Senate, Supervision, Detention and Incarceration of Deportable Aliens, S. 1232, S.2293, and S.1720*, March 23, 24, 1942, pp. 41–46, pp. 56–57.

108. Letter, Milton Eisenhower to Marvin McIntyre, May 15, 1942, OF 4849 (WRA).

109. ACLU, *Newsletter*, May 11, 1942, p. 3.

110. Letter, Alfred H. Bingham, George S. Counts, John Dewey, Sherwood Eddy, Harry Emerson Fosdick, Frank P. Graham, Mary W. Hillyer, John Haynes Holmes, James Wood Johnson, Louis and Ada Krahl, Harry W. Laidler, Rt. Rev. Mons. Luigi G. Ligutti, Reinhold Niebuhr, Clarence E. Pickett, Harold Rugg, Mark Starr, Norman Thomas, Ernest Fremont Tittle, Oswald Garrison Villard, and Mary E. Woolley to President Roosevelt, April 30, 1942, rpt. in CWRIC papers, pp. 25129–25130 (reel 22, pp. 884–885). See also Letter, Mary Hillyer to Carey McWilliams, April 23, 1942, Japanese American Files, Carey McWilliams Papers, Hoover Institution.

111. Robert Shaffer, "Cracks in the Consensus: Defending the Rights of Japanese Americans During World War II," *Radical History Review* 72 (June 1998): 84–120.

112. Letter, ACLU to FDR, March 20, 1942, rpt. in Daniels, *American Concentration Camps*, Vol.3 *February 19, 1942–March 31, 1942*.

113. For more on the British experience with enemy aliens see, for example, Arnold Krammer, *Undue Process* (London: Rowan & Littlefield, 1987), pp. 18–21. The Churchill quote is from Adamic, *Dinner at the White House*, p. 41.

114. Letter, FDR to Herbert H. Lehman, June 3, 1942, OF 133 (Immigration).

115. See Memorandum for the Commanding General, from Col. Joel F. Watson, Office of the Judge Advocate, April 23, 1942, rpt. in CWRIC Papers, p. 5211 (reel 4, p. 894).

116. Letter, FDR to Culbert Olson, May 25, 1942, OF 197-A (Japan).

117. Monroe Deutsch, Proposed Speech for the President, in Laughlin Currie, Memorandum for the President, May 27, 1942, Cited in Weglyn, *Years of Infamy*, pp. 108–109.

118. Letter, Milton Eisenhower to the President, June 18, 1942, OF 4849 (WRA).

119. Letter, Unidentified [John Bird?]) to John Province and Dillon Myer, December 1, 1942, Chron File, 2.2.911, RG 210, WRA Papers, NA.

120. Peter Irons, *Justice at War*, pp. 108–110ff.

121. Letter, John Haynes Holmes, Edward L. Parsons, Mary Woolley, Arthur Garfield Hays, and Roger Baldwin to FDR, September 8, 1942, rpt. in "President Roosevelt Asked for Statement to Reassure Nisei," *Pacific Citizen*, September 8, 1942, p. 1.

122. Memorandum for General Watson from MDT, April 22, 1942, OF 133 (Aliens).

123. Memo, Grace Tully to Milton S. Eisenhower, June 16, 1942, OF 133-A (Immigration).

124. Letter, Milton Eisenhower to John McCloy, October 13, 1942, WRA Papers, C102, BL.

125. Letter, Secretary of the Navy to the President, October 17, 1942, OF 4849 (WRA).

126. TenBroek, Barnhart, and Matson, *Prejudice, War, and the Constitution*, p. 167.

127. S. L. A. Marshall, cited in "Reveal Gen. Marshall's Support of Nisei," *Pacific Citizen*, January 25, 1947, p. 1.

128. General John L. DeWitt, Memorandum to Col. Theodore J. Koenig, GSC, Military Utilization of United States Citizens of Japanese Ancestry, July 23, 1942, Records of the Secretary of War, RG 107, NA, rpt. in CWRIC pp. 5171–5194 (reel 14, pp. 853–877).

129. Letter, Commandant, Military Intelligence Service Language School, to Mr. E. M. Rowalt, Acting Regional Director, WRA, October 3, 1942; Letter, Major Karl T. Gould to WRA, October 22, 1942, Chron File, October 1942, WRA Papers, RG 210, NA. By the end of 1942, 179 Japanese Americans had joined military intelligence units.

130. John McCloy, Memorandum for the Secretary of War, October 15, 1942, Records of the Secretary of War, RG 107, NA, rpt. in CWRIC p. 13779 (reel 12, p. 356).

131. Handwritten Note, undated, RG 407 (Adj. Gen. 1940–1942 Classified), AG 291.2, NA, rpt. in CWRIC Papers, p. 13760 (reel 12, p. 337).

132. Draft Letter, Secretary of War to the President, October 14, 1942, with Stimson's handwritten notes, undated, RG 407 (Adj. Gen. 1940–1942 Classified), AG 291.2, NA, rpt. in CWRIC Papers, pp. 13761–13764 (reel 12, pp. 338–341).

133. Ibid. While Stimson stopped short of basing his estimation of Nisei fighting ability on their innate Japanese character, he did rely on racial physical characteristics: "Almost without exception, they are taller than their parents, while possessed of the usual agility and endurance." Ibid.

134. Ibid.

135. *Personal Justice Denied*, p. 187.

136. Donald E. Collins, *Native American Aliens: Disloyalty and the Renunciation of Citizenship by Japanese Americans during World War II* (Westport, CT: Greenwood Press, 1985), pp. 22–23.

137. Verbatim Report, WRA Staff Conference, Washington DC, 9:30 A.M., November 12, 1942, Main Office Files, WRA Papers, BL, pp. 453–454.

138. John Franklin Carter, Report on Plan to Organize German and Italian Nationals for Armed Service, October 19, 1942, JFCF.

139. Letter, Henry L. Stimson to John Franklin Carter, November 4, 1942, Office of the Secretary of War, Entry 47, Box 22, ASW 342.18, Enlistment of Japanese Americans, rpt. in CWRIC Papers, p. 5701 (reel 5, p. 379).

140. FDR, Memorandum for the Secretary of War, November 17, 1942, PSF (War Department). Also RG 107, NA, rpt. in CWRIC Papers, p. 2871 (reel 3, p. 82).

141. Ibid. Emphasis in original.

142. Harold Ickes Diary, November 22, 1942, HIP.

143. Laughlin Currie, Memorandum for the President, December 18, 1942, Laughlin Currie Papers, Hoover Institution, Stanford University; also summarized in Routing Memo, OF 4849 (WRA).

144. *Personal Justice Denied*, p. 190.

145. Harold Ickes Diary, January 9, 1943, p. 7376, HIP.

146. FDR, Letter to Henry Stimson, February 1, 1943, OF 4849 (WRA). Elmer Davis came up with the comment that Americanism was not a matter of race.

147. Routing Memorandum, March 8, 1943, Marvin McIntyre to Gov. Sidney Osborn, OF 197-A (Japan); "President's Secretary Notes Nisei Sacrifice in Evacuation," *Pacific Citizen*, March 25, 1943, p. 1.

148. Letter, M. M. Tozier to Dorothea Lang [sic], May 21, 1942, WRA Correspondence File, RG 210, 21.011, NA.

149. ACLU, Confidential Memorandum on Conferences in Washington by Dr. Alexander Meiklejohn and Roger N. Baldwin, September 15 and 16, 1942, ACLU files, NAACP Papers, Series B-1, LC.

150. Letter, Henry L. Stimson to Mary W. Hillyer, May 25, 1942, cited in Post War World Council circular letter, June 12, 1942. Post War World Council Folder, Organizations File, NAACP Papers, Series A, LC. See also "Secretary of War Speaks on Evacuation," *Pacific Citizen*, June 18, 1942, p. 1.

151. "Biddle Opposes Detaining Nisei," *Rafu Shimpo*, March 25, 1942, p. 1.

152. "Biddle Speech Dropped on Italy," *New York Times*, October 15, 1942, p. 3.

153. Eleanor Roosevelt, "My Day," July 5, 1942, Eleanor Roosevelt Speeches and Writings File, FDRL. The column was actually sent to the White House by Charles Kikuchi, a sociologist then interned at the Tanforan "assembly center." See Charles Kikuchi, *The Kikuchi Diaries: Reports from an American Concentration Camp* (Urbana: University of Illinois Press, 1973), p. 167.

154. "Nisei Loyalty to U.S. Stressed by WRA Official to Congress," *Pacific Citizen*, July 16, 1942, p. 1. Eisenhower repeated as a "personal opinion" his private estimate to Roosevelt that the Nisei were 80 to 85 percent loyal and that 50 percent of the Issei were passively loyal.

155. Eisenhower, *The President Is Calling*, p. 121.

156. Emmet John Hughes, *The Ordeal of Power* (New York: Dell, 1962), p. 24.

5. Covering a Retreat

1. For a critical analysis of Myer's "scattering" policy, see Richard Drinnon, *Keeper of Concentration Camps: Dillon Myer and American Racism* (Berkeley: University of California Press, 1987), pp. 55–58.

2. Drinnon, *Keeper of Concentration Camps*, p. 61; Attorney General's Council, Thirty-First Meeting, September 1, 1943; Fifty-Third Meeting, September 6, 1944, Minutes of Attorney General's Council Meetings, pp. 24, 41, Box 2, FBP.

3. Kenneth D. Ringle, Unpublished Memorandum, Factors Making the Kibei a Dangerous Group, May 27, 1942, rpt. in CWRIC Papers, pp. 19563–19579 (reel 17, pp. 114–131). Ringle later anonymously published substantially the same memorandum in *Harper's* magazine as "The Japanese in America: The Problem and the Solution," *Harper's* 185 (October 1942): 489–497.

4. Michael John Wallinger, "Dispersal of Japanese Americans: Rhetorical Strategies of the War Relocation Authority," p. 86; Jacobus tenBroek et al., *Prejudice, War, and the Constitution*, pp. 160–161.

5. Ibid. Although Biddle did not testify, he privately agreed that segregation was necessary to isolate "trouble makers" in the camps. Attorney General's Council, Fifteenth Meeting, March 10, 1943. Attorney General's Council minutes, Box 2, FBP.

6. Letter, Dillon Myer to Henry L. Stimson, March 11, 1943, RG 338-X-1.020 (War Department); RG 107, Box 7, ASW 014.311 (WDC), NA, rpt. in CWRIC Papers, pp. 12772–82 (reel 11, pp. 683–693).

7. Dillon Myer, letter to John McCloy, March 12, 1943, RG 338-X-1.020 (War Department); RG 107, Box 7, ASW 014.311 (WDC), NA, rpt. in CWRIC Papers, pp. 12763–12765 (reel 11, p. 685–687).

8. U.S. Committee on Wartime Relocation and Internment of Civilians, *Personal Justice Denied*, pp. 221–222.

9. Edward Ennis, Memorandum for the Attorney General Re: Japanese Relocation, April 15, 1943, OF 133-A (Aliens).

10. Irons, *Justice at War*, pp. 207–214.

11. Letter, Henry L. Stimson to Dillon Myer, May 10, 1943, RG 107, ASW 014.311, rpt. in Daniels, *American Concentration Camps*, Vol. 7, *1943*.

12. Letter, Dillon Myer to the Secretary of War, June 8, 1943, RG 107, ASW 310.8 (6–8–43) (Secret), NA, rpt. in CWRIC Papers, pp. 12976–82 (reel 11, pp. 801–806).

13. Ibid. See also Henry Stimson, Letter to Eleanor Roosevelt, May 21, 1943, ERP, Section 70, Correspondence with Government Departments, Stimson 1943.

14. Dillon Myer, Press Conference, May 14, 1943, Public Statements by Director, WRA Papers, BL (reel 21, p. 33).

15. Harold Ickes Diary, March 19, 1942, p. 6453; Harold Ickes Diary, March 20, 1943, p. 7561, HIP.

16. Ibid., January 9, 1943, p. 7346.

17. Ibid., February 21, 1943, p. 7479.

18. Ibid., March 20, 1943, p. 7565.

19. Letter, Secretary of the Interior to the President, April 13, 1943, OF 4849 (WRA).

20. Letter, Milton Eisenhower to the President, April 22, 1943, OF 4849 (WRA).

21. Ibid.

22. Letter, President to the Secretary of Interior, April 22, 1943 (draft), April 24, 1943 (signed), rpt. in Roger Daniels, *American Concentration Camps,* Vol. 6, *1943* "Archival Documents, 1943."

23. Letter, Eleanor Roosevelt to Flora Rose, June 16, 1942, Group 100 (Personal Correspondence), ERP.

24. Letter, Clarence Pickett to Eleanor Roosevelt, February 12, 1942, Series 100, ERP; Letter, Eleanor Roosevelt to Clarence Pickett, May 23, 1942, National Japanese American Student Relocation Council Papers, Hoover Institution; Greg Robinson's Interview with Togo Tanaka, June 2000; Letter, Robert Patterson to Eleanor Roosevelt, May 23, 1942, Eleanor Roosevelt Correspondence, Robert Patterson Papers, LC; Letter, Eleanor Roosevelt to FDR, July 20, 1942, described in Routing memo, Presidential Memorandum for Dillon S. Myer, July 30, 1942, OF 133 (Aliens); Letter, Dillon Myer to Eleanor Roosevelt, August 10, 1942; Letter, Malvina Thompson to Dillon Myer, August 20, 1942; Series 70, Correspondence with Government Officials, ERP. For Eleanor Roosevelt and Japanese Americans generally, see Allida Black, *Casting Her Own Shadow: Eleanor Roosevelt and the Shaping of Postwar Liberalism* (New York: Columbia University Press, 1996), pp. 88–96.

25. Letter, John Tolan to Eleanor Roosevelt, March 1, 1943, Series 70, ERP; Editorial, *Honolulu Star-Bulletin,* May 19, 1943, p. 7; Letter, Eleanor Roosevelt to Joseph P. Lash, April 13, 1943, rpt. in Joseph P. Lash, *Eleanor: Eleanor Roosevelt and Her Friends* (Garden City, NY: Doubleday, 1982), p. 458.

26. Eleanor Roosevelt, "My Day," syndicated column, April 27, 1943; Timothy Turner, "First Lady Here to Visit Hospitals," *Los Angeles Times,* April 27, 1943, p. 1.

27. Letter, Morris L. Ernst to FDR, April 15, 1943, OF 197 (Japan).

28. Morris Ernst, Letter to Hon. Harlan F. Stone, March 6, 1943, Harlan Stone Papers, LC, rpt. in CWRIC Papers, pp. 6772–6775 (reel 6, pp. 358–361).

29. Hon. Harlan F. Stone, Letter to Morris Ernst, March 17, 1943, Harlan Stone Papers, LC, rpt. in CWRIC Papers, pp. 6772–6775 (reel 6, pp. 358–361).

30. Letter, Morris L. Ernst to FDR, April 15, 1943, OF 197 (Japan).

31. Ibid.

32. FDR, Memorandum for Morris Ernst, April 24, 1943, OF 197 (Japan).

33. Irons, *Justice at War*, pp. 245–247; Sidney Fine, "Mr. Justice Murphy and the Hirabayashi Case," *Pacific Historical Review* 32, no. 2 (May 1964): 255.

34. "Robertson Accuses Internees Coddled," *New York Times*, May 7, 1943, p. 12.

35. "Dies Group Opens Hearings On Japanese Americans," *Pacific Citizen*, June 24, 1943, p. 1.

36. "Dies Group Says Interned Japanese Are among Best-Fed Civilians in World," *New York Times*, June 1, 1943, p. 6.

37. Dillon Myer, "Statement on Testimony of Harold H. Townshend before the House of Representatives Subcommittee of the Special Committee on Un-American Activities, Los Angeles, California, May 26, 1943, 2:00 P.M.," July 1943, enclosed with letter, Dillon Myer to Eleanor Roosevelt, July 19, 1943, Series 100 (Personal Correspondence), ERP.

38. "The New Deal's Worst War Scandal," *New York Journal-American*, June 20, 1943.

39. Warren G. Edward White, *Earl Warren: A Public Life* (New York: Oxford University Press, 1982), p. 73.

40. "Warren Sees Grim Peril in Release of Japanese," *Los Angeles Times*, July 2, 1943, p. 1.

41. "Jap Troops Reported Here," *Los Angeles Times*, May 14, 1943, p. 1; "Representative Answers Pro-Jap Sentimentalism," *Los Angeles Times*, May 21, 1943, p. 2.

42. WRA File, Box 1, Aubrey Williams Papers, FDRL. See also War Relocation Authority/Office of War Information Press Release, June 3, 1943, OWI-Minorities File, Philleo Nash Papers, Harry S. Truman Library, Independence, MO (hereafter HSTL).

43. Eleanor Roosevelt, "My Day," Syndicated Column, April 27, 1943.

44. Dillon S. Myer, "An Autobiography of Dillon S. Myer" (1970), pp. 200–201, Regional Oral History Office, BL.

45. Ibid.

46. "John McCloy Sees Place for Japanese in California," *Pacific Citizen*, May 13, 1943, p. 1.

47. Letter, Henry L. Stimson to S.B.M., June 9, 1943, WRA Papers, reel 20, p. 11, BL.

48. "U.S. Inspector General Asks Tolerance for Evacuee Group"; "General Probes Arizona Demands on Evacuees," *Pacific Citizen*, July 31, 1943, p. 4.

49. Senate Resolution 166, July 6, 1943, *Congressional Record*, Senate, July 6, 1943, p. 7363.

50. Attorney General's Council Meeting, July 7, 1943, Attorney General's Council minutes, p. 22, Box 2, FBP.

51. Hon. Dillon Myer, Memorandum for the President, July 14, 1943, OF 197 (Japan).

52. Telephone Conversation, Mr. McCloy and Colonel Bendetsen, 10 July 1943, p. 1, RG 107, ASW 014.311 (WDC General), NA, rpt. in Daniels, *American Concentration Camps* Vol. 7, *1943*.

53. U.S. Senate, 78th Congress, First Session, Document Number 96, "Message from the President of the United States Transmitting Report on Senate Resolution No. 166 Relating to Segregation of Loyal and Disloyal Japanese in Relocation Centers and Plans for Future Operation of Such Centers," September 14, 1943, p. 2.

54. "The Right to Return," editorial, *Pacific Citizen*, September 18, 1943, p. 4.

55. FDR, Letter to Congress, October 11, 1943, OF 133 (Immigration).

56. "Gen. DeWitt Gets Distinguished Service Medal from President," *Pacific Citizen*, September 11, 1943, p. 4.

57. Letter, Dillon Myer to John J. McCloy, October 16, 1943, RG 107–47–9, ASW 014.311 (Permits), NA, rpt. in CWRIC Papers, pp. 811–812 (reel 1, pp. 763–764).

58. Letter, John J. McCloy to General Delos Emmons, November 5, 1943; Letter, General Delos Emmons to John J. McCloy, November 10, 1943, RG 338-X-1, 020 War Department, RG 107, Box 9, ASW 014.311 (Permits), NA, rpt. in CWRIC papers, pp. 802–807 (reel 1, pp. 754–759). See also "Jap Questionnaire," *Pacific Citizen*, December 11, 1943, p. 4.

59. The details of the Tule Lake disorder are dealt with most completely in two otherwise widely conflicting sources, Weglyn, *Years of Infamy*, pp. 160–164, and in Page Smith, *Democracy on Trial* (New York: Simon and Schuster, 1995), pp. 323–326.

60. "Two Kinds of Japanese," *New York Times*, November 20, 1943, p. 12.

61. "Results of Our Reader Poll," *Los Angeles Times*, December 6, 1943, p. 1; "War Relocation Authority Doubly in Hot Water," December 7, 1943, p. 2. The bias in the poll can be deduced from comparison with a Gallup Poll of some 3,000 people nationwide taken at the beginning of 1943 (before Roosevelt and Stimson spoke up on behalf of loyal internees). The Gallup Poll asked simply if the respondent thought that the Japanese who were

moved from the Pacific Coast should be allowed to return after the end of the war: 61 percent, including 53 percent in the evacuated states, answered affirmatively (although 25 percent of the latter would allow only U.S. citizens), while 31 percent in the Pacific Coast states answered negatively (to 17 percent nationwide). "Gallup Polls Shows Majority of West Coast People Favor Return of Citizen Japanese," *Pacific Citizen*, January 6, 1943, p. 1.

62. A *New York Times* article spoke disdainfully of the year-long campaign by congressional committees and West Coast lobbying groups such as the American Legion and the Native Sons and Daughters of the Golden West. These groups had labored to get the camps in the hands of the military, "which positively has not wanted them," on the mistaken theory that military control would automatically end the leave clearance program. "WRA Under Increasing Fire," *New York Times*, November 28, 1943, p. 10.

63. "West Coast Congressmen Ask Ouster of Dillon Myer," *Pacific Citizen*, December 14, 1943, p. 2.

64. See Letters to the President, March 1944, OF 4849 (WRA); Routing Memo, Memorandum, President to the Director of the Budget, February 9, 1944, OF 197-A (Japan).

65. Letter, General Delos Emmons to John J. McCloy, November 10, 1943, RG 338-X-1, 020 War Department, RG 107, Box 9, ASW 014.311 (Permits), NA, rpt. in CWRIC papers, pp. 806–807 (reel 1, pp. 736–739).

66. Francis Biddle, Memorandum for the President, November 10, 1943, CF (Justice Department), Box 76, rpt. in Weglyn, *Years of Infamy*, p. 163.

67. Attorney General's Council, Thirty-Fifth Meeting, November 19, 1943, Attorney General's Council Minutes, p. 29, Box 2, FBP.

68. Francis Biddle, "Racial and Cultural Minorities," Address to Jewish Theological Seminary, November 11, 1943, cited in "WRA Has No Right to Intern Nisei Citizens, Says Biddle," *Pacific Citizen*, November 27, 1943, p. 1; and rpt. as "Democracy and Racial Minorities," *Common Ground* 4, no. 2 (Winter 1944): 3–12.

69. "WRA's Role in Relocation of Evacuees Misunderstood, Biddle Tells Dies Group," *Pacific Citizen*, December 18, 1943, p. 5.

70. Morton Grodzins, Notes of Interview with Attorney General Biddle, October 13, 1943, Evacuation Study, JERS Papers, A7.02, BL; "Attorney General Opposes Stern Measures Proposed against Japanese Americans," *Pacific Citizen*, December 4, 1943, p. 6.

71. Attorney General's Council, Thirty-Eighth Meeting, December 9, 1943, Attorney General's Council minutes, p. 30, Box 2, FBP.

72. Note for the Secretary of the Interior from Walter Gellhorn, December 9, 1943, Department of Interior Correspondence, Notes, and Memoranda, Box 161, Abe Fortas Papers, Yale University.

73. My account of this meeting is drawn from Cabinet notes by Ickes, Biddle, and Vice President Henry Wallace. See Harold Ickes Diary, December 19, 1943, p. 8474, HIP; Francis Biddle Cabinet Notes, December 17, 1943, Box 1, FBP; John Morton Blum, ed., *The Price of Vision: The Diary of Henry Wallace, 1942–1946* (Boston: Houghton Mifflin, 1973), p. 281.

74. Blum, *The Price of Vision*, p. 281.

75. Francis Biddle, Memorandum for the President, December 30, 1943, OF 4849 (WRA).

76. Ibid.

77. James Byrnes, Memorandum to the President, January 4, 1944; Harold Smith, Memorandum to the President, January 28, 1944, OF 4849 (WRA).

78. Undersecretary of the Interior (Abe Fortas), Memorandum for the Secretary, January 15, 1944, WRA Files, HIP.

79. Letter, Rep. George Outland et al. to FDR, January 28, 1944; FDR, Memorandum for the Director of the Budget, February 9, 1944, OF 197-A (Japan).

80. Harold Ickes Diary, January 23, 1944, p. 8571, HIP.

81. Harold Smith, Journal, February 16, 1944, Harold Smith Papers, FDRL.

6. Equal Justice Delayed

1. Public Statement, Harold L. Ickes, April 13, 1944, Department of the Interior Information Service sheet, WRA Papers, HIP.

2. Letter, Abe Fortas to Dillon Myer, March 31, 1944, Abe Fortas Undersecretary Files, Box 1, Interior Department files, NA, cited in Bruce Allen Murphy, *Fortas: The Rise and Ruin of a Supreme Court Justice* (New York: Morrow, 1988), p. 57.

3. Abe Fortas, Memorandum for the Secretary of the Interior, February 22, 1944, WRA Files, HIP; Captain John Hall, Memorandum for Mr. McCloy, March 2, 1944, RG 107, ASW 014.311 (WDC Segregation), NA, rpt. in CWRIC Papers, p. 790 (reel 1, p. 742).

4. Dillon Myer, Memorandum for the Secretary of the Interior, March 9, 1944; Abe Fortas, Memorandum for the Secretary of the Interior, March 9, 10, 1944, WRA Files, HIP.

5. Letter, John J. McCloy to Francis Biddle, February 25, 1944, cited in Irons, *Justice at War*, p. 265.

6. "Relocation Centers Quiet," *New York Times*, January 29, 1944, p. 2.

7. Irons, *Justice at War*, pp. 281–285.

8. Henry L. Stimson, Foreword, in U.S. Army, *Final Report on Japanese Evacuation from the West Coast* (Washington DC: Government Printing Office, 1943).

9. Assistant Secretary of War, Memorandum for the Secretary of War, March 17, 1944, RG 107–47–9, ASW 014.311 (Permits), NA, rpt. in CWRIC Papers, pp. 798–805 (reel 1, pp. 751–758).

10. Assistant Secretary of War, Memorandum on the Return of Persons of Japanese Ancestry to the West Coast to Be Read by the Secretary of War to the Cabinet, March 17, 1944, RG 107–47–9, ASW 014.311 (Permits), NA, rpt. in CWRIC Papers, pp. 795–797 (reel 1, pp. 747–749).

11. John J. McCloy, Memorandum for the Chief of Staff, May 8, 1944, RG 107 ASW 014.311 (Permits), NA, rpt. in CWRIC Papers, pp. 792–794 (reel 1, pp. 744–746).

12. "A Friend of the American Way: An Interview with Herbert V. Nicholson," in Arthur A. Hansen and Betty E. Mitson, eds., *Voices Long Silent: An Oral Inquiry into the Japanese-American Evacuation,* Japanese American Oral History Project, California State University, Fullerton, 1974, pp. 139–140.

13. Harold Ickes Diary, April 4, 1944, p. 8720, HIP; Dillon Myer, Memorandum, Bringing the Relocation Program to a Conclusion, April 5, 1944, WRA File 8, Papers of Undersecretary of the Interior Abe Fortas, RG 48 772, NA.

14. Memo, Abe Fortas to Harold Ickes, April 6, 1944, RG 48, Box 12, NA, cited in Laura Kalman, *Abe Fortas: A Biography* (New Haven: Yale University Press, 1990), p. 82.

15. Letter, R. B. Cozzens to Dillon Myer, April 14, 1944; Letter, Philip Glick to Maurice Walk, April 17, 1944, WRA files, RG 210, 41.333, 41.134, NA; Dillon Myer, Memorandum, Revocation of Military Orders Excluding Japanese Americans from Pacific Coast Areas, May 15, 1944, RG 48, Box 12, WRA 3, NA. Fortas also proudly reported that the army judge advocate general's office adopted the speech as required reading for its course on international law. Note for the Undersecretary from "J," April 26, 1944, WRA File, HIP.

16. Letter, Harold Ickes to C. G., May 15, 1944, WRA Papers, HIP.

17. "Mayor Laguardia Protests Relocation in New York City or Eastern Seaboard States as Military Peril," *New York Times,* April 27, 1944, p. 1; "LaGuardia and Racism," *Pacific Citizen,* May 13, 1944, p. 5.

18. "Ickes Blasts New York Mayor, Two Governors for Biased Views on Evacuee Question," *Pacific Citizen,* April 29, 1944, p. 2; "LaGuardia Silent on Federal Group's Request," *New York Times,* April 28, 1944, p. 8. LaGuardia's statement also ushered in a series of public protests by liberal groups, including the ACLU and the NAACP.

19. Harold Ickes Diary, April 28, 1944, p. 8828, HIP.

20. Ibid., p. 8854, HIP.

21. Ibid. See also Myer, Revocation of Military Orders Excluding Japanese Americans from Pacific Coast Areas.

22. Chief of Staff (George Marshall), Memorandum for John J. McCloy, May 13, 1944, RG 107, ASW 014.311 (Permits), NA, rpt. in CWRIC Papers, p. 791 (reel 1, p. 743).

23. John J. McCloy, Memorandum for the Chief of Staff, May 8, 1944, RG 107, ASW 014.311 (Permits), NA, rpt. in CWRIC Papers, pp. 792–794 (reel 1, pp. 744–746).

24. Abe Fortas, Memorandum for the Secretary of the Interior, May 16, 1944, WRA File, HIP.

25. Letter, Dillon Myer to Jonathan Daniels, January 15, 1944, OF 4849 (WRA).

26. Harold Ickes Diary, March 20, 1944, p. 8720, HIP.

27. Routing Memorandum, citing Letter, Ingram M. Stainback to FDR, December 14, 1943, and Letter, FDR to Ingram Stainback, January 4, 1944, OF 133 (Immigration).

28. Geoffrey Ward, ed., *Closest Companion* (Boston: Houghton Mifflin, 1995), pp. 285–289. See also Robert H. Ferrell, *The Dying President* (Bloomington: University of Indiana Press, 1998).

29. Ferrell, *The Dying President*. See also Marquis W. Childs, "I've Got This Thing Simplified," *American Heritage*, April 1957, pp. 38–39, 91–93.

30. Henry Stimson Diary, May 17, 1944, pp. 3–4, HLSP.

31. Abe Fortas, Memorandum for the Secretary of the Interior, May 18, 1944, WRA Files, HIP.

32. Francis Biddle, Cabinet Notes, May 26, 1942, Box 1, FBP; Henry Stimson Diary, May 26, 1944, pp. 3–4, HLSP; Harold Ickes Diary, May 28, 1944, pp. 8937–38, HIP.

33. Attorney General's Council, Fifty-First Meeting, May 10, 1944, Attorney General's Council minutes, p. 40, FBP.

34. Henry Stimson Diary, May 26, 1944, p. 4, HLSP.

35. Harold Ickes Diary, June 4, 1944, p. 8964, HIP.

36. Letter, Harold L. Ickes to FDR, June 2, 1944, OF 197 (Japan).

37. Dillon Myer, "Plan for Bringing the Relocation Program to a Conclusion," p. 1.

38. Dillon Myer, Memorandum for the Undersecretary of the Interior, June 2, 1944, Box 2, Dillon Myer Papers, HSTL.

39. Harold Ickes Diary, June 10, 1944, p. 8982, HIP.

40. FDR, Memorandum for the Under Secretary of State, June 8, 1944, OF 4849 (WRA).

41. Stettinius's manuscript diary for June 9 and June 10, 1944, in the University of Virginia makes no mention of Japanese Americans. Thomas M. Campbell and George C. Herring, eds., *The Diaries of Edward Stettinius, 1943–1976* (New York: New Viewpoints, 1975), pp. 77–82.

42. Edward Stettinius, Jr., Memorandum for the President, June 9, 1944, OF 4849 (WRA).

43. Letter, Harold L. Ickes to FDR, June 2, 1944; Memorandum, FDR to E. R. Stettinius, Jr., and Harold L. Ickes, June 12, 1944, OF 4849.

44. "Military Situation on Coast Will Determine Any Change in Exclusion Order, Stimson Says," *Pacific Citizen*, June 17, 1944, p. 1.

45. Jonathan Daniels, *White House Witness, 1942–1945* (Garden City, NY: Doubleday, 1975), p. 229; President's Appointment Diary / White House Usher's Log, June 13, 1944, FDRL.

46. Daniels, *White House Witness*, p. 229.

47. John McCloy, conversation with General Delos Emmons, June 13, 1944, cited in Kai Bird, *The Chairman: John J. McCloy and the Making of the American Establishment* (New York: Simon & Schuster, 1992), p. 171.

48. Letter, Clarence Pickett to Eleanor Roosevelt, June 19, 1944, Clarence Pickett Correspondence 1944, Section 70 (Correspondence with Government Departments), ERP.

49. Letter, Eleanor Roosevelt to Clarence Pickett, June 18, 1944. Clarence Pickett Correspondence, Series 100 (Personal Correspondence), ERP; Memo from Miss Randolph to Mr. White, June 21, 1944, Eleanor Roosevelt Correspondence, NAACP Papers, Series II-A, LC.

50. Letter, Eleanor Roosevelt to Walter White, June 17, 1944, Walter White 1944, Section 100 (Personal Correspondence), ERP.

51. Letter, Clarence Pickett to Walter White, June 29, 1944, Nisei File, NAACP Papers, Series II-A, LC.

52. Harold Ickes Diary, June 24, 1944, p. 9027, HIP; Letter, Edward Joyce to Anna Roosevelt Boettiger, June 26, 1944; Letter, Anna Roosevelt Boettiger to Edward Joyce, June 29, 1944, Edward Joyce Correspondence, Anna Roosevelt Halsted Papers, FDRL.

53. Letter, Abe Fortas to John J. McCloy, June 16, 1944, Chron File, June 1944, WRA Papers, RG 210, NA. Also RG 107, NA, rpt. in CWRIC Papers, p. 2152 (reel 2, p. 857).

54. Letter, John J. McCloy to Abe Fortas, June 20, 1944, RG 48, Box 12, WRA 4, NA, rpt. in CWRIC Papers, pp. 6491–6492 (reel 6, pp. 110–111); Letter, John McCloy to Major General H. C. Pratt, July 25, 1944, ASW 014.311 (SDC Permits-Enter-Live), NA, rpt. in CWRIC Papers, p. 385 (reel 1, p. 380).

55. Memo, Commander Western Sea Frontier (Admiral D. W. Bagley) to

Commander in Chief, U.S. Fleet, September 15, 1944, RG 338–1–5, 291.2/37 WDC, NA, rpt. in CWRIC Papers, p. 615–616 (reel 1, pp. 571–572); Letter, Harold Ickes to James Forrestal, June 21, 1944; Harold Ickes to James Forrestal, September 5, 1944; Harold Ickes to Henry L. Stimson, October 28, 1944; WRA Papers, RG 210, 22.912, NA. There is astounding evidence of collusion between the army's operations division and Los Angeles Mayor Fletcher Bowron (a powerful advocate of the evacuation) to lobby the Supreme Court to approve continued exclusion as a military necessity after the threat of invasion had passed, on the grounds that the return had the potential to disrupt war production. Letter, Lt. Col. J. G. Schneider, Assistant Chief of Staff, Army Operations Division to the Commanding General of the Army Air Forces, November 6, 1944, RG 107?, NA, rpt. in CWRIC Papers, p. 664 (reel 1, p. 621).

56. Harold Ickes Diary, cited in Bill Hosokawa, *JACL: In Quest of Justice* (New York: William Morrow, 1982), p. 253.

57. Memo, Abe Fortas to William D. Hassett, September 8, 1944, OF 4849 (WRA).

58. Letter, Gen. C. H. Bonesteel to John J. McCloy, July 31, 1944, RG 107, ASW 014.311, NA, rpt. in CWRIC Papers, pp. 4397–4398 (reel 4, pp. 185–186).

59. Memo, Abe Fortas to William D. Hassett, September 8, 1944, OF 4849 (WRA).

60. Charles Fahy, Oral History Memoir, Columbia University Oral History Program, p. 178, cited in Irons, *Justice at War*, p. 365.

61. FDR, Speech, Puget Sound, WA, August 12, 1944, President's Speech File 1944, OF 1820. See also citation in Thomas H. Green, *What Roosevelt Thought* (Lansing: Michigan State University Press, 1958), p. 166.

62. FDR, Columbus Day Address to the American Republics, rpt. in *New York Times*, October 13, 1944, p. 15.

63. Francis Biddle Cabinet Notes, November 10, 1944, Box 1, FBP.

64. Henry Stimson Diary, November 10, 1944, p. 2, HLSP.

65. Letter, Harold Ickes to Francis Biddle and John J. McCloy, December 6, 1944, Correspondence with War Department, WRA Papers, BL.

66. Henry Stimson Diary, November 20, 1944, p. 2, HLSP.

67. Dillon Myer, Memorandum for the Secretary, December 4, 1944; Harold Ickes, Memorandum for Mr. Dillon Myer, December 5, 1944; Dillon Myer, Memorandum for the Secretary, December 14, 1944, WRA Files, HIP.

68. "Return of Nisei," *San Francisco Chronicle*, November 19, 1944, p. 1.

69. Letter, John McCloy to Francis Biddle, November 17, 1944; Letter, Francis Biddle to John McCloy, November 20, 1944, RG 107, ASW 014.311 (WDC), NA, rpt. in CWRIC Papers, pp. 660–661 (reel 1, pp. 618–619).

70. "Variety of Interpretations Seen in Press," *Rocky Shimpo,* December 4, 1944, p. 1.

71. John McCloy, Letter to Hon. Clarence Lea, December 6, 1944, WRA Box 8, Papers of Undersecretary of the Interior Abe Fortas, RG 48, Box 772, NA.

72. Henry L. Stimson, Memorandum for the President, December 13, 1944, PSF, PCF (Stimson). Also in RG 107, ASW.011, NA, rpt. in CRWIC Papers, pp. 9622–9628 (reel 8, pp. 596–602).

73. Memorandum, Robert Rogue to Colonel H. A. Gerhardt, December 14, 1944, RG 107, ASW 014.311 (WDC Permits to Enter-and-Live), rpt. in CWRIC Papers, p. 621 (reel 1, p. 577).

74. Letter, John McCloy to Abe Fortas, December 29, 1944, War Department records RG 107–47–7, ASW 014.311 (EDC Misc.), NA, rpt. in CWRIC Papers, pp. 605–606 (reel 1, pp. 561–562).

75. U.S. Department of the Interior, *Annual Report of the Director of the WRA to the Secretary of the Interior, Fiscal Year Ending June 30, 1945* (Washington, DC: Government Printing Office, 1945), p. 278; Wallace Stegner, "The Nisei Come Home," *New Republic,* July 9, 1945, pp. 45–46.

76. "Ickes Assails Anti-Niseism," *Baltimore Sun,* May 14, 1945, p. 4. Ickes's stand received supportive comment from such diverse newspapers as the *Philadelphia Bulletin,* the *Cleveland Plain Dealer,* and the *Washington Post.*

77. "Citation Awarded," *Rocky Shimpo,* March 12, 1945, p. 1.

78. Ansel Adams, *Born Free and Equal* (New York: U.S. Camera, 1944), pp. 102–103.

79. Harold Ickes, Memorandum to the President, December 28, 1944, OF 4849 (WRA).

80. The President, Memo for Mrs. Roosevelt, March 6, 1945 re February 19, 1945 letter from Miss Statire Biggs, OF 4849 (WRA).

81. U.S. Commission on Wartime Relocation and Internment of Civilians, *Personal Justice Denied,* p. 15.

82. For a defense of Roosevelt's decision to delay lifting exclusion on this basis, see Page Smith, *Democracy on Trial,* p. 370.

83. See, for example, "California Lieut. Governor Charges 'New Deal' Seeks to Return Evacuees to Coast Area," *Pacific Citizen,* September 2, 1944, p. 3; "War Department Denies Decision to Relax Restriction after Election," *Pacific Citizen,* October 14, 1944, p. 1.

84. "Deutsch Questions Dewey over Statement on Coast Evacuees," *Pacific Citizen,* September 30, 1944, p. 7.

85. Jay Franklin [John Franklin Carter], *The Catoctin Conversation,* p. 175.

86. FDR, Interview with Frederick Boyd Stevenson, *Brooklyn Eagle,* July 18, 1920, p. 6.

87. Henry Wallace Diary, May 22, 1943, University of Iowa (microfilm copy in LC).

88. See Larry Tajiri, "Goodbye to Little Tokyo," *Common Ground*, spring 1944; Togo Tanaka, "Letter to the Editor," *Gila River News-Courier*, June 1943.

89. Eleanor Roosevelt, cited in Weglyn, *Years of Infamy*, p. 174.

90. Letter, Dillon Myer to Carey McWilliams, March 7, 1946, Japanese-American Files, Box 4, Carey McWilliams Papers, BL.

91. Letter, Harold Ickes to Senator Guy Gordon, March 12, 1945; Memorandum, Harold Ickes to Dillon Myer, March 27, 1943, WRA Files 1945, HIP. See also "Ickes Believes West Will Not Tolerate Evacuee Persecution," *Denver Times*, April 7, 1945, p. 1.

92. Letter, Secretary of War to the President, July 7, 1942, OF 197-A (Japan).

93. Ironically, although the WRA was accused by anti-Japanese forces, with some justice, of having a "sociological" interest in the evacuees, it was McCloy who told Alexander Meicklejohn of the ACLU that he was interested in establishing the camps and studying the internees as "guinea pigs." Letter, John J. McCloy to Alexander Meicklejohn, September 30, 1942, Japanese Evacuation Research Study Papers, 67/14,E.1.020, BL. See also Richard Drinnon, *Keeper of Concentration Camps* (Berkeley: University of California Press, 1987), pp. 18ff.

7. The President of All the People?

1. Henry Stimson Diary, February 25, 1942, HLSP. For Stimson's racial bias see, for example, Irons, *Justice at War*, p. 363; Drinnon, *Keeper of Concentration Camps*, pp. 34–35; Godfrey Hodgson, *The Colonel: The Life and Wars of Henry Stimson, 1867–1950* (Boston: Northeastern University Press, 1990), pp. 248–251. See also Mitziko Sawada, "Research Memo on Henry Stimson Diaries," October 18, 1981, rpt. in CWRIC Papers, pp. 19734–19766 (reel 17, pp. 267–299).

2. Henry Stimson Diary, September 15, 1942, HLSP.

3. Henry L. Stimson and McGeorge Bundy, *On Active Service in Peace and War* (New York: Harper's, 1948), p. 406.

4. "Nisei Given Chance to Prove Loyalty," *Arizona Republic*, April 27, 1943, p. 7.

5. "Stimson Raps Critics of U.S. Nisei Policy," *Pacific Citizen*, October 30, 1943, p. 1; "Secretary Stimson Describes Attack on Nisei GI as 'Outrage,'" *Pacific Citizen*, April 7, 1945, p. 2.

6. FDR, cited (without date) in Michael Kammen, *A Machine That Would Go of Itself: The Constitution in American Culture* (New York: Vintage, 1987), p. 320.

7. Richard Hofstadter, *The Age of Reform: From Bryan to F.D.R.* (New York: Knopf, 1955), pp. 20, 316, is probably the most influential defense of Roosevelt's pragmatism. See also William E. Leuchtenberg, *Franklin D. Roosevelt and the New Deal* (New York: Harper & Row, 1963); Reinhold Niebuhr, *The Irony of American History* (New York: Scribner's, 1952); and Arthur Schlesinger, Jr., *Age of Roosevelt* (series) (Boston: Houghton Mifflin, 1956–1960).

8. Arthur Schlesinger, Jr., review of *The Secret Diary of Harold Ickes, New Republic*, December 7, 1953, pp. 14–15, cited in James MacGregor Burns, *Roosevelt: The Lion and Fox, 1882–1940* (New York: Harcourt Brace Jovanovich, 1956), p. 371.

9. Frank Freidel, *FDR: Launching the New Deal*, p. 501.

10. Burns, *Roosevelt: The Lion and the Fox*, p. 373.

11. See Jim Bishop, *FDR's Last Year* (New York: Morrow, 1974); Bernard Asbell, *When FDR Died* (New York: Holt, Rinehart, 1961).

12. *Personal Justice Denied*, p. 459.

13. John J. McCloy, Testimony, in *Hearings before the Subcommittee on Administrative Law*, p. 145. See also testimony of Colonel Frederick Bernays Wiener, ibid., p. 705.

14. Telegram, Japanese Americans Citizens League to President Roosevelt, December 7, 1941, cited in Allen Bosworth, *America's Concentration Camps* (New York: Norton, 1967), p. 46; "New Yorkers Organize to Help Japanese in General," *Rafu Shimpo*, December 17, 1941, p. 1, *Doho*, December 11, 1941, p. 1.

15. Togo Tanaka Diary, December 20, 1941, Togo Tanaka Papers, JERS, reel 6, BL.

16. Masthead, *Rafu Shimpo*, February 9, 1942, p. 1.

17. Tokie Slocum, Fred Tayama, statements at United Citizens Federation Meeting, February 19, 1942, Togo Tanaka Journal, JERS, reel 6, p. 335, BL. See also Audrie Girdner and Anne Loftis, *The Great Betrayal* (New York: Macmillan, 1969), p. 102.

18. Larry Tajiri, "On Franklin D. Roosevelt," *Pacific Citizen*, April 15, 1946, p. 4; Daniel L. Okimoto, *American in Disguise* (New York: Walker-Weatherhill, 1971), p. 38.

19. Togo Tanaka Journal, March 1, 1942, JERS, reel 6, p. 347, BL.

20. See, for example, "Alien Japanese Sends Letter, Poem to President Roosevelt," *Pacific Citizen*, December 10, 1942, p. 1; "Letter to President Gets Results for Evacuee Youth," *Pacific Citizen*, November 19, 1942, p. 1; "22-Year-Old Evacuee, Born in Japan, Writes to President, Pleads for Chance to Fight," *Pacific Citizen*, February 11, 1943, p. 1.

21. Frank Hijikata, Editorial, *Tulean Dispatch,* May 27, 1943, p. 2.

22. "Military Necessity," Editorial, *Pacific Citizen,* February 5, 1944, p. 2.

23. "New York Nisei Committee Backs Roosevelt for 4th 4 Year Term," *Rocky Shimpo,* November 3, 1944, p. 1; Dyke Miyagawa, "New York Japanese Americans Sponsor Rally for Roosevelt," *Pacific Citizen,* November 4, 1944, p. 3.

24. Sandra C. Taylor, *Jewel of the Desert: Japanese-American Internment at Topaz* (Berkeley: University of California Press, 1993), p. 198.

25. Kiyoshi Okamoto, Letter to Norman Thomas, February 10, 1943, Correspondence file, Norman Thomas Papers, New York Public Library.

26. Diary of Kasen Noda, May 13, 1943, July 28, 1943, February 12, 1945, in Takeo Kaneshiro, comp., *Internees: Relocation Center Memories and Diaries* (New York: Vantage Press, 1976), pp. 45, 48, 73.

27. See, for example, "YBA Holds Memorial for Roosevelt," *Colorado Times,* April 17, 1945.

28. "Death of an American," *Pacific Citizen,* April 14, 1945, p. 1.

29. "The Task Completed," *Rocky Shimpo,* April 15, 1945, p. 1.

30. Frank "Foo" Fujita, *Foo: A Japanese-American Prisoner of the Rising Sun* (Denton: University of North Texas Press, 1993), p. 270.

31. "Evacuees in Relocation Camps Hold Special Memorial Rites in Honor of Late President," *Pacific Citizen,* April 21, 1945, p. 2.

32. Taylor, *Jewel of the Desert,* p. 213.

33. "Evacuees Attend Memorial," *New York Times,* April 14, 1945.

34. George Takei, *To The Stars: The Autobiography of George Takei, Star Trek's Mr. Sulu* (Pocket Books, 1995), p. 158.

35. Girdner and Loftis, *The Great Betrayal,* p. 477.

36. Bill Hosokawa, *Nisei* (New York, William Morrow, 1969), p. 246; Bill Hosokawa, *The JACL in Quest of Justice,* p. 355; John Tateishi, *And Justice for All: An Oral History of the Japanese American Concentration Camps* (New York: Random House, 1984), pp. xvi, xxvii; Michi Weglyn, *Years of Infamy,* p. 73; William Minoru Hohri, *Repairing America* (Pullman: Washington State University Press, 1988), p. 22.

37. Satoru Tsufura, Letter to Greg Robinson, December 23, 1998.

38. Norman Mineta, "Interning 'Nonaliens' in '42 Was an Act of Racism," *New York Times,* February 24, 1983, I, p. 24.

39. Harry S. Truman, Letter to Eleanor Roosevelt, December 23, 1945, Eleanor Roosevelt Correspondence File (microfilm), HSTL.

40. Harry Truman, address to 442nd Regimental Combat Team, Washington, D.C., July 15, 1946, cited in Lyn Crost, *Honor By Fire: Japanese Americans at War in Europe and the Pacific* (Novato, CA: Presidio Press, 1994), p. 306.

ACKNOWLEDGMENTS

I HAVE REAPED the benefit of count-
less people's labor during the making of this book.
This volume would have been impossible without the
research and organizational efforts of those who have
documented the internment. Particularly useful were
the microfilmed Papers of the U.S. Commission on
Wartime Relocation and Internment of Civilians,
compiled by Aiko Yoshinaga-Herzig and the CWRIC
staff from archives across the country. I also relied on
American Concentration Camps, a nine-volume collec-
tion of government documents edited by the eminent
historian Roger Daniels.

The staff at numerous archives put me on the trail
of useful sources. In particular, I am grateful to Lynn
Bassanesse and Robert Parks at the Franklin D. Roosevelt Library for their helpfulness. I am also indebted
to the staffs of the Hoover Institution, the Bancroft
Library at the University of California, Berkeley, the
Library of Congress, the National Archives, the Harry
S. Truman Library, and the Isamu Noguchi Foundation. I located important published sources at The

New York Public Library and at the libraries of the University of California, Santa Barbara, and of New York University.

Many people assisted me on this project and deserve particular mention. Robert L. Beir's indefatigable interest in Franklin Roosevelt helped ignite my own, and his enormous private library of Rooseveltiana was a useful research resource. Marco Mariano shared his criticisms and ideas and provided research assistance at the FDR Library. Lillian Robinson was generous with "auntular" advice and compelling insights on race and liberalism. Heng Gun Ngo assisted with my research and graciously put up with my Roosevelt obsession. *Aku cinta mu.* Yi-Chun Tricia Lin's invitation to address her Asian-American studies class offered me a first chance to discuss my project, and her continuing interest made the work more fun. Ian Robinson sacrificed frequent-flyer miles to send me to the West Coast for two essential research trips. Michael Massing, Shirley Geok-Lin Lim and Charles Bazerman, Ian Robinson, Tracy Robinson, and Ken Feinour provided housing during research trips. Peter Eisenstadt and Claude Sirlin offered crucial encouragement.

Darline Levy read the entire manuscript, and her uncanny sense for the weaknesses of my argument pushed me to rethink and sharpen many points. Sanae Moorhead gave me invaluable friendship and encouragement, and she brought me into contact with many Nisei. Senator Alan Cranston, Jean Esaki, John Fuyuume, Joy Gee, Yuri Hata, Ike Hachimonji, Bill Hosokawa, Anne Howden, Motoko Ikeda-Spiegel, Chieko Inouye, Grace (Mrs. Chihiro) Kikuchi, Sue Kikuchi, John Kiyasu, Hisako Kobayashi, Milton R. Konvitz, Mich Kunitani, Masao Matsumoto, Kim Nagano, Mr. and Mrs. James Naka-mura, Miné Okubo, Pat Okura, Arthur M. Schlesinger, Jr., Kaye Sugiyama, Anne Sumida, Togo Tanaka, Satoru Tsufura, Michi Weglyn, Mitsuye Yamada, Hisaye Yamamoto, and George Yuzawa shared their experiences with me in letters or interviews. John Blum, Richard Drinnon, Clare Gorfinkel, Max Holland, Stuart David Ikeda, Peter Irons, Priscilla Long, Effie Lee Morris, and Robert Shaffer provided assistance on sources. Judy and Rus-sell Baker, Ana Daniel, J. J. Johnson, Ronald Seely, Heng Wee Tan, and Yoshi Yamamoto read all or part of the manuscript.

Professors Thomas Bender and Marilyn Young of the History Department at New York University provided essential advice and support throughout this project. Professors John Kuo Wei Tchen, Robin D. G. Kelley, and David Reimers also made suggestions on my manuscript. The students in Professor

Tom Bender's Dissertation Seminar, especially Terri Collins, Laurent Jean-pierre, and Amy Richter, read chapters and provided thoughtful critiques, as did my students at George Mason University, notably Jeremy Tucker, Jay Mykytiuk, and Heather Waole. In the last stages of revision, Professor Blanche Wiesen Cook gave me the benefit of her wise counsel on expanding my coverage of Eleanor Roosevelt's involvement with Japanese Americans.

I am indebted to my agent, Charlotte Sheedy, for championing my work and to my editor at Harvard University Press, Joyce Seltzer, for her help in reshaping it. I am also grateful to Susan Wallace Boehmer at HUP for her sensitive editing of the final draft.

Lastly and most importantly, I owe a tremendous debt to my parents, Toni and Ed Robinson. Both provided moral and financial support, read the entire manuscript, and gave advice on interpretation. Although the book is dedicated to them in gratitude for producing me, its contents were shaped in large part by their interventions.

INDEX